bodies in code

interfaces with digital media

mark b. n. hansen

 Routledge
Taylor & Francis Group
New York   London

Routledge is an imprint of the
Taylor & Francis Group, an informa business

contents

the author

Mark B. N. Hansen teaches cultural theory and comparative media studies in the English department and is on the Committee for Cinema and Media Studies at the University of Chicago. He is author of *Embodying Technesis: Technology beyond Writing* (Michigan 2000) and *New Philosophy for New Media* (MIT 2004), as well as numerous essays on cultural theory, contemporary literature, and media. His essay, "The Time of Affect, or Bearing Witness to Life" appeared in *Critical Inquiry* in Spring, 2004. He has coedited (with Taylor Carman) *The Cambridge Companion to Merleau–Ponty* and is currently coediting two volumes: *Critical Terms for Media Studies* (with W. J. T. Mitchell) and *Neocybernetic Emergence* (with Bruce Clarke). His current projects include: *The Politics of Presencing*, a study of embodied human agency in the context of real-time media and computing, *Becoming Human*, an ethics of the posthuman, and *Fiction after Television*, a study of the novel in the age of digital convergence.

preface

Bodies in Code: Interfaces with Digital Media forms the middle volume of what I now conceive to be a trilogy devoted to new media as the contemporary phase of human technogenesis (coevolution of the human with technics). This book follows *New Philosophy for New Media*, in which I make a case for the crucial role of embodied framing in the production of images out of information, and precedes *The Politics of Presencing*, in which I will position new media as a source for the technical contamination of embodied time consciousness. *Bodies in Code: Interfaces with Digital Media* focuses specifically on embodiment, exploring it for itself. In the pages that follow, I thus turn directly to the most developed phenomenology of the body—that of French philosopher Maurice Merleau–Ponty—to discover technics where its developer did not see it: namely, as a correlate of the protosensory, infraempirical functioning of tactility that, as Merleau–Ponty's project advances, becomes increasingly fundamental.

My explicit aim is to show how Merleau–Ponty's final ontology of the flesh, with its postulation of a fundamental indifference between body and world, requires a technics—a theory of the originary technicity of the human. Because the human is essentially a being distributed into nonoverlapping sensory interfaces with the world, it is characterized by a certain "gap" or "divide"—by what Merleau–Ponty calls an *écart*. As I show, the most primordial form of this *écart* is the transduction between embodiment and specularity, the transduction that informs the emergence of the visual from primordial tactility. This transduction (a relation that is primary with respect to its terms) is an instance (indeed, it is the protoinstance) of the inherence of technics within embodied life. Accordingly, technicity, understood in its broadest sense as a relation to exteriority, as exteriorization, is not and cannot be something merely added on to some "natural" core of embodied life.

Rather, it must be understood to be a constitutive dimension of embodiment from the start.

As was the case with *New Philosophy for New Media*, I have benefited from the thought-catalyzing work of a diverse host of contemporary artists whose varied use of digital media has pointed the way toward an introjection of technics into embodiment. For me, new media art has helped to clarify the stakes of thinking technics in relation to Merleau–Ponty's philosophy. As an aesthetic mediation of digital technology, it has introduced technical dimensions of embodiment literally unimaginable to this philosopher, and indeed unimaginable to any philosopher writing and thinking in the middle of the twentieth century. Accordingly, in the long first section devoted to the transduction of technics and embodiment, I have endeavored to capture the crucial role played by art in my thinking by devoting a series of concrete analyses to specific artworks. My hope is that these analyses will counterbalance and enliven the more theoretical discussions of embodiment, specularity, intercorporeity, and indivision of the flesh that they punctuate.

In contrast, the focused analyses in Part II are offered as exemplary instances of "bodies in code," a term designating embodiment as it is necessarily distributed beyond the skin in the context of contemporary technics. Each of the topics explored here—nonocularcentric virtual environments, racial stereotyping in the context of the digital commons, the architecture of infospace, and the deformation of the contemporary novel by nonliterary media—presents a singular process through which embodiment is actively produced in conjunction with flexible new media artifacts.

My hope is that *Bodies in Code* will help remind us of the vital and indispensable role played by embodiment in any human experience, even that of "virtual reality" and, more generally, the virtual in the manifold forms in which it appears in our contemporary culture. With the fading of the hype surrounding virtual reality 10 years ago, we are now in a perfect position to analyze the deep correlation between embodiment and virtuality and also to take stock of how much the virtual has been absorbed into everyday life.

I wager here that this changed perspective indicates an acceptance of, or at least a readiness to accept, the inherence of the virtual within human life as an embodied form of the living. Accordingly, as I seek to affirm here, the virtual is by no means limited to contemporary digital technologies (even if it has a certain elective affinity with the digital), but rather stretches back to the proto-origin of the human. Once it is understood in this way, the conjunction of the virtual with the powerful technologies of the digital computer can then be seen to furnish a rich source for experimentation with and expansion of the scope of human embodiment.

I wish to thank the following journals for permission to reprint material that appeared in earlier versions: *Critical Matrix*, which published an earlier version of Chapter 2 (Fall 2001); *Sub-Stance*, which published a shortened, earlier version of Chapter 3 (2004); *Configurations*, which published an earlier version of Chapter 4 (Spring 2002); and *Contemporary Literature*, which published an earlier version of Chapter 5 (Winter 2004). I wish to thank the artists for permission to reproduce images of their work and, more importantly, for creating the work in the first place.

I owe thanks to an innumerable number of friends, colleagues, and students, whose insights, criticisms, and comments have shaped my thinking about new media and challenged me to think beyond the point at which my own proclivities would have kept me.

I remain especially grateful to my wonderful family—Wilson, Michael, and Mimi—whose dedication allowed me time to work when I needed it most and whose love kept me motivated to continue.

I dedicate this book to my mother, Dr. Yvonne Hansen, whose speculative instinct clearly informs (epiphylogenetically or otherwise) my own.

Mark Hansen

Introduction

From the Image to the Power of Imaging: Virtual Reality and the "Originary" Specularity of Embodiment

1. ALL REALITY IS MIXED REALITY

According to a recent article in *The New York Times*, the (near) future of television will witness a triumphant conquest of virtual reality, a realm of experience that, with its cumbersome gear and prohibitive costs, we have grown accustomed to considering as distinct from normal perceptual reality.[1] Though we "see the world in three dimensions," the article notes, "throughout most of history, we've only been able to depict it in two." While this Achilles heel of representationalism has long inspired experiments involving perceptual trickery—and indeed might be credited as inspiration for an entire tradition in Western art—only in the past half century has scientific and artistic attention focused on the total simulation of perceptual reality, on the projection of images in three dimensions. The fruit of this attention, however, has recently undergone a minor revolution, as the article explains:

Until recently no one had come up with a better solution to this problem than goofy eyewear. When Rover sent back images from Mars, NASA scientists studied them wearing much the same glasses that audiences in '50s movie palaces donned to watch "It Came from Outer Space." Within the realms of industry, that's been changing, as what's known as stereoscopic imaging has become a big business involving everyone from drug researchers doing molecular mapping to car designers building next year's SUV…. the ever-evolving high-tech revolution is finally moving 3-D entertainment to the next stage.

Stereoscopic imaging, the article goes on to explain, generates "natural three dimension" using a principle called "multiplexing." Multiplexing does for three-dimensional perception what cinema and video did for two-dimensional perception: by delivering 300 images per second (30 images a second from ten different angles), it adds a stereoscopic or depth dimension to the illusion of motion generated by its technological precursors. With the ever increasing speed of home entertainment devices, delivery of three-dimensional content has now become practicable, even if its realization seems to loom fairly far out on the horizon.

What is particularly interesting about this story—at least for my purposes here—is its congruity with the more specific technical paradigm emerging from recent virtual reality research and art experimentation: the paradigm (to borrow a term from artists Monika Fleischmann and Wolfgang Strauss) of "mixed reality." Having tired of the clichés of disembodied transcendence as well as the glacial pace of progress in head-mounted-display and other interface technology, today's artists and engineers envision a fluid interpenetration of realms. Central in this reimagining of VR as a mixed reality stage is a certain specification of the virtual. No longer a wholly distinct, if largely amorphous realm with rules all its own, the virtual now denotes a "space full of information" that can be "activated, revealed, reorganized and recombined, added to and transformed as the user navigates … real space."[2]

What comes to the fore in this reimagining is the central role played by the body in the interface to the virtual. With the convergence of physical and virtual spaces informing today's corporate and entertainment environments, researchers and artists have come to recognize that motor activity—not representationalist verisimilitude—holds the key to fluid and functional crossings between virtual and physical realms. In what amounts to a position statement for the mixed reality movement as a whole, Fleischmann and Strauss speak of "turning the theory on its head that man is losing his body to technology"; as they see it, "the interactive media are supporting the multisensory mechanisms of the body and are thus extending man's space for play and action" (cited in Grau, 219).

To be sure, this recognition of the primacy of embodied motor activity simply ratifies on a vastly broader scale the position of early VR pioneers like Myron Krueger and of cutting-edge perception research-ers like Paul Bach y Rita, who insist on the poverty of our ocularcentric metaphysical tradition and its representationalist aesthetics.[i] From the standpoint opened up by these and like-minded artists and engineers, what is truly novel and promising about contemporary consumer elec-tronics is not the possibility they open for creating ever more immersive illusory spaces, but rather the expanded scope they accord embodied human agency.

The massive increases in processing speeds ushering in today's microcomputing revolution thus serve less to revitalize the dream of per-fect simulation than to underwrite a more expansive and fluid *functional* interpenetration of physical and virtual spaces. Although today's venture capitalist is inclined to reference the "evolution [of humanity] toward ever more sophisticated representations of reality,"[ii] for a media artist like Myron Krueger, the development of three-dimensional simulations puts us in touch with our most primitive perceptual capacities: "... the human interface is evolving toward more natural information. Three-dimensional space is more, not less, intuitive than two-dimensional space.... Three-dimensional space is what we evolved to understand. It is more primitive, not more advanced [than two-dimensional space]."[3]

Thus, although Krueger and today's venture capitalist admittedly share a desire for a more natural interface, their respective understand-ings of how such a desire might be realized could not be more distinct. For the latter, "natural three dimension" denotes a more immersive, data-rich *visual* simulation. In contrast, for Krueger, "natural informa-tion" means information produced through an extension of our natu-ral—that is, embodied, perceptuomotor—interface with the world.

By capturing the difference between the industrial and the aesthetic interest in advances in contemporary media technology, this distinction perfectly expresses the defining principle of mixed reality as a second generation in virtual reality research: its eschewal of representational-ism and embrace of a functionalist perspective rooted in perceptuomo-tor activity. For this reason, today's mixed reality movement has marked affinities with what Krueger has long designated as "artificial reality" (as opposed to the HMD paradigm synonymous, for him, with the term "virtual reality"). Indeed, as I shall argue in Chapter 1, Krueger stands as a kind of father figure for the entire mixed reality paradigm.

It can hardly come as a surprise, then, that Krueger has recently described this terminological difference in terms highly reminiscent of the latter's challenge to earlier conceptions of virtual reality: "Whereas the HMD folks thought that 3D scenery was the essence of reality, I felt that the degree of physical involvement was the measure of immersion."[iii,4] On Krueger's account, one of the crucial components of physical involvement was lack of bodily encumbrance and, in a testament to the prescience of his thinking, the mixed reality environments now ubiquitous in our world do require a nonencumbered interface.[iv] The theoretical underpinnings of Krueger's alternate vision of "artificial reality" have found their practical fruition in today's mixed reality environments, and the "first generation" model of VR as a disembodied hyperspace free of all material constraints simply no longer has any purchase in our world.

Following from this defining principle of mixed reality are several important corollaries that serve to differentiate it from earlier conceptions of virtual reality and predecessor technologies. First, the mixed reality paradigm radically reconfigures a trait that has characterized virtual reality from its proto-origin as the representationalist fantasy par excellence: namely, a desire for complete convergence with natural perception. This trait serves to distinguish it from all *discrete* image media, including cinema, which, as underscored by Gilles Deleuze's correction of Bergson's criticism of the "cinematic illusion," function by breaking with natural perception.

Such a break (at least on Deleuze's reading) grants cinema the capacity to present the world from a nonhuman perspective and thus opens a properly autonomous machinism; by contrast, the functional homology linking virtual reality technologies with natural perception supports a prosthetics that functions to expand the scope of *natural* perception, to tap the technics at its core. In its fantasy form, though certainly not in reality, virtual reality works—or rather would work—like an externalization of neuroscientist Antonio Damasio's analogy for consciousness: if consciousness can be likened to a "movie-in-the-brain" with no external spectator, then virtual reality would comprise something like a movie-outside-the-brain, again, importantly, with no external spectator.[5]

4

The mixed reality paradigm differs most saliently from this fantasy in its deployment of the functional homology between virtual reality technologies and perception: rather than conceiving the virtual as a total technical simulacrum and as the opening of a fully immersive, self-contained fantasy world, the mixed reality paradigm treats it as simply one more realm among others that can be accessed through embodied perception or enaction (Varela). In this way, emphasis falls less on the *content* of the virtual than on the *means of access* to it, less on what is perceived in the world than on how it comes to be perceived in the first place.

Bluntly put, the new mixed reality paradigm *foregrounds the constitutive or ontological role of the body in giving birth to the world.* For today's researchers and artists, virtual reality serves to highlight the body's function as, to quote phenomenologist Maurice Merleau–Ponty, an "immediately given invariant," a "primary access to the world," the "vehicle of being in the world."[6] The body forms an ultimate background, an absolute here, in relation to which all perceptual experience must be oriented. That is why virtual reality comprises something of a reality test *for the body*; as philosopher Alain Millon points out, it "puts into place constraining apparatuses that allow us to better understand the limits and the weakness [but also the powers] of the body."[7]

A further corollary of the functionalist perspective of mixed reality follows closely upon this focus on the ontological or constituting function of embodiment: the role of self-movement as the bodily—or better, the tactile—face of perception. Insofar as it yields a doubling of perception, this tactile dimension serves to confer a bodily—that is, sensory—reality on external perceptual experience (whether it is "physical" or "virtual"). It generates a felt correlate of perception that is part of the functionalist understanding of embodied agency. Together, these two corollaries—the primacy of the body as ontological access to the world and the role of tactility in the actualization of such access—effect a passage from the axiom that has been my focus thus far (*all virtual reality is mixed reality*) to the more general axiom that *all* reality is mixed reality.

In one sense, this passage simply recognizes what, with Brian Massumi, we can consider to be the priority (or the "superiority") of the analog—especially, though by no means exclusively, where digital technologies are in play.[v] "Always on arrival a transformative feeling of the outside, a feeling of thought," sensation is the being of the analog. This is the analog in a sense close to the technical meaning, as a continuously variable impulse or momentum that can cross from one qualitatively different medium into another. Like electricity into sound waves. Or heat into pain. Or light waves into vision. Or vision into imagination. Or noise in the ear into music in the heart. *Or outside coming in.* Variable continuity across the qualitatively different: continuity of transformation. (135)

Understood in this sense, the analog creates reality out of the fusion or mixing of realms, out of transformation; not surprisingly, the body forms its primary agent: "If sensation is the analog processing by body-matter of ongoing transformative forces, then foremost among them are forces of appearing as such: of coming into being, registering as becoming. The body, sensor of change, is a transducer of the virtual" (135).

Situated against the backdrop of this understanding, the sensory integration of or interface with a concrete virtual domain (distinct from the virtual as a source of potential) would form one (particularly illustrative) instantiation of a more general sensory pattern: transformative integration of the force of the outside, of the virtual. That is why Massumi's conception of the analog conditions of virtual reality experience perfectly anticipates the contemporary shift to the mixed reality paradigm:

> The sight-confining helmets of early virtual reality systems have given way to immersive and interactive environments capable of addressing other-than-visual senses, and looping sense modalities more flexibly and multiply into each other, packing more sensation into the digitally assisted field of experience—and with it, more potentialization. (142)

Because experience as such is "analog processed," there can be no difference in kind demarcating virtual reality (in its narrow, technicist sense) from the rest of experience; again, all reality is mixed reality.

2. THE POWER OF IMAGING AND THE PRIVILEGE OF THE OPERATIONAL

Let us now take a step backward to recognize the larger cultural transition in which the shift to mixed reality is embedded. The period from the early '90s until today has witnessed a veritable cascade of interest in the topic of the body, one that reached its apogée with the triumph of the cultural constructivist paradigm. It might be useful to align this triumph with a moment in the development of what (following the importation of post-structuralism into the English-speaking world) came to be called, simply, "theory." Such a moment occurred—as Eve Sedgwick and Adam Frank's 1995 polemical attack on neo-Foucauldian constructivism highlights—when theory became synonymous with antiessentialist constructivism.

Condensed into a single claim, Sedgwick and Frank's compelling, if massively reductive, argument runs as follows: the specification that _____ (fill in with appropriate object domain) is "discursively constructed" rather than "natural" *is precisely what constitutes theory.*[8] "[T]hat specification," Sedgwick and Frank claim, "is today understood to constitute *anything* as theory": "'theory' has become almost simply coextensive with the claim (you can't say it often enough), *it's not natural*" (513). Despite the distraction of its polemical fervor, this criticism manages to capture the thoroughgoing hostility to anything biological that literally permeated the ethos of theory—that is, of poststructuralism following its productive, if also (multiply) deformational, confrontation with homegrown feminist, race, gender, and queer theoretical enterprises.

The years following this triumph of the constructivist paradigm have witnessed several waves of further rumination on the topic of the body, fueled by "inputs" as diverse as cybercultural studies and Luhmannian sociology. Yet, despite a common concern with the limitations of the antibiological imperative of cultural constructivism and a perception that making good on this concern was part of their driving purpose, these latter-day theories of the body have to date hardly succeeded in producing a viable—not to mention widely palatable—account of the role played by biological embodiment in cultural experience, identity, and community. Leaving aside speculation on the reasons for this failure, which are no doubt complex enough to merit a study of their own, I would like instead to postulate that the shift to a mixed reality paradigm in our contemporary technoculture (that is, in our contemporary culture) brings with it an opportunity to revalue the meaning and role accorded the body within the accepted conceptual frameworks of our philosophical tradition.

With its functionalist model of perceptuomotor activation, the mixed reality paradigm exposes the primacy of what, with Merleau-Ponty, we might call motor intentionality for the constitution of "reality." Although this primacy is certainly not new (indeed, it coincides, as Krueger's earlier cited claim suggests, with the proto-"origin" of the

7

human as a distinct species), the specific conditions of mixed reality (namely, the fusion of the virtual and the physical) bring it to the fore with unprecedented clarity and force. Today's exemplary mixed reality situations—interrupting a meeting to get data from a digital database, comparing a two-dimensional architectural drawing with a real-time three-dimensional visualization, acquiring an image of oneself through the social prosthesis of common sense that is contemporary television—all have as their condition the abandonment of the dream of total immersion, i.e., the representationalist form of verisimilitude. Thus, they literally beg the question of their possibility: what makes the passage from one realm to another so seamless, so unnoticeable, so believable?

The answer, as we have seen, is the capacity of our embodied form of life to create reality through motor activity. However, the crucial point here—and this is what makes mixed reality so promising—is that this question *did not need to be posed* so long as perceptual experience (with only atypical exceptions) remained within a single experiential frame—so long, that is, as experience typically occurred within a single perceptual world as a coupling to a single form of extension or homogeneous outside.

This, it should be obvious, is precisely what has changed with mixed reality, understood as one of those events, dear to Walter Benjamin, where a quantitative amplification self-modifies into a qualitative difference.[vi] As the experiential correlate of contemporary technics, mixed reality comprises a norm determining what perception is in the world today. Put another way, today's mixed reality paradigm makes ubiquitous (specifically as a technical phenomenon) what we might think of as the experiential condition of mixed reality—that is, mixed reality as the condition for all real experience in the world today. In this function, mixed reality opens a domain of "transcendental sensibility" (Deleuze) or of the "sensible-transcendental" (Irigaray)[9]. This transcendental domain, paradoxically, is entirely *within* the empirical world, though invisible to traditional philosophical modes of capture, and deploys technics as its nonsupplementary core or "essence."

If, in a certain sense, mixed reality specifies how "media determine our situation" (following Friedrich Kittler's media-theoretical deepening of Foucault's epistemo-transcendental historiography[10]), it does so in a way that foregrounds, not (as in Kittler) the autonomy of the technical, but precisely its opposite: the irreducible bodily or *analog* basis of experience which, we must add, has *always* been conditioned by a technical dimension and has *always* occurred as a cofunctioning of embodiment with technics. Here, the transcendental function of mixed reality as a specification (our contemporary specification) of technics is to stimulate or provoke the power of the body to open the world.[vii]

We must struggle to comprehend, then, how mixed reality can be *both* a minimal condition for experience of *and* a concrete moment in the history of human technogenesis in which the constituting or ontological dimension of embodiment is incontrovertibly exposed. (This is equally to fathom how mixed reality can harbor a "generic" technical element of experience, a technical–transcendental structure, at the same time as it demarcates a concrete technical stage of the history made possible by such a structure.) Let us say that mixed reality appears from the moment that tools first delocalized and distributed human sensation, notably touch and vision. (Following paleontologist Andre Leroi-Gourhan, this would mean from the "origin" of the human.[viii]) Placed in this context, mixed reality, then, designates *the general condition of phenomenalization* ensuing from the "originary" coupling of the human and the technical. It names an originary condition of real experience, a condition which can only be thought under the category of the transcendental because it can only be known through its effects.

To think our situation today, we must ask what happens when the transcendental structure underlying mixed reality—mixed reality as the technical conditioning of experience as such—gets exposed through and as the concrete technical configuration that specifies its being in the world today. Otherwise put, what remains unprecedented in the history of mixed reality (that is, of experience as such), and what is thus singular about our historicotechnical moment, is precisely the becoming-empirical, the empirical manifestation, of mixed reality as the transcendental–technical, the condition for the empirical as such.

Blindspot (1991), a recent work by American artist Tim Hawkinson, perfectly captures this leveling of the divide between the empirical and transcendental structures of mixed reality (see Figure 0.1). *Blindspot* is an anatomically arrayed photographic portrait of all the surface areas of the artist's body that he cannot see with his eyes. It brilliantly interweaves a paradigmatic expression of the minimal condition of mixed reality—the externalization of the gaze afforded by a reflective surface—with the technical condition of our being-in-the-world today: namely, our being subjected to and made subject by the technically-supported

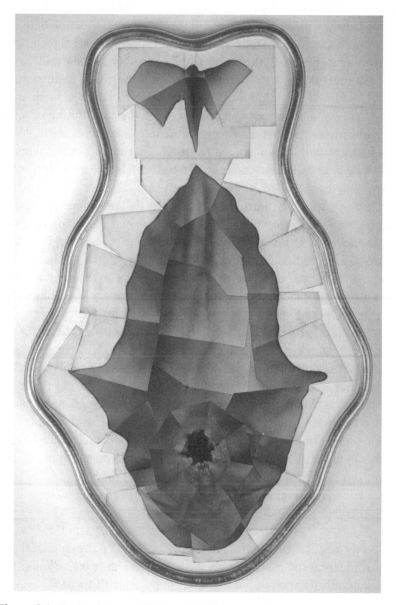

Figure 0.1 Tim Hawkinson, *Blindspot* (1991), photomontage capturing body surfaces not visible through natural perception. (Courtesy of the artist and the Whitney Museum of American Art.)

and technically-generated gaze of others, by the images of ourselves (including images through which we see ourselves) produced by and through society and the media.[ix]

Hawkinson's (critical) intervention into the terrain more or less owned by Lacanian theory is singular because of its rigorous commitment to sustaining the collapse of the boundary separating the empirical and the transcendental. *Blindspot* recognizes—indeed celebrates—the inescapability of a cofunctioning of "natural" perception and technically extended perception; it thus appropriates (or better, restores) the external imaging of the body as part of the body's constituting power.

Blindspot does not simply present an image of Hawkinson's body; rather, it images his body *from the standpoint of that body* (or better, of the organism that appears as that body). The image—which depicts what he *can't* see with his eyes—forms the strict correlate of what he *can* see and what, for that reason, does not require depiction. At the limit, then, the image of the body presented in *Blindspot* is not an image of the body, but rather an expression of the power (a power of imaging) that belongs to the embodied organism insofar as it is an "originarily" technical being.

Hawkinson's image thus makes common cause with French philosopher Raymond Ruyer's dismissal of the body as a merely scientific—that is, objectivized and external—entity, a kind of epiphenomenon of (radical) subjectivity:

> We are therefore, like all beings, pure subjectivities. Our organism (excluding the nervous system) is a set of subjectivities of a different order from conscious subjectivity. We are an object only in appearance; our body is an object only abstractly, in the subjectivity of those who observe us (or even, partially, in our subjectivity, when we see ourselves in a mirror or when we encounter ourselves as a particular image in our visual field). We are not, and other beings are not any more than us, really incarnate. Mind–body dualism is illusory *because we do not have a body*, because our organism is not a body.[11]

Despite appearances, Ruyer does not so much deny the (physical) reality of embodiment as displace it in favor of an ontological understanding of radical, indeed "originary," subjectivity. The body as object, along with incarnation and "conscious subjectivity," belongs to a derivative ontological plane, one that emerges from the primordial subjectivity—or, rather, the set of subjectivities—comprising the (human) organism.[x]

11

Like motoric embodiment discussed early, as well as Ruyer's later concept of the "absolute survey," the organismic perspective is absolute in the sense that it opens access to everything—to the world, to other bodies, to my body as object.

Ruyer conceptualizes his understanding as "reversed epiphenomenalism," meaning a reversal of the doctrine that subjectivity is an epiphenomenon of physical, material properties. For Ruyer, these latter (that is, the entire physical world, including that peculiar materiality known as consciousness) are simply epiphenomena of primary subjectivity.[xi] In this respect, Ruyer's work radicalizes the perspective of autopoietic theory, with its categorical and concept-defining privilege of the *operational* perspective of the organism over any *observational* perspective.[xii] For Ruyer, a primordial dimension of the living not only remains inaccessible from an external standpoint but also can only be (as philosopher Michel Piclin puts it) "felt from within."[12]

By assimilating the external image of the body to the perspective of the organism, Hawkinson's *Blindspot* might be said to depict the operational perspective for an age of total technical mediation (of *exposed* mixed reality) like ours. In so doing, *Blindspot* lays bare the technical element that inhabits the originary subjectivity of reversed epiphenomenalism: it reveals that self-experience today necessarily encompasses the power of imaging as a power of the organism (in this respect, it actualizes what has always been potentially the case). With its technical support in our world today, imaging has become what it has always been potentially: an aspect of *primary* self-experience (and not simply a derivative of the image of oneself held, and thus mediated, by the other).

Viewed in this context, Ruyer's own dismissal of the mirror image (a concrete figure for the minimal condition of mixed reality) can be seen as part of the technophobia characteristic of Western metaphysical discourse.[xiii] Eschewing such technophobia, Hawkinson announces in works like *Blindspot* that concrete technical conditions for self-experience today necessarily include the "internal observational" perspective made possible—*as a power of imaging*—by technical image mediation.

To anticipate an argument from Part II of this book, *Blindspot* thus pronounces the nonpathological generalization of the social–technical–psychological condition of psychasthenia, meaning "a state in which the space defined by the coordinates of the organism's body is confused with represented space".[13] If such a confusion has become normative for our experience in the world today—and what else is at stake in the technical exposure of mixed reality?—this is not because the organism has lost its perspective to that of external images (the gaze of the other), as *all* constructivist theories allege, but rather *because technical progress has exposed imaging as the crucial organismic dimension that it has always potentially been.*

With this conclusion, we are now in a position to fathom how the mixed reality paradigm (together with the second generation of virtual reality technologies that comprise its technical support) contributes to a revalued conceptualization of the body. With its picture of an originarily technical organismic perspective, this paradigm effectively repudiates all *externalist* accounts of the body, including constructivist theories that have recently held sway in critical discourse. It thus offers an affirmative model of bodily agency that conceives of the embodied organism's constitutive coupling with the social (paradigmatically, the technically mediated world of images, including linguistic images) in a fundamentally different manner than does (for example) Judith Butler's theory of performative iteration. The latter, *in the final instance*, subordinates the agency of the body (the force of iteration) to the content of the social images that, following the paradoxical operation of (linguistic) performativity, open up the space of its exercise.[xiv]

On the mixed reality paradigm, by contrast, coupling with the domain of social images occurs *from within the operational perspective* of the organism and thus comprises a component of its primordial embodied agency. One crucial consequence of this difference is the principle of indirection, loosely modeled on the autopoietic principle of organizational closure. This principle states that the organism undergoes change by reorganizing in reaction to external perturbation.

More precisely, because external images (including ones that are fantasized, i.e., of endogenous origin, as well as other images explicitly "from the operational perspective") have an impact on the organism *as part of its primordial operation*, they cannot be said to modify the organism *directly* (they do not comprise an informational input). Rather, they affect the organism *indirectly*, through the self-reorganization it undergoes in response to perturbation from the outside. Therefore, operating beneath the complex reappropriation of social images that Butler conceptualizes as performativity is a yet more primordial level of bodily, or organismic, processing. The latter forms nothing less than the enabling transcendental—the technical–transcendental—structure for the effects that Butler describes.

3. VIRTUAL REALITY AS EMBODIED POWER OF IMAGING

The potential promise of second-generation virtual reality/mixed reality for rethinking culture through embodiment reverberates throughout Alain Millon's recent discussion of the role of the body in media environments. Indeed, according to Millon, it is "across the virtual body that our culture constructs its own body image." That is why the conceptualization of the virtual body is a directly political issue, one that will determine not only the image but also the degree of agency our culture is willing to accord the body.

By postulating an opposition between "the cyberbody of cyberculture" and the "virtual body of computer modelization," the body "supposedly liberated from spatiotemporal constraints" and the body "immersed in these limits," Millon is able to specify the terms in which the externalist–internalist distinction comes to inhabit virtual reality, and, through it, the world itself (9). Thus, he asks:

> Is the virtual body simply a body without a corporeal envelop, a body without weakness, a body of pleasure without desire, in the end, a body without life? Isn't it rather a body in power, a body that anticipates all the forms but also all the thoughts to come, a body that furnishes the opportunity to pose the question of the person and its status, but also of its proper limit? (15)

Ultimately at stake in this questioning and in the distinction it supports are the irreducibility and priority of interior life, of the primordial organism, of the operational perspective. Millon makes this clear when he claims that the body "is not an envelop but an aggregate in which desire, suffering, and need find their place" (40); the body, he writes, forms an "obstacle and a resistance to all forms of transparence" and is living only "when it is opaque, complex, confused, flexible, and in perpetual mutation" (16). "In this perspective," he continues, "if there is a need for a liberation of the body, it is uniquely to affirm a more powerful interior life, all the while continuing to understand that the body remains … a presence" (40).

It is precisely the primordial operation of the organism that is at stake in the cultural debates surrounding the virtual body and it is entirely to Millon's credit that he understands this to be of direct concern to the social and cultural significance accorded the body: "The analysis of the virtual body … thus participates in a more global reflection on the manner in which our culture understands the body … [and] especially the way in which … it constructs a singular image of this body." Here, virtual reality is shown to comprise a chance for our culture to affirm the body as the primordial agency that it is, one that, as we have seen, includes imaging as part of its constituting power. The analysis of the virtual body thus constructs an "object that is a dense and opaque body, a body that has its limits and its weaknesses, an intimate body and one that, especially, refuses transparence and total clarity [*netteté*]" (18).

Forging such a cultural image of the body is crucial if we are to forestall the instrumentalization of the body and all that follows from it, above all the foreclosure of being-with or the finitude of our form of life.[xv] Far from being a mere "instrument" or the first "medium" (as some versions of posthumanism allege[xvi]), the body is a primordial and active source of resistance; indeed, it is as resistance—as the "living expression of something simultaneously organization and obstacle to its organization"—that the body forms the source of excess supporting all levels of constitution (or individuation), from the cellular to the cosmic.[xvii] As source of excess, the body possesses a flexibility that belies any effort, such as that of cyber-cultural criticism (and behind it, of cultural constructivism), to reduce it to a passive surface for social signification. The body is, affirms Millon, "an entity that becomes a person, a creative subject, a being or an individual according to the circumstances" (59).

As a technology that lays bare the enabling constraints of the body (that is, the body's *necessity*), virtual reality comprises our culture's privileged pathway for laying bare mixed reality as a technical–transcendental structure, which is equally to say, for exposing the technical element that lies at the heart of embodiment. To see why, let us turn to a pair of mixed reality works that correlate the contemporary generalization of psychasthenia—the confusion of the organismic with the representational and the ensuing exposure of imaging as a dimension of the organism—with the concrete context of virtual reality technologies.

In *Rigid Waves* and *Liquid Views*, Monika Fleischmann and Wolfgang Strauss present two technical mirrors for the self which function less to reflect the social gaze than to potentialize technical vision as a dimension of organismic being. Both works engage the myth of Narcissus and Echo to undermine the autonomy and closure of the visual register; to do so, both specifically, though differentially, interrogate the act of disappropriation and disembodiment involved in the "mirror image" (and also in the psychoanalytic interpellation it supports—namely, Lacan's famous "mirror stage"). The first work, *Rigid Waves* (1993), reproduces the apparatus of the mirror image only to decouple self and reflection (see Figure 0.2). As the artists explain, *Rigid Waves*

Figure 0.2 Monika Fleischmann and Wolfgang Strauss, *Rigid Waves* (1993), digital interactive work that disjoins the mirror image from the self, thus freeing "autonomous" self-images. (Courtesy of the artists.)

transforms the acoustic mirroring of Narcissus and Echo into visual form. Narcissus gives up his body to his mirror image. The "self" becomes another (body). His own movements are only an illusionary echo. As the observer approaches the mirror, he is confronted with a mirror image that does not correspond to his normal perception of things. He sees himself as an impression, as a body with strangely displaced movement sequences and, ultimately, as an image in the mirror that smashes as soon as he comes too close. He is unable to touch himself. A small camera hidden in the picture frame is used to place the observer in the image. The computer-controlled projection surface is controlled by an algorithm that calculates the distance to the observer. *Rigid Waves* is a virtual mirror which does not reflect but rather recognizes. Sight and movement, approaching and distance are triggers for the unusual images. This is an attempt to see oneself from the outside, to stand side by side with oneself and to discover other, hidden "selfs." In this fractured mirror, we are able to find ourselves, our "self" has been liberated. But how will I ever recognize myself again?[14]

Rigid Waves operates a disjunction of self from mirror image or, rather, of mirror image from self, thereby replacing the integrationist operation of mirror identification with the disintegrationist creation of autonomous self-images—images of the self unstuck from the self they image. The mobile spectator is empowered to control the changes the image undergoes, but cannot coincide visually with the image (because movement generates distortion) or touch the image (because proximity causes the image to shatter into pieces).

Situating perception between two perceptual limits (the distance required to see, on the one hand, and the distance required to touch, on the other), *Rigid Waves* thus liberates the self, as the artists proclaim, in an act of dispossession that leaves motility as compensation for loss of visual mastery. Their anxious query—"How will I ever recognize myself again?"—expresses the structure of transcendence inherent in motility as an existential dimension of human being. Because movement always displaces the self, thus preventing it from coinciding with itself, movement can only provisionally—or, perhaps better, only partially—compensate for the loss of visual identification.

Not surprisingly, the second installation, *Liquid Views: The Virtual Mirror of Narcissus* (1993), aims to complete this compensation (See Figure 0.3). It does so by coupling motility (specifically, tactile motility) directly with the deformation of the mirror image so that the

Figure 0.3 Monika Fleischmann and Wolfgang Strauss, *Liquid Views* (1993), digital interactive work that confronts the viewer with the scattering of his or her image. (Courtesy of the artists.)

17

viewer never loses control over the disintegration of the (self-)image. Thus, if *Rigid Waves* works to unfasten the self-image from the self (and vice versa), *Liquid Views* proffers a compensatory interface that reasserts—albeit, on radically different sensory terms—the embodied viewer's control over the body-image correlation. Again, let us allow the artists to describe the work:

> The central theme of *Liquid Views* is the well in which Narcissus discovers his reflection. He initially sees water as someone else, as another body. Like the small child in the various "mirror stages" described by Lacan, he decides to recognize his fictive body as himself. This installation has the objective of arousing the observer's curiosity and seducing him to undertake actions that bring him into contact with his senses.... Instead of pressing keys and buttons, the observer must experiment with his own sense of touch.... Attracted by the sounds of water and a room of shimmering lights, the visitor approaches the virtual well. Seeing the image of himself he is tempted to touch it. Touching the image with his fingertip, the image in the water breaks up. Drawn by the sensation triggered by touching his own image in the water, the observer immerses himself in the situation. (Fleischmann and Strauss, "Images")

What is striking about the experience of *Liquid Views* is that the image's scattering, far from ending engagement (as we might expect), in fact catalyzes a transition to another realm—to the realm of the disintegrated image. That is precisely why Fleischmann depicts the installation as an effort to open the access to the self closed up by Narcissus' "drowning in himself": "The central theme is the transition from the upper to the lower world.... The Narcissus of the media age is watching the world through a liquid mirror that questions our normal perception."[15] If this means that the "mirror becomes the actor," it acts *necessarily* in conjunction with the embodied spectator, whose immersion in the situation is enabled by the self-reflexivity characteristic of touch as the most primordial of the senses, as the root of premodal sensation.

The spectator's touch—touch as trigger for the image's scattering—materializes the power of imaging qua dimension of organismic being. Transformed from an external, visual image of the self into an internal correlate of the organism's imaging potentiality, the mirror of Liquid Views thus comprises what Fleischmann and Strauss call an "unsharp interface," an operator of the fusion of realms constitutive of the mixed reality paradigm: "The interface is not interpreted as such. It goes unnoticed and is not consciously perceived. These natural references turn *Liquid Views* and *Rigid Waves* into virtual reality." (Fleischmann and Strauss, "Images")

What makes these two works singular in the present context is the way that they support the opening of virtual reality not as a technical apparatus enabling some prescripted play, but rather as a *technically triggered experience of the organism's power of imaging*, an experience of imaging as an inherently technical, originary element of the organism's being. Here virtual reality is not built on a virtual reality support, so each work must produce the virtual; and because they can only do so through the interaction they trigger, we can rightly conclude that human experience actualizes the virtual potential of these art works. Accordingly, what these works add to the expression of Hawkinson's *Blindspot* is the direct incorporation of the concrete technologies supporting mixed reality: together, *Rigid Waves* and *Liquid Views* facilitate a comprehension on the part of the observer that his or her engagement with virtual reality technology *is* the contemporary manifestation of what can only be an originary correlation with technics.[xviii]

Commenting on an earlier work, Fleischmann and Strauss describe the transition from (external) image to (internal) imaging power, from the observational to the operational perspective, that informs such a comprehension. This transition renders their mixed reality works *allegories* of mixed reality as the minimal condition of phenomenalization:

> While the observer is only the onlooker, this "looking" is a kind of movement. It embodies "active observation." From a certain moment when the observer becomes immersed in the action, his "passive onlooking" is replaced by "active observation." The observer discovers that he—and not the artist—is the one creating the situation. When the situation changes and the observer becomes a player, he suddenly begins to identify himself with the situation. Observation becomes more than merely consumption.[16]

By catalyzing a coincidence of observational and operational perspectives, virtual reality artwork, as Fleischmann and Strauss describe it, perfectly captures the transformation at issue in the recuperation of imaging as a fundamental, existential power. When observation ceases to be consumption, imaging takes its proper place *within* the organism's primordial operation as a general condition of phenomenalization.

Contrasted with Hawkinson's *Blindspot*, therefore, *Rigid Waves* and *Liquid Views* expand the agency of the operational perspective because they directly incorporate the concrete technologies supporting mixed reality. More precisely, by placing the organism into relation with the image as a dimension of its operation and by supporting the disjunction between embodiment and imaging (i.e., the otherness and the disintegrating function of the image), *Rigid Waves* and *Liquid Views* facilitate the actualization of the organism's potential to extend its bodily boundaries and to expand the scope of its bodily agency.

What is then singular about these two works as exemplars of digital art and as mediators for digital culture is their use of the concrete technology of virtual reality *to stage a disconnection of the (fundamentally motile) body schema from the (fundamentally visual) body image*. In the experience of *Rigid Waves* and *Liquid Views*, the viewer is technically enabled to utilize the excess of the body schema over the body image to increase his agency as an embodied being.

Such technical mediation of the body schema (of the scope of body–environment coupling) comprises what I propose to call a *"body-in-code."* By this I do not mean a purely informational body or a digital disembodiment of the everyday body. I mean a body submitted to *and constituted by* an unavoidable and empowering technical deterritorialization—a body whose embodiment is realized, *and can only be realized,* in conjunction with technics. As I shall argue in this study, it is precisely through the vehicle of bodies-in-code that our contemporary technoculture, driven by digital technologies, comes to constitute a distinct concrete phase in our contemporary technogenesis (our originary yet historico-technically differentiated coevolution with technics).

Indeed, if we take the experience of *Rigid Waves* and *Liquid Views* as exemplary of this phase, we can immediately comprehend how digital technologies, as the contemporary expression of the originary technical mediation of the human, broaden what we might call the sensory *commons*—the space that we human beings share by dint of our constitutive embodiment. This is because digital technologies:

1. Expand the scope of bodily (motor) activity; and thereby
2. Markedly broaden the domain of the *prepersonal*, the organism–environment coupling operated by our nonconscious, deep embodiment; and thus
3. Create a rich, anonymous "medium" for our enactive co-belonging or "being-with" one another; which thereby
4. Transforms the agency of collective existence (of individual and collective individuation, to use French philosopher of technology Gilbert Simondon's terminology) from a self-enclosed and primarily cognitive operation to an essentially open, only provisionally bounded, and fundamentally motor, participation.

To think of the body as a *body-in-code*, then, is simultaneously to think of human existence as a *prepersonal* sensory being-with. As we will see, this is largely responsible for the promise of the digital, understood not as some autonomous moment in the history of technology but rather, first and foremost, as a stage in the ongoing technogenesis of the human.

To conceptualize this particular stage of our technogenesis—and the particular technical expansion of prepersonal bodily function that digital technologies facilitate—we will need to draw extensively on philosophical and psychological exploration of the "body schema" and the skin as a generalized sense organ. We will also need to develop a fundamentally or "essentially" technical phenomenology of the body, one that takes as its primary task the elucidation of the originary technical basis of embodied experience. Part I of my study is devoted to this task. Not surprisingly, it progresses through and attempts to update the work of Maurice Merleau-Ponty, the phenomenologist most committed to the ontological dimension of (human) embodiment.

The discussion begins with two crucial and interrelated concepts of Merleau-Ponty's *Phenomenology of Perception*—namely, the absolute priority of the phenomenal body (largely akin to the operational perspective of the organism) and the primary role accorded bodily motility (i.e., the body schema) in the constitution of a systemic coupling between organism and environment. The argument ultimately aims to conceptualize a technics on the basis of (and adequate to) the chiasmic correlation of being and world that forms the heart of Merleau-Ponty's final unfinished project, as documented particularly in *The Visible and the Invisible* and *Nature*. In contrast to the clearly delineated (and still subordinate or secondary) dimension of technics associated with Merleau-Ponty's exploration of motor intentionality in the *Phenomenology* (a dimension famously telescoped in the example of the blindman's stick), such a technics must be capable of supporting—of *being*—the *medium* of human individual and collective individuation.

The theoretical argument of Part I gives way in Part II to a logic of singular exemplarity. In the four chapters of this section, theoretical analysis will be made immanent to sustained exploration of notable instances of digital culture—singular instances in which a "body-in-code" functions to open the digital as a medium of prepersonal commonality. In line with our effort to restore virtuality as an originary technical element of human being and to expose mixed reality as its contemporary phenomenological dimension, these four chapters will implicitly narrate a progression backwards from the most artificial (and narrow) conception of virtual reality to the most natural (and broad) conception.

Thus these chapters will move from the brilliantly unconventional virtual environments of artist Char Davies (Chapter 2) to the imaginary reality of fiction as exemplified in Mark Danielewski's recent novel, *House of Leaves* (Chapter 5). The Internet as the medium for contemporary community (Chapter 3) and architectural space as a predigital and originary mixed reality (Chapter 4) will instance two intermediary points along the continuum connecting these poles. Singly and as well as a whole, these Chapters will "exfoliate" crucial aspects of the essentially analog basis of the virtual that necessarily installs it, to recall Massumi's argument, as the vehicle for any (concrete) technical contribution (including that of the so-called digital) to our ongoing and constitutive technogenesis.

PART

I

toward a technics
<u>of the flesh</u>

bodies in code, or how primordial tactility introjects technics into human life

Artificial realities are based on the premise that the perceptual intelligence that all men share is more powerful than the symbol manipulation skills that are the province of the few.

Myron Krueger[1]

1. "MAKE USE OF WHAT NATURE HAS GIVEN US!"

If Myron Krueger deserves to be heralded as the pioneer of interactive media art, this has more to do with the aesthetic qualities of his interactive platform than its undeniable technical contribution. From the beginning, Krueger's interest concerned the *enactive* potentialities afforded by the new media and not their representational or simulational capacities. He recalled this commitment in a recent interview:

In 1970, I considered HMDs (head mounted displays) and rejected them because I thought whatever benefit they provided in visual immersion was offset by the encumbering paraphernalia which I felt would distance participants from the world they were supposed to feel immersed in. When I pondered what the ultimate experience would feel like, I decided that it *should be indistinguishable from real experience.* It would not be separated from reality by a process of suiting up, wearing gear, and being tethered to a computer by unseen wires.... Rather than limiting your participation to a single hand-held 3D pointing device, your image would appear in the world and every action of your body could be responded to instantaneously. Whereas the HMD folks thought that 3D scenery was the essence of reality, I felt that *the degree of physical involvement was the measure of immersion.*[2]

In an artistic (and engineering) career wagered on this commitment, Krueger has quite literally sketched out an alternative trajectory to that followed by mainstream virtual reality research, art practice, and cultural ideology. Rather than investing in the simulational power of the image and the ocularcentric paradigm of immersion, Krueger has staked everything on the constructive power of (human) embodiment. For him, virtual reality technologies are important, indeed momentous, not because they lend new, stronger material support for the image (whether it is conceptualized in the frame or the panorama traditions), but precisely because they extend the body's power to construct space and world.

In this deployment, technologies work to expand the body's motile, tactile, and visual interface with the environment; to do so, they call upon—and ultimately, refunctionalize—the body's role as an "invariant," a fundamental access onto the world, what psychologists and phenomenologists have called the "body schema." In this way, digital technologies lend support to a phenomenological account of embodiment and expose the technical element that has always inhabited and mediated our embodied coupling with the world. Indeed, as we shall see, they add a technohistorical basis to the claims of those contemporary researchers who not only align the body schema with proprioception but also propose this latter as a sixth (and more fundamental or somehow originary) sense.

This subordination of technics to embodied enaction motivates (and licenses) me to position Krueger as the precursor—and first practitioner—of second-generation virtual (or mixed) reality. Together with the more interesting digital artists of today (indeed, in many cases, as a direct inspiration to them), Krueger views and deploys the virtual less as an alternate, body-transcending space than as a new, computer-enhanced (if not in some important sense, computer-facilitated) domain of affordances for extending our evolutionarily accomplished interface with the world. Understood against this background, Krueger's renegade act of renaming can be seen to mount an aesthetic, indeed properly philosophical, challenge to the mainstream. As Krueger explains, the term "artificial reality" more aptly captures how "virtual reality" functioned, not simply or primarily as a technical platform, but rather as a "metaphor for what was happening throughout our society" (Turner).

Yet, if Krueger's theory and work resonate with the second-generation paradigm of mixed reality, this is due less to his original aim (provoking the flat-footed humanism of the art world[i]) than to the singular convergence of the "artificial" and the "natural" in the electronics technologies ubiquitous in our world today.[ii] This is a reality not lost on Krueger, who has recently noted: "Since I was arguing for convenience, naturalness, and obviousness, my concepts were well-positioned for technological advances as they unfolded. Since 99% of applications are 2D and 99% of 3D applications are driven by 2D interfaces, there has been very little immediate interest in HMD immersion systems in the general office environment," not to mention the world beyond. As if echoing (or ventriloquizing) the proponents of the mixed reality paradigm, Krueger speaks of a "progression towards external realities" driven by the technical development of low-cost projectors and organic LED displays that can be ubiquitously embedded in the environment; rather than withdrawing from the physical domain, today's digital technologies are literally virtualizing the physical.

Krueger's calculated defense of the artificial notwithstanding, the operative principle of his research and artistic experimentation could easily be summarized in the form of a practical maxim: *make use of what nature has given us!* "In our physical reality," Krueger observes, "We use our bodies to interact with objects. We move our bodies or turn our heads to see better. We see other people and they can see us. We have acquired a consistent set of expectations through a lifetime of experience" (148). Making use of this evolutionarily realized heritage will allow us to adapt to our ever more rapidly changing technical environment because such heritage provides a stable background against which to assimilate new interactional spaces and share new affordances: "Any system that observes these conventions will be instantly understood by everyone on the planet" (148).

More than a simple desire to buck the technicist trend, Krueger's work is informed by his conviction that the best way for us to bring technologies to bear on human existence—to shepherd our ongoing technogenesis as it undergoes its most accelerated phase to date—is to channel them through our evolutionarily acquired embodiment. This explains his lifelong commitment to a humanist model in which human interaction (encompassing interaction with the self, with others, and with machines) prevails over any notion of technicist instrumentalization. Krueger's environments function practically, following the characterization of Howard Rheingold, as "laboratories for finding out how humans might harmonize with" technical environments whose sway is (and has always been) inescapable.[iii,3]

The benefits of such an artistic (and scientific) program are twofold: On one hand, human embodiment serves to "naturalize" technical modifications of the world (and, potentially, of the body); on the other hand, these modifications provide an important source for decoupling or deterritorialization by which the body's habitual intercourse with the world gets disturbed and (potentially) expanded. Embodiment accommodates and self-reorganizes in the face of the ever expanding scope of technics in our world today.

In a series of works culminating in the ground-breaking video projection system *Videoplace*, Krueger has sought to materialize his conviction that "the focus of interface research should be on human nature, not on the transient computer" (Krueger, "An Easy Entry," 147). This conviction has led him to construct environments that eschew the logic emanating from computer code in favor of emergent logics rooted in social conventions. Never an end in itself in Krueger's work, the computer is always a vehicle for exploring and expanding embodied (human) interaction with the world and with other human beings. "In the ultimate interface," he stresses, "input should come from our voices and bodies and output should be directed at all our senses. Since we will also interact with each other through computers, the ultimate interface should also be judged by how well it helps us to relate to each other" (147).

This principled emphasis on human embodiment as mediator between computer and world represents something new in the history of our technogenesis: in its role as primary access to a (now) highly technologized lifeworld, embodiment serves to couple body and world, as well as to actualize the potential of digital (virtual reality) technologies to modify the lifeworld (and, thereby, to infiltrate that primary enactive, world-constitutive coupling). Embodied enaction is, quite literally, the agent through which technics has an impact on life and the lifeworld.

If Krueger's entire career seems dedicated to exposing nothing more or less than this primacy of embodied enaction, the latter—as he points out—ushers in an important, and enabling, margin of indetermina-tion: "The logical consequence of this thought process [yielding the conception of the ultimate interface] was the concept of an artificial reality in which the laws of cause and effect were designed to facilitate the functions that interested the user" (148). It would hardly be an exag-geration to claim that this margin of indetermination—one directly tied to technics—comprises *the* operative principle of Krueger's embodied aesthetics of new media. The new technical environments afford noth-ing less than an opportunity to *suspend* habitual causal patterns and, subsequently, to *forge* new patterns through the medium of embodi-ment—that is, by tapping into the flexibility (or potentiality) that char-acterizes humans as fundamentally embodied creatures.

That this principle comprises the explicit focus of Krueger's first, predigital responsive environment amply attests to its centrality in his aesthetics. *Glowflow* (1969) is a light–sound environment—a room with four horizontal light tubes running along its walls—that deploys visual and auditory means to disturb the visitor's habitual mode of perceiving space (see Figure 1.1). The room is entirely dark except for the multi-colored phosphorescent light tubes which form the only visual point of reference for the visitor. Movement within the darkened space inevitably causes the visitor to step on floor sensors that release into the tubes light and sound elements from one of four enclosed light columns (one per tube). Outside of this element of interactivity, the pigments running through the tubes remain arbitrarily determined.

What proved compelling about the environment and most capti-vated Krueger's aesthetic interest was the way that viewers inevitably, one might even want to say "naturally," attempted to make sense of the environment by coupling intentional gestures (e.g., speaking or moving) with the (mostly arbitrary) patterns of light in the tubes. As Krueger recounts in *Artificial Reality 2*,

> If a tube started glowing after [the visitors] spoke, they would assume that their speech had turned it on. If a sound occurred after

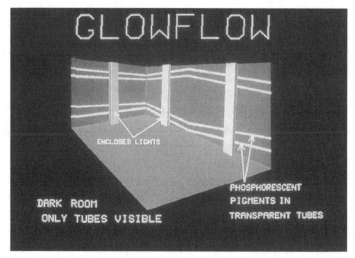

FIGURE 1.1 Myron Krueger, *Glowflow* (1969), light–sound reactive environment that deploys visual and auditory means to disturb the visitor's habitual mode of perceiving space. (Courtesy of the artist.)

they hit the wall, they would assume that striking the wall would elicit more sounds. Often, they would persist in the behavior long after the result should have convinced them that their hypotheses were incorrect.[4]

This emergent and unexpected phenomenon alerted Krueger to the possibility and value of exploiting the margin of indetermination afforded by experience with new technologies and media environments.[iv] As Söke Dinkla has observed,

The behavior of the visitor comprised efforts to figure out the rule system of *Glowflow*. The process of rational clarification of cause and effect proceeded precisely opposite to its normal pattern: an effect would dictate its cause and not the reverse [*Einer Wirkung wurde eine Ursache zugeschrieben und nicht umgekehrt*]. Such exploratory behavior is typical when it is a question of accommodating oneself to foreign surroundings whose rules are unknown. (67)

In one way or another, all of Krueger's environments exploit this technique of disturbing habitual cause and effect couplings to domesticate novel experiential domains through the primary medium of embodiment.

With his subsequent (and properly digital) environments, however, Krueger added a crucial element to this technique of domestication: the calculated feedback of new sensory experiences into embodied enaction for the express purpose of expanding the latter's agency (together with the scope of its coupling with the environment).[v] What made this possible and served to distinguish Krueger's environments from the majority of art environments from the 1960s was Krueger's insistence on clarifying for the visitor precisely how his or her actions called forth reactions from the environment. Because this insistence is due, in part at least, to the analytical precision afforded by the computer as a material support for the interactive environment, it yields a specific, technical (but not technicist) conception of interactivity: "dealings [*einen Umgang*] with the computer in which the receiver/user is able clearly to correlate her actions with the reactions of the system" (Dinkla, 70). Such correlation, affirms artist Simon Penny, comprises "the first and fundamental law of the aesthetics of interactive installation" (Simon Penny, email to the author, January 3, 2006).

On this conception, interactivity can be distinguished from prevailing notions of the period and from more contemporary technicist visions. It is at once more codified than the radically open-ended environments of process art and happenings and yet more open and flexible than the preprogrammed response repertoires that one finds in so-called interactive cinema and hypertext. What is crucial in Krueger's conception of interactivity, as in his humanist conception of artificial reality more generally, is the privilege accorded embodied (human) agents. Differences notwithstanding, the point of all of his environments is to facilitate new kinds of world-construction and intersubjective communication. If these environments do still serve as interfaces *to* the computer, they do not do so, as do all technicist conceptions of the "Human–Computer Interface" (including the mouse and the graphical-user interface), by instrumentalizing—and thus reducing—embodied enaction; here, rather, it is the technology that remains instrumentalized and human action that gets privileged.

From 1970 to 1984 (when he ceased development of his interactive platform, *Videoplace*), Krueger devoted himself to the task of producing an environment that would realize the potential of the computer to expand human capacities for embodied enaction and communication. Not surprisingly, this realization—accomplished in *Videoplace*—proceeded through several discrete stages, each of which marks an important advance in the transfer of agency from the computer to embodiment in open-ended feedback with itself.

Metaplay (1970) combined closed-circuit (video) technology with the computer to explore the conditions for the correlation by the visitor

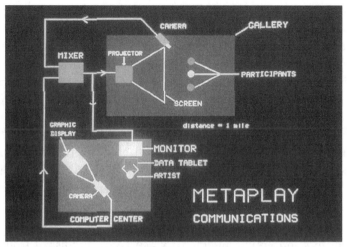

FIGURE 1.2 Myron Krueger, *Metaplay* (1970), interactive environment, functional diagram. (Courtesy of the artist.)

of her actions and the system's reactions. This environment established a real-time communication circuit between participants in a gallery, who encounter a projected two-dimensional image of their bodies, and the artist who, located in a separate space, employs a data-tablet and pen to draw directly on the projection screen, thereby provoking responses from and stimulating further interaction with the visitors (see Figure 1.2). As Andy Cameron has recently pointed out, *Metaplay* offered Krueger an opportunity to "explore the kinds of interactions which he had been unable to explore in *Glowflow*—an interaction which is *explicit* and which is capable of engaging people within a new kind of aesthetic experience."[5]

Rather than the amorphous and nondirected action–reaction couplings that spontaneously (and most often erroneously) emerged in *Glowflow, Metaplay* clarifies the correlation of (visitor) action and (system) reaction precisely by isolating it and embedding it within a tightly coupled, clearly delineated circuit. To achieve this isolation, the environment sacrifices the autonomy of response. As Cameron notes, because the technology to create a truly interactive computer-supported responsive environment was unavailable (at least to Krueger), he was forced "to *simulate* interactive technology, using people behind a screen [the artist, in the case of *Metaplay*] to provide the system responses. In this odd and oddly productive reversal of the classic Turing test, the "participants would think they were interacting with an interactive environment, but in fact they would be interacting with concealed human beings" (Cameron, 18).

What the environment gains from this sacrifice is the creativity of indirection, here instantiated in the margin of indeterminacy emerging in the space between Krueger's doodlings and the visitor's responses. Because the action–response circuit involves something beyond what can be contained in or determined by any technological interface— something *unpredictable* from the system's perspective—it privileges creativity over technicity. As Cameron suggests, this achievement—generating a working prototype of a new kind of communication with the paltriest of resources—is Krueger's most impressive: "By prototyping the experience, rather than the technology, ... Krueger was able to explore the aesthetic space of an interactive installation before the technology existed" (Cameron, 18).

When the source of indirection is subsequently integrated into the technical circuit, as it is in *Psychic Space* (1971), it simply cannot betoken any kind of break with Krueger's thoroughgoing privileging of the aesthetic over the technical. Rather, what is at stake here is a (partial) restoration of autonomy to the responsive environment, a restoration accomplished through the incorporation of feedback—and with it, of the element of *unpredictability*—as an internal aspect of the installation's solicitation and process-based generation of experience (see Figure 1.3). In this sense, *Psychic Space* marks a monumental accomplishment: the *extrinsic* source

FIGURE 1.3 Myron Krueger, *Psychic Space* (1971), interactive environment. (Courtesy of the artist.)

of creative indirection—Krueger's doodlings—is replaced by an *intrinsic* and *ineliminable* source—the embodied viewer's self-movement.

The operative technical element of this intrinsic feedback circuit is the use of motion sensors (in the place of the artist's external intervention); by placing the visitor into real-time interaction with data capturing the movement of her reactions within the environment, *Psychic Space* transforms embodied movement into the source of creative indetermination and, consequently, into the aesthetic focus of the environment. Dinkla emphasizes the (relative) novelty of this configuration:

> [*Psychic Space*] confronts the visitor … with the graphic, projected image of a lozenge that follows her movement. Just as Krueger moved the pen across the data tablet in *Metaplay*, now the visitor *can couple herself to the graphic symbol through her embodied movement*. The fact that the visitor engages in communication by way of her body stands in stark contrast to the typical interchange with the computer from this time …. (Dinkla, 73, emphasis added)

Although the visitor is initially invited to focus on the lozenge's function as a symbol of her self, the lozenge soon becomes enclosed by a small square that, triggered by the visitor's effort to move beyond this confine, then becomes a maze within which she is beckoned to wander freely. The aesthetic interest of the environment is thus shifted from the feedback circuit to the interactive possibilities that it facilitates.

In stark contrast to typical computer games, these possibilities offered by *Psychic Space* are not guided by any clearly defined goal and do not culminate in the successful accomplishment of a task. Rather, the environment is designed in such a way as to hinder the viewer's progress toward any such goal; for example, the computer will suddenly readjust the configuration of the maze at the moment when the visitor is nearing its exit, or it will shift the output generated by the visitor's movement so that it correlates with horizontal rather than vertical movement of the graphic symbol. In sum, the computer here functions to perturb the natural tendency of the primarily motile visitor to pursue a prescribed goal and thereby to foreground the flexibility and generativity of unreflective, learned social rules against the rigidity of the explicitly coded "if–then," rules governing the operation of computers (as well as the predominant visions of human–computer interface at the time).

As Dinkla puts it, *Psychic Space* "automatizes" socially coded, embodied behavior by prototyping its deployment as a source of creative feedback for adaptation to constantly changing situations (74). In this way, the environment continually solicits the visitor to affirm her agency, which is to say, the fact that the remapping and extension of *her* movement into this new space is the environment's driving purpose.

Videoplace, Krueger's interactive platform, marks a further and, in some sense, ultimate, stage in the restoration of autonomy to the responsive environment, understood as encompassing—and indeed as the interactional domain structurally coupled to —the embodied visitor. Like *Psychic Space, Videoplace* works by capturing an image of the visitor's movement, only in this case the image presents the outline of the visitor's body processed (and distorted in various ways) by the computer. Several different programs facilitate viewer interaction with the schematic traces of her bodily movement; for example, they allow her to fill in the space within the lines with colored images of body parts or to interact with temporally divergent and continually reverberating captures of her movement (see Figure 1.4).

More than anything else, *Videoplace* is differentiated from Krueger's earlier responsive environments by the technical and aesthetic accomplishment of complete action–response synchronicity. Here, the computer does not react to the visitor with a discrete response that in turn triggers an action on the part of the visitor (and so on); rather, because

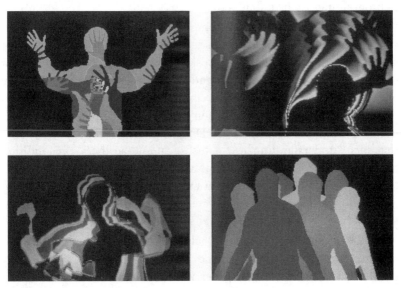

FIGURE 1.4 Myron Krueger, *Videoplace* (1974–1975), interactive environment/ platform, interaction sequence. (Courtesy of the artist.)

the computer's activity—some programmed modification of the data capturing the visitor's movement—coincides absolutely with that movement it becomes (or is experienced as) *an indissociable part of its agency*. This accomplishment of synchronicity shifts the aesthetic interest of the environment from the clarification of the visitor–system correlation (Krueger's guiding concern up to this point) to the newfound capacity for expanded agency:

> On account of the synchronicity [of the movement of the video image] with the movement of the [visitor's] body, it is no longer a question of distinguishing between the activity of the system and the activity of the visitor. The computer system's role as interaction partner fades into the background, and it now makes itself available as an instrument [*Instrumentarium*] for the visitor to use. (Dinkla, 82)

The accomplishment of synchronicity is accompanied by a displacement of the artist as programmer and a wholesale inversion of the problematic of simulation. With the shift away from the visitor–system correlation to the action of a now unified single enactive "system-agent," the function of programming undergoes profound transformation from a close-looped technical element to an open-ended social capability. As Dinkla argues, the environments supported by *Videoplace* are designed "to learn from the visitors." Krueger's goal, she continues, was "to delegate his role as programmer to the public" (78).

With this shift in aesthetic emphasis comes an equally profound shift in technical emphasis that is definitive for the entire trajectory of media art that I am attempting to sketch here. Rather than calling on the user to adapt to the computer and to learn its language (as is the case with most HCI systems), here the computer is called upon to "learn to understand the natural means of communication" employed by embodied humans: in this case, gestures (Dinkla, 78). It should be clear by now that such "understanding" is the technical and aesthetic precondition for the synchronicity of system and visitor action. Without it, the visitor–system correlation could never move beyond the stage of clarifying exploration; it could never be directed to the world of action and could never become creative in the proper sense.

Thus, *Videoplace* ultimately achieves nothing short of a wholesale humanistic dissolution of the infamous—and for many, highly problematic—Turing test (together with Turing's abstract conception of a general-purpose computing machine). Far from maintaining an emphasis on the behavioral indiscernibility of human and computer and on the general problem of simulation, *Videoplace* seeks to engineer a human–computer cooperation so seamless that functional synchronicity becomes possible in practice. Put another way, *Videoplace* replaces the observation of behavioral output central to the Turing paradigm of simulation with a functional criterion: the operational "congruence of actions of the user and reactions of the system" (Dinkla, 83). Its purpose is neither epistemological nor ontological—to fool a human observer—but purely functional: to integrate the computer as seamlessly as possible into the motor activity of embodied human agents.

Given *Videoplace*'s eschewal of "visual similarity" as a criterion of function, it is hardly surprising that the payoff of its functional dissolution of the Turing paradigm would be a capacity for coupling motor activity to graphic symbols and effects that bear no direct resemblance to the human body. In this respect, *Videoplace* realizes a degree of flexibility unprecedented in aesthetic mediations of the body (even within Krueger's work): by coupling the motile body with graphic elements that do not visually imitate or simulate it, *Videoplace* opens a disjunction between the body image and the body schema. More exactly, by deploying sensors to capture the movement of the body through a concrete space and in conjunction with a virtual element, it displaces the body image—that is, a predominately visual representation of the body, a primary resemblance—and offers in its place a new, representative but not representational "image," a graphic symbol that attains its force only through its inclusion within the body schema, through its motor coupling with embodied enaction.

For Dan Cameron, this displacement explains how Krueger is able to bring "a new category of beauty" into the world. By "making the body proprioceptively aware of itself, and of its relation to the artwork and to other viewers," Krueger manages to "reconfigure" the "representation" of the "human image" in a decisive way (Cameron, 24). In sum, the displacement of the body image by the generative activity of the body schema is what makes Krueger's art so powerful an intervention into digital culture. In stark contrast to the fatalism of critics like Baudrillard and Kittler for whom the abstract generality of digital code marks a fundamental and irremediable departure from the phenomenological ratios governing human experience, Krueger places human embodiment in a position to constrain the "referencelessness of digital code," thereby installing it as the agent whose action actualizes the (abstract) potential of code.[vi]

We are now in a position to see why Krueger's work, perhaps more than the work of any other digital artist, exemplifies the twofold movement informing the concept of the "body-in-code." Although Krueger's environments subordinate computer code to the more supple codings of human interaction, thus introducing a significant element of flexibility, they also deploy computer code to trigger or catalyze expansions of embodied agency. On this exemplary model, a body-in-code can be defined as a body whose (still primary) constructive or creative power is expanded through new interactional possibilities offered by the coded programs of "artificial reality."

Because of the way in which it challenges our received conceptions of embodiment—most significantly, by refusing to oppose embodiment to technics and by conjoining the two in a highly productive, functional manner—Krueger's work not only exemplifies the way in which technologies support the world-constituting function of embodiment in the world today, but also urges a fundamental reassessment of phenomenology in light of technics. In so doing, Krueger's work does not so much stand against phenomenology as guide us in the task of assessing the radically creative scope of embodiment in our highly technologized world. Like the art it inspired (directly and indirectly), Krueger's environments give us impetus to challenge the more conservative assumptions informing phenomenology and in this way help to bring out its more radical promise for thinking what I elsewhere call "technical life."

2. BODY SCHEMA AS POTENTIALITY

Notwithstanding the truly disastrous mistranslation of *schema corporel* by "body image," Merleau–Ponty's chapter on "The Spatiality of One's Own Body and Motility" from *The Phenomenology of Perception* offers an account of the body schema as a flexible, plastic, systemic form of distributed agency encompassing what takes place within the boundaries of the body proper (the skin) as well as the entirety of the spatiality of embodied motility. In so doing, as we shall see, Merleau–Ponty opens the possibility of categorically distinguishing the body schema from the body image and thus of putting the former—hitherto a mere object of scientific exploration—to properly philosophical work.

The distinction runs as follows: Whereas the body image characterizes and is generated from a primarily visual apprehension of the body as an external object, the body schema emerges from what, with autopoietic theory, we have called the operational perspective of the embodied organism. As such, it encompasses an "originary," preobjective process of world constitution that, by giving priority to the internal perspective of the organism, paradoxically includes what is outside its body proper, what lies in the interactional domain specified by embodied enaction. Three important consequences follow from this distinction: first, the body is always in excess over itself; second, this excess involves the body's coupling to an external environment; and third, because such coupling is increasingly accomplished through technical means, this excess (which has certainly always been *potentially* technical) can increasingly be actualized only with the explicit aid of technics.

This means that Merleau–Ponty's phenomenology of embodiment is, from the beginning, a philosophy of embodied technics in which the excess constitutive of embodiment—the horizon of potentiality associated with the body schema—forms a ready conduit for incorporating the technical at the heart of human motility. Accordingly, one of our pressing tasks here will be to think this "originary" technics as it might have been (but was not) developed by Merleau–Ponty, to think this technics beginning from but moving well beyond Merleau–Ponty's limited conception of prosthetics as the extension of bodily habit. In doing so, however, we must never lose sight of the fact that Merleau–Ponty—with the ontological conception of the body schema and its later extension-dissolution in the concept of the flesh—himself gives us the means to do so.

More than any other commentator on the philosopher, Shaun Gallagher emphasizes the centrality of the body schema–body image distinction for Merleau–Ponty's break with "classical" (Husserlian) phenomenology. According to Gallagher, the distinction correlates with the task of thinking "the human body on both sides of the intentional relation"; thus, the body image designates the body as the object or content of intentional (or noetic) consciousness, whereas the body schema characterizes the body as a "prenoetic" function, a kind of infraempirical or sensible–transcendental basis for intentional operation. "In contrast to the intentional (and sometimes conscious) nature of the body image, a *body schema* involves an extraintentional operation carried out prior to or outside of intentional awareness."[6] More explicitly still,

> [It] involves a system of motor capacities, abilities, and habits that enable movement and the maintenance of posture. The body schema

is not a perception, a belief, or an attitude. Rather, it is a system of motor and postural functions that operate below the level of self-referential intentionality, although such functions can enter into and support intentional activity. The preconscious, subpersonal processes carried out by the body-schema system are tacitly keyed into the environment and play a dynamic role in governing posture and movement. Although the body-schema system can have specific effects on cognitive experience, it does not have the status of a conscious representation or belief.[7]

Gallagher goes on to explain how the operations of the body schema "provide specific conditions that constrain perceptual consciousness." Not only does he thereby situate it as the condition of possibility for phenomenologically accessible experience, but also—more importantly for our purposes—he makes it available as a source for the indirect modification of that experience.

One crucial consequence of Merleau–Ponty's principled and philosophical distinction between body image and body schema is, as Gallagher points out, a methodological limitation on the phenomenological method: "The prenoetic role of the body schema is impenetrable to phenomenological reflection" (233). If this limitation requires a (nonreductive) appeal to the empirical sciences, as Gallagher suggests, it also, more consequentially, marks the operation of a "transcendental sensibility" at the heart of Merleau–Ponty's phenomenology of embodiment and, specifically, of his concept of the "phenomenal body."

This is just what is at issue in Merleau–Ponty's characterization of the body schema as a "law of [the body's] constitution": such a characterization is meant to capture the fact that

> The spatial and temporal unity, the inter-sensory or the sensorimotor unity of the body is, so to speak, *de jure*, that it is not confined to contents actually and fortuitously associated in the course of experience, that it is in some way *anterior to them and makes their association possible*."[8]

This is equivalent to saying that the motile or "phenomenal" body, the body as body schema, precedes and informs the constitution of the objective domain (including the body as object, or the body image) and the correlative demarcation of the subjective:

> Our bodily experience of movement is not a particular case of knowledge; it provides us with a way of access to the world and the object, with a "praktognosia," which has to be recognized *as original and*

perhaps as primary. My body has its world, or understands its world, without having to make use of my "symbolic" or "objectifying" function. (140, emphasis added)

Elsewhere, Merleau–Ponty speaks of the body schema as a "system of equivalents," an "immediately given invariant," a "general medium for having a world" (141; 146).

This conception of the phenomenal body as a kind of primary access to the world (a world that includes the body) resonates with the privilege of the operational perspective granted the living (human) organism in autopoietic theory. Specifically, it establishes the phenomenal body and its operational perspective, not as a correlate of the objective body and the observational perspective, but rather as the source of both perspectives, indeed of the very possibility of having a perspective as such:

> It is not a question of how the soul acts on the objective body, since it is not on the latter that it acts, but on the phenomenal body. So the question has to be reframed, and we must ask why there are two views of me and of my body: my body for me and my body for others, and how these two systems can exist together. It is indeed not enough to say that the objective body belongs to the realm of "for others," and my phenomenal body to that of "for me," and we cannot refuse to pose the problem of their relations, *since the "for me" and the "for others" coexist in one and the same world*…. (106, emphasis added)

As the primarily active potential that gives the "for me" and the "for others," the phenomenal body thus constitutes a (preobjective and presubjective) ontological figure that exceeds the scope of the *Phenomenology's* stated objective of rethinking consciousness through embodiment and consequently anticipates the perspective of Merleau–Ponty's final ontology of the flesh. Indeed, because of the use to which it puts the scientific concept of the body schema, the phenomenal body comprises something more akin to Massumi's "body without an image"[vii] or philosopher José Gil's "infralinguistic body"[viii] than to any version of the body image, including the mirror image and the famous "mirror stage."

Like the body without image and the infralinguistic body, the phenomenal body specifically draws on the intermodal or infraempirical dimension of the body schema, following Henry Head's original definition, as an unconscious postural model of the body underlying and conditioning exteroceptive sensory experience and preceding the reign, and even the differentiation, of the visual as a distinct (exteroceptive) sense.[ix]

As Gallagher suggests, the phenomenal body expresses the complexity of the body schema as an intermodal, pre-experiential potentiality:

> The body schema consists of certain functions that operate across various parts of a complex system responsible for maintaining posture and governing movement. The first set involves the input and processing of new information about posture and movement that is constantly provided by a number of sources, including proprioception. A second set involves motor habits, learned movement patterns ("motor schemas" or programs). The final set of functions consists of certain intermodal abilities that allow for communication between proprioceptive information and perceptual awareness, and in integration of sensory information and movement. (Gallagher and Cole, 376)

As the expression of the body schema, the phenomenal body fully invests in the ontological power of *proprioception*, as it has been conceptualized generally by recent scientists and philosophers and linked specifically to the body schema.[x]

Because it is responsible for linking protosensory bodily sense (proprioception) with perception and motility (and indeed for correlating these latter), the body schema is a source of embodied potential. Such a realization is central to Merleau–Ponty's analysis in the *Phenomenology*; it renders that analysis more interesting and far more continuous with the later ontology of the flesh than even the best of Merleau–Ponty's commentators have been willing to admit.[xi] The host of functions encompassed in the body schema facilitate what Merleau–Ponty names "potential movement"— that is, the capacity of the normal body to relate simultaneously to a series of potential situations and to exist, in a sense, beyond its actuality, in virtuality. Thus:

> Each stimulus applied to the body of the normal person arouses a kind of "potential movement," rather than an actual one; the part of the body in question sheds its anonymity, is revealed, by the presence of a particular tension, as a certain power of action within the framework of the anatomical apparatus. In the case of the normal subject, the body is available not only in real situations into which it is drawn. It can turn aside from the world, apply its activity to stimuli which affect its sensory surfaces, lend itself to experimentation, and generally speaking take its place in the realm of the potential. (108–109)

Merleau–Ponty even goes so far as to associate the normal experience of embodied enaction with a certain actualization of the potential: "The normal person *reckons with* the possible, which thus, without shifting from its position as a possibility, acquires a sort of actuality" (109). Because of the ontological work performed by the body schema, human beings experience the virtual as a kind of "fringe" of the actual; they "live" the potentiality of their embodiment outside the empirical space of simple actuality.

In an analysis that anticipates and coincides with Gil's treatment of the body as the "spatializer of space," Merleau–Ponty goes on to derive from the ontological dimension of embodied potentiality a conception of movement and, by implication, of space as fundamentally abstract:

> Abstract movement carves out within that plenum of the world in which concrete movement took place a zone of reflection and subjectivity; it superimposes upon physical space a virtual or human space. Concrete movement is therefore centripetal whereas abstract movement is centrifugal. The former occurs in the realm of being or of the actual, the latter on the other hand in that of the virtual or the nonexistent; the first adheres to a given background, the second throws out its own background. (111)

Its apparent dependence on actual or concrete movement notwithstanding, abstract movement expresses an ontological power—the power of the phenomenal body—that lies at the origin of, and therefore conditions, all concrete spatial experience. In this sense, abstract movement parallels Gil's conception of bodily exfoliation, whereby the body expands its "abstract posture" to occupy concrete space and transform it into abstract space.[xii] Indeed, Gil's term, "abstract posture," perfectly captures the productive plasticity of the body schema in Merleau–Ponty's analysis because, in both cases, a fundamental dedifferentiation of the boundary separating the body from space, a double invagination of inside and outside, is at issue.

3. TECHNICS AND THE DISSOLUTION OF THE BODY IMAGE

If the key question, as Gil suggests, is the "essential way the body 'turns onto' things," then technics can hardly be excluded from the primary operation of the phenomenal body. Merleau–Ponty seems to grasp this crucial point in his analysis of the blind man's stick. Like the feather in the woman's hat or my unreflective sense of my car's width, the stick does not function as an explicit, cognitively assessable enhancement of the body image, but rather as an immediately practical, unthematizable expansion of the body schema:

The blind man's stick has ceased to be an object for him, and is no longer perceived for itself: its point has become an area of sensitivity, extending the scope and active radius of touch, and providing a parallel to sight. In the exploration of things, the length of the stick does not enter expressly as a middle term: the blind man is rather aware of it through the position of objects than of the position of objects through it. The position of things is immediately given through the extent of the reach which carries him to it, which comprises besides the arm's own reach the stick's range of action.... To get used to a hat, a car or a stick is to be transplanted into them, or conversely, to convert them into the bulk of our own body. (143)

Merleau–Ponty concludes that habit "expresses our power of dilating our being-in-the-world," which today more than ever means "changing our existence by appropriating fresh instruments" (143). Lodged in the "body as mediator of the world," habit comprises a "rearrangement and renewal of the corporeal schema," the "motor grasping of a motor significance" (145/142/143). Importantly, what happens in such schematic rearrangement is a passage between the body proper and the world of things, an increase in power and scope of the body's coupling to (and indifferentiation from) the environment. This is what Gil means when he speaks of the body "turning onto" things: at stake is a "transplantation" of the body into things and an "incorporation" of things into body that, with each new habit and thus each new prosthesis, leaves the boundary between them that much less discrete.

It can hardly come as a surprise, then, that the "general bodily synthesis" carried out by habit perfectly describes, in its function as hinge linking the motor and the perceptual,[xiii] the accomplishment of human–computer synchronicity in Krueger's *Videoplace*. By transforming the perceptuomotor coupling in a way that is immediate and in a certain sense transparent, Krueger's environment can be said to achieve a bodily synthesis, a "rearrangement and renewal of the corporeal schema" in its motor and its perceptual dimensions. Like Merleau–Ponty's description of the blind man's stick, what is crucial here is the total and seamless integration of the technical element into the perceptuomotor body schema:

But habit does not *consist* in interpreting the pressures of the stick on the hand as indications of certain positions of the stick, and these as signs of an external object, since it *relieves us of the necessity of* doing so. The pressures on the hand and the stick are no longer given; the stick is no longer an object perceived by the blind man, but an

instrument *with* which he perceives. It is a bodily auxiliary, an extension of the bodily synthesis. (152)

Taking up Krueger's project of extending the body schema into the
uncharted terrain of "artificial reality," we might well ask what happens when the entirety of the perceptuomotor environment becomes
virtual—that is, when the technical extension of the body schema is so
massive that it affects every aspect of our access to the world?

In his virtual reality environment, *Traces* (1998–1999), Austra-
lian media artist Simon Penny presents us with just such a situation.
A project originally designed for networked CAVEs (computer-
assisted virtual environments), *Traces* generates a world—that is,
a space of sensorimotor interaction—out of the three-dimensional
traces of body movement captured by four cameras mounted in the
four corners of the CAVE (see Figure 1.5). In this way, it privileges
the "bodily, temporal, and kinesthetic sensibilities" of the participant
over the illusionism of traditional virtual reality spaces as the vehicle
for achieving immersion and the conferral of reality. For Penny, this
confrontation with mainstream VR research is necessary to probe

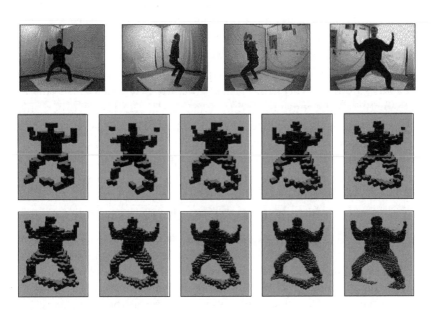

FIGURE 1.5 Simon Penny, Traces (1998–1999), networked interactive virtual
reality environment. (Courtesy of the artist.)

the promise of new technology and to pinpoint its humanistic basis. As he explains,

> *Traces* is an immersive art project which uses the CAVE stereo-immersive environment for an unorthodox purpose. While most virtual worlds are based on a paradigm of virtual navigation through texture mapped worlds, *Traces* has no "world" and no navigation. The aesthetic/theoretical goal of *Traces* is to focus the attention of the user onto their [*sic*] own sense of embodiment through time. The bodily behavior of the user generates real-time graphics and sound. The technical goal of *Traces* is wireless full-body interaction without the use of standard trackers, joysticks and wands, and without icons, menus or graphical pointers of any kind.[9]

With this nod to Krueger's legacy of "unencumbered VR," Penny forth-rightly announces his well-nigh philosophical (indeed properly phenom-enological) commitment to constructing virtual reality on the basis of our evolutionarily acquired power of embodiment.

This commitment imposes several constraints that form the very strengths of his project. First, he must eschew the use of illusionist tricks and software tools built according to the simulation paradigm: "Unlike other VR projects, I have no interest here in illusionistic texture mapped models, the illusion of infinite virtual space or building 'virtual worlds.' All attention is focused on the ongoing behavior of the user."[10] Second, he must forego the illusion of proximity in his realization of a telematic, networked experience; unlike the work of Paul Sermon (which achieves telematic copresence through the superposition of video images of par-ticipants' bodies), *Traces* emphasizes "the highly technologically medi-ated nature of the communication. The users never see each other, only the results of each other's behavior. The user interacts with gossamer spatial traces which exhibit the dynamics and volumes of bodies...." (Penny). Finally, and perhaps most consequentially, Penny must move away from the default perspectival interface of VR environments, the reduction of the user's body to a "single point, a viewpoint, or the end of a "pointer," which, he notes, "effectively erases the body from the computational system":

> My goal is to build a system with which the user can communicate kinesthetically, where the system comes closer to the native sensibili-ties of the human, rather than the human being required to adopt a system of abstracted and conventionalized signals (buttons, mouse clicks, command line interface ...) in order to input data to the sys-tem. (Penny)

Like Krueger before him, Penny values the evolutionary accomplishment of embodiment and deploys it as the basis of his work and his larger philosophy of mediation.

Unlike Krueger, however, Penny is in a position to benefit from the marked advancement in computer technology that is supporting our seamless entry into an exposed mixed reality environment. (In an email to the author (1/3/06), Penny notes that his vision system was built from the ground up, using a standard desktop computer (a 166 MHz pentium 2), and that it owes its effectiveness to "good, clear design, some very clever coding by Andre [Bernhardt], and very economical video processing solutions." It does, however, take advantage of the technically-advanced CAVE, which ran on "turbocharged" SGI hardware and which formed an enabling background for Penny's bricolage.) Thus, in contrast to Krueger's technically crude, floor-embedded motion sensors, *Traces* uses a sophisticated camera system to "capture the full extent of the user's body as usable input data" (Penny et al.). This difference yields a vast expansion in the scope of what is synchronized with the computer. Now the entire body schema—the coupling of body proper and environment—is generated by the technical system.

One interesting result of this progress, which is indissociably technical and aesthetic, is that synchronicity becomes artifactual—that is, it becomes describable in technical terms and necessarily bound to concrete technical apparatuses.[xiv] In *Traces*, the artifactuality of synchronicity appears with Penny's strategic gambit (closely related to his repudiation of visual illusionism) to eschew spatial resolution in favor of temporal resolution. At a rate of fifteen captures per second, *Traces* manages to sustain a sensorimotor verisimilitude that is responsible for conferring reality on the wholly *sui-generis* experience it offers. Only present latently in Krueger's *Videoplace*, this explicit temporal threshold comprises the minimal condition on which a technically generated deployment of the body schema can become creative: although "of a low spatial resolution," the real-time body model developed in *Traces* is "of a high temporal resolution" with the result that "the user experiences no 'latency,' or lag, between their [sic] movements and the virtual structures created" (Penny).

Penny's strategic gambit has significance well beyond the *Traces* project. Indeed, it exposes nothing less than the general condition—a minimal temporal threshold—for all technical (re)deployments of the body schema. This condition marks a crucial break with the (restricted) vision of technics central to Merleau–Ponty's embodied phenomenology. Whereas the blind man's stick merely extends the *spatial* range of the body schema (and of the motor intentionality it yields), *Traces* fundamentally redeploys the body schema—that is, the *temporality* of embodied enaction—toward the purpose of creating a world out of the primary data of bodily motility.

Traces thereby reveals that the power of the body schema to disclose a world—and along with it, the entire ontological register of the "phenomenal" body with its privileged operational standpoint and orientation via *proprioception* and intermodal communication—is a temporal power, or better, a power that can be exercised only within certain temporal boundaries. Because temporal boundaries are necessarily set into place by artifactual technologies—by those technologies that support the being in the world of time today, including the time of consciousness—*Traces* demonstrates that the disclosive power of the body schema is an essentially technical power, that it simply cannot be dissociated from or thought independently of its concrete technical support, and that, in the end, it emerges only through the technology that makes it possible in the first place.

Obviously, such a general condition for the technical (re)deployment of the body schema calls for a more radical thinking of technics than we find in Merleau–Ponty's vision of prosthetics in the *Phenomenology*. Perhaps the best way to capture what is at stake here is to return, briefly, to the relation (and differences) between body image and body schema. Once again, Shaun Gallagher proves an insightful guide insofar as he manages to explain how prosthetics function to disjoin the unconscious body schema from any consciously experienced, intended (or noetic) body image.

> When the body does appear in consciousness, it often appears as clearly differentiated from its environment. Body image boundaries tend to be relatively clearly defined. The body schema, in contrast, can be functionally integrated with its environment, even to the extent that it frequently incorporates certain objects into its operations—the hammer in the carpenter's hand, the feather in the woman's hat, and so forth. Under these circumstances one's perception of body boundary may end at one's finger tips even when a particular schema projects itself to include the hammer that one is using. (Gallagher and Cole, 372)

It is interesting that this perceptual differentiation between self-representation

48

(body image) and enactive spatialization (body schema) *can no longer be made in virtual environments like that of Penny's Traces.* The reason is not simply that the prosthetic function is so fundamental that it has an impact on the visual or representational body image as well as the motile body schema,[xv] but rather *that the difference between them—and with it, the role of representation—has been entirely effaced.* Put another way, in such environments, whatever experience one has of one's body proper does not take the form of a (representational) image, but rather emerges through the *representative* function of the data of body movement, the way these data ("naturally," as it were) represent one's body.

The experience of one's body proper is thus given through the *same material* as is one's experience of motility: namely, traces of body movement captured at or above a minimally sufficient temporal speed. Here, then, we encounter a *body-in-code* in a completely literal sense, meaning a body image that is indiscernible from a technically generated body schema. Describing the networked model of his project, Penny perfectly captures this productive technical fusion of image and schema. In the networked *Traces*, he explains:

> Each CAVE will use multi-camera machine vision to build real-time body models of participants. These body-models will then be used to generate abstracted graphical bodily traces in the other CAVEs. If, for instance, three CAVEs are networked, then a participant in CAVE A will interact in real time with image traces of participants in CAVEs B and C. These traces will not … be accurate sculptural representations but will be used to drive complex algorithmic processes which will give rise to changing 3D graphical traces which indicate the presence, gesture and movement of the remote participants. Hence a person may be represented as a moving ghostlike, transparent and wispy trace. (Penny)

If a similar algorithmic procedure underlies the self-described dimension of "user experience" in the *Traces* system, it not only witnesses the collapse of the body image and body schema, but also exposes this collapse as the condition of possibility for the creative deployment of the technically enactive body schema.

Not surprisingly, the experience proposed by Penny and his collaborators for users of *Traces* is designed specifically to accommodate the gradual adjustment of the body schema to its total technical mediation. A first phase of interaction, "Passive Trace," places users into feedback with traces that passively follow their movements and that gradually float and fade away. A second phase, "Active Trace," allows users to build their own structures; still generated as traces of user movement, these traces are amplified by a cellular automaton algorithm that, in the words of the designers, makes them "sparkle." Finally, in a third phase, "Chinese Dragons," the user's movements throw off small abstract creatures (resembling Chinese dragons), which initially maintain the momentum of the movements that generate them but eventually begin to behave autonomously, flying through the space and chasing behind the viewer. (Penny notes in an email (1/3/06) that the "Chinese Dragons" interaction was a very early, if not the first, attempt to utilize basic life behaviors (flocking, etc.) in an immersive interactive 3D context.)

In the passage through these phases, the user's body schema—the means of access to, indeed of production of, this virtual world—undergoes progressive deterritorialization, bringing home the fact that this feedback with the traces of one's bodily movement *is* an enactive representative of the body, *is* the body image. In this scenario, one simply cannot differentiate the boundaries of a body proper from the entire interactional domain generated through bodily movement. The functions informing a consciously experienced body image that would be separate from the interactive coupling of the body schema simply do not apply in this world.

To appreciate this technically facilitated fusion of image and schema, we would do well to follow Alphonso Lingis when he conceives of the body image (in a well-nigh Bergsonian manner) as an "emanation" from the postural (body) schema, rather than a separate and distinct representation of the body. Lingis suggests:

> What psychologists have improperly named "body image" is not something projected by an act of imagination when we detach our perception from things; it emanates from the mobilized posture and extends about it. The body in mobilizing into a posture situates the levels where other viewing positions lie and emanates an "image" of itself as something visible, tangible, audible in that space.[11]

In this respect, the body image is distinctly derivative—it is a minimally distanced (and predominately visual) apprehension of the self, paradigmatically performed by the other, but also, of course, by the self confronting itself, as it were, as an other (that is, from an observational perspective[xvi]).

This characterization of the body image as an emanation (along with the differentiation of image and schema it supports and derives specifically from Merleau–Ponty) helps to clarify Paul Schilder's claim that we perceive our body image in the same way as others perceive it. For Schilder (the psychologist *par excellence* of the body image and the source for much of Merleau–Ponty's analysis), this is almost an analytical postulate, insofar as it is (or seemed to him to be) necessary to ward off the specter of *Einfühlung* and projective identification:

> The perception of the bodies of others and of their expression of emotions is as primary as the perception of our own body and its emotions and expressions. Our own body, as all the previous discussions show, in sensory perception is not different from the sensory perception of the bodies of others.... Just as we have rejected the idea of *"Einfüh-lung"* we have to reject the idea that we arrive at the knowledge of the bodies of others and their emotions by projecting our body and our feelings into other personalities.... [T]here is a continual interchange between our own body-image and the body-image of others.[12]

Conceiving of the body image (as it is used here) as an emanation from the body schema allows us to grasp the extent of Merleau–Ponty's philosophical break with empirical psychological theory. From his perspective, the noetic, representational body image is a derivative of—an emanation from—a more primitive, prenoetic bodily activity. Although it is true that there is continual interchange between our body image and the body image of others, the reason is far more profound than Schilder imagines. Body images (to the extent they exist as separable representations) enjoy such interchange only because they are emanations of body schemas which operate in a common, intercorporeal interactional domain. The (representational) commonality of the body image is an emanation from the (enactive) commonality of the body schema.

If an appreciation of this profound structure of intercorporeality is missing from Schilder's analysis, the reason is that Schilder lacks any understanding of the operational privilege that defines the phenomenal body on Merleau–Ponty's account. For him, everything takes place at the level of observation, meaning ultimately that he lacks the resources to differentiate embodiment as an ontological operation from its representation in the form of an image. (In this respect, Schilder's theory resonates with the concept of psychasthenia that will be central in Chapter 2.) This lack explains Schilder's failure to differentiate the body image from the body schema in any principled, categorical manner, as well as the waves of confusion that have ensued as this failure was perpetuated by his successors and, in the process, gradually effaced.

Because of its explicit concern for the problematic of perspective, Penny's *Traces* comprises a perfect occasion to confront this confusion and to demonstrate, specifically, how the technical deployment of the body schema makes its exposure all the more urgent. Penny's description of the "user experience" dimension of the project makes clear the centrality—indeed the privilege—accorded the operational perspective in the production and perception of the world and, specifically, of whatever body image it may sustain:

> The user enters the CAVE. A small cubic virtual room with an hemispherical dome is rendered exactly onto the walls of the CAVE in simple shading. This enclosure immediately negates the illusion of infinite space found in many virtual worlds. It is a cozy space. As the user moves, volumes appear in the space which are representations of the space passed through by the body parts of the user. These volumes have a life span, they become more transparent over a period of about a minute, then disappear. After a minute or two, another set of volumes appear in the space. These are volumes created by the remote user. Users can create volumes in response to each other. After a while, this volume-building behavior changes. The user can create self-contained floating volumes, blobs or particles. Simultaneously, a small four-paned window appears in the back wall of the CAVE. Beyond this window the user can see another room exactly like the one she is in. In it is a very abstract moving anthropomorphic volume. This is the body model of the remote user, perhaps also with some blobs. The wall between the spaces dissolves, leaving the two users in a longer room. The users find that their blobs can be thrown and have a trajectory. They bounce off the walls. Slowly the blobs or particles begin to have their own dynamic, graphical and acoustic behavior. The particles can traverse the whole space, while the users are confined to their original part. The particles interact with each other with some sort of gravitational behavior. The space becomes populated with swarms of autonomous chattering things. Slowly it becomes more difficult to generate particles, and they die off. Projection intensity dims and the experience is over. (In an email to the author (1/3/06), Penny clarifies that this description belongs to his proposal for the Cyberstar 98 Competition and does not represent the project as realized. It does, however, eloquently, even poetically, express the privilege of the operational perspective that, *willy nilly*, does inform the actual project.)

52

This third-person description manages to capture the transductive identity between the user's bodily action in the environment and the (algorithmically processed) imaging of the traces of his or her movement. Not only does neither one exist without the other and outside of their relation (the definition of transduction, according to Gilbert Simondon[xvii]), but also, as the description of the interaction's cessation makes clear, both are wholly dependent on the environment's technical deployment of the body schema—that is, the operational perspective of the user. This is precisely why the artist only discovered the significance of the problematic of perspective during the exhibition of *Traces*. As Penny notes:

> An amusing aspect of the graphics development was the transition from the 3rd person view (while developing off-line) to the first person view in the CAVE. Solutions which were very satisfying in the simulation mode were useless in first person. For example, if a person is moving forwards, the trace is developing behind her and she can't see it! Worse, if she moves even a voxel backwards, her head is encased in a form which is the head location at the previous time step, so she can't see anything! (Penny et al., citation modified)

This discovery taught Penny that, at the limit, all descriptions of the environment (including the user's description of her body image within it) depend on (and are subordinate to) the bodily activity of the user. For this reason, it seems, Penny is able to appreciate the significant ergodic dimension of the work, a dimension linked directly to the demands made on the body schema of the user.[xviii]

4. SPECULARITY BEYOND THE MIRROR-IMAGE

Conceptualizing the body image as an emanation from the body schema asserts the derivative status of the body image (and of the image, per se, as an ontological category[xix]) and—even more importantly for our present concerns—puts the category of the visual (the "nobility of vision," to use Hans Jonas' felicitous term) into question. I shall return to Jonas' critique of vision in Chapter 2; in the present context, Merleau–Ponty's derivation of vision from touch is my ultimate concern. Indeed, what follows can be understood as an effort to explicate the following passage from one of the most enigmatic but also most pregnant working notes of *The Visible and the Invisible*:

The flesh *is a mirror phenomenon* and the mirror is an extension of my relation with my body.... To touch oneself, to see oneself, is to obtain ... a specular extract of oneself. I.e. fission of appearance and Being—*a fission that already takes place in the touch* (duality of the touching and the touched) and which, with the mirror (Narcissus) is only a more profound adhesion to Self.[13]

What is the meaning of this primacy apparently granted touch as the originary source of the fission of Being and its "specular extract"? In what sense can we say that the mirror image, far from being the source of fission, rather belongs to touch, expands its originary self-belonging/self-differentiating across an essential distance?

Given the correlation of the body schema with the later conception of the flesh[xx] and the more general continuity it marks between the exploration of the ontological power of the "phenomenal body" in the *Phenomenology* and the later, explicit turn to ontology, we would do well to explore such questions—and the apparent privilege of touch—beginning from Merleau–Ponty's analysis of child development in his seminar on "The Child's Relations with Others." Merleau–Ponty's analysis in this seminar is guided by his conviction that the child's visual apprehension of her body—that is, the visual image of the body presented in the mirror, neither exhausts the child's experience of her body nor directly concerns the ontological dimension of such experience. "The child's visual experience of his own body is," Merleau–Ponty observes, "altogether insignificant in relation to the kinesthetic, cenesthesic, or tactile feeling he can have of it."[14]

To explain the fact that the child nevertheless does assimilate the visual image of her body to the interoceptive image of it and also, more generally, that she "comes to identify as bodies," indeed as "animated ones," her body and the bodies of others, Merleau–Ponty invokes a certain commonality of experience that comes simply from the fact of embodiment: "If I am a consciousness turned toward things [it would be better to say a body turned towards things, MH], I can meet in things the actions of another and find in them a meaning, because they are themes of possible activity for my own body" (117).

Just as this presupposes a "reform" in the notion of the psyche (which can no longer be viewed as something accessible only to myself and not seen from the outside), it also requires a reform in our conception of our body: "If my body is to appropriate the conducts given to me visually and make them its own, it must itself be given to me not as a mass of utterly private sensations but instead by what has been called a 'postural' or 'corporeal' schema" (117). This capacity is what Henri Wallon calls "a 'postural impregnation' of my own body by the conducts I witness". Thus, explains Merleau–Ponty:

> I can perceive, across the visual image of the other, that the other is an organism, that that organism is inhabited by a "psyche," because the visual image of the other is interpreted by the notion I myself have of my own body and thus appears as the visible envelopment of another "corporeal schema." (118)[xxi]

This ontological privileging of the body schema over the visual image of the body ultimately informs Merleau–Ponty's refunctionalization of Lacan's famous "mirror stage" and, with it, the entire role of the specular (of which the mirror image is only a particular concrete dimension). Lacan, as is well known, posits the mirror stage—the concrete experience of seeing in the mirror image—as the crucial moment in the complex transition of the infant from a "fragmented body image" into an "orthopaedic" totality.[xxii] This accomplishment yields a net gain in organization and a concomitant development of the ego (and super-ego); however, it also marks, or at least prefigures, the advent of "paranoic alienation," the alienation of the imaginary ego that occurs as this latter is "deflect[ed] … into the social"—that is, subjected to the symbolic order (Lacan, 5). From this point onwards in Lacan's picture, the subject enters into a perpetual struggle for recognition in the eyes of others, which is equally to say, a struggle against its lack, its dependence on the symbolic, and, finally, its fundamental or essential incompleteness.

In his comments on the specular image and on Lacan's theory specifically, Merleau–Ponty makes clear the extent of his agreement with Lacan: he too recognizes that self-alienation arises in the passage from the fragmented body to the unified body image, the body image as form or *gestalt*. What distinguishes Merleau–Ponty's commentary, however, is his effort to understand this alienation, not as an inaugural source of paranoia, but as a productive and ongoing dimension of the phenomenal body—what I have earlier called the *imaging power* of the organism.

Two principles are fundamental in Merleau–Ponty's analysis—the nonidentity between the interoceptive and the specular and the primacy of the former as the source of their relation. Not surprisingly, these two principles emerge as the "solutions" to two concrete problems faced by the infant as she seeks to understand the discord between her "natural" and necessarily incomplete view of her body and the complete view given by the mirror image[xxiii]:

It is a problem first of understanding that the visual image of his body which he sees over there in the mirror *is not himself,* since he is not in the mirror but here, where he feels himself; and second, he must understand that, not being located there, in the mirror, but rather where he feels himself interoceptively, he can nonetheless be seen by an external witness *at the very place at which he feels himself to be* and with the same visual appearance that he has from the mirror. In short, he must displace the mirror image, bringing it from the apparent or virtual place it occupies in the depth of the mirror back to himself, whom he identifies *at a distance* with his interoceptive body. (1964, 129, first and last emphases added)

Far from comprising a wholesale displacement of identification from the interoceptive to the specular self and from the body as a "collection of confusedly felt impulses" to the unified body image, the specular image rather marks the advent of a more complex self-relation, one that requires the recognition of a certain doubling of the self and compels a massive spatial extension of the body's primary tactility.[xxiv] The child must learn to recognize the specular image "as being *of* oneself, yet not identical *to* oneself," to employ the felicitous distinction suggested by feminist philosopher Gail Weiss, and the means to do so is a bodily occupation of the visible, a "touching" across an essential distance.[15]

What is at stake in the specular image is, accordingly, less a drama of identification, as Lacan suggests, than a particular stage in a process that is, from the very beginning, defined by schism, "fission," *écart.* Instead of marking a fundamental trauma that at once or continuously gives birth to the subject (as Lacan, Butler, and a host of feminist critics following in their wake have variously contended), the mirror stage belongs within a broader developmental trajectory and concretely instances the more fundamental experience of essential separation that Merleau–Ponty will increasingly identify with embodied (human) being. With this in mind, it is important to emphasize that, far from occasioning some transcendence of primary tactility (bodily feeling), the mirror stage not only is ontologically rooted in it but also comprises a concrete valence of its power (i.e., imaging power).

Although he insists on situating the schism of the mirror stage as an instance of a broader developmental trajectory of the phenomenal body, Merleau–Ponty is also, like Lacan, keenly attentive to the specific accomplishments, to the well-nigh existential leap, it makes possible. Yet, whereas, for Lacan, the schism yields the fundamental, desire-generating alienation of the specular "I" into the social "I," for Merleau–Ponty it allows the child to enter into a space of intercorporeality: "What is true of his own body, for the child, is also true of the other's body. The child himself feels that he is in the other's body, just as he feels himself to be in his visual image" (134). For Merleau–Ponty, that is, the specular image and the "gaze of the other" belong together as an integral phenomenon. Far from occasioning paranoiac alienation, then, the specular image facilitates a vast expansion in the child's embodied agency precisely because it allows the child to enter into the space of the social and into social relations with others. Weiss explains how this happens:

> [T]he specular image offers the child a new perspective not only on her/his own body and her/his being-for-others (what we may call an "outside-in" perspective) but *simultaneously* allows the child to project her/himself outside of her/his body *into* the specular image and, correspondingly, into the bodies of others (an "inside-out" perspective). Although the former may indeed be a source of profound alienation, it is the latter, especially, that provides the ground for strong *identifications with others*, identifications that expand the parameters of the body image and accomplish its transition from an interoceptive, fragmented experience of the body to a social gestalt. In emphasizing the child's new understanding of visibility and spatiality, Merleau–Ponty displaces Lacan's emphasis on the temporal conflation of a future, complete "I" with the present incomplete sense of self, a fundamental *méconnaissance* that is, for the latter, the source of deception that provides the necessary basis for the constitution of the "I." What Merleau–Ponty offers instead is the development of an intracorporeal spatiality accomplished through the mirror stage that provides a more positive and productive account of the formation of the body image (and of the I) as an intersubjective phenomenon that need not be grounded in deception. (13)

For all its keen attention to Merleau-Ponty's divergence from Lacan, this account fails to capture the essential adherence of the visual image—and the power of imaging as such—to the ontogenesis of the phenomenal body. Put another way, Weiss stops short of carrying the analysis through to its ultimate point (that is, of returning to the origin of intercorporeality: namely, the commonality of the body schema). Following Merleau–Ponty's initial (previously cited) remarks on the essentially public dimension of embodied life, it is the commonality of the body schema that grounds the incarnation of the distance opened by the mirror image and of the distance separating us from the images of the other's body.

The commonality of the body schema, in short, produces a form of being-with that is indifferent to its trigger, indifferent to whether it concerns one's mirror image or the image of the other. That this comprises a fundamental, ontological form of being-with is assured by the fact that it precedes the distinction of self and other. It thereby correlates with an account of primary narcissism that, unlike Freud's highly fraught notion,[xxv] corresponds to the installation of the schism, the *écart*, at the heart of bodily life, prior to its differentiation from an object world.

One crucial consequence of this fundamental domain of being-with is the dedifferentiation of the mirror-image and the image of the other and an ensuing generalization of specularization not simply beyond the visual, but as the very originary basis of all embodied experience. Indeed, this generalized specularity underlies the isomorphism of access to the mirror-image and image of the other in Merleau–Ponty's account of the so-called mirror stage. In both cases, the body schema forms a medium through which the feeling body opens out—exfoliates itself, to recall Gil's term—into the space between it and the image.

This self-exfoliation, this bodily occupation of the distance opened by the visible, brings the image back to the feeling body and, accordingly, makes it more than a mere surface reflection, makes it a true specular image, a true double of the self, and even more generally, an occasion for the *specular* doubling of the body's primary sensibility.[xxvi] In this sense, the child's experience of his or her mirror-image simply exemplifies a broader experience of specularity, and the integrality or unity of experience that persists across the mirror-stage characterizes embodied life in general, insofar as this is fundamentally split between the tactile and the visual:

> In the case of the specular image, instead of a second body which the child would have and which would be located elsewhere than in his tactile body, there is a kind of *identity at a distance*, a *ubiquity* of the body; the body is at once present in the mirror and present at the point of where I feel it tactually. But if this is the case, the two aspects that are to be co-ordinated are not really separated in the child and are in no way separated in the sense in which all objects in space are separated in adult perception.... The reduction to unity is not a cataclysm, if it is true that there is no veritable duplicity or duality between the visual body and the interoceptive body in spite of the phenomenon of distance that separates the image in the mirror from the felt body. (139–140)

If the distance introduced by visual experience does not cleave embodied being in two, that is because the latter's "possession" of the visible through the body schema itself emerges out of an "originary" installation of schism, of *écart*, at the very heart of being.[xxvii]

5. ALL EXTERIORIZATIONS ARE EXTERIORIZATIONS OF THE SKIN

If the self-exfoliation of the phenomenal body occasioned by the specular image is a thoroughly technical process, it does not, however, *introduce* technics into embodiment as if for the first time. No more a fall into technics than (*pace* Lacan) a fall into social alienation, worldly specularization merely instances the concrete technical conditions for the phenomenalization of embodiment at any given historical moment in what philosopher Bernard Stiegler has called the history of the supplement.[xxviii] If there is a history of specularization, that is precisely because embodied life is "essentially" technical, because the generalization of specularity always already implicated in the concrete operation of the body schema finds its enabling, sensible–transcendental or infraempirical condition in the *écart* constitutive of sensibility. We could equally say that technologies are always already embodied, that they are in their own way "essentially" embodied, if by this we mean that they mediate—that they express—the primordial fission, the gap, within the being of the sensible.

Such an understanding of the primordial technicity of life as sensible *écart* resonates in interesting and productive ways with the psychoanalytical conceptions of the skin ego (Didier Anzieu) and the primary, *passive* containing function of the skin (Esther Bick). Part of an effort to unpack the domain of *transcendental sensibility* underlying and conditioning Kleinian object relations, Anzieu and Bick (working simultaneously but separately!) invest the skin as a kind of primary passivity that, long before the advent of the mirror-stage and even before the incorporation of the mother's breast, serves to bind together "parts of the personality not as yet differentiated from parts of the body."[16] "The thesis," explains Bick, "is that in its most primitive form the parts of the personality are felt to have no binding force among themselves and must therefore be held together in a way that is experienced by them passively, by the skin functioning as a boundary" (55). However, she abruptly notes:

> This internal function of containing the parts of the self is dependent initially on the introjection of an external object, experienced as capable of fulfilling this function.… Until the containing functions

have been introjected, the concept of a space within the self cannot arise.... The stage of primary splitting and idealization of self and object can now be seen to rest on this earlier process of containment of self and object by their respective "skins." (55–56)

In his commentary on Bick, Anzieu brings out the fundamental differentiation—the presence of a primordial sensory *écart*—that informs Bick's conception of the passive integrating function of the skin:

But this internal function of containing the parts of the Self is dependent initially on the introjection of an external object capable of fulfilling the function. This containing object is usually constituted in the process of feeding [in its dual aspect of nipple in mouth and touching of skin].... The containing object is experienced concretely as skin. If the containing function is introjected, the baby may acquire the concept of a "space within the self" and accede to a splitting of Self and object, each being contained in its respective skin.[17]

If we substitute "skin" for "containing object" here, we encounter, in an only apparent tautology, the most fundamental form of the *écart* constitutive of the being of the sensible: "the skin [= introjected containing object] is experienced concretely as skin." In the mode of primary passivity, the infant thus experiences the skin from the "inside" (the feeling of having "a space within the self") *and* from the "outside" (though via the *introjection* of the skin as boundary), as "agent" *and* as "patient." This happens without support from—and thus prior to—the series of differentiations (self–other, inside–outside, psychic space–objective space, etc.) that such experience would seem to require but will in effect performatively produce.

Because of this fundamental, preobjective, prespatial duality or reversibility, the skin constitutes the locus and support for a primordial materialization of the sensible, for the most basic form of the *écart* of the sensible. Recalling our earlier comments on primary narcissism, it is important to emphasize once again (with Merleau-Ponty) that this basic form of *écart*—the skin as the locus and support for primary narcissism—is always already differentiated, but differentiated amodally, prior to sensory differentiation (at a more basic level than the separation of the distinct senses).

As this primordial differentiation of the skin, the sensory *écart* is essentially technical. Viewed from the perspective of the human being of today (the normal adult as it has evolved, genetically and culturally, up to the present), this essential technicity can (perhaps only) be understood through the trajectory of exteriorization it makes possible and which constitutes the "epiphylogenetic" evolution of the human.[xxix] It can (perhaps only) be understood, that is, *as the sensible–transcendental ground for exteriorization as such.*

That is why I have emphasized the coupling of embodiment and technics: the technologies that saturate our contemporary world, in this respect no different from the earliest flint chipping tools used by protohumans, are so many exteriorizations of our fundamental sensory *écart.* What Bick's and (particularly) Anzieu's work on the skin helps us to see, however, is that this epiphylogenesis of the human, its evolution through means other than life, is made possible by the primordial *écart* and, more specifically, by the fundamental anaclitic indifferentiation of the *écart,* its occupation of the cusp between the biological and the psychic *prior to their actual differentiation.*

A concept describing the way that psychic functions "lean on" biological functions (Freud's word is *Anlehnung,* literally "leaning on"), "anaclisis" is central to Freud's conception of psychoanalysis insofar as it depicts the psyche in continuity with the body and with the biological functioning of the organism. If anaclisis is, for Anzieu, arguably the most fundamental principle of the Freudian revolution, this commitment has the effect of making psychic phenomena intrinsically technical or, perhaps more exactly, of rendering the passage to the psychical nothing less than the sensible–transcendental condition for technical exteriorization as a "transcendence" of genetic law.

In contrast to Jean Laplanche, who reserves anaclisis for explaining how organic functions of self-preservation provide a support for sexual drives, Anzieu generalizes its application to the entirety of psychic life: "The psychical apparatus develops through successive stages of breaking with its biological bases, breaks which on the one hand make it possible to escape from biological laws and, on the other, make it necessary to look for an anaclitic relationship of every psychical to a bodily function" (96). As the most diffuse and primitive organic (sensory, or better, protosensory) locus—the locus for the "attachment drive" (following John Bowlby's ethology-inspired broadening of early infant experience beyond the oral phase of the sexual drive)—the skin encompasses the entirety of biological and psychical function, initially (as we have seen) in an undifferentiated state (a state of virtual differentiation). It thereby forms the basis for a conception of the ego, the skin ego, that is far more primitive than Lacan's mirror stage, Winnicott's analysis of the mother's face, and Klein's introjection, and is primitive, *categorically*, because it designates the (in)differentiation of the psychical and the biological.

Indeed, Anzieu defines the skin ego as a transitional stage *between* the psychical and the biological—the psychic *and* embodied inhabitation of the caesura of their fundamental (dis)juncture. It is a

> mental image of which the Ego of the child makes use during the early phases of its development to represent itself as an Ego containing psychical contents, on the basis of its experience of the surface of the body. This corresponds to the moment at which the psychical Ego differentiates itself from the bodily Ego at the operative level while remaining confused with it at the figurative level. (40)

As Victor Tausk's analysis of the "influencing machine" attests,[xxx] the skin ego comprises a stage in which the operational function of anaclisis is ahead of its properly psychic function—a stage in which the body operates through a fundamental differentiation that it does not yet experience as such. It thus marks the fundamental sense in which, as Freud put it, the ego is "first and foremost a bodily ego," "not merely a surface entity," but "the projection of a surface," the projection of "bodily sensations ... springing from the surface of the body" (Freud, 16).

The skin, in sum, is the most primordial locus and expression of the indifferentiation of the biological and the psychical marked and overcome by the function of anaclisis. That is why it supports the proto-origin of specularity, of self-relation/heterorelation, as the fundamental sensible *écart*. This *écart* is essentially technical because it is the sensible–transcendental condition for all exteriorization. As it is expanded and deepened by Anzieu, the Freudian theory of anaclisis shows that the passage to exteriorization is only possible because of a passage *within* embodied being, the passage opened by anaclisis and the primordial indifference it marks as well as overcomes, indeed marks in the very process of overcoming.

By helping us discover the essential technicity of the skin ego as the primordial support of anaclisis, Anzieu's analysis refunctionalizes Bick's conception of the "second muscular skin," uncovering its non-pathological generality and, more importantly, making it speak to our contemporary technogenesis and the challenges it poses to our efforts to understand our agency in the world today.[xxxi] From Bick's more narrow clinical perspective, the second muscular skin, or "'second-skin' formation," occurs when there is a "'disturbance in the primal skin function'"; in this formation, "dependence on the object is replaced by a

pseudo-independence, by the inappropriate use of certain mental functions, or perhaps innate talents, for the purpose of creating a substitute
for this skin container function" (56).

Given our investment in the body schema as the empirical agent of
generalized specularity, it is extremely consequential that "this faulty
skin-formation produces a general fragility in later integration and
organizations. It manifests itself in states of unintegration as distinct
from regression involving the most basic types of partial or total unintegration of body, posture, motility, and corresponding functions of
mind, particularly communication" (59). Indeed, its correlation with
the body schema is so fundamental that Bick is led to characterize it as
a "muscular shell" (59).

Clearly discerning the correlation of this second muscular skin with
technics—it is variously referred to as a "substitutive prosthesis," an
"*ersatz* muscularity," a "protective prosthesis" (193/195)—Anzieu modifies Bick's theory by proposing a more generalized, normative function
of the second-skin formation:

> The second muscular skin is abnormally overdeveloped when it has
> to compensate for a serious insufficiency of the Skin Ego and to fill in
> the faults, fissures and holes in the first containing skin. Yet everyone
> needs a second muscular skin, as an *active* protective shield supple-
> menting the *passive* protective shield constituted by the outer layer of
> a normally constituted Skin Ego. (195, emphasis added)[xxxii]

Anzieu gives the example of sports and clothing, noting in particular the penchant of patients to protect themselves from psychoanalytic
regression through pre- and postsession work-outs. Bearing in mind the
technical function of the second muscular skin, however, we might do
better to connect it with the specter of "psychasthenia" precisely as it has
been linked to contemporary media culture.[xxxiii] Faced with the assault
of media images that aim precisely to "confuse … the space defined by
the coordinates of the organism's own body … with represented space,"
it makes perfect sense that the organism would adopt a muscular skin, a
protective shield, in order to ward off the dissolution of its identity that
comprises the contemporary condition of generalized psychasthenia.

Our discovery of the essential technicity of the skin as the indifferentiation of the biological and the psychical (as the primordial *écart*
of the sensible) allows us to differentiate another genealogy of technics
that diverges fundamentally from this muscular model. The muscular apparatus of the generalized second-skin formation is driven by

aggressiveness[xxxiv]—as is, obviously, the massively predominant view and deployment of technology in our culture; however, the fact that today's technologies are nonetheless exteriorizations of the skin means that, underneath the (still) pathological cathexis of aggressiveness, these technologies are necessarily correlated with the self-preservative, attachment-centered technical genealogy of the skin as primary containing function. Indeed, in light of the anaclitic indifference instantiated by the primary skin function, we can understand the second muscular skin formation as, first and foremost, an expression of the fact—defining a perfectly general technical condition—that *all exteriorizations are exteriorizations of the skin.*

Accordingly, what the psychoanalytic perspective helps us appreciate (and here it supplements phenomenology, as Merleau–Ponty was well aware) is the concrete (infra)empirical operation, in the life of the adult, of the first containing skin. Indeed, the origin of the skin ego, the first containing skin, in the undifferentiated, protosensory *écart* constitutive of the sensible entails its essential withdrawal from phenomenological manifestation. Such a withdrawal characterizes adult life first and foremost only because it is a purely general, sensible–transcendental condition of all life, of life as such.

Confronted with an artwork that expressly stages a regression from the muscular model of media consumption to some kind of (re)inhabitation of the primary skin as the core of our essential technicity, we thus have due cause to be wary, but also to be intrigued. How can a reversal of the phylogenetic trajectory of embodied life ever lead us back to that which is by definition phenomenologically inscrutable?

Describing her computer sound and video installation, *Bodymaps: artifacts of touch* (1996), artist Thecla Schiphorst announces her desire to create a sensory interface with the human capacity for amodal tactility, the operation of which is logically, if not *per force* chronologically and developmentally, prior to the differentiation of the senses (see Figure 1.6). Noting the work's technical infrastructure—its use of "a specially designed sensor surface ... which can detect touch, pressure, and the amount of forced applied" to it—Schiphorst explains its function:

> [T]hese sensors lie beneath a white velvet surface upon which is projected images of the artist's body. The surface yearns for contact and touch. Its rule base is complex and subtle, impossible to decode. Its effect is disturbing, erotic, sensual and subjective. The intention of the work is to subvert the visual/objective relationship between the object and the eye, between click and drag, between analysis and

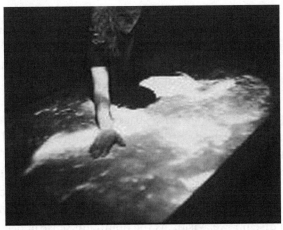

FIGURE 1.6 Thecla Schiphorst, *Bodymaps: artifacts of touch* (1996), computer sound and video installation. (Courtesy of the artist.)

power, to create a relationship between participant and technology that transgresses rules of ownership and objectivity and begs questions of experience, power and being.... The work ... constructs a space inhabited by the body *as mediated by technology*. The *Bodymaps* installation employs electric field sensor technology, in which the viewer's proximity, touch, and gesture evoke moving sound and image responses from the body contained and represented within the installation space. Images of the body ...of the artist ... are projected onto a horizontal planar surface. The opaque projection surface is a container for the body, and is the site and source for the physical and cultural conditions and objects or artifacts which reference this containment. The surface is covered in white velvet creating a sensual and unexpected texture which leaves "traces" of the hand prints that are left behind, creating a relationship to memory, an inability to escape the effects of one's touch. As the viewer places their [*sic*] hands closer to the surface or skin of the installation, a complex soundscape responds to their proximity and movement. The image shudders. The viewer becomes participant through the sense of touch. There is no escape from entering the "third space" between objective seeing and subjective feeling.... This work invites relationship through an experience grounded in proprioceptive knowledge, skin sense feeling, listening through touching, seeing through hearing, together integrated through attention.[18]

Bodymaps assembles all of the topics we have been discussing here—the mirror-image, the image of the other's body, technics, touch, the skin—and configures them so as to underscore the productive potentiality the body schema offers for *restoring a tactile interface with the world*. The "third space" at issue here is not some intermediate space that somehow splits the difference between operational and observational perspectives, but rather is more like the sensible–transcendental spatiality—the power to spatialize—that Merleau–Ponty, Gil, and Massumi all accord the phenomenal body.

Bodymaps opens such a third space by reversing the psychogenetic process through which the child comes to acquire a normal adult perspective on the world. Accordingly, whereas Bick correlates the development of body schema function with a healthy first containing skin, *Bodymaps* exploits the (relative) primordiality of the body schema within the register of empirical experience (recall its prenoietic dimension) as a means to disempower vision as the dominant sense (a necessary prerequisite) and thereby to create what we might call (thinking of Ong's "second orality") a "second primary tactility," a partial restoration of the primordial dimension of the skin. This is why the work instances the experimental, as Massumi would put it, somewhere in between—that is, *beneath* the division between—the analog and the digital. *Bodymaps* uses technics to "connect and interfuse different spheres of activity on the same operational plane." Yet, if it thereby creates "startling effects" by "using proprioception as the general plane of cross-referencing,"[xxxv] it does so in a way that underscores the primordial technicity of embodiment (and the originary embodiment of technics).

Bodymaps, we can now specify, exemplifies the use of technics to expose the originary technical element of being, the *écart* constitutive of the being of the sensible. This technical exposure is accomplished through Schiphorst's use of technics to set the embodied enaction of the viewer into feedback with its sensible–transcendental grounding. *Bodymaps*, explains Schiphorst, "uses video images of my own body *and* images of a digital body whose movement is 'captured' from my own movement." It thus uses—indeed *interfaces*—two distinct kinds of image: images of the *body in movement* and images of the *movements of the body*. Schiphorst clarifies her aim here:

> I am especially interested in how the knowledge of movement and of the body can affect and inform the design of electronic computer technology *and* the works created with (or through) that technology. All movement in the video images … was created *from within the body*, as was dictated by elemental states such a[s] drowning, floating, shivering, crawling, uncovering, hiding. This technique used

knowledge gained in physical techniques, ... through movement practices and training. (Schiphorst)

By combining these two distinct kinds of movement in a single interactive installation, Schiphorst is able to deploy the tension between two perspectives—the observational and the operational, the "statistical body" and the "incommensurable body"—to catalyze a potentialization of the body rooted in the function of the body schema beyond or beneath vision. As she explains, the "tension between these coexisting polarities or conditions (one imposed from without, and the other mute, subversive, willed from within) construct maps that define the path of possible inhabitable and inhabited regions of body space."

In this way, *Bodymaps* effects a direct interface not simply with the *image* of the other's body (which, recall, was sufficient to ground intercorporeality on Merleau–Ponty's account), but with the *very traces of movement that constitute the direct expression—indeed, the very activity—of other's body schema.* This has a significant impact on the constitution of intercorporeality because, rather than having to infer the embodiment of the other and fill in or incarnate the visual distance by bringing the image back to the (feeling) body, the embodied viewer here is confronted with the other's schema directly—that is, *independently of its body image.*

Schiphorst goes so far as to attribute movement—that is, motile *activity*—to the technically inscribed body: thus the viewer, in her vision, "enters the field of consciousness of the body, where the body's image becomes aware of the viewer's gaze and physical presence." A body with such awareness (which can no longer be a mere "consciousness") can, obviously, no longer be a mere image. What this means is that the normally dominant (the most noble) sense of vision becomes purely instrumental—a mere means to a deeper, fundamentally tactile and proprioceptive (which is to say, amodal) interface; vision is bypassed as (an essential dimension of) the constitution of (inter)corporeality *qua* generalized and common medium. That is why *Bodymaps* can aptly be described as a "tactile dialogue with the image."[xxxvi,19]

6. PRIMORDIAL TACTILITY

Bodymaps exemplifies the capacity of tactility to effectuate the concrete potentialization of the body schema—the becoming-common of the phenomenal body. What exactly is it about tactility that allows it to be the medium (and not simply the privileged sense, that is, one sense among others) for the partial regression back to the primordial skin formation as concrete, *infraempirical* operator of the *écart* of the sensible? The answer to this question will come in the wake of yet another differentiation, one which is, from the (infra)empirical perspective, opened by the sensible–transcendental *écart*, certainly the most fundamental of all: namely, the differentiation of touch as a distinct sense from touch as a protosensory (amodal) power, of touch proper from primordial tactility.

In his development of the skin ego as the "agent" of a generalized anaclisis, Anzieu privileges the tactile precisely as the point of oscillation, the pivot, between the sensible–transcendental *écart* and the infraempirical ground of experience:

> In relation to all the other sensory registers, the tactile possesses a distinctive characteristic which not only places it at the origin of the psyche, but allows it permanently to provide the latter with something which one might also call the mental background. This is the backdrop against which psychical contents [*contenus*] stand out as figures, or alternatively the containing envelope which makes it possible for the psychical apparatus to have contents. (84)

In this figuration, the tactile comprises the modality for the reversibility of psychic life, for a higher order reversibility grounded in the primordial anaclitic indifference of the skin. Yet, to function as a kind of privileged *über*-sense, an "infrasensory sense," the tactile must continue to harbor something of the more primordial skin container function. Thus, tactility is at once the most primitive sense formation *and* the sensible–transcendental origin of the sensible per se; it must simultaneously instance two divergent ontological formations and must also bridge the gap between them, forming some kind of passage across the empirical–transcendental divide.

This is precisely why Anzieu furnishes two apparently incompatible accounts of the tactile, both of which, however, serve to foreground the reflexivity of sense. On one hand, there is the reflexivity of touch as a distinct sense:

> The skin possesses a structural primacy over all the other senses and this is true for a least three reasons. Firstly, it is the only sense organ that covers the whole body. It itself also contains several distinct senses (heat, pain, contact, pressure ...) whose physical proximity entails psychical contiguity. Lastly, as Freud allusively remarks (1923), touch is the only one of the five external senses which possesses a reflexive structure: the child who touches the parts of its body with its

finger is testing our two complementary sensation[s], of being a piece of skin that touches at the same time as being a piece of skin that is touched. It is on the model of tactile reflexivity that the other sensory reflexivities (hearing oneself make sounds, smelling one's own odor, looking at oneself in the mirror), and subsequently the reflexivity of thinking, are constructed. (61)

On the other hand, there is the protoreflexivity—the protorevers-ibility—of the primordial skin, which only gradually gives rise to the sensible as a differentiated field structured above all through sensory doubleness or reversibility:

The skin, which is a system of several sense organs (perceiving touch, pressure, pain, heat) is itself closely connected with the other organs of external sense (hearing, sight, smell, taste) and with the awareness of body movement and balance. In small babies, the complex sensitiv-ity of the epidermis (to touch, heat and pain) remains for a long time diffuse and undifferentiated. Subsequently, however, it transforms the organism into a sensitive system that is capable of experiencing other sensations of the skin (the associative function) or differentiat-ing them and localizing them as figures emerging against the back-ground of the overall body surface (the screen function). (14)

Rather than relating to each other as abstract transcendental condition and organ of possible experience, as they would on a Kantian approach, these two determinations demonstrate how tactility—primordial tactil-ity—forms the sensible–transcendental condition of its sensory function, how it, in effect, bootstraps itself into experience. This is what I mean by "primordial tactility," and, given the peculiar dissolution of the empiri-cal–transcendental divide it performs, it is entirely fitting that it has, as its distinct phenomenality, the intersensorial domain normally experienced only by synaesthetes and very young infants, but that, as Brian Massumi has shown, every so often ruptures the smooth fabric of the actual, thus reminding us of its constitutive coupling to the virtual.

Anzieu, for his part, unpacks the psycho–physio–genetic basis of the so-called "fringe of the virtual," thereby tracing the manifest privilege that touch enjoys in empirical life directly and irrevocably back to the anaclitic function of the skin:

The Skin Ego is a psychical surface which connects up sensations of various sorts and makes them stand out as figures against the origi-nal background formed by the tactile envelope: this is the Skin Ego's function of *intersensoriality*, which leads to the creation of a 'common sense … whose basic reference is always to the sense of touch. (103)

What is decisive about Anzieu's contribution here is his insistence on the necessary integration of primary tactility as the medium of the amodal. Far from a hidden transcendental cause, primary tactility is necessarily at work *in every sensory event*; as the source for the differentiation of the senses, it is also the glue that gathers them into a system, the system of the sensible:

> [T]he repressed primary tactile communications are not destroyed (except in pathological cases), but are preserved as a backcloth upon which systems of intersensory correspondences come to be inscribed; they constitute a primary psychical space, into which other sensory and motor spaces may be fitted; they provide an imaginary surface upon which the products of later operations of thought may be set out. Communication at a distance through gestures and subsequently by the spoken word requires not only the acquisition of specific codes, but also the preservation of this original echotactile backcloth to communication, and its more or less frequent reactivation and re-use. (152–153)

Anzieu's insistence here allows us to demarcate a domain of the infraempirical more primordial than the *infralanguage* (Gil): namely, the *infratactile* or *infratactility*. "Echotactile communication," he tells us, "remains the original source of semiosis," which means that primordial tactility—infratactility—demarcates a prelinguistic domain and function beneath the operation of the infralanguage. The latter, accordingly, can be no more than a metaphoric extension or transformation (rather than the sensible–transcendental source of metaphor). "Feedback loops with the environment" are formed very early in the infant's development, insists Anzieu: These are audio-phonological in nature; they relate to crying in the first instance and then to vocalizations ... and are the first stages in the acquisition of semiotic behavior. In other words, *the acquisition of pre-linguistic signification* (of crying and then of sounds during babbling) *precedes the acquisition of infralinguistic signification* (of mimicry and gesture) (165, emphasis added).

Recognizing that chronological succession need not imply structural derivation, we can nonetheless affirm Anzieu's insistence here for the precise reason that it follows directly from the generalization of the anaclitic function by which, as we have seen, the sensible is revealed to have always already been specular—that is, constituted on the basis of a fundamental *écart*. For its part, the derivation of language (and of the *infralanguage*) from a more primordial *infratactility* supports the reciprocal coupling of embodiment and technics that we have located at the heart of the sensible. If language is a specification of technics, a historicotechnical specification of *différance* (as Stiegler puts it), then it is only fitting that it emerge from out of the infratactile, the protodifference of the sensible.

7. SEEING THROUGH THE HAND

As a premodal or amodal dimension of the infraempirical that bootstraps itself into phenomenological existence, primary tactility or *infratactility* comprises a kind of primitive or not yet differentiated, virtual, or potential reversibility out of which arises not simply the division of the senses, but more fundamentally, the divisions that comprise *sensation per se* (activity–passivity, experiencing–experienced, subject–object, etc.). *Infratactility* would thus seem to furnish a source for the reversibility that, according to Merleau–Ponty's famous analysis of the chiasm, characterizes the "flesh." Indeed, it helps us to understand the apparent inconsistency in Merleau–Ponty's conception of reversibility, its teetering in the balance between something that cannot quite occur in fact and yet must, by right, be possible:

> To begin with, we spoke summarily of a reversibility of the seeing and the visible, of the touching and the touched. It is time to emphasize that it is a reversibility *always imminent and never realized in fact*. My left hand is always on the verge of touching my right hand touching the things, but I never reach coincidence; the coincidence eclipses at the moment of realization, and one of two things always occurs: either my right hand really passes over to the rank of the touched, but then its hold on the world is interrupted; or it retains its hold on the world, but then I do not really touch *it*—my right hand touching, I palpate with my left hand only its outer covering. (1968, 147–48)

By what right, however, is the reversibility always imminent? What agency, what materiality, what form of being supports this imminence? This is a crucial question precisely because it foregrounds the divide separating the phenomenal domain, in which reversibility occurs as the experience of "double sensation," from the infraempirical domain, where reversibility remains *in potentia*.

If we follow Merleau–Ponty in making the move from imminence to double sensation as *experienced*, we obtain a certain conceptualization of the *écart* (the "fission," "gap," or "spread") constitutive of sensation. Specifically, the *écart* would seem to comprise the fundamental principle

71

of the body's belongingness to the world (and of the complementarity of phenomenalization and ontology):

> But this incessant escaping, this impotency to superpose exactly upon one another the touching of the things by my right hand and the touching of this same right hand by my left hand, or to superpose, in the exploratory movements of the hand, the tactile experience of a point and that of the "same" point a moment later, or the auditory experience of my own voice and that of other voices—this is not a failure. For if these experiences never exactly overlap, if they slip away at the very moment they are about to rejoin, if there is always a "shift," a "spread" [*écart*], between them, this is precisely because my two hands are part of the same body, because it moves itself in the world, because I hear myself both from within and from without. I experience—and as often as I wish—the transition and the metamorphosis of the one experience into the other, and it is only as though the hinge between them, solid, unshakeable, remained irremediably hidden from me. But this hiatus between my right hand touched and my right hand touching, between my voice heard and my voice uttered, between one moment of my tactile life and the following one, is not an ontological void, a non-being: it is spanned by the total being of my body and by that of the world.... (148)

The *écart* in this sense is a marker of reversibility as a necessary condition of phenomenal experience, of sensation *per se*. It is nothing other than the fundamental dehiscence that explains the body's need for the world (and also the world's need for the body, being's need for manifestation or phenomenalization). As such, *écart* also prevents the body from achieving pure immanence; it is that which renders it an essentially incomplete "unity;" a process of individuation that will never be fully accomplished.

The necessity for such an understanding of the body-world coupling and of its rootedness in the *experience* of the *écart* has been demonstrated by Renaud Barbaras in *The Being of the Phenomenon*. The divergence between touching and touched is the condition for the being of the tangible world (and something similar can be said for vision and for hearing—that is, those other senses characterized by doubleness):

> [T]he touch is produced only insofar as it is immersed in a body; it advents only as this very corporeality. The touch is itself, that is, sentient, only to the degree that it is unaware of itself in or as the world that it reaches. The incarnation of touch corresponds to the fact that its object is not clearly laid out in front of it but is given only as the obscure presence of a tactile world, the presentation *as* tactile world of a dimension that is non-presentable by itself. The absence of this

dimension to the world responds to the absence of touch to itself, that is, to its carnal being. ... touch can proceed only from a subject which is its own absence, which is outside of itself.[xxxvii,20]

This understanding of the necessary correlation of body and world—and thus of the *écart*—as a function of the reciprocal impossibility of pure reflexivity and pure corporeity goes together (at least on Barbaras's account) with a privileging of vision as the most noble of the senses. Indeed, Barbaras begins his reconstruction of *The Visible and the Invisible* by positing the "primacy of vision." He claims:

> Vision alone gives us access to the world as world.... In hearing or touch, the object does not have access to this exteriority and autonomy: in touch, occurring through physical contact, the thing is experienced "at the tips of the fingers" rather than outside of the one sensing, and I hear the sound "in the ear" rather than situating it in space. In the two cases, the perceiving body is referred back to itself; it fails to forget itself in favor of a pure exteriority. (149)

Things are otherwise in the case of vision: "there is," claims Barbaras, "'more world' in vision, since the sensed is given vision only as split off from sensibility, as resting in itself." (149)

As compelling as such an analysis would appear to be, it does not fully accord with the role Merleau–Ponty assigns touch—or, rather, the double sensation of tactility—in some of the final working notes included in *The Visible and the Invisible*. Thus, despite his insistence that vision and touch are fundamentally divergent, that they disclose or construct distinct, *nonsuperposable* universes, Merleau–Ponty accords to both an irreducible openness, a fundamental access, to the world as world:

> To touch *oneself*, to see *oneself* ... is not to apprehend oneself as an object, it is to be open to oneself, destined to oneself (narcissism) Nor, therefore, is it to reach *oneself*, it is on the contrary to escape *oneself*, to be ignorant of *oneself*, the self in question is by divergence (*d'écart*), is *Unverborgenheit of the Verborgen* as such, which consequently does not cease to be hidden or latent. (249)

In both cases, moreover, this openness or access to world as world emerges because of the asymmetry that lies at the heart of the reversibility constitutive of double sensation. That is why the *écart* is the condition for the transduction of body and world that informs Merleau–Ponty's conception of the flesh. "In fact," continues the same working note:

> I do not entirely succeed in touching myself touching, in seeing myself seeing, the experience I have of myself perceiving does not go

beyond a sort of *imminence*, it terminates in the invisible, simply this invisible is *its* invisible, i.e., the reverse of *its* specular perception, of the concrete vision I have of my body in the mirror. The self-perception is still a perception, i.e., it gives me a *Nicht Urpräsentierbar* (a non-visible, myself), but this it gives me through an *Urpräsentierbar* (my tactile or visual appearance) in transparency (i.e., as a latency). (249–50)

In a yet more radical reflection on the transduction of body and world, Merleau–Ponty clearly positions the *écart* constitutive of touch, the *écart* between the touched and the touching, as the source for the opening of the world, for the "untouchable," and, by extension, for the "invisible":

To touch and to touch oneself (to touch oneself = touched–touching) They do not coincide in the body: the touching is never exactly the touched. This does not mean that they coincide "in the mind" or at the level of "consciousness." Something else than the body is needed for the junction to be made: it takes place in the *untouchable*. That of the other which I will never touch. (254)

In this further rumination on the *imminence* of the reversibility of double sensation, Merleau–Ponty lays bare the true *ontological* basis for the failure of the body to coincide with itself: Noncoincidence or "embodied alterity" is simply a primary condition of the being of the body. This ontological fact is precisely what makes the body part of the flesh and also, of course, what grounds the body's self-transcendence, its fundamental adherence to the world. Beneath the reciprocity of pure reflexivity and pure corporeity, activity and passivity, consciousness and matter, lies the primordial *écart* of tactility which, as Merleau–Ponty's descriptions attest, must be understood as a first (and "originary") embrace of alterity, "an original of the *elsewhere*, a *Selbst* that is an Other" (254).

The fundamental self-alterity of the body goes together with a triangulation of self, things, and world, and it informs a primordial negativity of tactility, or put otherwise, tactility as the source of the body's negativity (and hence of its transcendence in immanence, its self-transcendence toward the world):

To touch is to touch oneself. To be understood as: the things are the prolongation of my body and my body is the prolongation of the world, through it the world surrounds me—If I cannot touch my own movement, this movement is entirely woven out of contacts with me—The touching oneself and the touching have to be understood as each the reverse of the other—The negativity that inhabits the touch (and which I must not minimize: it is because of it that the body is not an empirical fact, that it has ontological signification) ... is the *other side* or the *reverse* (or the other dimensionality) of sensible Being.... (255)

This ontological signification of the body explains why the radicalization of the body-world transduction that is constitutive of the flesh—which is also a radicalization of the *écart*—coincides with a passage back from the phenomenal domain of sensory separation (common sense) to the infraempirical domain. As the protodivision of primary tactility, the *écart* generates a protoreversibility—a reversibility prior to and independent of any actual terms to be reversed—that forms the sensible–transcendental condition for sensation.

In the wake of this radicalization of the flesh and of the écart of primary tactility, Merleau–Ponty is led to abandon the parallelism of touch and vision that holds sway throughout the chapter on the chiasm and the working notes directly related to it. Although this appears only by implication in the working notes, it emerges as a decisive motif of Merleau–Ponty's exploration of the human body in the third and final lecture course on *Nature*. What *is* firmly established in the working notes, however, is the derivation of vision from tactility on which the lectures build.

Thus, for example, we see Merleau–Ponty continuing the same note just cited (and cited earlier at the beginning of Section 5) by correlating vision with touch (or better, with tactility as the agent of embodied self-affectivity). He observes:

The flesh *is a mirror phenomenon* and the mirror is *an extension* of my relation with my body. Mirror = realization of a *Bild* of the thing, and I–my shadow relation = realization of a (verbal) *Wesen*: extraction of the essence of the thing, of the pellicle of Being or of its "Appearance"—To touch oneself, to see oneself, is to obtain such a specular extract of oneself. I.e. fission of appearance and Being—a fission that *already* takes place in the touch (duality of the touching and the touched) and which, with the mirror (Narcissus) is only a more profound adhesion to Self. (255–256, some emphases added)

We can now understand this passage in its full profundity: it expresses the rootedness of touch and vision as differentiated (and nonoverlapping) senses from a more primordial self-relation of the body that is at the same time (because of its noncoincidence) a self-transcendence: primary tactility.

In *Nature*, the double sensation of touch is explicitly accorded the ontological task of opening the body onto the world, and vision is explicitly positioned as a (higher order) derivation from it. What emerges as the crucial component of this more profound understanding of tactility is the demarcation of a bodily interiority, which is certainly significant in light of our previous exposure of the correlation of the skin boundary and primary tactility. Asking how the body can "have a reference to something other than itself," Merleau–Ponty quickly comes to what is distinctive about tactility: its boundedness "within" the body:

> It [the body] is open in a circuit with the world, but it is open. It sees itself; it touches itself. The hand that I touch, I sense, could touch that which touches it. And this is no longer true past the limits of my skin. The block of my body thus has an "interior" which is its application to itself. By this application, it has not only affective states closed on itself, but also correlations [?]—the sensibles and the world. The flesh (the touching touched, as an innate body) as the visibility of the invisible (the touching hand, the look).[21]

This delimitation of a bodily interiority and a skin boundary comprises the payoff of Merleau–Ponty's deepening of the *Phenomenology*'s analysis of the body as our access to the world as such. To say that the body is "the measurement of the world" or a "*standard of things*" is, simply, to recognize that its specificity, its singularity, as a kind of being (and as a part of Being) comes from its interiority, from its application to itself (its self-affection), which is, simultaneously, the agency for its openness to the world (hetero-affectivity). This complex self-relation, moreover, informs the duality of sensation characteristic of touch and vision as differentiated (nonoverlapping) senses.

Thus, when Merleau–Ponty discovers the condition of possibility for the duality of sensation "in the relation of the body to itself," noting that "it is here that there is the touched–touching," he is simply unpacking the significance of primary tactility's role as the strict correlative to the skin boundary and the primordial interiority it demarcates (223). Primary tactility is that in virtue of which sensory reciprocity can "break down" or "collapse"; it is the source of the "identity of touching and touched" that, as the analysis from *The Visible and the Invisible* made clear, can never appear in actuality, in the realm of empirical life, even as it expresses the ontological principle of bodily life as fundamentally noncoincident with itself, as sundered by its essential openness to the world.

In *Nature,* Merleau–Ponty explicitly recognizes the asymmetry between touch and vision and the resultant need to modify this understanding if it is to fit the case of vision. If this recognition marks a break with the procedure of *The Visible and the Invisible,* that is precisely because it makes way for an introduction of technicity into the heart of the flesh (the being of the sensible). For what now becomes distinctive about vision is its explicit dependence on a technical artifact, as Merleau–Ponty's analysis makes clear:

> This ["that-is-openness to things" constitutive of the flesh] has been analyzed in the order of touching—there would be changes to make in order to apply this to vision. The eye cannot see the eye as the hand touches the other hand; it can be seen only in a mirror. The gap is larger between the seeing and the seen than between the touching and the touched. A segment of the invisible is encrusted between the eye and itself as a thing. It is maybe only in the other that I see the eye, and this meditation means that the eye is above all seeing, much more seeing than seen, a more subtle flesh, more nervous. But if it were not visible, it would not see, because it would not be a point of view, it would not have planes, depths, orientation.... (223–224)

Vision, in other words, is of a different nature than touch, and this difference is captured by the fact that vision requires a technical artifact—the mirror—in order to attain the reflexivity that is, on Merleau–Ponty's understanding, characteristic of sensation. Recalling (from our earlier analysis of "The Child's Relations with Others") that the mirror image cannot be equated with the specular image, we can now appreciate the derivative nature of vision *and of the mirror as a technical mediation of sensation.* Because of its dependence on the technical artifact (the mirror), vision cannot be originary; indeed, the passage from touch (as a distinct sense) to vision represents a concrete exteriorization (and a technical artifactualization) of the specular whose initial, more primary phenomenalization occurs as and in the duality of embodied self-relation (touched–touching). In a certain sense, we can say that the mirror takes the place of the embodied hand, with all the modifications attendant upon this shift, of which the most important is certainly the fact that reciprocity is no longer embodied as interiority, but rather supported by the gaze of the other.

If touch maintains a privileged relation with primordial tactility, that is precisely because the specific reciprocity it involves remains *within* the body (even when the body is extended through prostheses, at least of the sort Merleau–Ponty envisions and discusses). In a sense, the experience of collapse, the "kaleidoscopic change" that ensues as the moment of identity approaches, harbors within itself some trace of the primordial *écart* of the sensible, of the reciprocity constitutive of primordial tactility. As if in direct proportion to its disenfranchisement within ordinary (adult) perception, touch would seem to enjoy an immediacy, a unity, that owes more to bodily interiority than to the body's coupling to a world: "Touching immediately touches itself (the 'bipolarity' of the *Tastwelt*)." By contrast, "vision breaks this immediate (the visible at a distance, outside the limits of my body) and reestablishes the unity by the mirror, in the world" (278).

The passage from touch to vision is, for all that, less of a shift from one to another sense than a complexification of sensation that inaugurates vision *at the same time as* it extends the scope of touch. That is how Merleau–Ponty explains the "captation of the tactile body by the visual image." Addressing Paul Schilder's example of my sensing the contact of my pipe in my hand in the mirror, Merleau–Ponty speculates on the

> place of the imaginary of seeing: By seeing and its tactile equivalents, the inauguration of an inside and an outside and their exchanges, of a relation of being to what is however forever outside: The spatiality of the body is an encrustation in the space of the world (I *find* my hand starting from its place in the world, not starting from the axis of coordinates of my body ...). (278)

In effect, the coordination of vision and touch expands the *Tastwelt* so that my hand gives access to a felt space there where it is, with this space becoming incorporated as part of the reciprocity of touch. In so doing, this coordination facilitates the construction of situation-specific boundaries between inside and outside that need not coincide with the skin and that, accordingly, open the body to technical expansion.

Yet, if the body can be thus opened to technical expansion—whether via the mirror of specular vision or the expanded *Tastwelt* of what (with Massumi) we might call "movement-vision"—it is only because embodiment is essentially and orginarily technical. To see why, we have only to pass from the correlation-in-fact between touch and vision (which institutes an empirical technicity) to their correlation-in-principle (which entails an originary technicity). In the wake of such a passage, we begin to see that the transductive correlation of touching–touched and seeing rests upon a yet more primordial transduction, a transduction that, for the human as form of life, is entirely originary: the transduction of the *écart* as condition of embodiment and as source for the technical.

Embodiment and technicity thus comprise two divergent, yet entirely complementary (indeed, strictly correlated) expressions of the negativity of (human) being as Merleau–Ponty understands it. If neither one is the cause of the other (which is just what transduction here means), then neither one can be understood as a fall or a contamination (or even a humanization) of the other, as traditional and (now) posthumanist accounts would, variously, have it. Indeed, they each occasion an originary form of transcendence and thus, together, furnish the (double) condition for the emergence of the human as a form of life—that is, as "sensing sensible," that part of the flesh endowed with "*Empfindbarkeit*," the capacity to sense (224).

Although the shift to vision may in fact *expose* the essential technicity of being in a particularly clear manner, it manifestly does not inaugurate that technicity. This is crucial if we are to grasp the correlation of embodiment and technicity in its full originity. Along with embodiment, technicity is there from the origin (which is equally to say that it inhabits primordial tactility) and, like embodiment, is a dimension of the essential specularity of the sensible being of the flesh. That is why the strict correlation of the two distinct, empirical senses of vision and touch comprises nothing other than a manifestation of this originary correlation. As a being conditioned by the transduction of embodiment and technicity, by the double *écart* of primordial tactility, the human is and will always remain split, inhabiting the two separate, incompossible yet superposed worlds of the tactile and the visual.

Only because humans are embodied beings are they able to conjoin these divergent worlds of sense: embodiment is the condition for a phenomenalization of being (for a form of the living) that emerges in the gap between touch and vision. Here, then, is the deep reason why we must not simply oppose touch and vision, but rather must attempt to think their transduction and, most crucially, must assume the consequences of its emergence out of the originary transduction of the *écart* as condition of embodiment and source for the technical.

For if vision does mark a massive expansion of exteriorization, we must remember that it does so not by breaking with touch, but rather by extending touch beyond the boundary of the skin. Likewise, if touch gives rise to interiority, it also—and for this very reason—inaugurates the relation to the outside constitutive for all exteriorization. To say

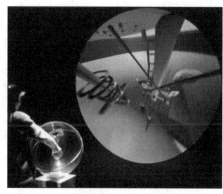

FIGURE 1.7 Agnes Hededüs, *Handsight* (1992), interactive virtual reality interface system. (Courtesy of the artist.)

that the human is split between the tactile and the visual is, in a certain sense, to say that the human is, from its origin, embodied *and* technical; the proto-origin of tactility and vision is the *écart*, the hinge or gap in which embodiment is conjoined with technicity, interiority with exteriorization.

As the compression of its title announces, Agnes Hegedüs's *Handsight* (1992) proffers a performative allegory of this transductive coupling of vision and touch. *Handsight* comprises three separate elements: a hand-held "eyeball" interface that tracks hand position; a transparent sphere with an iris-shaped opening for the hand; and a round projection screen, initially displaying an image of an eye, that opens into a virtual world. Functioning as a single, integrated visual system, *Handsight* requires the viewer to initiate and control the operation of vision through the hand; only by manipulating the eyeball interface within the transparent sphere is the viewer able to access the virtual world projected in the eye-shaped screen on the wall in front of him or her (see Figure 1.7).

By routing the function of vision through the instrumentality of manual manipulation, Hegedüs compels the viewer–user of her work to see with the hand, thus foregrounding—in a particularly enactive way—the presence of tactility in vision. And by coupling this form of tactile vision with the virtual, Hegedüs displaces the focus from the differences and similarities between the physical and the virtual worlds, revealing instead how the virtual comprises an extension of the essential technicity of embodied life. If the work carries out "the reembodiment of the senses," as Hegedüs contends, the reason has everything to do with the transductive coupling of vision and touch.[22] *Handsight* is able directly to map virtual vision on tactility precisely because it channels vision through an interface—the tactilely manipulable eyeball—that correlates to a visual point of view *within* the virtual world it views. "Hand motions," explains Hegedüs, "are translated instantly (i.e., in 'real time') into a moving-point-of-view like an 'endoscopic eye' (endo—within, e.g., capable of penetrating an interior space) exploring a virtual world."[23] The sphere (and the work as such) ultimately provides the viewer "an endo-spatial enclosure whose manual exploration maps directly into the representation of the virtual domain" (Hegedüs, "Handsight").

Coupled in this way with "the endo-spatial enclosure," the virtual is positioned as the payoff, not of some autonomous technical accomplishment (as so many recent discussions seem to maintain), but rather of the transductive coupling of vision and touch. If the virtual here comprises a deterritorialization of the visual via its exteriorization of the body's interiority, like vision, it is deeply bound up with embodiment. Indeed, the virtual is less a new domain of vision proper than a technical extension of sensation that serves to expose tactility's role in inaugurating the coupling of interiority and exteriorization and, with it, the essential technicity of sensation.

What the work exteriorizes, then, is not some autonomous domain of the visual, but, as Hegedüs insists, the domain of interiority: the work transforms "an ordinarily inaccessible interiority or psychic space of transcendence … into an externalized virtual space that can be entered and explored" (Hegedüs, [Description]). Given our earlier discussion of the transduction of interiority and exteriorization, it is interesting that this passage to exteriorization is doubled by the inverse movement, as Anne-Marie Duguet explains:

> [T]he eye, an object in the exterior, becomes a detecting subject in the interior of the sphere where it executes the points of view that are given to it by the hand. One is thus confronted with an extraordinary mobility and instability of the look; the scene regresses [*se retourne*] to a simple game of digits, the objects turn around and traverse one another without resistance.[24]

Duguet's analysis helps to underscore how *Handsight*, by making the hand into the operator of the eye's movement, introduces a distancing into tactility and thus allows reflection on the transduction—and perhaps, ultimately, on the indifferentiation—between tactility and vision.

In the end, *Handsight* works by reorienting attention from the virtual world to which it allows access to the means of access; thus, Hegedüs concludes:

> [T]he "endoscopic eye" or virtual camera is inducted symbolically into the mind itself, not in order to reveal some objective reality, but to display parts of a symbolic system laden with historical and personal resonance. Once entered, this virtual space becomes larger than its apparent container, seemingly monumental, offering a subjective point-of-view onto precipitous declines and vertiginous shifts of position governed by the visitor's own hand. (cited in Duguet)

What can this virtual space be, if not the capacity of embodied human life to exteriorize its interiority, and thus, equally, an expression of the latter's essential and originary technicity?

8. WORLDSKIN

The transductive correlation of vision and touch that emerges in Merleau–Ponty's final lectures on nature entails a fundamental transformation of the closely intertwined conceptions of the body schema and of intercorporeality. Putting into question the distinction between the body as a thing and as my point of view on things, Merleau–Ponty would now appear to be capable of moving beyond the impasse presented by the *écart* (the failure of reversibility). Eschewing the alternative that informs reversibility, he insists that the body is "both: thing-standard as flesh" (*Nature*, 224). This means that the body schema has now become something more than simply the agent of the body's access to the world: if "to sense my body is also to have its posture in the world" (224), this is because the flesh of the world is only phenomenalized in the flesh of the body (or, as Merleau–Ponty puts it, because "the flesh of the body makes us understand the flesh of the world" [218]).

The corporeal schema has, accordingly, been transformed from an organization of the individual body into a form of generality or commonality that directly characterizes the flesh of the world, the world as flesh:

> The relation with the world is included in the relation of the body with itself. The relation of my two hands = the exchange between them; the touched hand is given to the touching hand as touching; they are the mirror of each other—something analogous in the relation with the things: they "touch me" just as much as I touch them. Not surprising: They are that on which the synergy of my body opens; they are made of the same stuff as the corporal schema; I haunt them at a distance,

they haunt me at a distance. I am with them in a relation of *Einfühlung*: my within is an echo of their within.

What follows from this reinscription of the body schema in the flesh of the world is a conception of intercorporeity that eschews the mediation of the image of the other in favor of a generality of sensibility, a sensible commons that is not simply a common sense:

> But as a result, the corporal schema is going to be not only a relation to the things and to an *Umwelt* of things, but also a relation to other corporal schema. Among the things, there are living "similars." These are going to insert themselves in the circuit of my hand to my hand. The coupling of my two hands = recognition of a "behavior" in which appears a "thing"; the active hand lives at a distance from the other. Likewise, the coupling of my hand and the hand of another: my corporal schema as an animal of conducts lives at a distance in the living exterior. There are [sic] among them a carnal relation, an extension of the narcissism of the body. This narcissism is also an opening to generality: I live the offered behaviors as my own, and I see them animated by a corporal schema. The flesh also resolves the problem here: it is because I perceive that the other is possible for me as an other perceiving the same sensibles that I perceive. Massive flesh of esthesiology, flesh of co-perception made subtle, of identification between corporal schemas. My corporal schema is projected in the others and is also introjected, has relations of being with them, seeks identification, appears as undivided among them, desires them. Desire considered from the transcendental point of view = common framework of my world as carnal and of the world of the other. (224–225)

This sensory generality furnishes a deeper foundation for what had earlier been the basis for intercorporeity: namely, the image of the other. Just as the elucidation of primordial tactility as a protoreversibility deepens, rather than displaces, the role of vision and its complex articulation with technicity, the sharing of body schemata serves to ground the commonality of the visible. It thus explains why the visual experience of the other (of the other's image) can yield intercorporeity. For this reason, Merleau–Ponty can invoke "an opening of my body to other bodies: just as I touch my hand touching, I perceive others as perceiving. The articulation of their body on the world is lived by me in the articulation of my body on the world where I see them." What is more, this sharing of embodied schematism introduces a reversibility at the heart of intercorporeity: "my body is also made up of their corporeality. My corporal schema is a normal means of knowing other bodies and these know my body. Universal-lateral of the co-perception of the world" (218).

Because this reciprocity between my body and the body of the other comprises an emanation from the protoreciprocity of primordial tactility, it operates an extension of the *écart* into the domain of collective experience. Just as the *écart* marks a failure of reversibility between the hand as touched and as toucher—a failure which *expresses* the originary form of the *écart* as transduction of embodiment and technics—it likewise opens an irreducible asymmetry in the reversibility between my body and the body of the other. And just as the duality of sensation (and of primordial tactility) brought with it a fundamental chance—the chance for a coupling with the flesh of the world and with things—the asymmetry that informs collective intercorporeity (the sensory common) opens the chance for an at once more concrete and more generalized coupling with technics.

Accordingly, the very means facilitating my body's opening to the flesh of the world and to things give concrete expression to the transductive correlation of primary tactility, to the *écart* as condition of embodiment and source of technicity. Today's digital technologies and the mixed reality aesthetic that they support thus function to actualize the potential of technicity to be a *medium* for being. Through them, the transduction constitutive of primary tactility—the transduction of embodiment and technics, of interiority and exteriorization—becomes actualized as a technically specific and technically facilitated intercorporeal commonality.

Now it should be clear that Merleau–Ponty's theorization of technics—limited to the conception of discrete prosthesis—fails to grapple with the technical "essence" of the human that, as I have suggested, lies at the heart of his conception of primary tactility and the structural coupling of the flesh of my body and of the world. To grasp this dimension of technics, then, we must turn to Gilbert Simondon, the French "bio–techno–phenomenologist" and student of Merleau–Ponty's, whose work takes up the thread of the latter's unfinished final project and discovers, as the necessary correlate of a complex theory of physico–bio–social individuation, a convergence of the biosocial with the technical.

On Simondon's understanding, individuation is an ongoing and interminable process, ranging from the physical (the process of crystallization is his key example) to the social; in all cases, it crucially involves a relation to the "preindividual," the domain of "metastable" potentiality.

With his specific distinction between the subject and the individual within the process of human individuation, Simondon develops an account of the human as a living being constitutively in excess of itself and necessarily endowed with a collective dimension. Schematically put, the subject is the individual viewed from the standpoint of its ongoing individuation (or genesis) and thus through its constitutive relation to the metastable domain of the "preindividual"; the individual, by contrast, is the subject frozen at a specific moment of this individuation and cut off from the source of its (hetero)genesis, from the domain of potentiality.

The subject and the individual are connected via a disjunction: The subject encompasses the individual which in turn forms an element in the subject's individuation. This means that the individual and the subject exist at different levels of being and that, because they do, the subject can undergo a (relative) "disindividuation" which, far from marking its dissolution as a subject, comprises the condition of possibility for the discovery of its latent collective dimension. With this discovery, the subject is able to resolve the tension generated by its constitutive excess over itself (experienced as affectivity) and, by putting itself in question through a confrontation with the preindividual it carries within it, can undergo a new (collective) individuation. Indeed, on Simondon's account, every psychosocial individuation requires a relative disindividuation of the already individuated beings that comprise its elements. This disindividuation is simply the condition of possibility for the non-individuated potential (the preindividual) they each contain to be freed for a subsequent, higher order individuation. Not only does the subject perdure through these stages of individuation, but also—as one of their constitutive elements—it evolves in and through them.

What renders Simondon's conceptualization a crucial continuation of Merleau–Ponty's excavation of the technicity of the living is his correlation of individuation with technics understood as a quasi-autonomous domain of being—what Bernard Stiegler has called "organized, inorganic matter"—between the organic and the inorganic.[25] On Simondon's account, technical objects are like living beings in that they must be understood from the perspective of their genesis or progressive individuation; yet, they differ from living beings in that, far from being given initially as concrete individuals, they only tend toward the concrete.

Nonetheless, by establishing that technical objects are the ever changing bearers of a genesis, Simondon accords them a certain autonomy from the human. Though never entirely separable from human evolution, their evolution occurs through relations internal to the domain of technicity and is only punctuated by human intervention. For this reason, technical objects are able to constitute a medium for the biologically and psychically individuated human being to interpenetrate nature, as Simondon claims:

> [T]hrough technical activity, the human creates mediations, and these mediations are detachable from the individual who produces and thinks them. The individual expresses itself in them, but does not adhere to them. The machine possesses a sort of impersonality which allows it to become the instrument of another human. The human reality that it crystallizes in itself is alienable, precisely because it is detachable.... The technical object, conceived and constructed by the human, does not limit itself to creating a mediation between the human and nature.... It accords its human content a structure similar to that accorded natural objects and permits the insertion of the natural effects of this human reality into the world.... A convertibility of the human into the natural and of the natural into the human is instituted through the technical schematism.[26]

Put in Merleau–Pontyian terminology, this mutual interpenetration of the human and the natural could be said to actualize the *écart* of primary tactility—the gap between embodiment and technicity—that yields the asymmetrical interpenetration of the flesh of my body and the flesh of the world.

In fact, this connection to the primordial *écart* is precisely why technics can facilitate the convertibility that allows biologically and psychically individuated human beings to participate in a *transindividual* collective individuation:

> [T]he technical world offers an indefinite affordance [*disponibilité*] of groupings and connections. For it is the result of a liberation of human reality crystallized in the technical object. To construct a technical object is to prepare an affordance ... beyond the interindividual relation which is not maintained through an operational activity, a mental and practical universe of technicity is instituted, in which human beings communicate through what they invent. The technical object understood according to its essence—the technical object such that it has been invented, conceived and desired, and taken up by a human subject—becomes the support and the symbol of that relation we want to call *transindividual*.... By the intermediary of the technical object, an interhuman relation is thus created that forms the very model of *transindividuality*. What is meant by this is a relation that does not

86

place individuals into relation by means of their already constituted individuality, ... nor by means of what is identical in every human subject, ... but by means of the charge of preindividual reality, of this charge of nature that is conserved with the individual being and that contains potentials and virtuality. (246–248)

By correlating *transindividual* individuation with technics, Simondon crucially expands Merleau–Ponty's conception of intercorporeity as a "commonality" of the body schema, as a "common framework of my world as carnal and of the world of the other" (*Nature*, 217/225). Indeed, the connection between the body schema and technics—the "technical schematism" as a medium for the mutual convertibility of human and nature—is precisely what conditions Merleau–Ponty's extension of the body schema to the point of its dissolution, to the point where it no longer serves to specify the boundaries of the body's interiority but rather to mark its ontological interpenetration with the flesh of the world.

Fittingly, this extension comes at the end of the final course on *Nature*, at the moment when the human relation to technics would (perhaps) "naturally" arise:

The corporal schema as incorporation. The corporal schema is that. Finally thus (above all by the vision of the self) a relation of being between:

- My body and the world
- The different aspects of my body; a relation of ejection
- Introjection, a relation of incorporation

It can be extended to the things (clothing and the corporal schema). It can expel a part of the body. It is thus not made of determined parts, but it is a lacunary being (the corporal schema is the hollow on the inside)—includes accentuated, precise regions, and other vague regions. (The hollow and the vague regions are the point of insertion of imaginary bodies.) Sensoriality (above all by vision) intentionally implies incorporation, that is, a functioning of the body as a passage to an outside, by its "orifices." Other consequence: As my image captures my touching, the visual image of the others captures it also: they are also the outside of me. And I am their inside. They alienate me and I incorporate them. I see by the eyes of the other → the world. (278–279)

In this culminating recapitulation of the various elements of our previous excavation of primary tactility (note especially the complex imbrication of vision and touch as the foundation of intercorporeity), Merleau–Ponty affirms the essential technicity of the bodily schema. By doing so, he furnishes a conception of the commonality of being that can embrace what Simondon has shown to be its necessary technical expression.

It should come as no surprise, given our focus here, that an elective affinity exists between this dissolution of the schema—together with the ensuing concept of "indivision" (279)—and the virtual. What remains to be shown is how Merleau–Ponty's excavation of the transductive *écart* of primordial tactility serves to expose embodiment at the heart of virtual reality (and thus to confer on the latter its unavoidable status as mixed reality). That I shall do this through examination of a digital artwork should also come as little surprise. Indeed, like many other artworks discussed here, Maurice Benayoun's *Worldskin* (1997, in collaboration with musician Jean-Baptiste Barrière) offers a performative allegory of the passage from the domain of the image—here in the form of the virtual as the exemplary instance of the technical mediation of specularity in our world today—to the domain that informs it and (on account of our originary technicity) depends on it: namely, the domain of tactility, motility, and embodiment.

Commissioned by Ars Electronica for the CAVE environment (a three-dimensional projection space encompassing three adjacent walls, floor, and ceiling), *Worldskin* foregrounds the crucial previously discussed distinction between operationality and observation, participation and documentation (see Figure 1.8).[xxxviii] The environment consists of imagery of recent war zones divided into two modes of interface: a three-dimensional world comprising sky and ground planes and a series of two-dimensional digital "cut and pastes" of mass media images of tanks, aircraft, buildings, and innumerable soldiers and war victims. Participants wear wireless LCD glasses which allow them to perceive and navigate seamlessly in the (passively) immersive projection space.

To interact with the environment, however, participants must make use of three still cameras hanging from the ceiling. When a participant points and shoots one of these cameras, the entire field captured by the pyramid-shaped aperture is transformed into a blank space. This destruction of the image is in turn doubled and reinforced by Barrière's audio: at the moment at which the camera is snapped, the background noises of war give way to a sonic transform in which the sound of the camera clicking is abruptly replaced by sounds of guns being fired. Each exposure is subsequently printed to paper in the form of a blank

FIGURE 1.8 Maurice Benayoun, Worldskin (1997), interactive CAVE environment deploying photographic interface. (Courtesy of the artist.)

silhouette, providing the viewer with a material trace of his or her unique intervention into this archive environment.

In *Worldskin*, two divergent contemporary image technologies instantiating two longstanding aesthetic traditions—photography and virtual reality—are pitted against one another. The express intention is to catalyze a jump from the superficial level of the image as a neutralizing "capture" of the world to a deeper level where it forms a trigger for the viewer's active engagement with his or her agency in the world. In this way, as I propose to demonstrate here, *Worldskin* advances a plea of sorts for a model of technics that would affirm, express, and indeed condition the dissolution of the body–world separation in our world today.

That this model crucially involves a critique of the ontology of observation as it is technically instantiated in photography—and that such a critique is undeniably a political project—becomes clear when we read Benayoun's description of the work:

> Armed with cameras, we make our way through a … landscape … scarred by war-demolished buildings, armed men, tanks and artillery, piles of rubble, the wounded and the maimed.… Like so many tourists, we [visit the land of war] with camera in hand. Each of us can take pictures, capture a moment of this world that is wrestling with death. The image thus recorded exists no longer.… We take pictures. First by our aggression, then feeling the pleasure of sharing, we rip the skin off the body of the world. The skin becomes a trophy, and our fame grows with the disappearance of the world.… Taking pictures expropriates the intimacy of … pain while, at the same time, bearing witness to it. This has to do with the status of the image in our process of getting a grasp on this world. The rawest and most brutal realities are reduced to an emotional superficiality in our perception. Acquisition, evaluation and understanding of the world constitute a process of capturing it. Capturing means making something one's own; and once it is in one's possession, that thing can no longer be taken by another.… The picture neutralizes the content. Media bring everything onto one and the same level. Physical memory-paper, for example, is the door that remains open to a certain kind of forgetting. We interpose the lens ("objectif" in French) between ourselves and the world. We protect ourselves from the responsibility of acting. One "takes" the picture, and the world "proffers" itself as a theatrical event.… The world falls victim to the viewer's glance, and everyone is involved in its disappearance. The collective unveiling becomes a personal pleasure, the object of fetishistic satisfaction. We keep to ourselves what we have seen (or rather, the traces of what we have seen). To possess a printed vestige, to

possess the image inherent in this is the paradox of the virtual, which is better suited to the glorification of the ephemeral.[27]

This agonistic face-off with photography yields a fundamental reorientation of virtual reality technology that exposes virtual reality—at least as it exists in the world today—as mixed reality, as a dimension or property of the "real" world. Normally understood to be a form of passive immersion, a distancing fascination that insulates "first world" spectator–citizens from the real, as Žižek famously contended in his denunciation of Western reactions to 9/11,[28] virtual reality here becomes a technical interface to the world that succeeds because it taps into the transductive coupling of embodiment and technicity constitutive of the human.

The viewer's presence in this environment—her capacity to act within it—accordingly becomes a function of the technical distribution of her embodiment, of her exteriorization into the various effects of his or her intervention within the environment. To the extent that this distribution coincides with the transformation of the image from the superficial representation of the visible (the image of the body of the other) to the material traces or indices of the viewer's kinesthetic movement (the blank spaces and the paper print-outs which uniquely inscribe the viewer's position and orientation toward the images), it constitutes a paradoxical form of "embodied disembodiment." I would suggest that this disembodiment perfectly expresses the contemporary (technically specified) form of the "indivision" invoked by Merleau–Ponty at the end of his exploration of the human body in *Nature*.

That such embodied disembodiment (or disembodied embodiment) instances the process of informational framing explored at length in *New Philosophy for New Media* fully attests to its role as an actualization, in and for the technical epoch of digital immateriality, of the originary indivision of the flesh (primary tactility). *Worldskin* calls on the viewer to coproduce images from information in conjunction with a digital environment, and its CAVE infrastructure inverts the relation of vision and touch so that, as Anne-Marie Duguet puts it, "the look does not 'touch' the image so much as the image touches the entire body" (210). However, precisely because it deploys this inversion *as the vehicle for the viewer's disembodiment, Worldskin* perfectly expresses (in the act of performatively exposing) the contemporary (technical) dissolution of the divide between interiority and exteriorization, the flesh of my body and the flesh of the world.

Through its particular specification of the process of informational framing, the work thus *produces* the experience of embodied disembodiment, meaning that it actively dissolves (in order to reconstitute anew) the differentiation according to which embodiment and disembodiment have been set into opposition in our culture and in Western thinking more generally. To be yet more precise, *Worldskin* catalyzes a *double* transformation in the economy linking embodiment and disembodiment. On the one hand, the technical extension of vision (and of memory) carried out by photography is repurposed *as a functional element of the viewer's embodied agency within the digital environment*: the viewer literally acts through the camera, which is equally to say that the camera alone allows his or her embodiment to matter here. On the other hand, the viewer's embodied movement within the environment—the actual kinesthetic activity—is exteriorized (or distributed) in the technical traces created by his or her intervention into the image space. To the extent that these traces (the modifications of the images as well as the paper print-outs) inscribe the singular movement of the viewer, they literally comprise "embodied disembodiments," material extensions of the viewer's embodied agency that, while remaining correlated with the latter, nonetheless function autonomously from it.

The aesthetic impact of this double transformation is perfectly emblematized by the work's redeployment of photography as a vehicle for the viewer's direct engagement in the (present) moment of interaction (or intervention) with the environment. As Anne-Marie Duguet has astutely pointed out, *Worldskin* playfully—though altogether seriously—asks its viewers to "photograph the virtual" (211). Because photography—the indexical medium par excellence—simply has no purchase in the domain of the virtual, what hangs in the balance is the status of what Roland Barthes long ago called the "photographic referent," the photograph's material inscription of the "that has been" [*ça a été*], the unique convergence of the real and the past. *Worldskin* in effect stages a dissolution of this function and, with it, a critique of photography's role as storage medium, as the exemplary form of what Bernard Stiegler has called "tertiary memory" (the memory of that which has not been lived by present consciousness but yet conditions its temporalization). More specifically, *Worldskin* aligns the storage function of photography (and of tertiary memory more generally) with the insulated, distanced stance of the first-world image consumer. When it compels viewers to destroy the tertiary image—here invested specifically as the material support for this self-protective stance—*Worldskin* accordingly suspends photography's storage function. In the process, it redirects attention from the content of the image to its capacity to trigger embodied activity that paradoxically yields disembodiment as its material trace.

If photography provides a source of the preindividual and of the generic commons, as Stiegler has suggested,[29] it is not because it forms an archive of discrete memories whose adoption by individual consciousness necessarily informs the latter's temporalization (and the possibility for collective temporalization). On the contrary, the deployment of photography in *Worldskin* makes clear that it is the process of exteriorization which forms the source of the preindividual. That is why, again, the ensuing disembodiment is not so much opposed to embodiment as it is to its strict complement; bluntly put, disembodiment is the condition of possibility for embodied human life to sustain its (life-sustaining) contact with the preindividual.

Rather than offering an opportunity for the adoption of archived tertiary memories, *Worldskin* thus facilitates a self-reflexive *experience* of one's embodied agency in the world. To the extent that it exteriorizes embodied agency (thereby disembodying it), the work manages to separate it from the viewer's ongoing, constitutive, autopoietic embodiment and thus allows it to be *fed back* into the latter via a recursive coupling that comprises the contemporary correlation—the new economy as it were—between embodiment and disembodiment.

To the extent that we increasingly act in informational environments and in conjunction with informational agents, *Worldskin* thereby exposes nothing less than the general condition for embodied agency in our world today. With the ubiquitous infiltration of digital technologies into daily life, embodied agency becomes conditioned (necessarily so) by a certain (technical) disembodiment. Embodied disembodiment (or disembodied embodiment) accordingly forms a strict complement to the ontology of mixed reality conditioning all real experience. Just as all virtual reality is mixed reality, so too is all embodied life constitutively disembodied. Understood in this context, virtuality thus forms the basis for the convergence of the living and information underway everywhere today.

Such an understanding lies at the heart of Benayoun's endeavor in *Worldskin*, as can be discerned from his extended discussion of the constitutive impurity of virtuality:

> When we come to understand that virtuality is, at the origins, a property of the "real" world, we should admit that the exchange

between fiction and reality would be balanced only if the dynamic and symbolic properties of the virtual representation become part of the physical world. This explained that, having been a matter of experiment, in search of specific properties that would only belong to the medium, VR and VE are becoming, like the art of using them, more and more impure. This impurity might characterize the mature stage of the medium, and the merging of the virtual and the physical world is probably the extension of the human trend of converting the objective environment into an informational system.[30]

That this conversion informs *both* the integration of virtuality into the "real" world *and* the disembodying exteriorization of human embodiment only confirms the urgency of rethinking embodied agency in the age of digital immateriality. Because contemporary technics facilitate a dissolution of the body–world distinction (an "indivision") that is fundamentally informational in its (im)materiality and because human embodied activity is, in some way, the agent of this dissolution, we can no longer constrain embodiment to the body, can no longer contain it within the (organic) skin. We must—as Benayoun's title suggests—extend it into a "worldskin." As a concept for the contemporary technically facilitated indivision of the flesh, worldskin perfectly captures the complementarity between informational environment and disembodied embodiment that—as a technically specific actualization of the transduction of primordial tactility—ensures the "essential" embodiment of the former no less than the "essential" technicity of the latter.

9. THE TELE-ABSENT BODY

No contemporary media artist has been more directly concerned with this complementarity between informational environment and disembodied embodiment than Mexican-Canadian artist Rafael Lozano–Hemmer. In a series of performance installations collectively titled "relational architecture," Lozano–Hemmer has variously deployed information technology to energize urban space. Defined as "the technological actualization of buildings and public spaces with alien memory," relational architecture aims to transform "the master narratives of a specific building by adding and subtracting audiovisual elements to affect it, effect it and re-contextualize it."[31]

Accordingly, Lozano–Hemmer's relational architecture installations deploy media interventions into existing architectural space precisely as a means of triggering embodied reactions (reactions which, as we shall see, tap into the disembodiment constitutive of embodiment). When these reactions subsequently enter into resonance with the media transformations triggering them, they establish feedback loops in which embodiment and information mutually catalyze one another's ongoing evolution, rendering it a coevolution that perfectly expresses the contemporary stage of the technogenesis of the human.

Explaining that the "real motivation behind relational architecture is the modification of existing behavior," Lozano–Hemmer stresses the creativity of this recursivity: Relational artworks, he maintains, "create a situation where the building, the urban context and the participants relate in new, 'alien' ways." A relational work can be considered successful, he explains, if its intervention "actively modifies the point of dynamic equilibrium between the public's actions and the building's reactions, and vice versa," thereby generating "chaotic ... or emergent behaviors."[32]

Functioning together in this way, embodiment and information generate temporary transformations of built urban space that are simultaneously collective individuations of embodied human actors. By taking "indivision" to its ultimate point—the point where embodiment and information, functioning transductively, operate to "dematerialize" the environment—Lozano–Hemmer's project forcefully demonstrates that embodiment today can only be conceived *as collective individuation,* as an individuation that requires a certain disembodiment of embodied individuals. The reason for this is simple: Because human embodiment no longer coincides with the boundaries of the human body, a disembodiment of the body forms the condition of possibility for a collective (re)embodiment through technics. The human today is embodied in and through technics.

Just such a realignment of the basis of embodiment is at issue—in a fully performative manner—in Lozano–Hemmer's *Re:Positioning Fear— Relational Architecture 3* (1997; see Figure 1.9). Designed as an intervention into one of Europe's largest military arsenals, the Landeszeughaus in Graz, Austria, the work consists of two components: an archive of "Internet relay chat" (IRC) sessions devoted to the discussion of contemporary fears and a "tele-absence" installation involving projection of shadows and text on the facade of the Landeszeughaus' inner courtyard.

By linking the legibility of the text (the projection of the IRC sessions) with the projection of amplified shadows of participants'

FIGURE 1.9 Rafael Lozano–Hemmer, Re:Positioning Fear (1997), "tele-absence" installation. (Courtesy of the artist.)

bodies, Lozano–Hemmer directly correlates disembodiment with the informational transformation of the spatial environment. In this respect, he literally creates a "body-in-code," as I have been developing the concept here, and in the process correlates the concept with a certain margin of disembodiment. Because the text only becomes legible against the background of an amplified shadow, the embodied participant's transformation into shadow forms the enabling condition for the transformation of the physical façade into informational space. This latter in turn becomes the stimulus for continued participant interaction via the shadow interface, and an evolving feedback loop is established.

By calling this a "tele-absence" interface, Lozano–Hemmer foregrounds the complex imbrication of disembodiment and information that will ultimately yield a higher order (collective) form of (technically supported) embodiment:

> Even though the IRC sessions could have been projected on the arsenal by covering most of the façade, an interface was designed to prevent all of the text from being visible at one time. The interface is called "tele-absence" and it consists of an "active" shadow that reveals the text on the building. To read the building, a participant standing in front of it must wear a small wireless sensor and walk around the courtyard. As he or she walks, two pigi 7kW Xenon light sources track his or her position and project his or her shadow onto the façade of the Zeughaus. By using robotic lighting control, the shadows were focused dynamically so that regardless of the participant's proximity to the lamps the shadows were always crisp and well defined. The final effect was a "dynamic stencil" whereby the shadow of the participant was an active architectural element which "revealed" the IRC texts that appeared to be within the building, as though the shadow was a cutout or an x-ray of the building. ("Re: Positioning Fear")

Defined as "the technological acknowledgement of the impossibility of self transmission ... the celebration of where and when the body is not" ("Re:Positioning Fear"), tele-absence is less a simple disembodiment of the self-present human body than it is its re-embodiment in different, expanded form—namely, as an amplified shadow that is simultaneously the trigger for the dynamic informatization of a static physical building. In his commentary on the work, Brian Massumi astutely discerns the complexity of Lozano–Hemmer's dance with (dis)embodiment:

> If you think of the shadow ... as casting "absence" as a potential next action, ... the "where and when the body is not" becomes "where the body may relay," and "the impossibility of self transmission" becomes a reminder that every stretch of the body is not just a displacement of it but a becoming. A body cannot transmit itself. But it can project its vitality. Its activity may take on a new dimension.

Massumi's perspective here perfectly captures the indifferentiation of absence and presence, of embodiment and disembodiment, that characterizes human life in the informational age: "Seen in this way," he continues, "'tele-absence' is perhaps not so different from 'teleembodyment,' the term relayed into in later work."[33]

Given my aim of introducing technics into Merleau–Ponty's final phenomenology, it is hardly incidental that Lozano–Hemmer's tele-absent extension of embodiment (and its qualified embrace of disembodiment) breaks with the model of prosthetics which, as we have seen, informs (and compromises) Merleau–Ponty's explicit thinking of technics. Lozano–Hemmer's work makes clear that such a model simply cannot forego privileging the individual body and thus cannot tap the potential of technics to support "alien" forms of embodiment that do not coincide with the body and its potential prosthetic extensions.

As a contribution to Lozano–Hemmer's larger project of producing a new collective individuation of embodiment, *Re:Positioning Fear* takes the first step of disembodying the individual body, thus opening the possibility for a break from the prosthetic model of technics. This is precisely why Lozano-Hemmer insists that "the shadow is not an avatar, an agent, nor an alias of the participant's body" but rather "projected darkness, a play of geometries, a disembodied bodypart." As a negation of the body's static positivity, the shadow does not so much act in its stead as open its potential to be otherwise, thereby transforming it into "a site of telematic activity."

This material transformation of the body is what, for Lozano–Hemmer, serves to differentiate relational architecture in general from its virtual counterpart:

> Virtual buildings are data constructs that strive for realism, asking the participant to "suspend disbelief" and "play along" with the environment; relational buildings, on the other hand, are real buildings pretending to be something other than themselves, masquerading as that which they might become, asking participants to "suspend faith" and probe, interact and experiment with the false construct. Virtual architecture tends to miniaturize buildings to the participant's scale, for example through VR peripherals such as HMDs or CAVEs, while relational architecture amplifies the participant to the building's scale, or emphasizes the relationship between urban and personal scale. In this sense, virtual architecture dematerializes the *body*, while relational architecture dematerializes the *environment*. ("Relational Architecture")

On this understanding, virtual architecture makes common cause with the model of technics as prosthetics: because it retains the scale of the individual body, it simply cannot overcome the division between body and world except through the illusion of simulation; in Lozano–Hemmer's vision, this illusion serves to dematerialize the body. By contrast, relational architecture undoes this division and promotes "indivision" precisely by dematerializing the environment, by transforming it into a cocreation of embodiment and information, of bodily performance extended through information and of information embodied in such extension. What is thereby promoted is a model of technics as medium-for-individuation.

This model of technics foregrounds the complementarity of the two forms of individuation at issue in Simondon's conceptualization and in Lozano-Hemmer's relational works: the individuation of the (human) individual and collective individuation. The latter—specifically, the form that Simondon calls "transindividuation"—allows us to grasp how a certain disembodiment (understood as the individual's constitutive coupling to the preindividual) is a dimension of embodiment, as we have been maintaining for some time now. (In Simondon's parlance, transindividuation would be said to *resolve* the paradox of the human individual as a form of embodiment that is constitutively disembodied.) It is from the standpoint of transindividuation—an embodiment that is *super-individual* and also necessarily technical—that the excess of the individual over itself, the excess of its (preindividual) potentiality over its (individual) actuality, can be seen to be a constitutive dimension of its embodiment as an individual. In this respect, transindividuation can be said to be the ultimate expression of the primordial *écart*. In transindividuation, the originary transduction of embodiment and technicity constitutive of the human comes to yield nothing less than a technical embodiment of the indivision of the flesh, a technically embodied commons in which my body acquires its autonomy only through its participation in a larger process of embodiment.

The model of technics as medium-for-individuation thus forms the strict correlate of a view of the human that refuses to divorce technicity from embodiment and that therefore embraces disembodiment as a dimension of embodiment and as a potential for its extension beyond the body. If this model invests the *écart* constitutive of the human as the operator of human–machine interchange, it thereby gains a vastly expanded space of embodiment capable of encompassing technical extensions of the (human) body no less than concrete materializations of informational potentiality.

In this respect, my effort to introduce technics into (indeed, at the very core of) Merleau–Ponty's ontology of the flesh differs fundamentally from Gail Weiss' superficially similar attempt to position the *écart* as a "space of disincorporation that makes incorporation possible" (120). Insofar as it retains the separability of the body as body, Weiss' conception of technics is fundamentally a prosthetic one, on which technics befall the human from the outside and function merely to extend the scope of its proper embodiment. As what makes the disincorporation of this body possible, the *écart* opens a space of noncoincidence outside the body (between the body and its outside) rather than an originary noncoincidence (the transduction of embodiment and technicity) *within* the body. That is why, on her account, the *écart* is the condition that allows "for human beings to 'interface' with machines, ... to become one with our familiar, mass-produced or even 'one-of-a-kind' prostheses (e.g., glasses, clothes, artificial limbs, moussed-up hair, cars, watches, etc.)" (120). For Weiss, in sum, the *écart* names the condition for a prosthetic extension of the already individuated human being; from our Simondon-inspired perspective, by contrast, the *écart* expresses the originary technicity of the human, the condition that has now, with today's digital technologies, made real the co-individuation of technics and embodiment in the form of technically facilitated transindividuation.

Taking up the accomplishment of *Re:Positioning Fear* (the disembodying of the individual body), Lozano–Hemmer's *Body Movies—Relational Architecture 6* (2001) constitutes the artist's attempt to produce a transindividuation through technical disembodiment and subsequent reembodiment on a transformed scale and via an informational circuit (see Figure 1.10). Like the earlier work, *Body Movies* uses a tele-absence interface—namely, the projection of shadows cast by participants' bodies—to which it adds some new elements. These include the capacity for simultaneous, collective, indeed collaborative, participation; a role for body images; and a more direct assault on the culture industry and its domination via the circulation of mass illusion.

The work, which played from August 31 to September 23, 2001, in the Schouwburgplein in Rotterdam, consisted of the projection of over one thousand prerecorded portraits (captured in Rotterdam, Madrid, Mexico, and Montréal) onto the façade of the Pathé Cinema building. Powerful xenon lights placed at floor level totally washed the images out except when they were blocked by passersby whose bodies cast shadows of variable size (from 2 to 22 m high, depending on how proximate they were to the light sources) onto the façade, thereby rendering visible the otherwise hidden images. The locations of the shadows were continuously monitored in real time by a camera-based tracking system and, each time the shadows matched all the portraits in a given scene, the computer automatically updated the scene with a new set of portraits.

In his description of the work, Lozano–Hemmer stresses the way in which *Body Movies* encourages participants to embody the massive

FIGURE 1.10 Rafael Lozano–Hemmer, *Body Movies* (2001), "tele-absence" installation. (Courtesy of the artist.)

portraits (by superposing their shadows on them) only to frustrate this attempt by immediately replacing the images once they are so embodied. Linking this paradoxical structure to his effort to "introduce 'alien memory' as an urban catalyst," Lozano–Hemmer unequivocally characterizes the interactional space of the installation as a space in which the body "does not belong"—that is, as a space that cannot be inhabited by means of the body image, of the body as an image, and of the image as the medium of the commonality between bodies, intercorporeity.[34] More clearly than in *Re:Positioning Fear*, the disembodiment of the body is carried out via a performative critique of the superficiality of the body image. Still, as was the case in the earlier work, what remains instrumental in the interface is the role of the shadow as a negation of the body's positivity, as a disembodied anti-image of the body, which can achieve agency within the informationally energized space of the installation solely because and insofar as it disembodies the individuated body.

In contrast to *Re:Positioning Fear*, however, this disembodiment is here deployed in the service of a broader aesthetic aim—that of creating the possibility for a form of communion rooted in a technically facilitated kinesthetic space, a technically generated space of intercorporeity that embodies the indivision ensuing from the dissolution of the corporeal schema. To this end, *Body Movies* expressly solicits collective participation and, through it, the emergence of unpredictable behaviors. As Alex Adriaansens and Joke Brouwer describe it, *Body Movies* invited people on the square, up to 50 of them at a time, "to embody different representational narratives," thereby allowing them to create "a collective experience that nonetheless allowed discrete individual participation (Adriaansens and Brower)."

What this invitation facilitated can be gauged from the documentation video on Lozano–Hemmer's Website (http://www.fundacion.telefonica.com/at/rlh/video/bodymovies.html), which features various games involving disparity of scale and, interestingly enough, wholly unrelated to the prepackaged images highlighted by the various shadows at play. This hints at the work's success at guiding participants away from simple mimetic identification with the body image and toward creative play with their disembodied shadows in this new space of indivision. An experience is thereby facilitated that is entirely unprecedented; in the words of one Dutch participant, there is a possibility for "a strange kind of communication with people you've never met," one where "you're all together but you're also separate" (interview from the video cited earlier).

Creating the possibility for such communion—for a truly impersonal communication or, better (following Walter Benjamin), for the "communicability" that underlies and facilitates communication—is the ultimate aim, and the ultimate accomplishment, of Lozano–Hemmer's relational aesthetic. What is truly inspiring about his work is the way that it facilitates communion: namely, through the use of the most advanced configuration of technics and embodiment imaginable, one in which technics is treated as an originary dimension of embodiment and embodiment is understood to be a creation of bodily performance of and through information.

"Computers can communicate very efficiently; but they can't engage in communion," notes Candian theater director Robert Lapage. Explaining his own preference for catalyzing "collective experiences rather than using individual interfaces for solitary participation," Lozano-Hemmer reaffirms Lepage's affirmation of communion. For Lozano-Hemmer, what is crucial "is people meeting and sharing an experience," people "coming together," and indeed, "coming together in the flesh." If the contemporary phase of our (human) technogenesis makes such *physical* communion increasingly difficult, it simultaneously opens more radical possibilities for communion. As Lozano-Hemmer's work perfectly illustrates, such possibilities stem from our investment in technics as a means for overcoming the atomic isolation of the body. They give us a chance to live the "indivision" of body, its immanence to the flesh of the world.

In sum: By glimpsing and helping us to glimpse what such living might be, Lozano-Hemmer's relational works make good the promise, "contained" in the primordial *écart*, for a form of life—transindividuation—that exploits the originary indifferentiation of embodiment and technicity to the point at which human technogenesis parts company with the organic (human) body. It does so, however, without losing its constitutive concern for the human as a form of the living.

PART

II

locating the virtual in contemporary culture

embodying virtual reality

tactility and self-movement in the work of char davies

VR is a literal enactment of Cartesian ontology, cocooning a person as an isolated subject within a field of sensations and claiming that everything is there, presented to the subject.

Richard Coyne

The possession of a body in space, itself part of the space to be apprehended, and that body capable of self-motion in counterplay with other bodies, is the precondition for a vision of the world.

Hans Jonas

You are floating inside an abstract lattice not unlike the skeletal wireframe models familiar from three-dimensional graphics. You have no visible body at all in the space in front of you, but hear a soundscape of human voices swirling around you as you navigate forward and backward by leaning your body accordingly. Soon the Cartesian gridlines melt away as a forest clearing centering around a great old oak tree appears. Everything in your visual field seems to be constructed of light: branches, trunks, leaves shimmer with a strange luminescence, while in

FIGURE 2.1 Char Davies, Osmose (1995), virtual reality environment. (Courtesy of the artist.)

the distance there appears a river of dancing lights. Leaning your body forward, you move toward the boundary of the clearing and pass into another forest zone. You are now enfolded in a play of light and shadow, as leaves phase imperceptibly into darkened blotches and then phase back again, in what seems like a rhythmic perpetuity. Exhaling deeply causes you to sink down through the soil as you follow a stream of tiny lights illuminating the roots of the oak tree.

Soon you sink into an underworld of glowing red rocks that form a deep, luminous cavern beneath the earth. Exhaling again, you sink still further, encountering scrolling walls of green alphanumeric characters that (you will later learn) reproduce the 20,000 some lines of code upon which the world you are in is built. Longing for the vivid images above, you take in a deep breath and hold it, waiting to ascend. After passing once again through the clearing, you enter another world of text, encountering quotations from philosophical and literary sources that seem to bear directly on your experience. "By changing space, by leaving the space of one's usual sensibilities," one passage informs you, "one enters into communications with a space that is psychically innovating … we do not change place, we change our Nature."[i]

The attention you have been lending to your breathing makes you feel angelic and fleshy: while you float dreamlike, unencumbered by the drag of gravity, your actions are syncopated with your breathing in a way that makes your bodily presence palpable, insistent. Meanwhile, you find yourself floating back down to the clearing, no longer driven to explore, but meditative, content simply to float wherever your bodily leaning and breathing patterns will take you. Now acclimated to the new sensorimotor demands of this interactional domain, you can effortlessly explore the different spaces contained in this world, choosing to follow the river of lights as if swept along by a swarm of fireflies or, alternately, to step into the big oak tree and see its blood-red sap coursing around you or, again, to dive into a pool of shimmering water and let yourself sink into its engulfing embrace.

Yet just at that point when you begin to see the fuzzy pixelated organic forms around you morph into a field of resonant luminosity, you are suddenly thrust outside the world, looking upon what now appears as a gray, bean-shaped blob floating against an empty background. When you realize that you cannot return, you are flooded with a combination of resignation and melancholy which soon gives way to a sense of awe, to a wonder that you have somehow lived the immaterial.

If your experience is anything like that of the many thousands of other "immersants," you will feel that you have lived through something vastly different from what normal life brings and also quite different from what other forms of "virtual reality" afford or, at least, what you imagined them to afford. Here you have lived in harmony with a virtual lifeworld and have felt the dissolution of the hard boundary of the skin that, in ordinary experience and most certainly in most forms of virtual experience, so insistently prevents fluid interchange with the surrounding space. You have let your visual faculty become subordinate as you gained confidence in maneuvering with body movement and breathing. Perhaps most strikingly, you have let the experience of spatial navigation penetrate into your body via the immediately felt physiological modifications produced by the inhalation and exhalation that triggered your vertical movement as well as the bodily leaning that triggered your horizontal movement.[ii]

As several commentators have pointed out, the work just described— Char Davies' *Osmose* (1995)—is highly atypical for what currently goes under the rubric "virtual reality art."[iii] Davies' work eschews many of the familiar trappings of computer-based worlds, virtual reality, and game environments, including the primacy normally accorded to detached vision, the use of a joystick or other manipulable navigational tool, the orientation toward a goal, and the hard-edged simulation of a perspectival space. What results is a tactile aesthetics that, as Jennifer Fisher puts it, strives to "deepen the sense of subjective embodiment" by foregrounding the function of bodily modes of experience. "At a time when much VR technology effects a visual dominance and corporeal abstraction," Fisher continues, Davies' solicitation of tactility "both implicates and creates an 'embodied' spectator."[1]

Davies' *Osmose* is, in the words of another commentator, "the first major immersive VR environment to 'resist' simulation of perspectival space and to attempt to heal the rift between vision and body inherent in conventional virtual reality."[2] Davies herself is credited, by no less an authority than (VMRL inventor) Mark Pesce, with "redefin[ing] our place in cyberspace and mak[ing] the virtual world seem more human than our own."[3] Davies likens her work's difference from more traditional VR environments to the difference between illustration and evocation: "When art evokes," she says, "it's drawing on the experiences of the user. It becomes interactive on a much more subtle level. To me, *Osmose* looks at immersive space as a place where we can explore what it means to be embodied conscious beings."[4]

My aim in this chapter is to draw out further what makes Davies' art atypical, if not in fact unique, for work that invests in the concrete technology of virtual reality as a means of constituting (one kind of) body-in-code. By purposely deploying low resolution in the HMD, Davies' work actively counters the conventional VR emphasis on vision: indeed, as we shall see, her work compels the viewer–participant to reconfigure her sensory economy, such that (at the very least) vision becomes thoroughly permeated by tactility and proprioception. In the process, Davies successfully deploys the virtual reality interface toward an end—contemplative engagement—that moves it away from the instrumentalism associated with it (and for good reason, as we have seen) by prescient skeptics like Myron Krueger. Indeed, if Davies thus goes as far as possible, within the VR interface, in rendering irrelevant those elements that make it cumbersome and artificial, that is because she deploys VR toward an end that is thoroughly noninstrumental, meaning that it entirely eschews the interface with the physical world seemingly constitutive of today's mixed reality aesthetic. Yet, if Davies' work nonetheless supports the maxim that all VR is mixed reality, that is because it exposes the underlying constitution of the experience of the virtual in embodiment and, more specifically, in proprioception and tactility.

Davies' explicit desire to create an interface to the immaterial can be understood as a fulfillment of a hypothesis: to wit, that disenabling sensory stimulation from a richly material environment would lay bare the embodied processing that serves to confer reality on experience. In a recent commentary, Davies stresses the "hands-free and hands-off" emphasis of her work in a way that perfectly illustrates this retooling of the VR interface into a kind of laboratory for exploring embodiment: in perfect resonance with the movement from actual tactile experience to the embodied technicity of primordial tactility, Davies describes her aim to be that of catalyzing "the interior kinesthetic and proprioceptive experience of being a *lived* body *in* space, of *self*-movement *through* space, of being enveloped *by* space" (email to author). She further emphasizes her deliberate choice "not to involve haptic perception," meaning "hands-on or literal touching, skin to skin, surface to surface," so that she could catalyze an experience akin to the interlacing described by Merleau-Ponty—the interlacing "of one's own bodily surface with the visible surfaces of the other(s) … even though in a virtual environment these are immaterial." As a laboratory for testing the capacity of embodiment to generate reality, Davies' work thus restores virtuality as a dimension of embodied life, as a technicity within the living rather than a (mere) technical artifact that affects life from the outside.

For this reason, Davies' *Osmose* furnishes an exemplary instance of one kind of "body-in-code": an experience of embodiment that is specifically engineered to breathe life into the immaterial. As she puts it, her environments are designed to foreground the kinesthetic and proprioceptive dimensions of bodily self-movement "*in order to enable* a fuller (more real) experience of the virtual realm, doing so in such a way that they temporarily deautomate habitual perception and facilitate a 'seeing freshly.'" *Osmose* creates a body-in-code by harnessing embodied life in the service of conferring reality on the immaterial.

To explore Char Davies' work as a catalyst for the constitution of (one kind of) body-in-code, I shall undertake two relatively autonomous explorations, each of which will make a claim for the centrality of tactility in perception generally and for its specific function within the virtual reality interface. In a first section, I shall build up to an examination of how Davies' work deploys the role of tactility and proprioception in a way that effectively counters the overemphasis on vision on the part of scientists and artists working in virtual reality. Of particular interest will be the resonance between this deployment and philosophical and especially scientific work that supports our preceding claims concerning the emergence of vision from touch. This resonance will serve to underwrite a neo-Bergsonist claim that virtual reality realizes an aesthetic function insofar as it couples new immaterial domains of perception with the "reality"-conferring experience of touch (or what Bergson calls "affection").[5] In this way, Davies' work simply makes explicit something that forms a crucial dimension in every successful VR simulation: the role played by proprioception and tactility in generating what seems to be an exclusively visual—that is, virtual—simulation.

In a second section, I shall widen the divide separating a tactile aesthetic from a visual one by returning to the topic of the body image. Specifically, I shall enlist Davies' work in a continuing critique of the reduction of bodily experience—here, paradigmatically, of the body's fluid interface with space—to the body image. Insofar as it opens a non-representational and nonvisual affective and proprioceptive experience of the body, Davies' work once again brings to material fruition research in science and philosophy—in this case, by illustrating concretely how the living body exceeds the boundaries of the skin and encompasses parts of the environment.

For this reason, I argue that Davies' work expands the concept of "worldskin" in a way that addresses the complexity of our embodied experience of coupling to the contemporary technosphere. Specifically, her work deploys the confusion of self and space constitutive of the condition of "psychasthenia" in a way that counters its contemporary cultural currency as a simulational or image-based "disorder"[iv]; accordingly, in *Osmose*, this confusion becomes the catalyst for a reworking of the correlation between bodily and environmental space—a reworking that teaches us how to orient ourselves without needing to see ourselves (or to let the gaze of the other see us) as a point in space. Far from illustrating a confusion of the organism *with the representations* that surround it, the process triggered by Davies' work spurs a fluid, ongoing, and active interchange with the environment that has the effect of "transcending" the limited (representational) function of the "body schema" (its reduction to the body image). In this way, Davies' work concretely embodies the capacity of technics to facilitate an experience of the "indivision" of the flesh that Merleau–Ponty discovers at the heart of Being and that our previous discussion has now associated with the "originary" technicity (the *écart*) of primordial tactility.

1. THE PRIMACY OF SELF-MOVEMENT IN CONFERRING REALITY ON PERCEPTION

The rhetoric associated with virtual reality clearly conveys its privileging of the visual register of perception. More than a mere bias of a popular culture that constantly barrages us with the promise of perfect simulation and the lure of disembodied existence, this privileging informs the research aims of scientists interested in virtual reality technology. "The screen is the window through which one sees a virtual world," says VR pioneer Ivan Sutherland. "The challenge is to make that world look real."[6] Researcher Frank Biocca concurs, noting that "the long-term developmental goal of the technology is nothing short of an attempt … to fool eye and mind into seeing … worlds that are not and never can be." Our aim, Biocca continues, is to transform "[a]n array of light on a visual display [into] a lush landscape in the mind of the viewer."[7]

This privilege accorded the visual has so thoroughly seeped into the practical design of virtual environments (VEs) by scientists, artists, and game designers that it might be said to dictate a kind of de facto standard: hard-edged objects and shapes, distinct spatial demarcations (e.g., into rooms or subworlds), vivid, surreal image quality, and perhaps most centrally, the deployment of a familiar infrastructural Cartesian grid. Conjure up your mental image of virtual reality. What does it present if not some version of this visually optimized, sanitized space? Having by now been streamed and restreamed through all available cultural channels (movies being, perhaps, the most effective one), this standard picture has become so ubiquitous that most of us would not even think of questioning it.

However, rather than stemming from some necessity inherent in the technological interface or even in the makeup of our perceptual apparatus, this visual bias is, in fact, a complex artifact related to the motivating desires and scientific backgrounds of VR developers (largely male engineers) and, more generally, to the pervasive ocularcentrism of Western culture. In a recent study of space, identity, and embodiment in virtual reality, Ken Hillis has criticized the ocularcentrism characteristic of VR research by exposing the false promise of a multisensory interface with informational worlds. As he sees it, this rhetoric masks an underlying investment in the function of vision:

> Suggestions that VR's real promise is a corroboration among the senses fail to consider the disjuncture between subordination and corroboration. Subordination to the visual really points to the coordination (and domination) *by the visual* of our other bodily faculties and senses. VR privileges sight, and other senses play a subordinate role to it. (Hillis, xxii, emphasis added)

To a great extent this claim is borne out by the fact that all branches of VR research currently employ some kind of HMD as a means of empowering vision.

Hillis traces this overvaluation of the visual on the part of VR researchers to the seminal influence of the work of perceptual psychologist J. J. Gibson. Throughout his career, Gibson sought to theorize the way we directly perceive aspects of the world by picking up information from what he calls the ambient light.[8] As Jeremy Campbell explains:

> Gibson held that all the information needed for perception … is present in the structure of the light as it is reflected from objects and events in space. The objects and events give the light its specific organization as it reaches the eye. An observer is immersed, drenched in this information, and the perceptual system of the brain is attuned to pick up certain aspects of it, either by means of innate neural circuits or by the fine discrimination which comes with experience.[9]

As Hillis sees it, this notion of direct perception, together with the correlative notion that there are perceptual invariants immediately observable in the visual field, explains Gibson's impact among the VR research community.[v] Researchers saw in Gibson's work a mechanism for transferring perceptual experience characteristic of "real-world" perception to new, artificial environments: if real-world perceptual experience was grounded in biologically innate capacities to see perceptual invariants in the ambient light, all that would be necessary to carry perception into artificial environments would be to reproduce such perceptual invariants in the virtual domain.[vi]

One important facet of the complex influence of Gibson's work on VR research concerns Gibson's early theory of "texture-gradient mapping" which, Hillis suggests, furnished a model for the mapping of "perceptual invariance" onto virtual environments (Hillis, 15; see also 125). According to Gibson, we directly perceive distance insofar as we detect the differences in texture gradient of objects located at different distances from us. Thus, we recognize the distance of an object from its texture relative to other objects within our visual field: the finer the texture is, the closer it is to us; the denser the texture is, the more distant it is. The important point here is that texture gradient does not define a cue that our brains employ in processing what we have seen, but is *a spatial property of the environment itself.* Once again, Campbell explains why:

> For Gibson, invariants in the structure of light reaching the eye correspond to the stable features of the real world: the surfaces and edges of objects, ... the texture of the ground that grows more dense with distance. In spite of the fact that the image of an object on the retina may shrink in size as it recedes, the image is invariant with respect to the texture of its surroundings. (205)

No less than the privileging of hard-edged surfaces and objects, the liberal deployment of textural surfaces in VEs testifies to the effort to capitalize on Gibson's theory; indeed, both cases betray the same underlying logic: that building such visual invariants into artificial environments will function to attract the attention of our evolutionarily-attuned brains.

In his criticism of this strategy, Hillis accuses VR researchers of, in effect, *misapplying* Gibson's theory. Although innate perceptual invariants like texture gradients function, within Gibson's theory, as enabling constraints on how we perceive the environment, carried over into VEs they become the mechanism for an unhindered and limitless potential for visual interface with any environment imaginable (and, no doubt, many not yet imaginable). It is as if the simple presence of icons or representations of perceptual invariants (hard edges, texture gradients) within an environment were enough to transform it into a world not simply visually apprehensible to us, but rather one in which we can feel at home. What such logic ignores is the deep correlation of our visual system with other, nonvisual perceptual systems—a correlation that is, incidentally, foregrounded at each stage of Gibson's career.[vii]

If perceptual invariants do in fact exist and if they serve to inform us about the world, they do so only in conjunction with the panoply of perceptual processes constitutive of the kinds of beings we are. This means that the appropriation of Gibson does not pay sufficient heed to the evolutionary basis of his theory. Thus, although VR technology might well "permit users to see like birds" (or like anything whatsoever), a VE constructed on the basis of perceptual invariants "may confuse users precisely because they have not been 'hardwired' by evolution to fly like birds" (130). In sum: whereas Gibson's theory of perception (including the role played by perceptual invariants) is a holist one that encompasses (and is constrained by) the range of perceptual processes constitutive of our evolutionarily robust embodied being, its deployment in VE design is piecemeal and premised on an unthematized, and I think, wholly implausible, hope that vision can *by itself* reconstitute the richness of human perceptual function.

Another way to make this same objection is to focus somewhat differently on the concrete material difficulties involved in creating successful—that is, compelling—virtual environments. As Wann and Rushton point out, the limitless potential of the imagination to construct rich virtual environments is contravened by the reality of storage and computational limitations. The Gibson-inspired researchers believe they can "solve" these difficulties through texture-gradient mapping; by building in "objective" elements that simply transcribe perceptually invariant elements of the "real" world into VEs, they think they can mobilize, *through visual stimulation alone*, the perceptual modalities for which we have been evolutionarily hardwired.[viii]

In their interpretation of the storage and computational limitations necessarily encountered in designing VEs, Wann and Rushton outline a very different position. For them, the existence of such limitations immediately introduces a wedge or gap between "real-world" perception and perception in virtual environments that bears directly on the misapplication of Gibson just discussed. For these researchers, the presupposition that perception (including visual perception) involves the full panoply of perceptual systems—the presupposition informing Gibson's theory—*simply cannot be carried over to perception in VEs.* As a consequence, whereas perception in "natural settings" can be said to be "veridical" (i.e., indicative of properties of the environment), the principle informing the creation of virtual environments is, of necessity, "deception." Wann and Rushton explain:

> It is technically impossible to present an observer with a VE that has coherence across the perceptual domains (e.g., for vision and vestibular stimulation) ... [Consequently,] the emphasis has to be on presenting visual displays that are salient enough to induce the required percept and to establish what other sensory conditions may be necessary to maintain that illusion.[10]

What Wann and Rushton foreground here is the necessity, in creating compelling VEs, to rely on the embodied subject's *response* to the

116

stimuli presented as what generates the effect of "reality." Some degree of corroboration among different sensory registers is *always* involved in perception; however, within VEs, this corroboration plays an especially important function insofar as it constitutes the *primary* vehicle for overcoming effects of storage and computational limitations— effects that threaten to compromise the desired sense of immersion.

Wann and Rushton's position thus defines an approach to virtual reality at odds with the Gibson-inspired position just discussed. For them, what is crucial is not simulating a visually "realistic" environment in purely visual terms, but rather designing an environment capable of inducing a compelling sensorimotor correlation in the participant. As Held and Durlach point out in their discussion of telepresence, such a position stems from a conviction that the "best general-purpose system known to us (as engineers) is us (as operators)."[11] Such a view finds corroboration in no less an authority on artificial reality than artist and engineer Myron Krueger, who (as we have seen) has long held that "the ultimate interface would be the human body and human senses."[12]

All of these views advance a *functional* understanding of what makes VEs compelling. According to such an understanding, their purpose is "to augment the sensorimotor system of the human operator" (Held and Durlach, 234). Thus, rather than being defined strictly or even primarily by their "incorporation" of objectively "realistic" elements like perceptual invariants, VEs should be valued for their capacity to stimulate sensorimotor processes responsible for producing effects of "realism" or of presence.[ix] Held and Durlach make this point explicitly and in terms immediately relevant to design implementation:

> The most crucial factor in creating high telepresence is, perhaps, high correlation between (1) the movements of the operator sensed directly via the internal proprioceptive/kinesthetic senses of the operator and (2) the actions of the slave robot sensed via the sensors on the slave robot and the displays in the teleoperator station. (237)

Beyond simply specifying the means to mobilize the human body as the interface, such functional correlation emphasizes the active contribution made by proprioception and internal kinesthetic sense in creating the effect of presence.

In this respect, Held and Durlach introduce a fundamentally different understanding of telepresence than that proposed by the Gibson-inspired position. For the latter, as Hillis explains, the simulation of the hand's presence in the VE via the data glove "allows users to manipulate virtual objects" in a way that draws upon "Gibson's belief that we grab on to our world and make it part of our 'direct' experience" (15). This virtual extension of our hand stimulates the mapping of the virtual world onto internal human perception-structuring processes. The resulting experience of presence (or telepresence)—"experience of presence in an environment by means of a communications medium"—is, not surprisingly, informational at its core.[x,13] Like the "information pickup" involved in the visual experience of perceptual invariants, the virtual extension of perceptual mapping facilitated by the data glove simply opens the body to the reception of information emanating from a new, virtual environment.[xi] For Held and Durlach, by contrast, the telepresent hand would be less a hinge for mapping the information from a visually disclosed environment onto internal perception-structuring processes than one element in a necessarily broader sensorimotor coupling of the operator's body with the VE.

Beyond its consequences for concrete issues of VE design, the contrast of these two fundamentally divergent approaches illustrates the deep connection linking the privileged role of vision with the desire to explain "reality" in terms of information (or, more precisely, informational exchange between system and environment). In both cases, what is left out is the grounding role played by the body and by experiential modalities—tactility, proprioception, internal kinesthesia—proper to it. No less a visionary than Jaron Lanier (who coined the term "virtual reality") has diagnosed this double-barreled reduction as a form of "information disease." Encouraged by technology,

> People think of themselves as information entities that aren't real experiencers, and … gradually lose a sense of validity for everyday experiences … Technology has been so overwhelmingly successful that it serves for many people as the most creative metaphor for what they are. And so, … they lose the internal perspective, and tend to substitute an external perspective. With that goes the essentiality of life.[14]

Both of these postulates—the priority of vision and the informational perspective—are contested in another domain of inquiry that will return us to our original question concerning the uniqueness of Char Davies' deployment of virtual reality toward the noninstrumental constitution of a body-in-code. In his brilliant exploration of the phenomenology of the different senses, philosopher Hans Jonas underscores the necessary correlation among the senses— particularly between vision and touch— in the generation of perception. Ostensibly intended as a discussion of the "nobility of sight," Jonas's essay ("The Nobility of Sight") actually seeks to dethrone sight, or at least to delimit its specific privilege:

> Sight, in addition to furnishing the analogues for the intellectual upperstructure, has tended to serve as the model of perception in general and thus as the measure of the other senses. But it is in fact a very special sense. It is incomplete by itself; it requires the complement of other senses and functions for its cognitive office; its highest virtues are also its essential insufficiencies.[15]

In accord with this basic position, Jonas' demonstration pursues two main tasks: 1) to explain how, and at what cost, sight acquires its "nobility"; and 2) to embed sight within a larger sense ecology in which the role of other sensory modalities, and especially touch, is shown to be fundamental.

Schematically put, the privilege of sight stems from its role as the sense, *par excellence*, of "the simultaneous or the coordinated, and thereby of the extensive" (136). Unlike hearing and touch, which are both proximate senses that build up their manifolds in time, sight presents us with an "instantaneous survey of the whole field of possible encounters" (145). What is more, because of this unique capacity, sight is characterized by two additional factors that inform its alleged "nobility": the "*neutralization* of the causality of sense-affection" and "*distance* in the spatial and mental senses" (136). In sum, then, sight achieves its "nobility" because of its detachment from the domain of affective causality and sensory proximity.[xii]

This detachment accounts for a certain gain—namely, the concept of objectivity—"of the thing as it is in itself as distinct from the thing as it affects me," and with it, the "whole idea of *theoria* and theoretical truth." Yet it also involves a necessary loss: "the elimination of the causal connection from the visual account" (147). Despite the pretensions of sight to autonomy, this elimination introduces a certain insufficiency that requires supplementation from other sensory registers. In a way that effectively suppresses the "very feature which makes these higher developments (i.e., the concept of objectivity and theory) possible," this elimination fundamentally saps visual objects of any "force-experience" that could account for their interconnection with one another and with the observer:

> The pure form-presentation which vision affords does not betray its causal genesis, and it suppresses with it every causal aspect in its objects because their self-containedness vis-à-vis the observer

becomes at the same time a mutual self-containedness among themselves. *No force-experience, no character of impulse and transitive causality, enter into the nature of image,* and thus any edifice of concepts built on that evidence must show the gap in the interconnection of objects which Hume noted (147, emphasis added).

When he criticizes Hume and Kant for, effectively, "forgetting the body" (28), Jonas forcefully underscores the fact that this limitation of sight is not some voluntary whim, but rather a constitutive dimension of sight as a sensory modality: "The character generally suppressed [in accounts of perception] is *force* which, being not a 'datum' but an 'actum,' cannot be 'seen,' i.e., objectified, but only experienced from within when exerted or suffered" (31). The mistake of Hume and Kant (and the many philosophers and nonphilosophers alike who follow their lead) is to maintain belief in an objective autonomy of sight unsupported by the "lowlier" sensory modalities.

In this respect, Jonas's analysis helps clarify why the position of Gibson-inspired VR researchers is philosophically untenable: because it neglects the integral nature of sense, any *purely visual account of perception must necessarily fail.* Correlatively, his account elucidates the underlying logic informing the alternate approach pursued by researchers like Wann, Rushton, Held, and Durlach, and deployed concretely by Char Davies. For all of these individuals, the force-experience involved in tactility and proprioception furnishes *the "reality-generating" element* of perception. This is precisely Jonas' point when, contrasting it with touch, he declares sight to be the "least realistic" of the senses:

> Reality is primarily evidenced in resistance which is an ingredient in touch-experience. For physical contact is more than geometrical contiguity: it involves impact. In other words, touch is the sense, and the only sense, in which the perception of quality is normally blended with the experience of force, which being reciprocal does not let the subject be passive; thus touch is the sense in which the original encounter with reality as reality takes place. Touch brings the reality of its object within the experience of sense in virtue of that by which it exceeds mere sense, viz., the force-component in its original make-up. The percipient on his part can magnify this component by his voluntary counteraction against the affecting object. For this reason touch is the true test of reality. (147–148)

On this version of the priority of double sensation, success in generating compelling virtual experience is gained not by simulating visual images but by stimulating tactile, proprioceptive, and kinesthetic sensations.

Because of its *epochē* of external force, virtual reality forms something of a laboratory to test the reality-conferring function performed by tactility. Perception of a VE (here no different in kind from perception of a "real" environment, only purified of its material basis) is less an affair of informational pickup than one of channeling external through internal reality: "external reality is disclosed in the same act and as one with the disclosure of my own reality—which occurs in self-action: *in feeling my own reality by some sort of* effort *I make, I feel the reality of the world*" (148, emphasis added).

The stress on "effort" in this last line is significant insofar as it introduces the fundamental role played by voluntary self-movement in the ecology of perception. Although Jonas does lend a certain privilege to touch over sight (though certainly not to the point of suggesting a simple elimination of sight in favor of touch), this privilege stems not so much from touch as a specific sense as it does from its implicit conjunction with movement.[xiii] Put another way, Jonas' sense ecology involves a certain elevation of touch from a *mere* sense modality into a cross-modal synthesizing function. The commonplace account of perception as a conjunction of sight and touch is incomplete, Jonas remarks, "so long as 'touch' in this combination is taken as just another *sense*, only qualitatively different from sight, hearing, and smell." However, if we include in our understanding of touch the "fact of its being an activity involving *motion*," we add the complement of action to its "receptivity," thus elevating it, as it were, into a "spatial organizer" of the different sense species, "the synthesizer of the several senses toward one common objectivity" (153). The "reality-conferring" effect of touch—of what we might better call tactility—stems from this elevated function; specifically, it results from the "toucher's" newfound capacity to give form to perceptual experience:

> The tactile situation moves to a higher level when the sentient body itself becomes the voluntary agent of that movement which is required for the acquisition of this serial sequence of impression. Then touch passes over from suffering to acting: its progress comes under the control of the percipient, and it may be continued and varied with a view to fuller information. Thus mere touch-impression changes into the act of feeling. There is a basic difference between simply having a tactile encounter and *feeling* another *body*. ... The *motor* element introduces an essentially new quality into the picture: its active employment discloses spatial characteristics in the touch-object which were no inherent part of the elementary tactile

qualities. Through the kinesthetic accompaniment of voluntary motion the whole perception is raised to a higher order: the touch qualities become arranged in a spatial scheme, they fall into the pattern of *surface*, and become elements of *form*. (139–141)

Jonas' account of the spatializing power of the sensory body not only resonates with our previous exploration of Merleau–Ponty's concept of the phenomenal body, but also emphasizes the crucial shift from the empirical deployment of touch to its infraempirical basis in primordial tactility (what we earlier called *infratactility*). Once again, it is the incipient split between embodiment and technicity that creates the internal distance generative of double sensation.

Jonas' emphasis on the shift to self-movement within the process of sensation also resonates with the position of Held and Durlach discussed previously; indeed, it might be said to find empirical verification in Held's earlier experimentation with active and passive perception in kittens.[xiv] Once again, Jonas' theory furnishes a philosophical explanation for the crucial role of voluntary action in the development of normal sensorimotor coordination; such action, his analysis suggests, gives a spatial form to otherwise disparate perceptual data, thus making them consonant with a body's feeling of the reality of the world. Because of its account of the spatializing power, Jonas' work proves valuable for understanding how VEs function. Eschewing the purely theoretical understanding of perceptual situations that forms the starting point for most virtual reality projects, his account emphasizes how felt experience emerges from an internal action of the body, a self-movement of sensation that precedes, at least logically, the division of the separate senses.

Jonas brings home the extent of this difference by contrasting embodied perception with an imaginary case of a "winged seed sailing on the wind" that would perceive "a kaleidoscopic change with a definite but meaningless pattern" (155).[xv] What is lacking in this imaginary case is the recursive correlation between self-moving animal and environment central to embodied perception. Insofar as the animal "changes its place by an exchange of mechanical action with the resisting medium," the two evolve in tandem; moreover, the "muscular effort required means that the relative motion is more than a shift of mutual geometrical position: through an interplay of force the geometrical becomes a dynamical situation" (155). Embodied perception here occurs through a mapping of space *into* the body, through a conversion of an external, geometrical space into an internal, dynamic space. That is why proprioception "becomes a guide for the organism in the successive construction of spatial distance and direction out of the phases of the motion it actually performs" (155).

On Jonas' account, then, VEs generate an effect of presence or "reality" because they correlate a "virtual" perceptual stimulus with a "real" motor response (although one directed inward, toward the dynamics of proprioceptive space). The priority Jonas thereby lends to proprioceptively guided self-movement serves to correlate Henri Bergson's defense of affection with the tactile basis of vision. According to Bergson,

> The necessity of affection follows from the very existence of perception. Perception, understood as we understand it, measures our possible action upon things, and thereby, inversely, the possible action of things upon us. ... our perception of an object distinct from our body, separated from our body by an interval, never expresses anything but a *virtual* action. But the more distance decreases between this object and our body, ... the more does virtual action tend to pass into *real* action. Suppose the distance reduced to zero, that is to say that the object to be perceived coincides with our body, that is to say again, that our body is the object to be perceived. Then it is no longer virtual action, but real action, that this specialized perception will express, and this is exactly what affection is. Our sensations are, then, to our perceptions that which the real action of our body is to its possible, or virtual, action. (Bergson, 57)

What Jonas's analysis adds to this account is an explicit privileging of the tactile. Whereas Bergson deploys the irreducibility of affection as a means to differentiate virtual and real action (vision and touch), Jonas shows that every perceptual experience (vision *included*) must lead back to an action of the body on itself (self-movement). On his account, *infratactility*—the body's action on itself—makes the virtual actual. With its forceful emphasis on the tactile basis for all perceptual experience, Jonas' work (here in full resonance with the later Merleau-Ponty) thus clarifies how the reality-generating potential (or virtuality) of embodied self-movement can be lent to the most schematic artificial environments.

We can now specify precisely what constitutes the uniqueness of Char Davies' deployment of virtual reality technology to create a body-in-code. *Osmose* and her more recent *Ephémère* are designed expressly to catalyze a shift, as well as to compel self-reflexive recognition of the shift, from a predominately visual sensory interface to a predominately bodily or affective interface.[xvi] The characteristics we earlier singled out in differentiating her work from most other artistic and scientific engagements with VR technology can now be seen to reflect a deeper, properly philosophical dimension of her project. Thus, the diaphanous surfaces, the solicitation of bodily motion and breathing, and the non-goal-oriented nature of the environments do not just form the elements of an alternative approach to three-dimensional design. More centrally, they testify to a more fundamental shift in perceptual sensibility away from the entire Cartesian worldview so central to the development of three-dimensional computer graphics.

Davies characterizes this philosophical dimension as an experience of "being" rather than of "doing"[xvii] and correlates it with her well-documented immersion in scuba diving, the proximate inspiration for the breathing and motion interface as well as the diaphanous, shimmering surfaces. Yet, despite the Heideggerian rhetoric of withdrawal, the origin of Davies' quest to escape Cartesianism can be found, not insignificantly, in a more mundane, if not exactly everyday, personal experience: her early experimentation with her own extreme myopic vision as a source or catalyst for artistic creativity. She recounts,

> In this unmediated, unfocused mode of perception, I discovered an alternative (non-Cartesian) spatiality whereby "objects" had disappeared; where all semblance of solidity, surface, edges and distinctions between things—i.e., the usual perceptual cues by which we visually objectify the world—had dissolved. These were replaced by a sense of enveloping space in which there were no sharply defined objects in empty space, but rather an ambiguous intermingling of varying luminosities and hues, a totally enveloping and sensuous spatiality. (Davies and O'Donaghue, 1)

Davies' virtual environments might be understood as efforts to bring this private experience and, most centrally, its creative or catalytic dimension—namely, the eclipse of visual mastery of external space—into the public domain. In this respect, *Osmose* and *Ephémère* constitute environments that manifestly do not aim to simulate "real-world" perception (as Gibson-inspired VEs do), but rather to utilize the virtual domain as a medium for sharing what must be considered a liminal form of experience. The statement Davies furnishes to accompany the exhibition of both works at the SFMOMA show, 01010101, makes this difference altogether patent: "I imagine virtual space as a philosophical yet participatory medium, a visual/aural spatiotemporal arena wherein mental models or abstract constructs can be given virtual embodiment in three dimensions and then be kinesthetically explored by others through full body immersion and interaction, even while such constructs retain their immateriality."[16]

Moreover, because the environments involve the direct placement of the "immersant" into an atypical, indeed anti-"realistic," environment, the role of tactility or self-movement as the "reality"-generating sense becomes especially pronounced. Here, the primacy that Jonas lends touch as a sense-synthesizer helps explain why maneuvering through *Osmose* using bodily movements and breathing seems, in the words of one immersant, "so uncannily 'real'" (Wettheim, 2). Indeed, whatever effect of presence the installations produce must stem not from a withdrawal from the activity of movement and the contact with "force-experience," as Davies' occasional Heideggerian rhetoric might suggest, but rather from a heightening of self-movement and of the proprioceptive and internal kinesthetic senses of the "immersant," a restoration of the primitive anchoring of sense in protosensory tactility. Again, Davies' statement serves to clarify her intentions:

> My interest lies in going beyond VR's conventions of photorealism and joystick interfaces which situate the user as a probing hand (with gun) and disembodied eye among passive hard-edged objects in empty space. By working with the participant's breath as primary interface (enabling them to "float"), and using semitransparency as a means of evoking cognitive ambiguity, I have sought to reaffirm the role of the subjectively lived body within the virtual realm and deeply engage the participant's sensory imagination. (Davies, Artist's Statement)

In sum, rather than being about the realist simulation of an external environment, Davies' works are about experiential possibilities that explicitly foreground the kinesthetic and proprioceptive dimensions of bodily self-movement, the way in which self-movement or infratactility serves to confer (sensory) reality on perceptual experience. "It is my hope that the paradoxical qualities of bodily immersion in virtual space might lead to an experience of being-in-the-world freshly," concludes Davies (2001). In the succinct phrasing of Mark Pesce: "What you encounter in *Osmose* is yourself" (Pesce, cited in Davis, "Osmose," 4).

2. BEYOND THE BODY-IMAGE: EMBODYING PSYCHASTHENIA

In her 1992 book *Megalopolis*, Celeste Olalquiaga correlates experience in our contemporary technosphere with the psychological and ethological condition of *psychasthenia*:

> Defined as a disturbance in the relation between self and surrounding territory, psychasthenia is a state in which the space defined by the coordinates of the organism's own body is confused with represented space. Incapable of demarcating the limits of its own body, lost in the immense area that circumscribes it, the psychasthenic organism proceeds to abandon its own identity to embrace the space beyond. It does so by camouflaging itself into the milieu.... Psychasthenia helps describe contemporary experience and account for its uneasiness. Urban culture resembles this mimetic condition when it enables a ubiquitous feeling of being in all places while not really being anywhere. Architectural transparency, for example, transforms shopping malls into a continuous window display where the homogeneity of store windows, stairs, elevators, and water fountains causes a perceptual loss, and shoppers are left wandering around in a maze.... Dislocated by this ongoing trompe l'oeil, the body seeks concreteness in the consumption of food and goods, saturating its senses to the maximum.[17]

With certain adjustments, this account of psychasthenia as a mimetic condition for contemporary perception could perfectly well describe the experience of virtual reality, which also, as we have seen, functions via a dissolution of boundaries between self and environment. Davies has likened the intended experience of her environments to the condition of psychasthenia, noting that she has "deliberately sought to facilitate [the] intermingling, [the] dissolution, of the hard boundaries of the skin ... through the use of semitransparency, by allowing the immersant to effectively see-*through*, and even more importantly, self-move-*through* the surfaces of various visual elements" (email). To the extent that this experience is engineered to effect a "dissolution of boundaries, the confusion between inside and out, self and space," we can say that Davies' aim is (at least in part) to generate psychasthenia.

It is crucial, however, that we not overlook the marked differences between Davies' phenomenological embrace of psychasthenia and Olalquiaga's depiction of it as an image-based pathology. Olalquiaga views psychasthenia as the disempowering (because disembodying) result of our contemporary technosphere; Davies seeks to catalyze an experience of psychasthenia *as a means to disrupt the Cartesian worldview and to reestablish the embodied basis of all perception, vision included.* To appreciate how such a catalysis lies at the heart of Davies' work, we must dissociate psychasthenia from the narrow representationalist understanding of it that Olalquiaga and, following in her wake, Elizabeth Grosz, endorse. Indeed, insofar as it provides an alternative to Olalquiaga's reductive conception of psychasthenia as an image-based condition, Davies' work serves to question the basis of efforts by feminist theorists like Grosz and (as we have seen) Gail Weiss to route the correlation of embodiment and technics through the image. As we shall see, it does so in the interest of another, vastly different feminist engagement with virtual reality.

At issue here is the status of psychasthenia itself. Does it operate through disembodiment—that is, through a dissolution of the self into the image? Or does it produce a more complex interlacing of the body and the environment that, in some sense, reflects the technical conditions for life in our world today? For Olalquiaga, as I have already implied, the former is the case. That is why, despite her recognition that psychasthenia involves a recursive correlation between organism and environment, she effectively narrows the register of this correlation to the domain of representation. It is also why her account perfectly instances the privileging of the visual we have just analyzed. Like virtual perception in the hands of the Gibson-inspired VR researchers, Olalquiaga reduces the entire spatial problematic of psychasthenia to a narrowly representationalist framework. On her account, psychasthenia is a disorder that takes place exclusively in the visual register, through an inability to preserve a distinct body representation (a body-image) in the face of the proliferation of representations in the environment.

Grosz's account of psychasthenia likewise hypostatizes the domain of vision and the problematic of representation. Thus, she contends that mimicry, the paradigmatic instance of self-environment dissolution (and the topic of Roger Caillois' 1934 paper on psychasthenia), "is not a consequence of space but rather of the representation of space." Psychasthenia, she continues, "is a response to the lure posed by space for subjectivity. The subject can take up a position only by being able to situate its body in a position in space, ... a point from which vision emanates" (190–192).[xviii] Thus, in psychasthenia, "the primacy of the subject's own perspective is replaced by the gaze of another for whom the subject is merely a point in space, not the focal point organizing space" (193).

Like Olalquiaga, Grosz sees in psychasthenia a perfect figure for the contemporary technologized lifeworld or, to cite her more descriptive terminology, for the "deceptive simulations" of cyberspace. Insofar as it names a disturbance in the subject's capacity to differentiate itself *representationally* from its environment, psychasthenia marks a danger of contemporary culture—one that, for Grosz at least, has profound implications for the way in which gender has been written out of considerations of contemporary technological culture and, specifically, of virtual reality.

If psychasthenia is a danger in this sense (a danger endemic to our technoculture that is differentially experienced by differently gendered subjects), the reason is that it compromises the function of the body image as a mediator between self and world, body and environment, subject and space. Unable to represent one's position in space, and thus one's being, the psychasthenic subject suffers a kind of visual objectification: it becomes a mere point in a space projected by another.

Less obvious than the gender politics underwriting this understanding, however, is the prosthetic model of technics that lies behind it. For Grosz, as for Gail Weiss following in her wake, the body image functions to couple the subject and its biosocial environment and thus forms the proximate agent of any prosthetic modification of the human body. It is

> the condition of the subject's capacity not only to adapt to but also to become integrated with various objects, instruments, tools, and machines. It is the condition of the body's inherent openness and pliability to and in its social context.... It is the condition that enables us to acquire and use prosthetic devices (glasses, contact lenses, artificial limbs, surgical implants) in place of our sense organs.[18]

By insisting on the primacy of the body-image in mediating the interchange between subject and environment, Grosz ends up advancing a very conservative view of prosthetics: effectively, technological enhancements like virtual reality goggles (not to mention those she enumerates in the passage cited previously) can only have an impact on experience *insofar as they are mediated by the body image.* There is, for Grosz, no question that technological prosthetics might actually modify the way in which the senses work and, subsequently, the way in which the body experiences sensation; rather, as she puts it, prosthetic devices function "in place of our sense organs" as the vehicle of a substitute set of data for the body-image to compute.

Grosz's model thus remains incapable of accounting for any but the most straightforward deployments of VR technology (i.e., those in which the "coordinates" of the body-image are in no way disturbed). Likening the "deceptive simulation" of cyberspace to the "dysfunctional breakdown" of psychosis, Grosz positions psychasthenia as a purely negative condition, one that can only demarcate the limits of bodily experience rather than opening up its potential technical transformation. In sum: by narrowing the impact of VR experience to the way in which it confounds the body-image, Grosz effectively ensures its reduction to the status of disembodied simulation.

We have already had a chance to criticize this model of technics for what we might in fact call its superficiality—that is, its incapacity (or refusal) to reckon with the more primordial correlation of embodiment and technicity that we explored at length in Chapter 1. In our present context, we can add a more specific objection against its subordination of bodily action—of dynamic self-movement—to representation. By positioning the body image as the necessary link between inside and outside, Grosz invests it as the medium for the body to experience itself either "naturally" or as prosthetically extended. As the "link between our biological and cultural existences, between our 'inner' psyche and our 'external' body," the body image is taken to form the condition not only for the body's self-representation but also for its "capacity for undertaking voluntary action" (187).

As the basis for this model of technics, the body image thus becomes the condition of possibility for the prosthetic extension of the body, as well as for the experience of the biological body: "If it exists at all," Grosz notes, "the biological body exists for the subject only through the mediation of a series of images or representations of the body and its capacities for movement and action" (186). Given our earlier excavation of the "originary" transduction of embodiment and technicity, however, such an understanding would appear to produce a double reduction of biological embodiment and of technical embodiment. To the extent that these two poles of embodiment can only be articulated externally— through the mediation of the image and the medium of representation, they are effectively deprived of their anchoring in primordial tactility. In sum: rather than seeing psychasthenia as an expression of the "originary" condition for dynamic bodily self-movement in the concrete form of today's technics, Grosz can only understand it to mark a failure in the representational meshing of subject and body that, on her account, forms the condition for bodily activity.

Insofar as they explicitly capitalize on the decoupling of vision from dynamic self-movement that occurs in psychasthenia, Char Davies' virtual environments proffer a very different understanding of the psychasthenic condition of contemporary technoculture. For the same reason, they sketch out a vastly divergent feminist intervention into the domain of virtual reality, one that, to the extent it celebrates the dissolution of the schematic differentiation of body and world together with the resulting "indivision" of the flesh, would seem to have far more resonance with the work of Irigaray than with that of Grosz.[xix]

Given our extended analysis in Chapter 1, it should come as little surprise that the crux of this understanding centers on the inadequacy of the body image as a basis for intercorporeity and, ultimately, for thinking the technical conditions for the indivision of the flesh as it constitutes the real condition for experience in our world today. Insofar as they aim to reverse the reduction of the body to the image—that is, to reassert the role of dynamic self-movement *beneath* any experience of the image, Davies' environments thus draw on another dimension of psychasthenia: namely, the way in which it facilitates a tactile experience of the body's interpenetration with the environment.

For this reason, Davies' environments call on us to read Roger Caillois' original description of psychasthenic mimicry against its later appropriation by a certain feminist project. For Caillois, psychasthenia comprises a disturbance first and foremost in embodiment; it marks the organism's inability to live its experience from its (operational) perspective—that is, from some space proper to it:

> There can be no doubt that the perception of space is a complex phenomenon: space is indissolubly perceived and represented.... It is with represented space that the drama becomes specific, since the living creature, the organism, is no longer the origin of the coordinates, but one point among others; it is dispossessed of its privilege and literally *no longer knows where to place itself*. One can already recognize the characteristic scientific attitude and, indeed, it is remarkable that represented spaces are just what is multiplied by contemporary science. Finsler's spaces, Fermat's spaces, Riemann–Christoffel's hyperspace, abstract, generalized, open, and closed spaces, spaces dense in themselves, thinned out, and so on. The feeling of personality, considered as the organism's feeling of distinction from its surroundings, of the connection between consciousness and a particular point in space,

cannot fail under these conditions to be seriously undermined; one then enters into the psychology of psychasthenia. (Caillois)[19]

Linking psychasthenia to the ascent of the scientific world view and the representational ontology that Heidegger has analyzed, for example, in "The Age of the World Picture," Caillois presents it as a shift in the economy of embodiment and representation that comprises any lived experience of space. In the modern world, his argument runs, it has become particularly difficult for the living organism (the human being) to maintain its unique (operational) perspective against the manifold impersonal descriptions of space and the general triumph of the observational perspective they advance.

Thus, despite the centrality he accords representation, Caillois presents a far more complex account of psychasthenia than is recognized by Olalquiaga and Grosz. For him, psychasthenia is, irreducibly, a multisensory existential problematic affecting the organism not at the level of its visually apprehended symbolic significance, but rather at the more primitive level of embodiment where the impact of the representational indifferentiation is actually lived. That is why Caillois concludes his analysis by characterizing insect mimicry as a "sort of *instinct of renunciation*," an "*inertia of the élan vital*" (32), and it is also why he can liken it to the Freudian death drive: to the extent that it decouples representation from action, psychasthenic mimicry marks a certain disempowering of the organism.[xx] On Caillois' account, then, the "drama" of psychasthenia is fundamentally a part of a larger existential drama, part of the continually evolving, systemic correlation of the organism with its environment.

It is, however, undeniable that Caillois presents psychasthenia as posing a well-nigh Heideggerian danger; indeed, he positions it as the rigorous consequence of the concrete technical achievement of the "age of the world picture." Far from being a necessary conclusion of his analysis, however, this analysis would appear to stem from his (again, well-nigh Heideggerian) fear of the contamination of thinking by technics.[xxi] He thus betrays his adherence to an ontology of the individual that cannot withstand the revelation, currently being expressed in full force by our digital culture, that the human has always been technical. Rather than allowing for a co-becoming of the individual and space, as contemporary ethology most certainly would and as our introduction of technics into Merleau–Ponty's final work demands, Caillois can only see the "generalization" of space as a threat to the autonomy of the individual. In psychasthenia, as he puts it, space "seems to be a devouring force" (30). Caillois' limitation, in short, is his inability to give up the scientific world view, an inability that prevents him from seeing psychasthenia as a chance for a different conceptualization of the individual in its constitutive correlation with technics. That is why he is compelled, in the end, to thematize psychasthenia as a pathology of the visual register: "the body separates itself from thought, the individual breaks the boundary of his skin and occupies the other side of his senses. He tries to look at *himself from* any point whatever in space" (30).

Despite this limitation, Caillois' account does in fact open the possibility for thinking psychasthenia through contemporary technics or, better, for thinking our technoculture as the catalyst of a positive form of psychasthenia. Indeed, when he characterizes psychasthenia as an organism's active "assimilation to the surroundings," Caillois opens up a very different genealogy of technics than that presented by Grosz (and Weiss). Rather than restricting the impact of contemporary technologies like VR to a prosthetic function (one that, as I have pointed out, effectively reduces VR to the status of disembodied simulation), Caillois' account of psychasthenia opens up the potentiality of technics—a potentiality that has always been part of the human—to modify not only the content of our lived experience but also our mode of living.

One hint of this potential comes by way of Caillois' interpretation of Eugène Minkowski's phenomenological analyses of pathological temporality, where what is at stake is a shift from vision to tactility—that is, from geometrical perception of space to embodied constitution of space through dynamic self-movement:

> The magical hold … of night and obscurity, the *fear of the dark*, probably also has its roots in the peril in which it puts the opposition between the organism and the milieu. Minkowski's analyses are invaluable here: darkness is not the mere absence of light; there is something positive about it. While light space is eliminated by the materiality of objects, darkness is "filled," it touches the individual directly, envelops him, penetrates him, and even passes through him: hence "the ego is *permeable* for darkness while it is not so for light" … Minkowski likewise comes to speak of *dark space* and almost of a lack of distinction between the milieu and the organism: " Dark space envelops me on all sides and penetrates me much deeper than light space; the distinction between inside and outside and consequently the sense organs as well, insofar as they are designed for external perception, here play only a totally modest role." (30)[xxii]

In endorsing the description of what is, after all, a shift from percep-tion to affection, from vision to tactility, Caillois effectively opens the way for a deployment of psychasthenia *beyond the body-image*. Indeed, his interpretation of Minkowski underscores the capacity of tactility to operate the psychasthenic indifferentiation as an incorporation of touch, a passage from the domain of exteroception where touch (like vision) operates as an interchange with the environment to the undifferentiated experience of tactility as dynamic self-movement.

In this respect, Caillois's account of psychasthenia makes com-mon cause with our earlier analysis of Merleau–Ponty's final project. Indeed, the displacement of the "body schema" that underwrites Mer-leau–Ponty's final ontology—its dissolution into the "indivision" of the flesh—parallels the conceptualization of psychasthenia beyond the body-image. It does so to the precise extent that such a conceptualiza-tion necessarily displaces vision, as well as the division it supports, in favor of an undifferentiated ontology of dynamic self-movement. In this sense, what is important is what takes the place of the body-image, or more precisely, what can take place once the body-image is dethroned as the mediator of all bodily experience.

On this score, moreover, the conception of psychasthenia as an affirmative activity of the body finds support in recent neuroscien-tific research. Thus, for example, Antonio Damasio's differentiation between static and "on-line" body images makes salient just how much our experience of our bodies owes to direct real-time monitoring of its continuously changing states.[20] Although it is undeniable (as Damasio admits) that we do experience static images of our bodies, the fact that these provide scant information about our actual embodied states sug-gests just how much richer the (misnamed) body-image is than a mere representation of the body.

Because it gives a detailed account of spatiality as a constitutive modality of bodily experience (and not simply an effect of representations, even bodily representations), Merleau–Ponty's work helps us to correlate psychasthenia with an ontology of embodiment (of the flesh). In this way, it serves to highlight the insufficiency of the ontology of projection that forms the correlative of Grosz's deployment of the body image as media-tor between body and environment and that is derived, as we observed in Chapter 1, from a certain misreading of Freud's claim that the "ego is first and foremost a bodily ego ... the projection of a surface." Eschewing such a projective ontology from the very outset of his development of the "phenomenal body" in the *Phenomenology*, Merleau–Ponty shows himself to be concerned with articulating the specificity of his conception of the body-schema against other, reductive understandings, most notably, the body-image. The body-schema, specifies Merleau–Ponty, is more than simply a "continual translation into visual language of the kinaesthetic and articular impressions of the moment."[21] It is also more than a de facto synthesis of a particular set of bodily components, "a superimposed *sketch* of the body" (99). Rather, as we have seen, it is a "total awareness of my posture in the intersensory world, a 'form' in the sense used by Gestalt psychology" (100); or, more precisely still "a way of stating that my body is in-the-world," a "third term, always tacitly understood, in the figure-background structure" (101).

Far from being a mediator between the subject and the environment that would condition bodily activity (as it is for Grosz), the body-schema is thus cosubstantial with the activity of the body as a whole and is dynamically constitutive of the spatiality of the world. We might say that the body schema, like touch in the higher office accorded it by Jonas, comprises an *infraempirical* form: one that is immanent to bodily life without being reducible to its empirical contents and that, as we have seen, intertwines vision and touch in an irreducible cofunctioning that, in and of itself, indicts the more abstract, visual conception of the body-image.

The introduction of the body schema already makes clear the vast divide between Merleau–Ponty's motor-centered understanding of the body and the representationalist conception. Correlative with this divide is a vast difference in the role of space: whereas Grosz's (and Olalquiaga's) understanding of psychasthenia portrayed space as a geometrical, visual domain in which the subject fails to locate itself, for Merleau–Ponty (as we have seen), such a space is abstracted from a more fundamental space: the space constituted by the motor-intentionality of the body.

If, in one sense, this can be taken to mean that the body holds a certain priority over space (at least on the ontology at issue in the *Phenomenology*), it also means that the body does not stand opposed to space, as Caillois' analysis suggested. Rather, from the beginning in Merleau–Ponty, body and space are dynamically coupled so that changes in bodily motility (e.g., the blind man's stick) necessarily correlate with changes in lived spatiality, the sum of which is expressed in the body schema. With respect to psychasthenia, what Merleau–Ponty's analysis affords, then, is an account capable of explaining how the dissolution of the (representational) boundaries between body and space nonetheless accords with a certain bodily activity that functions to ground the recursive correlation of embodiment and technics within self-movement.

Ultimately, this understanding of the dynamic coupling of body and space undermines the function of the body schema as such, in the sense that it can no longer function to demarcate the body from the environment. That is why, as we have seen, the problematic of the body schema more or less falls away in Merleau–Ponty's final work as his interest shifts from the phenomenological-existential problematic of the body as source of space (and world) to the ontological problematic of the flesh and the body's immanent belonging to the world.

More important in the present context, however, is the resonance of this final dissolution of the body schema with Caillois' account of psychasthenia: Merleau–Ponty's final work furnishes a conception of the body's spatiality that can account for psychasthenia as an affirmative modality in which the indifferentiation between the body and the environment, the oneness of the flesh, is opened to experience. Indeed, in a much-cited passage from his chapter on "The Chiasm," Merleau–Ponty states:

> The body unites us directly with the things through its own onto-genesis, by welding to one another the two outlines of which it is made, its two lips: the sensible mass it is and the mass of the sensible wherein it is born and upon which, as seer, it remains open. It is the body and it alone, because it is a two-dimensional being, that can bring us to the things themselves, which are themselves not flat beings but beings in depth, inaccessible to a subject that would survey them from above, open to him alone that ... would coexist with them in the same world.... What we call a visible is ... a quality pregnant with a texture, the surface of a depth, a cross section upon a massive being, a grain or corpuscle borne by a wave of Being.[22]

As immanent to the world, the body is penetrated by the world in a fluid interchange. This interchange, as we have seen, is why Merleau–Ponty's final work is concerned with the problem of thinking the indifferentiation, the *indivision*, between body and world. Moreover, it perfectly expresses the condition, the *indivision*, of psychasthenia, as the (no doubt) rhetorical question orienting Merleau–Ponty's entire investigation makes altogether clear: "Where," he asks, "are we to put the limit between the body and the world, since the world is flesh?" (138).

By way of conclusion, let me now suggest in more concrete terms how Char Davies' *Osmose* and *Ephémère* function to catalyze an experience of psychasthenia and the oneness of the "flesh." Both environments are designed to effectuate a restoration of the power of embodied agency in the face of the "danger" of technically facilitated psychasthenia. By taking virtual reality as a laboratory for exploring the function of perception in a situation where there simply is no material, external world and hence no demarcation between self and environment, Davies in effect embraces the psychasthenic condition full-on. Thus, in contrast to Grosz (and Weiss), whose work attempts to restore some clear demarcation between body and environment, Davies seeks to catalyze a more primitive, undifferentiated form of self-movement as the activity that confers reality as such. By effectively drawing attention to the fact that all reality is virtual reality, her environments exemplify the way in which virtual reality technologies can support the constitution of a certain body-in-code and thereby participate in the aesthetic—mixed reality—that seemed to announce their obsolescence.

Davies has spoken of a "seminal" adolescent experience in a field that involved her loss of vision. Recalling her "near mystical manifestation of the confusion ... between inside and out, self and space," Davies cites her "desire to communicate that firsthand *bodily* experience to others" as her driving motivation and also as the reason why the "medium of immersive virtual space has proven more conducive" to her aim than any other medium. Because they deploy technics to effect a dissolution of the discrete boundaries characteristic of the body as a visually dominant agent, Davies' use of transparency, ambiguity, low-resolution imagery, and fog instance the essential technicity of the indivision of the flesh, as it informs Merleau–Ponty's final project. As Davies explains it, the use of immersive virtual reality technology allows her to catalyze a performative experience of the indifferentiation between bodily interiority and spatial exteriority, and thus, in some sense to compel participants to experience technical psychasthenia firsthand:

> As an artist, I ... have two choices: I can either unplug and never go near a computer again or I can choose to remain engaged, seeking to subvert the technology from within, using it to communicate an alternative worldview ... My strategy has been to explore how the medium/technology can be used to "deautomatize" perception (via use of semitransparency, seemingly floating through things, etc.) in order that participants may begin to question their own habitual perceptions and assumptions about being in the world, thus facilitating a mental state whereby Cartesian boundaries between mind and body, self and world begin to slip. (Davies and O'Donaghue, 3)

In accord with this aim, as Mark Pesce suggests, Davies manages to design a space "that contained no distinct boundaries between self and world," one that functions by engaging vision and touch as irreducibly interlinked sensory modalities, both centered on the bodily sensation that confers reality on all perception. In what he describes as a "direct assault on two fronts," Pesce contends that Davies' work simultaneously changes "what the eye would see" and "how the participant would move through the world" (Pesce, "Cathedrals," 2). The result is a use of the virtual reality interface to catalyze a profoundly affirmative and empowering experience of psychasthenia. That is why, to cite the experience of one participant, at some point in the immersion, "the border between the interface as a symbolized surface and the surface of the physiological body begins to blur."[23] As the visual (representational) boundaries between body and world dissolve in favor of an affective contact that foregrounds what Jonas called the "force-experience" characteristic of tactility—internal self-movement synchronized with the visual "perception" of the immaterial—what is brought to the fore is an energetic connection of the body with the world, their primordial *indivision.*

digitizing the racialized body, or the politics of common impropriety

In his recent study of the Internet, Mark Poster has argued for a radical approach that would do more than simply deploy new media as a "tool for determining the fate of groups *as they are currently constituted*."[1] As Poster sees it, the transformational potential of the new media stems from their impact on how human beings are interpellated as social actors. As it becomes increasingly mediated by the communication networks of the new media, interpellation comes to materialize a "self that is no longer a subject since it no longer subtends the world as if from outside but operates within a machine apparatus as a point in a circuit" (16). In this way, new media allow us to suspend existing cultural figurations of the self—"race, class, and gender, or citizen, manager, and worker"—in order to forge new cultural forms that have the potential to change "the position of existing groups ... in unforeseeable ways" (3).

In their call for a new "pedagogy" adequate to the technically facilitated phenomenon of globalization, Ella Shohat and Robert Stam appear to endorse just such a radical program. Specifically, they wonder whether the potential of digital technologies to "bypass the search for a profilmic model" might furnish the opportunity to "expand the reality effect exponentially by switching the viewer from a passive to a more interactive position, so that the raced gendered sensorial body could be implanted, theoretically, with a constructed virtual gaze, becoming a launching site for identity travel."[2] For Shohat and Stam, the important question is this:

> Might virtual reality or computer simulation be harnessed for the purposes of multicultural or transnational pedagogy, in order to communicate, for example, what it feels like to be an 'illegal alien' pursued by the border police or a civil rights demonstrator feeling the lash of police brutality in the early 1960s? (166)

Despite a shared enthusiasm regarding the potentiality of new media, it is the differences between these two positions that help to foreground exactly what *is* new about new media and to specify ways in which it calls on us to transform our techniques of cultural analysis. Thus, Poster's sensitivity toward the materiality of new media gives the lie to Shohat and Stam's easy subordination of interactivity to the demands of content-based practices of resistance; and his insightful (if ultimately insufficient) criticism of the concept of identity in the wake of digital mediation poses an insuperable obstacle for a media practice rooted in emancipative transformation via the category of identity.[i] On both counts, I would suggest, Poster's analysis issues the challenge for any transformative media practice in the postbroadcast age: to find a way of conceptualizing and deploying media that does not subordinate them to preconstituted categories of identity and subjectivity and that exploits their capacity to bring the "preindividual" dimension (following Gilbert Simondon's conception) to bear on the ongoing process of individuation.

It is precisely this challenge I propose to take on in this chapter. My focus will be the performance of race and ethnicity in cyberspace—specifically, the difference (and the opportunity) that might be said to distinguish the category of race as it comes to be cyberized. Following those critics who have argued that online interactions generalize the condition of passing hitherto associated with racial performance, I shall deploy race as a privileged *topos* for experimenting with the radical potentialities afforded by new media for transforming how we conceptualize identity in general. Because race has always been plagued by a certain disembodiment (the fact that race *is* manifestly a construction at the level of the image because visible racial traits are in no way reducible to organic, i.e., genetic, organization), it will prove especially useful for exposing the limitations of the Internet as a new machinic assemblage for producing subjectivity. For the same reason, it will help us to grasp and potentially to deploy the possibilities new media offer for experiencing community beyond identity.

My transformational engagement with race theory aims to redeem the generalization of passing on the Internet from the criticism that it functions negatively to erase the category of race.[ii] As I see it, the suspension of the social category of visibility in online environments transforms the experience of race in what is, potentially, a fundamental way: by suspending the automatic ascription of racial signifiers according to visible traits, online environments can, in a certain sense, be said to subject everyone to what I shall call a "zero degree" of racial difference. The certain universalization thereby effectuated, a universalization that certainly remains differential, divorces the image from the living body it would capture. It thereby exposes—in ways that are singular but somehow also common—the affective basis of racial signification and, more specifically, the radical disjunction between racial identity categories and the singularity of each body whose life is always in excess of any particular, fixed identity.

In two initial sections devoted to the phenomenon of online interpellation as a form of passing, I attempt to foreground the differences between raced and gendered interpellation in order to expose the bodily mediation that necessarily gives all interpellations their force. In a third section devoted to Frantz Fanon's analysis of racism as "corporeal malediction," I explore the crucial role that embodiment (specifically, the corporeal schema) plays as the root level where racism gains a foothold and also, necessarily, where racism must be universalized and attacked. Then, in two sections focused on the deployment of new media in the work of artist Keith Piper, I explore how race is experienced within a postbroadcast media environment and along a (potentially) universal continuum, first through the incommensurability of the static image of the black body and subsequently through the phenomenon of interpellative failure and the production of an affective bodily excess.

Finally, in a concluding section centered on the work of Italian philosopher Giorgio Agamben, I link this postinterpellative, affective experience of the constraints of race with an ethics of singularity predicated on the bankruptcy of the stereotyped media image and the categories of identity through which it previously performed its reifying cultural work. By showing how new media potentially facilitate an experience of community rooted in the commonality of the improper, I hope to give a glimpse of the radical promise they may hold for radically reconfiguring the obsolescent categories that clearly still function to introduce inequalities of all kinds and, beyond that, to obscure our shared singularity, our common status as beings radically in excess of our selves.

1. BEYOND SYMBOLIC INTERPELLATION: UNDERSTANDING DIGITAL PERFORMATIVITY

Cultural criticism has already recognized the potential of the Internet to usher in a postidentitarian politics rooted in the obsolescence of racial and ethnic categorizations. In her discussion of cyberspace in *Continental Drift*, for example, Emily Apter suggestively positions the Internet as the natural extension of postcolonial theory's complexification of identity, embodiment, and community *and* as its (potential) salvation from its internal contradictions. Welcoming the cyborg as the "quintessential 'hybrid' postcolonial subject," Apter sees the fluidity of cyberidentity as a chance for postcolonial theory to sublate what she understands to be its historically specific (thus provisional) embrace of emancipatory identity politics.[iii,3]

Abstracted from its narrow concern with redeeming postcolonial criticism, Apter's analysis of cyberculture as the vehicle for an "ironic screening of the subject" helps to expose the bankruptcy of the image as a basis for any representational or performative politics of identity that would function by linking agency to transgression via the category of visibility and the visibly marked body. More than any other figure, Italian philosopher Giorgio Agamben has explored this bankruptcy and its crucial position within the endgame of the society of the spectacle. For Agamben:

> [T]he absurdity of individual existence ... has become ... so senseless that it has lost all pathos and been transformed, brought out into the open, into an everyday exhibition: Nothing resembles the life of this new humanity more than advertising footage from which every trace of the advertised product has been wiped out.[4]

This total cooptation of the category of the individual explains why images of the ethnic other can today be nothing but fantasy projections of the same. They might look like the other, but they work only to the extent that they speak and think just like us.[iv]

As a new phase in the apotheosis of the becoming-image of capital, the technologies of cyberspace and the new media simply take the logic of the spectacle one step beyond globalized advertising and cinema, in effect emptying the spectacle of all promise from the start. Because online identity and the cyborging of the body are constructions through and through, whatever allure they may hold simply cannot be that of a fetish masking difference, but must rather be something more like an unapologetic celebration of the simulacral.

Such a possibility, however, is the unprecedented redemptive opportunity that, according to Agamben, must at all costs not be squandered:

> Because if instead of continuing to search for a proper identity in the already improper and senseless form of individuality, humans were to succeed in belonging to this impropriety as such, in making of the proper being-thus not an identity and an individual property but a singularity without identity, a common and absolutely exposed singularity—if humans could, that is, not be-thus in this or that particular biography, but be only *the* thus, their singular exteriority and their face, then they would for the first time enter into a community without presuppositions and without subjects, into a communication without the incommunicable. (65)

If the new media hold the potential to generate radically new forms of cultural existence, I would suggest that this is because and insofar as they facilitate this belonging to the improper, this process of forging the "whatever body." Where the society of the spectacle passively generates its own obsolescence—and thus functions as a *precondition* for the "coming community"—the new media *actively* invest the dimension of *the* thus, the dimension of bodily life that exceeds concrete embodiment and thus (potentially) evades the grasp of capitalism's wholesale investment of the image.

In this sense, we might say that the Internet completes the positive movement beyond the spectacle and the trap of identity bound up with its (empty) promise. More specifically still, we might say that it suspends the force of the image, of capital's "becoming-image," which forms the precondition for a reinvestment of the body *outside* the image. What permits the Internet to perform this crucial function is, to return to Poster's terminology, its deployment of machinic means for facilitating the performance of identity beyond the constraints imposed by physical appearance:

> The important question [in online communities] is the way identity is performed.... Participants are authors of themselves as characters, not simply by acts of consciousness, but by the interactions that take place on the screen. In these situations, ... mediated by the interface of computers and communications network, the body enters a new relation with the subject, a dissociated yet actual relation that

opens identity to new degrees of flexible determination. The body no longer constrains the performativity of speech acts to the extent it does in face-to-face relations. These digital authors enact an unprecedented type of performative self-constitution in which the process of interpellation becomes an explicit question in the communication. Instead of the policeman–teacher–parent–boss hailing the individual in a manner that occludes the performative nature of the communication, in online communities one invents oneself and one knows that others also invent themselves, while each interpellates the others through those inventions. Unlike earlier forms of mediated communication, digital authorship is *about* the performance of self-constitution. (75, emphasis added)

On Poster's account, online identity performance exemplifies a *post-ideological* and *postsymbolic* form of interpellation in which the artifactuality of identity is exposed by the technology that mediates it. Because it is effectuated by the *machinic* performativity of computer language, rather than the *symbolic* performativity of social institutions, online interpellation affords an unprecedented freedom to the digital author to invent herself, subject only to the constraints of the online medium.[v]

Despite its utter blindness to the social constraints that thoroughly permeate virtual spaces,[vi] Poster's analysis crucially foregrounds the *experimental* function of online identity play. If there is indeed a general awareness concerning the disjunction between online and actual identity, as he suggests,[vii] then what is at stake in online identity performance must be something quite different from the struggle for social recognition central to recent theories of performativity. Such a conclusion is implicit in Poster's definition of online interpellation as entirely borne by the words on the screen[viii]: so long as the body is entirely constituted from text, it can have no necessary analogical correlation with the flesh-and-blood body of the user outside the virtual space; put somewhat differently, it lacks all force to compel the subjection of this latter body.

Contextualized in relation to our concerns here, Poster's conception attains a crucial specificity: in materializing interpellation via a text-body, online identity performance does not bracket out the body per se so much as it suspends the constraint the body exercises as a *visible* signifier—as a receptive surface for the markings of racial (and gendered) particularity.

144

2. BEYOND VISIBILITY: THE GENERALIZATION OF PASSING

It is precisely on account of its specific *epochē* of the visual that online identity performance can be said to generalize the phenomenon of passing. By decoupling identity from any analogical relation to the visible body, online self-invention effectively places everyone in the position previously reserved for certain raced subjects: everyone must mime his or her identity.[ix] However, in generalizing the phenomenon of passing, the Internet does far more than simply materialize an already existent racial or ethnic problematic. In effect, it introduces a radically unprecedented condition of selfhood: what is fundamentally new about Internet passing is not its generalization of an epistemosocial problematic (the fact that there is no way to "tell if a character's description matches a player's physical characteristics," as Nakamura puts it), but rather its generalization of a situation in which *the only way to acquire an identity is to "pass,"* to perform or imitate a role, norm, or stereotype that is itself a cultural performance.[x]

In his analysis of the "ambivalent relationship of race and cyberspace," Thomas Foster contends that this kinship between online interpellation and passing allows us to understand "African-American culture ... as prefiguring the concerns of virtual systems theory." Online identification is like racial performance, Foster suggests, because it lacks any naturalizing norm that it might transgress and is thus *always already* "antifoundational":

> Histories of racial performance complicate the project of de-essentializing or denaturalizing embodiment.... Race has never been constructed *only* through "the corporealizing logic that [seeks] to anchor the indeterminacies of race to organic organization [...]" [citing Robyn Wiegman].... [Rather, as blackface shows,] racial norms have historically been constructed through the kind of antifoundational performative practices that have come to be associated with postmodern modes of cross-identification and gender-bending. By "antifoundational," I mean that in blackface performances it was not necessary to ground racial identity in a black body. Nor was it necessary to occupy a black body in order to be perceived by others as producing a culturally intelligible performance of "blackness."[5]

Like that of racial passing, the problematic of blackface demonstrates that raced identity has always been constructed as a disembodied mimicry, that it has always been a performance of pure convention, in the absence of any bodily foundation. It is thus closely akin to online performance because, in both cases, identity is *exclusively* bound to the imitation of culturally sanctioned signifiers. The paradox in which such performance results is aptly captured in the figure of the black minstrel imitating himself: to do so, he must, as Eric Lott puts it, "offer credible imitations of white men imitating him."[6] In online self-invention, as in blackface and racial passing, identity is always an imitation of an imitation: a purely disembodied simulacrum.

In this, both forms of passing differ fundamentally from gender performativity, where the strong motivation to resist all appeal to the body stems from the traditional identification of femininity with the body—that is, from the assurance that the body has always been (and will always be) there. To cite only the most famous example, in her account of interpellation, Judith Butler shows how the body emerges as an excess or residue *in the very act* in which it is materialized through a particular socially or institutionally sanctioned coding.[xi] The kinds of transgressive performative practice Butler valorizes function by making this bodily residue culturally intelligible, i.e., visible. Such a model of the body is precisely what is missing in the case of blackface performance, racial passing, and, we might add, online self-invention, whose similarity in this regard helps to show the limitations of a theory that builds bodily excess into the scene of interpellation and thus denies it any standing outside the interpellative act.

In these instances, the problem is that interpellation *works all too well*: the mimicry at work in all three requires a *wholesale* replacement of the lived body with a new prosthetic body—whether it is the text-body of Internet communities or the cultural image of the black body operative in blackface and passing.[xii] The absolute discontinuity between the materialized body and the lived body means that there simply is no possibility for embodiment to form a site of resistance *within* the process of interpellation; insofar as it constitutes a *prosthetic* body that *replaces* the lived body, passing can leave no bodily residue that could be made visible or otherwise rendered culturally intelligible.

For Thomas Foster, this transcendence of visibility makes cyberspace a promising frontier for reconceptualizing race. By altering the "accustomed grounding of social interaction in the physical facticity of human bodies," as Sandy Stone puts it, cyberspace opens possibilities for identity-performance that are not "simply expressive or mimetic."[xiii] Insofar as it dispenses with the category of visibility, cyberspace holds the potential to broker raced identity through means other than the imitation or expression (the visible or epidermal traits) of a body.[xiv] Yet, to stop there—and to see in the generalization of passing nothing more than the suspension of the constraint of visibility and the possibility for variant couplings of self and body thus afforded—is to underestimate its impact massively. The license passing affords us to try on other and multiple representational selves (the experimental function foregrounded by Poster) is at the same time a call into being of that heretofore invisible domain of our existence: the life of the body.[xv]

This is why it is important that online interpellation submits everyone—not just a particular subgroup—to the condition of having to pass; the generalization of this *condition* means in effect that the resulting abjection of the lived body from the space of intelligibility (visibility) can no longer be limited to certain subjects, but rather becomes a problem for all. If we all must imitate cultural images of how particular bodies should appear in order to acquire agency—if we must give up our singular bodily experiences to occupy a constituted textual body—*then we all must live the erasure of our lived bodies.*

We might say then that what is most significant about the transcendence of visibility in online interpellation is less the possibility it affords for new modes of *represented* agency than its exposure of the violence exerted on bodily life by generic categories of social intelligibility and by the politics of recognition—identity politics—that it subtends. By severing imitation from visual appearance, online passing allows cultural signifiers to appear as what they are: social codings that have no natural correlation to any particular body and that, for this reason, are and cannot avoid being profoundly reductive of bodily singularity.

3. "CORPOREAL MALEDICTION" AND THE "RACIAL–EPIDERMAL SCHEMA"

In a manner not dissimilar from the deployment of virtual reality by Char Davies, cyberspace—the site of today's online identity play—comprises a kind of laboratory for testing the contribution of embodiment, in this case, to our experience of living our "self" as racially marked. By bracketing out the visual markers that have given content to the process of racialization in our culture, cyberspace would seem to provide a "zero-degree" of racial identification, a certain universality rooted in the precariousness—what we have been analyzing under the concept of passing—of identity as a stabilization or fixation of embodied life (or, following Simondon, of individuation). So long as racialization proceeds *automatically*, as it were, from the availability of visual markers of race, it will perforce apply unequally to differently embodied individuals. However, as soon as this automaticity is interrupted—as I suggest it is by the generalization of passing requisite for agency in cyberspace—racialization is opened up for a certain exploration.

The important question thereby raised is whether this margin of indetermination and the exploration it facilitates can yield something positive. Does the generalization of passing—and the bracketing of the visual as the privileged register for racialization—simply subject all embodied individuals to the same conditions, to the same struggle for identity? Or, might it rather be an opportunity to challenge the assumptions underlying the application of racial signifiers to bodies, assumptions that include a static picture of the individual as well as a subordination of embodiment to the force of the image?

So long as we remain focused on the most literal spaces for identity play in cyberspace (the chat room, multiplayer video games, etc.), we will be unable to address this crucial alternative. That is, we will retain interpellation—the hailing of the embodied individual that confers identity and agency, always at the expense of some dimension of embodiment—as the category for thinking racialization. We will thus fail to capitalize on the excess of embodiment over interpellation that I propose (following Simondon and Michael Hardt) to call "affectivity" and that, as we shall see, forms the medium for an inclusive experience of impropriety, a collective "whatever body" (Agamben).

Because we need to think *beyond* interpellation, the generalization of passing that has been our focus thus far (and indeed, online identity play in general) can do no more than suggest a kind of technical readiness or even ripeness, an availability or disposition, to use Simondon's term (*disposition*), for a rethinking of the relation between embodiment and racialization. To pursue the avenue it opens, I shall thus turn to the work of Malta-born British artist Keith Piper, whose multimedia, multiplatform, archival synthesis of his work from 1980 onward, *Relocating the Remains* (1997), brilliantly deploys digital technics as a means of thinking—of compelling viewers to think—racialization beyond interpellation.

Piper's work constructs yet another body-in-code—this one concerned specifically with the dematerialization of cyberspatial interaction and community—that, to the extent it invests in the materiality of the digital, forms a complement to the online *epochē* of the visual. Because of its use of digital technics, Piper's work (as we shall see shortly) allows and perhaps even compels us to negotiate our relation to stereotyped media images—images that function by capturing embodied force—in ways that mobilize viewer affectivity as a mechanism for experiencing the excess of embodiment and for deploying it toward the forging of a collective "whatever body."

Before turning to this examination of Piper's digital practice, let me try to unpack and justify my claim that digital technics—here in the form of the Internet as the support for what is somewhat misleadingly called cyberspace—has, in some sense, prepared the way for a fundamentally different experience of racialization or, perhaps more accurately, for a new regime of individuation in which race matters differently.

To the extent that this new regime dethrones the image in favor of embodied excess, it might be helpful to conceptualize how race is lived at the level of embodiment. No critic has been more eloquent on this issue than Frantz Fanon, whose *Black Skin, White Masks* articulates a definitive critique of the neutrality underlying Sartre's theorization of anti-Semitism and, more generally, of the exploration of the body schema from Jean Lhermitte to (at least implicitly) Merleau–Ponty.

Fanon begins his analysis by foregrounding the specific difficulties black men and women encounter in their efforts to compose themselves as bodies: "In the white world," he writes, "the man of color encounters difficulties in the development of his body schema. Consciousness of the body is solely a negating activity. It is a third-person consciousness."[7] The clear implication here is that black men and women experience their bodies not directly, or firsthand, but as objectifications, in the mode of third-person consciousness; in sum, because they experience their bodies indirectly through images created by others, they are unable to construct coherent bodily schemas.

As a consequence, black men and women are deprived of the resources of embodiment as a ground and medium for the coupling of body and world, of the "slow composition of my *self* as a body in the middle of a spatial and temporal world" that "does not impose itself on me," but is rather "a definitive structuring of the self and of the world— definitive because it creates a real dialectic between my body and the world" (111). This deprivation of the resources afforded by a bodily schema is what Fanon refers to as "corporeal malediction," the estrangement of the self from itself, from its own constitutive embodiment.

The source of this malediction is, of course, the perverted or false dialectic between the black body and the world. To the extent that this dialectic is mediated not internally, as a direct structural coupling, but rather by white society and the values it imposes on black bodies, it can only be an interrupted and impotent dialectic, one that cannot secure the coupling of body and world theorized by Lhermitte (and Merleau–Ponty) and hence can only burden its "subjects" with extrinsic and disabling contents. These contents comprise another schema—the "historico-racial schema"—that operates not on top of, but *below* the corporeal schema; this schema interferes, terminally in Fanon's estimation, with the successful constitution of a physiological bodily schema.

Dramatizing his discovery that he has "sketched a historico-racial schema" of this sort, Fanon clarifies the additional burden faced by black men and women:

> The elements that I used had been provided for me not by "residual sensations and perceptions primarily of a tactile, vestibular, kinesthetic, and visual character" [citing Lhermitte, *L'Image de Notre Corps*], but by the other, the white man, who had woven me out of a thousand details, anecdotes, stories. I thought that what I had in hand was to construct a physiological self, to balance space, to localize sensations, and here I was called on for more. (111)

Specifically, he was called on to assume the burden of history, of the sedimented stereotypes (tertiary retentions) of his race. Continuing his dramatization, Fanon describes his discovery of this inexorable burden: "I could no longer laugh, because I already know that there were legends, stories, history, and above all *historicity* ..." (112). Inexorable or not, this burden proves overwhelming, as Fanon goes on to describe how his fractured "corporeal schema," already "assailed at various points," finally "crumbled, its place taken by a racial epidermal schema" (112).

With this passage from the "historico-racial schema" to the "racial epidermal schema," Fanon and the black men and women for whose experience he testifies truly and properly become objects:

> I was responsible at the same time for my body, for my race, for my ancestors. I subjected myself to an objective examination; I discovered my blackness, my ethnic characteristics; and I was battered down by tom-toms, cannibalism, intellectual deficiency, fetishism, racial defects, slave-ships, and above all else, above all: "Sho' good

eatin'." On that day, completely dislocated, unable to be abroad with the other, the white man, who unmercifully imprisoned me, I took myself far off from my own presence, far indeed, and made myself an object. (112)

No longer even aware of his body through third-person consciousness, Fanon now experiences himself, his body, solely from the perspective of the white man's gaze. Literally the object of the gaze of the other, Fanon can only live his embodiment as a flattened, one-dimensional racial epidermal schema:

> In the train, it was no longer a question of being aware of my body in the third person but in a triple person. In the train, I was given not one but two, three places. I had already stopped being amused. It was not that I was finding febrile coordinates in the world. I existed triply: I occupied space. I moved toward the other ... and the evanescent other, hostile but not opaque, transparent, not there, disappeared. Nausea ... (112)

One can hardly imagine a stronger expression of the fact, the historico-racial reality, that black bodies *do not live in the same space as other, white bodies*; they are, quite simply, barred from the intercorporeity that is, as we have seen, the very payoff of having a body schema on Merleau–Ponty's account.

In her commentary on Fanon, Gail Weiss astutely grasps the depth at which racial alienation occurs, stressing that:

> Social objectification should not be viewed as a subsequent influence upon the construction of an individual body image (i.e., coming into play only in the development of the ego-ideal or body image ideal), but is always already operative, and for those societally designated as "racial minorities," the internalization of this racial epidermal schema (whose inscriptive force penetrates the psyche through the skin) results in a (psychophysical) inferiority complex that no body image ideal, however positive, can ever completely overcome. (27–28)

Not only is objectification "always already operative" *within* the process of body image construction, but it also similarly contaminates the constitution of a body schema, which forms, as we have seen, the background for the construction of any body image, coherent or otherwise. Accordingly, the disturbance Fanon calls "corporeal malediction" is much more than a mere contamination of the black self's body image by racial stereotypes and the objectification they render unavoidable; it

151

is a disturbance in the bodily schema, in the process that would make possible the construction of a body image in the first place, that would accord black selves the agency to perform such a construction.

Thus, the corporeal malediction created by the imposition on black selves of a "racial epidermal schema" involves a reduction of the bodily schema to the image; this reduction, moreover, is distinct from, and far more fundamental than, for instance, Paul Schilder's (or, for that matter, Elizabeth Grosz's) conflation of body schema and body image. Here, what is at issue is a wholesale displacement of the physiological corporeal schema—the embodied basis for agency as such—by a racial epidermal schema whose content is stereotyped images of the black body imposed by white society. (This difference is marked by Fanon's differentiation between the "third person" and the "triple person." The former names a situation in which the self's bodily schema is impeded by the body image, i.e., the image of *his or her own* body; the latter describes a situation in which the self has lost its schema entirely—that is, any contact whatsoever with his or her embodiment—and consequently exists only as the bare living of a set of images imposed on his or her body from the outside.) What this means, ultimately, is that racism, on Fanon's account, occurs through the "expropriation" of the corporeal schema of black men and women, which is simply replaced by a set of contents, tertiary memories, and racial images permitting only the most hollow, automatic forms of agency.

However, what is at stake in Fanon's conceptualization of "corporeal malediction" is more than just an account of racism; indeed, with his firm insistence that racial difference concerns how racial difference is actually lived, his analysis has significant consequences for how we think identification as such. By demonstrating that racism operates fundamentally at the level of the bodily schema—as an impairment of the embodiment, of the corporeal agency, of certain bodies—Fanon's analysis advances an important claim about identification in general: namely, identification not only crucially involves subrepresentational processes of bodily life, but these latter—insofar as they comprise the processes *through which the effects of differences are actually lived or felt*—are what makes differences matter!

This stress on how difference is lived may in fact be the crucial difference between processes of racial and gender identification—if, for example, we think the latter with Judith Butler and view it fundamentally as a performative problematic involving the attempt to secure "a certain possibility for social existence," as she puts it in *Excitable Speech*.[8] Butler's nuanced analyses of the illocutionary force of linguistic utterances notwithstanding, it remains the case that the subject materialized through performative interpellation, even if it is produced in the act of its materialization, is from the moment of its materialization always already possessed of an intact, coherent bodily schema.

We might legitimately ask, then, if the becoming-object that Fanon describes is an interpellation at all. It is undeniable, as Diana Fuss argues, that "colonialism works in part by policing the boundaries of cultural intelligibility"[9]; however, the exclusion of the black man (and the black woman), as Fanon depicts it, is so categorical—he or she is "denied entry into the alterity that underwrites subjectivity" (which is the sense of Fanon's conception of the "triple person")—that any capacity to respond to the call of the other would seem to be vitiated from the get-go. The singularity of the black man (or woman) on Fanon's account stems from this last reality. Deprived of any capacity to respond, of any "self" that could be produced in responding to the call of the other, the black man (or woman) simply cannot be the *subject* of any interpellation, even one brought into being through the "violence of racial interpellation." Thus, in Fanon's reckoning, when the black man (or woman) hears the call of the other—"Dirty nigger!" or "Look, a Negro!"—he or she cannot even purchase some compromised social standing through identification with the racial slur. Instead, he or she spirals away along the perverted, empty dialectic of crushing objecthood, becoming the mute, impotent object of the system of racism.

As a contribution to the thinking of identification, Fanon's work thus provides a negative archaeology of the infrastructural embodiment necessary for a "politics of the performative" not only to succeed, but simply to be possible in the first place. If his work thereby underscores an important difference between racial and gender identification, it is because of his personal and historical demonstration that racial difference, indeed racism, is lived *at a deeper level* than gender difference (at least as contemporary feminists tend to conceptualize it); it does not concern cultural intelligibility, but rather the embodied preconditions for acquiring such intelligibility *in the first place*, the capacity to sustain, to live, to give body to, the subjectifications imposed upon it.[xvi] In sum, the "corporeal malediction" generated by racism yields the dispossession not only of the meaning of the body but also of the body itself, as Fanon's experience makes unbearably clear: "My body *was given back to me* sprawled out, distorted, recolored, clad in mourning in that white winter day. The Negro is an animal, the Negro is bad, the Negro is mean, the Negro is ugly ..." (113, emphasis added).

Although the imposition of the "racial epidermal schema" has the effect of turning the black self into an object, it nonetheless remains part of a larger dialectic; indeed, this devastating effect can only be the rigorous result—in a sense, the distorted remainder—of the dialectic of white identification. The question thus arises: what does the racial epidermal schema—the reduction of black embodiment to a racial image—do for and to the white self?

Fanon turns to this question in his effort to identify, extrapolating from and expanding Sartre's analysis of anti-Semitism, the constituents of "negrophobia." This leads him to a startling conclusion:

> Phobia is to be found on an instinctual, biological level. At the extreme, I should say that the Negro, because of his body, impedes the closing of the postural schema of the white man—at the point, naturally, at which the black man makes his entry into the phenomenal world of the white man. (160)

Fanon's point is that the black man—and with him, racial alterity, of which he is the exemplar—interrupts the mirror stage which functions to lend an imaginary integration, an illusory closure, to the postural schema. As Fanon sees it, this failure of the mirror stage to achieve its imaginary sublation of bodily fragmentation describes the actual workings of identification processes in the white world of his time, i.e., in a white world constituted on the basis of the system of racism.

Whether or not this renders Lacan's account of identification racist, it does serve to specify the privilege of the white man and to mark the limitations of that privilege:

> It would indeed be interesting, on the basis of Lacan's theory of the *mirror stage*, to investigate the extent to which the *imago* of his fellow built up in the young white at the usual age would undergo an imaginary aggression with the appearance of the Negro. When one has grasped the mechanism described by Lacan, one can have no further doubt that the real Other for the white man is and will continue to be the black man. And conversely. Only for the white man the Other is perceived on the level of the body image, absolutely as the not-self—that is, the unidentifiable, the unassimilable. For the black man, as we have shown, historical and economic realities come into the picture. (161, note, translation modified)

Once again, Fanon pinpoints the fundamental asymmetry of the identification process: the black self is simply deprived of any opportunity to participate in the dialectic of identification as described by Lacan. At the same time, however, insofar as the image of the black man constitutes absolute alterity within the white man's dialectic, it manages to exercise a degree of constraint on the latter. As that which refuses to be sublated in the dialectic of identification, resists integration into the corporeal schema and thus hinders its closure, the black body as absolute Other fundamentally interrupts the dialectic as Lacan describes it. On this account (i.e., from the white man's standpoint), racism stems from the need on the part of the white man to preserve the illusion of imaginary integration by denying the force of this interruption. Negrophobia is simply the result of such a projection: the image of the black man creates anxiety because it is "the corporeal reminder" of just how precarious the illusion of integration actually is to borrow a term from Gail Weiss.

To comprehend the reverberations of this interrupted dialectic—specifically, the qualified agency it would seem to assign the black man's image—we need to ask why, exactly, the black body has this role of absolute Other, exemplar for pure alterity. Fanon's reasoning here is admittedly complex, detouring as it does through psychoanalytical theorizing; however, what seems unequivocal throughout his analysis is the identification of the Negro with the "biological." "What is important," he specifies at the beginning of his analysis of negrophobia, "is to show that with the Negro the cycle of the *biological* begins" (161). Unlike the Jew who is persecuted as a member of a race, the Negro is persecuted "as a concrete personality": "it is in his corporeality that the Negro is attacked" (163). Again, unlike the Jew who stands for the "intellectual danger" of cultural displacement, the Negro "symbolizes the biological danger." By "projecting his own desires onto the Negro," the "civilized white man behaves 'as if' the Negro really had them."

Thus, concludes Fanon, "to suffer from a phobia of Negroes is to be afraid of the biological. For the Negro is only biological. The Negroes are animals. They go about naked. And God alone knows" (165). By identifying the Negro with the biological, Fanon in effect comprehends the absolute alterity of the black body *as the corporeal remainder of the biological itself*, as that dimension of the living (what Agamben has analyzed as *zoē* or "bare life") that simply cannot be denied, no matter how forceful and complex the mechanism of projection may be. In this respect, the

155

unassimilable black body is a living emblem of the excess of embodiment over its captation by the image (the dialectic of identification).

As such, racial difference (and here it again contrasts with gender difference) holds a certain potential for universalization: notwithstanding the fundamental asymmetry that permeates the concrete experience it conditions, racial difference as it structures life in our world today interrupts the dialectic of identification *in all cases*, albeit differentially. Despite the fact that some bodies (black bodies) are wholly deprived of the chance to acquire a coherent body schema and others (white bodies) are interrupted in their effort to achieve imaginary integration, the violence of both forms of deprivation stems from a common root cause: the imposition of the "racial epidermal schema" on black men and women.

As the process that transforms the black body into an inert image, this imposition is responsible for making the black self into an object just as it is responsible for rendering the black body an anxiety-inducing, phobic image. What this means, then, is that all parties—black and white alike—have an interest in overturning the reduction of the black body to a mere image, even if this interest is asymmetrical. What is at stake here, as Fanon's identification of the black body with the biological makes clear, is the excess of bodily life over any form of identification that would seek to contain it through identification with or explusion as an image.

4. FROM NEGROPHOBIA TO NEGROPHILIA

(Re)thinking identification with Fanon requires us to interrogate its racist foundation, which in turn requires us to recognize the universality of its scope without losing sight of the asymmetry of its actual impact. Now, as I have already mentioned, new media technology—as exemplified in the Internet and, specifically, in the generalization of passing in online identity play—prepares the way for such a vigilant recognition. By instancing the potential of new technically facilitated forms of community to suspend, at least within certain parameters, the overdetermination exercised by the (visual) image of the racial other, online identity play creates the possibility for a "zero-degree" of racial identification, a potential universality rooted in the precariousness of any identity as a fixation of embodied individuation.

156

In *Relocating the Remains*, Keith Piper deploys new media technology as a means to effectuate—differentially, to be sure—the universalization of the violence imposed by the "racial epidermal schema." The common target of what I propose to call his politics of affectivity is the image of the black man (the black man become image), or rather, the specific form it takes in a digital environment where it has been divested of the automaticity that, as Fanon highlights, renders him (and the black men and women for whom he stands) a "slave not of the 'idea' that others have of me but of my own appearance" (116).

The promise of the digital, then, is the promise of a certain *indetermination* in the correlation between racialization and the image, an indetermination that suspends the "overdetermination" of the black body "from without" and thereby positions the image as a static fixation of individuation—a reduction of embodiment, of the biological life common to all humans (116). Recalling our earlier discussion of Agamben, we might well say that Piper's work invests racialization as a concrete—and perhaps privileged—actualization of the contemporary bankruptcy of the image; in exposing the utter incongruence of the image of the black body with any form of embodied life, it announces the obsolescence of the image as a support for identification as such.

To the extent that it attacks the image as an adequate vehicle for the apprehension of the other, Piper's project would seem to take up Shohat and Stam's call to exploit the capability of digital technologies to "bypass the search for a profilmic model." Indeed, Piper relies extensively on digital compositing to create fragmented and conflicted images of black men—images which, through their lack of viability as objects of (either) identification or projective expulsion, lay bare the insidious workings of the racial epidermal schema. That is why, in the end, Piper's politics of affectivity gives the lie to Shohat and Stam's well-intentioned effort to deploy new media in the service of an empathic politics.[xvii]

Indeed, Piper is keenly aware that it is not the felicitous identification with the felt reality of the other that is important and potentially transformative, but rather the political force linked to the affect of incommensurability. In this sense, his use of new media in *Relocating the Remains* brings to the politics of bodily life what Gilles Deleuze's analysis of "third cinema" brings to the politics of memory. Just as the "intercessor" operates a movement beyond habitual memory into absolute memory, so too the experience of incommensurability resulting from the failure of identification with the stereotyped racial image

157

sparks a movement beyond habitual feeling networks into an affective confusion. Where the former opens the possibility to invent a new future (or a new people), the latter opens the possibility to live new affects, ones commensurate to the singularity or impropriety of life.[xviii]

Piper is perhaps the ideal figure for exploring the confrontation of new media technology and race theory. Not only has his artistic production coevolved with race theory and politics, taking inspiration from it and inspiring it in turn, but also his recent work acquires much of its resonance from its success at holding together the contradictions of racial identity, as well as those of identity. This is why Piper's critical engagement with race and media exemplifies the radical promise of new media. Indeed, his practice is perhaps most distinctive in its success at exposing and capitalizing on the intrinsic duality of technologies of containment and control like surveillance and cyberspace. Without disregarding the primary deployment of these technologies to target minority bodies—and indeed, by thinking their logic through to the limit—Piper attempts to make them available for postidentitarian identification on the basis of the singularity or impropriety common to us all.

Piper's complex project—which combines a gallery installation, a CD-ROM, and a Website and integrates much of his work from the mid '80s on[xix]—bears vivid witness to the role that technology plays as the facilitator for the politicization of affect, at least or especially when it is a question of race and ethnicity. Put bluntly, new media technology allows for a certain despecification of Piper's critical engagement with racial stereotypes and the paradoxical invisibility of the black (male) body. This despecification, in turn, allows for an opening up and complexification of the mode of address of his work. In an insightful essay on the project, Kobena Mercer pinpoints the operative mechanism for this technically facilitated despecification, arguing that Piper's turn to the digital allows him to treat the body as the focal site for a "double-voicing" of the "confrontational" and the "invitational," a site where resistance is always contaminated by identification, where activism is complicated by emotion.[xx,10]

Extending this analysis, I would suggest that Piper's concrete engagement with technology as a site of dedifferentiation and universality must be understood in the dual mode of confrontation and invitation. The result is a significant complexification: not only is the address to black subjects nuanced in a way that routes self-perception through perception by the other (that is, through the surveillant and/or consumerist gaze),[xxi] but also the address is opened in an unprecedented way to nonblack, nonminority white subjects. In short, not until Piper deploys the allegedly universal technologies of surveillance and cyberspace can his work truly address a white audience (and thus accomplish his goal, formulated in the early '90s, of liberating address from concerns of identity[xxii]). Accordingly, if *Relocating the Remains* can be said to culminate Piper's shift to a more nuanced and dialogic deployment of the "cut and mix" aesthetic, this is because it brings to fruition the universalizing of address that was always implicitly at issue in his turn to multimedia technologies.

At first glance, the spatial layout of *Relocating the Remains* would seem no more than an opportune vehicle for Piper to archive the impressive array of his artistic production. The three "virtual" rooms each house works corresponding to his three main areas of interest: the cultural imaging of the black body, the legacy of colonialism, and the racial politics of contemporary technology. Yet, doubling this homogenizing spatial division is a heterogenizing temporal logic that restructures the interrelations between works in order to foreground Piper's trajectory toward a multivalent mode of address. Following this logic, the three virtual rooms—*Unmapped, Unrecorded,* and *Unclassified* (organized from left to right)—might be thought of as designating distinct phases or levels of generality in Piper's effort to complexify his broadly Foucauldian racial politics.[xxiii]

Devoted to manifesting the multiple contradictions attaching to the cultural image of the black body (specifically, the black male body), *Unmapped* cites and mediates the most prominent area of the artist's interest from the mid '80s until the early '90s. Incorporating previous works, including *The Body Politic* (1983), with new material and a new interface entitled "Negrophilia" (encompassing spaces devoted to the "sight," "sound," and "feel" of the Negro), *Unmapped* charts the course leading from Piper's initial confrontations with black stereotypes (themselves much nuanced by the addition of animation and especially sound) to his later complex engagement with the paradoxical figure of the black athlete.

As a whole, this archive overwhelms the spectator with the irresistibility of the commodified image of the black male. Indeed, as something like a synecdoche for the entirety of this line of exploration, the image of the black athlete brings to a head the oversaturation that, as Mercer insightfully points out, is crucial to the efficacy of the stereotyped image. It is not simply that too much meaning is packed into the image, but rather that visibility has been thoroughly co-opted as a viable category of resistance: "The paradox is that the hypervisibility of black sportsmen like U.S. basketball star Michael Jordan perpetuates the spectacular otherness on which colonial fantasy turns, only this time in the service of multicultural commodity fetishism" (58).[xxiv]

Here, Piper's strategy would seem to be that of resisting the eviscerating of the image by capital, not by restoring content to the image of the black male athlete, but rather by reclaiming its empty promise as the source for the experience of affective confusion. However, the high degree of specificity attached to this act of reclaiming is most crucial. Although the exposure of the paradox of hypervisibility can certainly speak to all viewers, white and black alike, the concrete effect Mercer cites—namely, Piper's nuanced channeling of the commodified image through the channels that mediate each subject's self-image—here applies specifically to black (male, and to a lesser extent, female) subjects. Put another way, the emotional charge of these images—their capacity to induce affective confusion—will be limited to a narrow group among Piper's potential audience who are directly affected by the particular co-optation exercised in the capitalist exploitation of these stereotypes. This specificity, moreover, is interconnected in complex ways with the unique problematic of (in)visibility in the performance of race, what Fanon describes as the utter slavery of the black man to his appearance.

Devoted to the legacies of colonialism, the second virtual room, *Unrecorded*, marks a significant expansion of the affective dimension of Piper's project. Here, Piper takes the plurality inherent in colonialism's legacy as the basis for an interrogation of the concept of identity. Indeed, by articulating colonialism with contemporary technoscience, Piper opens up a vast continuum that potentially encompasses the interests of any potential viewer–participant, regardless of his or her given marks of particularity. No matter where one is positioned in relation to the Diaspora experience, no one can claim to be outside the sphere of its contemporary effects—that is, if these effects are taken as manifesting biases and violence built into the reigning epistemological discourses of the West. Put in a perhaps more positive light, we might say that Piper stages a deterritorializing of colonialism from an overly narrow historicism, thus revealing "the convulsions of a multicultural society in which the descendents of colonizers and colonized alike are mutually enmeshed in histories that are not yet fully known" (Mercer 18).

Like *Unmapped*, *Unrecorded* brings together prior work and new material, again supplemented with animation and sound. Two of the three prior artworks—*A Ship Called Jesus* (1991) and (now garbed in a colonial tapestry interface) *Go West Young Man*—exemplify Piper's strategies for interiorizing contradictions in order to make them emotionally resonant as well as inescapable. By melding the complex figure of the black father with the handing-down of tradition among the enslaved and colonized, the father–son dialogue of *Go West* lends an indeterminate historical dimension to the failure of the black father, implicitly inviting its audience (whoever that may be) to nuance any easy conviction regarding its cause.

Likewise, by exploring the historical coupling of slavery and Christianity, *A Ship Called Jesus* aims to expose the correlation between the desire for certainty and the experience of trauma and, subsequently, to challenge the certainties of its spectators. Named after a slave ship, "The Jesus of Lubeck," endowed by Queen Elizabeth I to Sir John Hawkins, the work juxtaposes its historical context—including a headstone and grave, made from shards of broken mirror, and a crucifix lightbox, both commemorating the victims of the Middle Passage—with three archives of contemporary material, including quotes from Margaret Thatcher on Britain's race fears ("An English Queen"), gospel music ("A Ship"), and the ventriloquized rhetoric of commerce ("A Pirate"). In this way, *A Ship Called Jesus* manages to generalize the trauma of slavery (without compromising its differential referentiality) such that any position of "fundamentalist certainty" (whether black nationalism, racism, or, interestingly enough, the denial of racism) can only appear as the symptom of trauma. In consequence, loss of certainty becomes a redemptive vehicle for a new, more open-ended ethnicization that has dispensed with the constraining binary categories of race as a historical substance.[xxv]

Extending this dispensation, the two remaining works featured in this space serve to link the intrinsic imbrications of colonialism and ethnicization with the other two domains of Piper's aesthetic interest. *Tradewinds* (1992) deploys the rhetoric of the black body—now projected as moving animations onto images of shipping crates—in order to introduce a historical dimension into the interrogation of the contemporary stereotype and thus, once again, to expand its scope. Conversely, a new work made specifically for the CD-ROM, *The Fictions of Science*, deploys a viewfinder interface, reminiscent of a camera, as a vehicle to access various spaces where the value-neutrality of different sciences—including the now suspect "science" of craniology—finds itself under question. Here, the colonial legacy is generalized insofar as it is shown to inhabit the classifying systems responsible for the knowledge institutions of our culture.[xxvi]

As differentiated from *Unmapped*, the works in *Unrecorded* compel *all* viewers to reflect on the precariousness and flexibility of their ethnicity; moreover, by exposing the complex historical connections that, through the agency of technology, interlink all particular destinies, they invite us all to reforge our ethnicity beyond the "obligation of an identity tethered to the signifying chain of history" (Mercer 62). If this potential forging of "new figures of ethnicity" represents an example of the process Poster calls "virtual ethnicity," it is one that reveals the relation between technology and ethnicization to be far more immanent than it is on Poster's account. As the mechanism for articulating figures of ethnicity that reflect their "electronic constitution in virtual spaces" (Poster 164), digital technology does not simply furnish a new, nonphysical place for memory, as Poster suggests.[xxvii] On the contrary, it brokers a new phase in the ongoing coevolution of the human and technology—in the technico–social–cultural differentiation, characteristic of the human species, that French anthropologist André Leroi–Gourhan names (in specific opposition to genetic differentiation) *ethnic* differentiation.

On this view, ethnicity has *always* been technical, in the sense that it coincides with the possibility for passing on nongenetically programmed memory that is external to the individual: ethnicity is, in Bernard Stiegler's terminology, "epiphylogenetic," evolution through means other than life.[xxviii] The works in *Unrecorded* foreground this coevolution of technology and ethnicization. By soliciting a confrontation and potential reforging of ethnicity in each user—one concretely premised on the complicity of colonization and slavery with technology—these works materialize the promise of "collective intelligence" in a manner that does justice not only to the freedom afforded by the virtual *but also* to the historically specific (though in no sense fixed or determinate) constraints that continue to differentiate subjects unequally and to burden them with differential tasks.[xxix]

5. MOBILIZING AFFECTIVITY BEYOND THE IMAGE

That the vehicle of Piper's universalization of address is technology appears most clearly in the final space, *Unclassified*, where two new works divergently take up and radicalize the immanent correlation of ethnicity and technicity.[xxx] By focusing on the racist deployment of surveillance technologies and the inequalities of access to cyberspace, *Tagging the Other* and *Caught like a Nigger in Cyberspace* bring a true universality of address to Piper's nuanced blend of the confrontational and the invitational, while at the same time tempering the indifference implicit in all visions of a technically instantiated collective intelligence. They do so by deploying the mechanism of technology as a universal form of address *in order better to foreground the fact of its differential application* (the burden of *Tagging the Other*) and, more importantly still, *to resituate the potential for community beyond ethnicity* (the burden of *Caught like a Nigger in Cyberspace*).

Tagging the Other adapts a 1992 video installation, resituating the four monitors of the original within the rectangular space of the computer screen. On these four "virtual" monitors, the work presents four black male heads, variously cloaked with a red band over the mouth, over the eyes, or with a target, and corresponding to a set of curious binaries (culture–ethnicity, subject–reject, other–boundaries, visible–difference) superimposed on the image and seemingly meant to expose the differential conditions of life in the "New European State." Clicking on each of the virtual monitors sets off a barrage of news clips reporting on topics like racist killing, the "Fortress Europe impregnable for black people," and the becoming extrageographic of life, as well as a music loop repeatedly intoning the incendiary imperative to "bring it on."

In yet another bid to destroy the certainty of conviction, this work confronts all viewers with the patent racism made invisible (to all but its immediate victims) by the neutrality of technological rhetoric. Yet, beyond simply drawing attention to this new reality, the work manages to place the viewer in the position of the surveilling gaze in a way that compels her to question her potential complicity with this situation. Interestingly enough, the target of this questioning is less one's participation in the technology of surveillance per se than the implicit ratification of limiting identity categories that such participation would seem to betoken: "Central to the piece," explains Piper, "is the framing and fixing of the Black European under a high tech gaze which seeks to

FIGURE 3.1 "Cyberspace: the New Frontier," from Keith Piper, *Caught like a Nigger in Cyberspace*, from *Relocating the Remains* (1997). (Courtesy of the artist and the Institute of International Visual Arts, London.)

classify and codify the individual within an arena in which *the logical constraints of race, ethnicity, nation and culture are fixed and delineated in a discourse of exclusion.*"[xxxi]

Because the effect of this strategy remains for the most part cognitive, at least for the nonblack viewer, the work cannot realize the universality of address I have been invoking here. Indeed, it is only with the realization of *Caught like a Nigger in Cyberspace*[xxxii]—modeled as a computer game whose ostensible goal is entry into cyberspace—that the affective logic so crucial to Piper's work from the early 1990s onward finally becomes the true driving force of his aesthetic. Initially challenging the viewer with the oscillating image of a black male and the injunction, "Click on to interrogate," *Caught like a Nigger in Cyberspace* subsequently invites the viewer to the "New Frontier" of cyberspace, extending "A Welcome Beneath the Silicon Sun for You and Your Family" (pasted against an image of a white couple and baby), and urging him or her to "apply within" (see Figure 3.1).

When the viewer clicks on this option, he or she is thanked for the application and invited to select one of three handles for entering cyberspace. Selecting "Al Gore Lookalike" yields immediate entry into

164

cyberspace and an invitation to play a game, "Infopoly," in which money endlessly and automatically circulates around a monopoly-like board. Selecting "Techhead" inserts the viewer in a circular loop of derogatory questions and accusations, such as, "Which part of 'mouse down' don't you understand?" "Looks like your KeyUpScript just keyed down," and "Read the fucking manual." Finally, selecting "Other" yields a screen informing the viewer that the application has been put on hold and advising of three possible courses: abandoning the application, waiting in a cyberspace waiting room, or a third option obscured by a red sign reading "Do not touch."

If the viewer is so bold as to disregard this injunction, a screen appears featuring a black man running and a sign reading "You are trespassing in cyberspace; we advise you to step the fuck back." This unequivocal message notwithstanding, the viewer is then invited to enter and, if she does so, is told that "our first defensive level" is being entered. This, it turns out, is a video game in which the goal is to avoid "low-flying jargon and insider speak." Informed that the mission is to "dodge the bombardment of techno jargon" and that she will be given five lives with which to survive 30 seconds of bombardment, the viewer is again asked whether she wants to play the game. Assenting to this invitation causes mathematical symbols to bombard the icon of a black male from all sides (see Figure 3.2).

Let me invoke my experience of the game to illustrate its affective impact. Having made my way to this point in the game, I dutifully used my mouse to control the icon in what turned out, again and again, to be a vain attempt to survive the assault. After each such attempt, I was greeted with the message, "You have just suffered death by techno jargon" and advised to leave by the nearest exit, yet offered the chance to

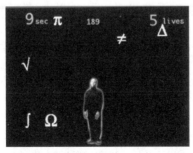

FIGURE 3.2 Barraged by Mathematical Symbols, from Keith Piper, *Caught like a Nigger in Cyberspace*, from *Relocating the Remains* (1997). (Courtesy of the artist and the Institute of International Visual Arts, London.

"try again." Finally, after countless failed efforts, I fortuitously dragged the mouse outside the game space entirely and waited while the timer clicked down to zero. Informed that I had "survived bombardment by techno jargon," I was asked whether I had seen enough or was hungry for more. Selecting the latter yielded a screen with a black male figure running from a viewfinder controlled by my mouse that informed me I was entering "Defensive Level II."

Using the viewfinder to fix my sights on the red target adorning the back of the black male figure, I clicked and was again asked whether I wanted to continue my mission; answering yes, I was then confronted with a building displaying the sign "Price of a Ticket" and flashing a red light at the location of the doorbell. Once again using the target to select this light, I clicked and entered a theater as the field zoomed into a screen displaying the message, "Seduction by Cyberspace: A Million Applications for a Brave New World," and showing six pictures featuring examples of high technology, including a stock trader, a comic book muscle man, a robotic auto factory, a combat soldier, a monitor displaying the logo, "Guerilla computing," and a photographer snapping a photo (apparently) of me.

Continuing to use the viewfinder interface, I clicked on each of these images in turn, only to be disappointed that the action thereby triggered consisted of nothing more than zooming into the image. Still energized from my earlier success at avoiding techno jargon, I felt trapped in this space of inaction, where my need for some outlet in an action was disappointed by my severely limited ability to frame the image from a purely classifying and analytic point of view. Once I became sufficiently exasperated with this protracted inaction, I selected the exit button and was brought to a screen featuring a smiling white woman thanking me for visiting cyberspace and urging me to "have a nice day."

Ostensibly aimed at securing the viewer entry into cyberspace, this game-like space is in fact designed to make affectively salient the vast disparities between those who control this new medium and those who are not wanted there and are urged, as one screen puts it with a self-effacing, almost parodic irony, to "find contentment in premodernity" (see Figure 3.3). In this sense, it functions much like Piper's earlier work, in which contradictions facing the black male subject are exposed for the viewer's consumption, except the anger informing that work has been replaced by a far more nuanced solicitation of an impossible emotional identification. Paradoxically, the vehicle for

FIGURE 3.3 "Find Contentment in Premodernity," from Keith Piper, Caught like a Nigger in Cyberspace, from Relocating the Remains (1997). (Courtesy of the artist and the Institute of International Visual Arts, London.)

this solicitation is the work's deployment of the specific, constrained temporality of the video game interface.

Generalizing from its impact on me, I would say that *Caught like a Nigger in Cyberspace* owes its efficacy to its success at confronting the viewer—black and white alike—with images that simply cannot be completed through action, at least not within the constraints the work imposes on our consumption. In this sense, the work functions in a manner akin to the cinema of the affection-image, following Deleuze's typology: like the affection-image, this mechanized interface with the image of the black body creates a crisis of the sensorimotor logic of the (movement-) image. If the affection-image ensues when the completion of the sensorimotor circuit is interrupted and received movement (sensation) and executed movement (action) are rendered incommensurable,[xxxiii] something like an affective-overflow occurs in our bodies when we are unable to correlate the sensations generated by the video game with some appropriate action on our parts.

Yet, in contrast to Deleuze's typology, affection here is not a modality of the cinematic image, but rather a "faculty" of our embodied singularity, and the source of our affective crisis is not an opening of the cinematic image to the force of time, but the concrete excess of our singular bodies.[xxxiv] Piper's *Caught like a Nigger in Cyberspace* extends the logic of affectivity *beyond* the image and it does so by deploying a postcinematic interface in which the power of time has been subordinated to constraints of the body's agency within a game-space. The work compels its viewer to live through the exclusion of certain bodies from cyberspace via the frantic temporal mode of a survival exercise, thereby mobilizing the disappointment of viewer expectations concerning the payoff of video game-playing (where some kind of clear victory is an always achievable goal) in order to deliver a message about racial inequality.

Put another way, the work utilizes the universal addressability of the video game[xxxv]—by which I mean above all its form as a simple, goal-directed temporal exercise—to produce an affective experience of the incommensurability of racial stereotypes: it is through the experience of seeing her expectations of victory disappointed that the viewer is brought to *feel* the inappropriateness of her efforts to "help" the black male figure overcome the burden of cultural stereotypes. Rather than an opportunity to experience "what it feels like" to be this figure, as Shohat and Stam propose, the viewer is made to feel the utter pointlessness of any effort that stops short of grasping the bankruptcy of the racialized image.

6. FORGING THE AFFECTION-BODY

We can now see clearly how Piper's project exploits the generalization of passing that forms the sociotechnical condition of possibility for online identity play. If we can say that passing within digital networks opens new opportunities for thinking identification, this is because and insofar as it gives concrete form to the essential impropriety of human life that is, as Agamben has shown, the basis for any collective individuation. To the extent that it deploys this concrete deployment of impropriety in the service of an affective universalization, Piper's work thus transforms a limited technical condition for identity production (passing within digital networks) into an opportunity to rethink identification. Whereas the generalized phenomenon of online passing simply exposes the bankruptcy of identity categories as a prosthesis for our bodily singularity, Piper's deployment of new media to catalyze an experience of impropriety turns this bankruptcy into an opportunity to think—and perhaps to live—singularity beyond identity.

More specifically, by catalyzing experiences of failed interpellation and affective confusion, Piper's work exposes a rich dimension of embodiment—affectivity—which is common to all. If affectivity is precisely the experience of one's incongruity with oneself (one's excess in relation to any fixing of identity), then Piper's work functions to link this fundamental singularity of the self with the fundamental singularity of the other (of all others), and thus to render singularity as such improper. In a simpler phrasing that is also more faithful to the phenomenology of the experience it affords, Piper's work confronts us with this incongruity *in the other*—the other's incongruity with itself—in a way that compels us to recognize it in ourselves.

Piper's work can thus be said to seize the opportunity glimpsed by Agamben: the opportunity to "appropriate the historic transformations of human nature that capitalism wants to limit to the spectacle, to link together image and body in a space where they can no longer be separated, and thus to forge the whatever body, whose *physis* is resemblance" (1993, 50). By re-embodying the image as bodily affect—as an affectivity always in excess of the image's desire to fix the body (and the body's captation by the image)—Piper's work seizes on the gap between image and body that, following Agamben, holds the potential for redemption understood as the opening to potentiality.

For Agamben, the hope for humanity can be found in this gap, the hope that comes from the emptying-out of the image by capitalism. Just as exchange capitalism of the early twentieth century performed the momentous work of redeeming the body "from the stigma of ineffability that had marked it for millennia," making it for the first time "something truly *whatever*," so too the apotheosis of exchange capitalism in the bankruptcy of the advertising image yields the rediscovery of the "fragile, slight human body" that it had for so long masked behind its "glorious body" (48). The ultimately fatal—and ultimately redemptive—paradox of the society of the spectacle thus takes shape in the gap between image and body:

> Never has the human body—above all the female body—been so massively manipulated as today and, so to speak, imagined from top to bottom by the techniques of advertising and commodity production: The opacity of sexual differences has been belied by the transsexual body; the incommunicable foreignness of the singular *physis* has been abolished by its mediatization as spectacle; the mortality of the organic body has been put in question by its traffic with the body without organs of commodities; the intimacy of erotic life has been refuted by pornography. *And yet* the process of technologization, instead of materially investing the body, was aimed at the construction of a separate sphere that had practically no point of contact with it: What was technologized was not the body but its image. (50, emphasis added)

The force of this "and yet" could not be clearer[xxxvi]: because it has so insistently invested the image as a wholesale prosthesis for the body, capitalism has left open a line of flight beyond it. This line of flight is the potentiality for reinvesting the body, reinvesting it beyond the categories of the spectacle (identity)—the potentiality, in short, for investing in the body's potentiality.

Relocating the Remains responds to this largely unprecedented opportunity by staging a confrontation with the image through which this line of flight can be rediscovered—by compelling its viewers to grasp *within themselves* this crucial gap between image and body. The affective confusion it brokers serves to catalyze a radical reconfiguration of the self beyond identity, its reconfiguration as a self rooted in the potentiality of the body, as a self essentially "out of phase" with itself.

Such being-out-of-phase with itself is, of course, the phenomenological correlate of Gilbert Simondon's conceptualization of individuation as an ongoing process continuously stretched between the domain of preindividual metastability and the never fully achieved constitution of the individual.[xxxvii] By offering an account of embodied life as an ongoing materialization of the human on the cusp between the individual and the preindividual, the actual and the potential,[xxxviii] Simondon's work thus fills in Agamben's purely formal conceptualization of the coming community, a "community without presuppositions and without subjects," with a concrete account of how collective individuation takes place. If it thereby furnishes the ontological basis for singularity beyond identity, it also puts to concrete use the potential that Agamben associates with life. Because it necessarily involves the disindividuation of the individual, collective individuation (transindividuation) taps what remains preindividual, improper, potential, "within" the human.[xxxix]

Given our interest in Piper's technically facilitated catalysis of affectivity as the "medium" for realizing postidentitarian communion, we cannot but find Simondon's theory of individuation fundamental. By conceptualizing affectivity as the experience, *within the individual*, of the preindividual, of its proper excess over itself (its impropriety), Simondon positions affectivity as the phenomenological correlate of singularity beyond identity. As Simondon develops it in *L'Individuation Psychique et Collective*, affectivity is that mode of bodily experience which mediates between the individual and the preindividual, the personal and the impersonal. Whereas perception appeals to structures already constituted in the interior of the individuated being,

> affectivity indicates and comprises this relation between the individualized being and preindividual reality: it is thus to a certain extent heterogeneous in relation to individualized reality, and appears to bring it something from the exterior, indicating to the individualized

being that it is not a complete and closed set [*ensemble*] of reality. (Simondon, *L'Individuation*, 108)

Affectivity thus furnishes the basis for a reconfiguration of singularity beyond identity (which Simondon names the "subject"): "the problem of the subject is that of the heterogeneity between perceptual worlds and the affective world, between the individual and the preindividual; this problem is that of the subject *as* subject [*en tant que sujet*]: the subject is individual and other than individual; it is incompatible with itself" (108).

Because it is incompatible, indeed, out of phase, with itself—because it is a subject of, and also subject to, affectivity—the subject (the human being) *must* participate in collective life. Collectivity—the experience of the common beyond identity—comprises the opportunity for the subject to coincide with itself: "the subject can coincide with itself only in the individuation of the collective, because the individuated being and the preindividual being that are in it cannot coincide directly" (108). It is, in short, affectivity that calls into being commonality beyond identity. Affectivity is the catalyst for collective individuation (or transindividuation), understood, as we have seen, as a distinct individuation, an individuation at a higher level that is not reducible to any set of individual individuations. Affectivity, in sum, furnishes the possibility for a "resonance" beyond or beneath the category of the individual (identity).

When Agamben invokes individuation as a concept of the subject adequate to the "absolute indetermination, [the] absolute indiscernibility between internal politics and exterior politics" that has, in the wake of the Gulf war and Yugoslavia, formed a "new figure of domination,"[11] he would seem to be acknowledging the need for just such a materialization of the impropriety constitutive of singularity beyond identity. As Agamben understands it, individuation serves to mediate the personal and the impersonal as two phases that are always in relation even though they are clearly separated:

> One could call the impersonal the order of the impersonal power [*puissance*] with which all life is in relation. And one could call desubjectivation this experience that one has every day of bordering on [*cotoyer*] an impersonal power, something which both exceeds [*dépasse*] us and makes us live. Hence ... the question of the art of living would be: how to be in relation [*en rapport*] with this impersonal power. How will the subject learn to be in relation with a power that does not belong to it, that exceeds it? (9)

Not surprisingly, the answer is: through affectivity[xxxx]—and not simply through the "use" of affectivity to keep ourselves open as subjects beyond the lure of identity-positions and figures of individuality, but, more fundamentally, through an *exposure* of affectivity insofar as it is *the essential impropriety, the utter singularity, common to us all.*

We can now discern how Piper's politicization of affect responds to and transforms racial politics. As a catalyst for precisely such an exposure, Piper's complex strategy addresses the contemporary reality of technologized racialization which, in a sense, can be said to derive its power from its appropriation of the force of the (visible) raced image. At the moment when the raced image has been emptied of its promise as the signifier of a positive difference (recall the hypervisibility of a black sports figure like Michael Jordan), it has become brutally effective as the signifier of racism. I would suggest that this coincidence is not in fact a coincidence and that the current proliferation of racializing (and racist) techniques—including surveillance, profiling, and facial identification—can be linked directly to the emptiness of the (visible) raced image.

Stripped of any positive meaning for the subjects that it would mark, the raced image can function all the more effectively as an instrument of control. Without power to interpellate subjects as raced subjects, the raced image can no longer broker processes of identify formation and struggles for social recognition and, in effect, remains in force solely as an instrument of social techniques for identification, classification, and exclusion. The result is a profound paradox of our contemporary moment: the subjects targeted by these racist techniques can only misrecognize themselves in the images that, for this reason, manage all the more effectively to exert their violence upon them. Is this not just an updating of the "corporeal malediction" that Fanon describes?

Building upon and moving beyond the eclipse of visibility at stake in the online generalization of passing, Piper's work takes up the challenge posed by this paradox. Piper seizes the empty husk of the raced image, not to rehabilitate it against capitalist fetishism, but to extract its redemptive kernel. In the various ways we have explored, he deploys this empty image as the catalyst for a reinvestment of embodiment beyond the image, for an exposure of the rootedness of life in a source—affectivity—that lies beyond identity and individuality and thus beyond the reach of commodification.

If Piper's work manages, even for an instant, to expose the bare singularity, the common impropriety, that binds us beyond identification, and if it does so for potentially any viewer, then it can be understood as a form of resistance to the principle informing today's technologized racism: the notion that human beings can (and should) be classified through categories of social visibility. Such resistance takes shape not as an external struggle by an oppressed group, but rather as a collective individuation rooted in the exposure of the affective basis of life, the excess of bodily life in relation to itself.

wearable space

Today's wearables ... might listen to you talk, watch your gestures, and sense changes in your heart rate, blood pressure, and electrodermal response ... emotion modulates not just autonomic nervous system activity, but the whole body—how it moves, speaks, gestures; almost any bodily signal might be analyzed for clues to the wearer's affective state. Signals that currently require physical contact to sense, such as electromyogram and skin conductivity, are especially well-suited to wearable technology. (Rosalind Picard[1])

Just as we can use an array of pixels to create any image we please within the confines of a screen, or a three-dimensional array of voxels to create any form within the confines of an overall volume, so we can create a precise sense-shape with an array or volume of appropriate sensels. Such a shape would be exact, but invisible, a region of activated, hypersensitive space. (Marcos Novak[2])

Let these citations stand for the two "poles" circumscribing current conceptions of wearable and ubiquitous computing. On one extreme, we encounter a sober, technical, yet nonetheless exciting prospect for a hitherto unimaginable fluidity between human body and computer: an extension of the body that takes advantage of the rich panoply of bodily signals and internal regulatory processes. On the other extreme, we brush against a visionary, perhaps truly alien, projection of a complete fluidity between body and space: a mutual embedding of both in the primary "medium" of sensation. What I am calling "wearable space" results from the superposition of these two poles: *space* becomes *wearable* when embodied affectivity becomes the operator of spacing.

Neither in itself sufficient to theorize wearable space, affective computing and the aesthetics of eversion foreground crucial components of this concept. The former emphasizes the superiority of an affective basis of interface between computer and body; the latter demonstrates how space is intimately correlated with sensory capacities of the body and yet also infinitely flexible and convertible through these same capacities. Each, that is, foregrounds in its own way the creativity of the affective body—the role of the body as at once a *source* for and *activator* of a rich affective constitution of space.

My aim in this chapter is to fill out this picture of wearable space by delving further into what happens when the body "spaces the formless," to borrow a phrase from architect Peter Eisenman.[3] If the defining material cultural shift of our time—the shift to the digital—has suspended the framing function performed by the (preconstituted) technical image (as I have argued in *New Philosophy for New Media*), then the task of clarifying the nature and extent of the coupling of body and space is particularly crucial at this moment in our coevolution with technology. The body—or rather, embodiment, the process through which bodies are produced—comprises the selective background on which information can be framed. Embodiment, accordingly, takes on a truly unprecedented responsibility: the responsibility of constraining and thereby specifying the process through which informational "objects"—images, space, events—are actually generated.

To understand how architecture is implicated in this new regime of embodied framing of information, let us consider a recent suggestion that architecture has dethroned cinema as the quintessential art of framing for our time. In *Earth Moves: the Furnishing of Territories*, architect and philosopher Bernard Cache boldly asserts the singular privilege of architectural images as the "urban texture that enfolds all other images." Cache defines architecture as

> the manipulation of one of these elementary images, namely, the frame. Architecture, the art of the frame, would then not only concern those specific objects that are buildings, but would refer to any image involving any element of framing, which is to say painting as well as cinema, and certainly many other things.[4]

Following Cache, could we not say that architecture, as *the* art of the frame, forms a correlate to embodiment, as the operator of framing, such that all embodied framing is, necessarily, architectural, and all architecture is, likewise, necessarily embodied? To what extent, indeed, does architecture's privilege as the generic art of framing stem from the fact that architectural framing unavoidably entails a negotiation among formal manipulation, built space, and embodied life? Unlike cinema and any other technical art in which framing is built into an apparatus, and unlike painting, in which the frame forms a material precondition, architectural framing occurs as a process that is contemporaneous with its reception or consumption. That is precisely why we can say that it is intrinsically (rather than contingently) embodied.

This correlation of architectural framing and embodiment entails a certain understanding of architecture's technical dimension: architecture in the digital age must do more than simply deploy the technical capacities of the computer in an effort to overcome constraints of form dictated by the properties of architecture's raw material. This is partly because buildings—even digitally designed buildings—must still be built; more fundamentally though, it is because they must still be inhabited, which is to say, calibrated to our embodied form of life. No amount of freedom from formal constraint can undo architecture's constitutive correlation with embodiment, even if it can shift the locus of embodiment from the pregiven materiality of architecture to the embodied experience of inhabitation triggered by built form.

Indeed, the more digitally deterritorialized the architectural frame is, the more central the body becomes as the framer of spatial information, as the source of its "autonomy" or "interiority," following the conceptualization of the formalist critics of the 1970s. Just as the body assumes a renewed importance in the aftermath of the digital explosion of the technical frame, so too does it counterbalance the digital dissolution of spatial form, offering an indirect and supplementary—but no less fundamental—means to couple deformation and inhabitation, formal play and real life. For this reason, architecture must reconceive its function for the digital age: as the art of framing *par excellence*, it must embrace its potential to bring space and body together in the creation of "wearable space."

To the extent that this vocation involves a double dematerialization—of architecture as built form and of embodiment as static body or rigidly bounded organism—architectural framing might be said to furnish a generic body-in-code as a strict correlate to the rematerialization I am here proposing to name wearable space. While wearable space designates the becoming-fluid of spatial form that results from the imbrication of architectural framing and embodiment, body-in-code names the

177

disembodiment–re-embodiment that ensues from this same imbrication. Wearable space is to architecture what body-in-code is to embodiment. Accordingly, if architecture *is* indeed the art of framing par excellence, is not its embodied correlate—the architecturally triggered body-in-code—in fact the generic form of embodiment, the process of disembodiment–re-embodiment that encompasses all other instances (including those we have focused on thus far) in which the body is distributed beyond its organic boundaries?

1. ENCOUNTERING THE BLUR

You slowly proceed down a hill toward an amorphous, cloudlike mass looming above the lake beneath you (see Figure 4.1). At the end of a long, narrow bridge heading off across the lake in front of you and terminating in the middle of what you can now discern to be a huge clump of fog suspended over the water, you come to a "log-in station," where you are invited to fill out a brief survey consisting of twenty more or less personal questions. Upon turning this in, you are handed a heavy translucent raincoat that, you are told, has been programmed with your

FIGURE 4.1 Elizabeth Diller + Ricardo Scofidio, view of log-in station, *Blur Building* (2002). (Courtesy of the artists.)

FIGURE 4.2 Elizabeth Diller + Ricardo Scofidio, view of fog-immersed interior of *Blur Building*. (Courtesy of the artists.)

"profile." Excited and a bit flustered, you hastily don the raincoat as you walk onto the narrow bridge and toward the dense mass of fog looming in front of you.

As you gradually become enveloped by the vaporous surround emitted from the fog mass, you lose visual and aural contact with the terrestrial environment you have just left and begin to immerse yourself in a cool zone made up of soft sounds of water spray and the semi-sweet smell of vapor. Upon reaching the end of the narrow bridge, you enter a space of indeterminate size, comprised entirely (or so it seems to you) of incredibly dense fog continuously billowing out all around you. Nestled into a densely packed, tactilely palpable, almost viscous medium in which the only thing you can sense with certainty is your body, you are struck by a vaguely uncomfortable feeling of constriction (see Figure 4.2).

Yet, you soon become accustomed to this oddly materialized space and, as you do so, you begin to perceive a forest of vertical red and green lights around you. Moving close to one of these lights, you notice that they are LED columns scrolling suggestive adjectives like "obsessive" and "passionate" which, you cannot help feel, are eerily apt descriptions of your personality. You notice too that your raincoat has started to glow with a faint blue-green hue; you also perceive a muffled ping reverberating at regular intervals and, as you concentrate on the sound, you realize that it is coming from your coat.

Feeling more and more at home in this weird, sensorily inverted world, you start to walk in the direction of a smaller, moving red light off in the distance. As you do so, the pinging noise emanating from your coat becomes more rapid and grows louder. Momentarily flustered by this, you look down at your coat and when you look up again, you see the blurred outlines of another person move toward you; you stop and, as you do, you notice that the red glow surrounding this person is becoming more intense as the distance between you diminishes. Excited and also a bit frightened, you perceive suddenly that the blue-green hue of your coat has become a red glow that is also gradually intensifying. Recalling the instructions you distractedly read at the log-in center, you realize that this person is someone whose profile bears affinity with yours. What flashes instantly to your mind is whether you will have the courage to talk to this person when he reaches you; overcoming your natural inclination to flee into the now altogether inviting neutrality of the fog, you steel yourself for contact.

Almost immediately, you find yourself face to face with this anonymous other, literally unable to look away from the intense red glow pervading the space between your respective raincoats. As if obeying the same program, you and your blurry interlocutor turn away at the same moment and, as your heart rate gradually slows, you attune yourself once again to the now decreasingly rapid and softer pinging noise, which, you realize in a flash, was also an index of your affinity to the other.

Making your way through the thicket of vertical LED columns looming at regular intervals out of the fog, you come to a stairway leading upwards and, as you ascend the stairs, you climb up out of the fog onto an observation deck (see Figure 4.3). There you are treated to breathtakingly clear views of land on one side and lake on the other. Reminiscent of an airplane's abrupt emergence from out of the clouds, this ascent restores the predominant function of vision in your sensory ecology and in so doing brings some much needed relief from the intense sensory demands of the fog environment. Still, after some time relaxing on this "Angel Deck," you find yourself drawn back to the vaporous surround oozing just beneath you.

Almost immediately upon redescending into the fog, the sonar ping from your coat becomes quite furious in its rhythm and you see a bright red blotch of color in front of you; stopping in anticipation of another face-to-face encounter with another anonymous "soulmate," you are altogether flabbergasted to find your entire body vibrating in response to what, you quickly discern, is a tactile reaction by your raincoat. Stunned by the intensity of this experience, you race back toward

FIGURE 4.3 Elizabeth Diller + Ricardo Scofidio, birds-eye view of observation deck, *Blur Building*. (Courtesy of the artists and www.beatwidmer.com.)

the exit. Stepping onto the exit ramp, you scurry to shore, shedding your raincoat and hurriedly taking a password that will allow you to access your experience from the comfort and safe distance of your home.

The experience just described is based on the original project proposal for Liz Diller and Ricardo Scofidio's *Blur Building*, a project developed for the Swiss Expo 2001 in Yverdon-les-Bains, Switzerland.[i] An architectural project for a building made of water, *Blur Building* is intended to undermine our ordinary sensory interface with the environment and with architecture by putting vision more or less out of play. The result, as you have just experienced, is a compelling attempt to engage other, less used sensory modalities—proprioception, tactility, hearing—in the task of navigating bodily through space.

The infrastructure of the *Blur Building* is an edifice 100 m wide by 65 m deep by 25 m high that is cantilevered up from the lake below and that forms the base out of which the mist cloud is projected as well as support for the Angel Deck observation platform. The mist cloud is produced by an artificial fog-making system that filters lake water into a dense array of high-pressure water nozzles regulated by computer and adjusted to actual weather conditions in the surrounding environment. The resulting fog mass is, as the architects put it, "a dynamic form that combines natural and artificial weather forces."[5] Into this dynamic mass is integrated a media environment whose function, again according to the architects, is to interweave architecture and electronic technologies, exchanging the properties of each for the other. Through the use of sophisticated technologies that "would be entirely invisible, leaving only their effects, … architecture would dematerialize and electronic media, normally ephemeral, would become palpable in space" (*Blur*, 44).

Fused with architecture in this way, electronic media are relocated from a high-definition context to a low-definition one, with the result that their typical and deeply rooted correlation with the sense of vision is almost wholly suspended: "The fog mass is primarily an experience of visual interference, thus the reliance on vision competes with *Blur's* most notable characteristic, obscurity" (195). Embracing this fact as a challenge for the project, the architects view the *Blur Building* as a kind of machine for "rebalancing the senses"; specifically, it furnishes an "immersive environment in which the world is put out of focus so that our visual dependency can be put into focus" (195). Beyond exposing the imbalance of our habitual sensory ecology, the project aims to substitute for the "focused attention of a visual spectacle" an alternative: the "attentuated attention of an immersive acoustic encounter" (198).

To this end, the architects structure disorientation into the *Blur* experience and equip the impaired, visually dependent visitor with a "braincoat," a raincoat with embedded technologies that forms "an acoustical prosthesis" to the body's natural system of navigation. Rather than forming a preexistent architectural ground for experience, the *Blur Building* can be said to result from the actual navigation of bodies inside the cloud of fog. The acoustically guided movement of prosthetically enhanced, blind bodies in a nonspace creates an *architecture of nothing*, an architecture that is as much *in* the bodily experiences as it is *in* the acoustic and tactile mappings of space which they trace.

Here, in sum and in an altogether literal sense, space is made wearable. Divorced from any fixed spatial form, space is directly coupled to the movement and experience of bodies. Less a "building" than a "pure atmosphere," the *Blur Building* is, as the architects put it, a "habitable medium," (325, 162). Yet, even as it integrates the two dimensions of wearable space I enumerated earlier—the prosthetic extension of the body's contact with the environment and the affection of space as a medium of sensation—the *Blur Building* opens up some crucial questions that deserve further examination. How exactly does what takes place inside the body—the triggering of affective, proprioceptive, and tactile dimensions of experience—contribute to the constitution of space in the *Blur* experience? Why does the *epoché* of the visual through the deployment of a dynamic amorphous fog mass engage an alternate spatial sense and with it an entirely different kind of space? What is it about the body that allows it to use the sensory excess of its movement in this nonspace to generate a profoundly intensive spatial experience? Finally, what is it about space—or better, about its contemporary conjunction with media—that permits it to be so fluidly worn?

2. THE ARCHITECTURAL BODY

Wearable space emerges out of the interlacing of body and architectural space. Nowhere has this interlacing been given better expression than in Japanese-American artist Arakawa's concept of the "architectural body." Defined, simply, as the conjunction of the "body proper" and the "architectural surround," this concept is meant to capture the recursive correlation literally intertwining the body with space. For Arakawa and his constant collaborator, Madeleine Gins, this correlation informs the very origin of the body:

> If the body is born into architecture and is from then on inextricable from it, why not take it up in its full scope as an "architectural body" (the body proper plus the architectural surround)?... If the basic unit of concern is the body, not an abstract body considered apart from impulses and movement, but the body in action, then will not the concepts most central to the living of a life be those formed—no matter how fleetingly—through architectural encounters?[6]

In sum, because the body always is a body in space—or better, a spatializing body—it is by necessity an architectural body. Starting from the position that having a body includes having a world, Arakawa and Gins elaborate a theory of world constitution through landing sites. Defined as "spots at which stimuli for and effects of sensory modalities ... are positioned" (157), landing sites express the field of action connecting a body with space:

> "The fabric of the world consists of a multitude, a plenitude, of sites.... Landing sites occur as a perceiver's perception, whatever that might be, lands *here* and *there* as the world.... A landing site is simultaneously an event and an event-marker. The concept of landing site

183

is basically a heuristic device for mapping how a person forms the world and situates herself within it.[7]

Landing sites are the concrete ways in which the body actively couples with space. Despite the emphasis on perception in the preceding passage, the world is in fact composed of three distinct types of landing site, each of which is integral to its constitution. *Perceptual* landing sites register the particular qualities of *heres* and *theres*, *imaging* landing sites fill in the gaps between areas of perceptual capture, and *architectural* landing sites afford an intimation of position.

In developing their concept of the architectural body, Arakawa and Gins have increasingly come to emphasize the role of nonperceptual, and especially, imaging, landing sites. Imaging landing sites form the necessary multisensory background within which any reality-conferring act of perception must be situated:

> A full picture or view of the world, the total *event-map* of what goes on in daily living, requires the collaboration of an imaging capability or imaging landing sites to fill in the gaps between perceptual points or areas of focus.... Imaging landing sites "generalize" the world.... without even an indeterminate size, ... they fall into line with whatever perceptual and architectural landing sites sketch out. Imaging landing sites act as amorphous accordings of more information in the cause of perception than is available at one glance.... By definition shapeless, imaging landing sites are, nonetheless, shape-defining, for without them the world would be made mostly of holes. (20)

Imaging landing sites, in short, are responsible for rendering space potentially embodied or "embodiable," for imbuing it with a sensory richness that catalyzes bodily response.

That is why Arakawa and Gins can insist that "tactile-imaging landing sites register texture or near-texture in the world at large" and that "kinesthetic-imaging landing sites confer on the world at large some of how it feels to be a kinesthetic-proprioceptive body" (*Reversible Destiny*, 157). More than simply the extension of a perception of a *here* or *there* to alternative variant perceptions, imaging landing sites render space affective. In the case of kinesthetic imaging, for example, a "kinesthetic spillover" occurs whereby the "body, through imaging, lends to all it perceives a modicum of kinesthetic endowment" (158). This capacity of the body to affect space is largely responsible for the fact that the world is *not* "kinesthetically neutral," but always already endowed with the

184

"kinesthetic context and feel of [the] sensoria" of embodied perceivers (159).

With this conception of space animated by the projections of the body—and not simply those which the body specifically perceives and intends, Arakawa and Gins expand the affective body beyond the bounds of Henri Bergson's seminal account. Bergson argued that perception, rather than being a spiritual activity that added something to the material world, was in actuality a result of material diminution: the subtraction, from the universe of images, of precisely those that are relevant to a particular body or "center of indetermination." According to Bergson, this subtraction is necessarily informed by the affection of the body, such that there can be no perception without affection.[ii] Yet, although Bergson understood affection to be a bodily correlate necessarily accompanying any act of perception, the affection of space by the body—and specifically by the body's imaging capability or imaging landing sites—projects affectivity *beyond the physical–physiological confines of the body*.

Such a projection yields what Bernard Cache (following Husserl) has called the "longitudinal" dimension of embodied perception:

> Perception consists of two parts that could be called frontal and logitudinal. The frontality of perceived images would result from their action being suspended with respect to us; from the break between their solicitation and our reaction—an interval between our automatisms. The second part would then be longitudinal as we constantly expose ourselves to out-of-body images in order to always redefine the present of our perception or the variable horizon of our contractile body. According to the frontal component, we see clear articulations drawn between the objects that solicit the reactions of our solid body; while longitudinally, each of these images continually interacts with the others and with us, as in a test of resonance. For we must produce the tone of our present in order to adjust the horizon of our contractile body and find the right pitch. Unlike the great frontal articulations, our longitudinal perception constantly folds and rubs the fabric of images against itself, thus allowing the texture of things to emerge. (147)

With this beautiful image of a perceiving body nurtured by the rich texture of images surrounding it, Cache expresses the importance of a tactile and affective background to perception. As he sees it, perception cannot merely designate the virtual action of the body upon things, as if it existed in a vacuum, but must also somehow integrate

185

the larger "milieu" of interactions within which the body necessarily finds itself located and which it experiences more as a tactile than a visual sensation.[iii] Accordingly, the body's capacity to act is never simply a property it possesses in isolation; it is always a recursive and constantly modulated function of its embeddedness within a rich "texture of sensation."

In Arakawa and Gins' terminology, the body can be said to experience the longitudinal dimension through its imaging capability. This, however, means that the longitudinal dimension is always in recursive correlation with the imaging body so that, to matter, space must enter the "variable horizon" of the body's imaging landing sites. The strict recursivity linking space and body informs the radical purpose to which Arakawa and Gins apply architecture: namely, throwing the body out of balance. Radical architecture furnishes architectural landing sites that challenge the body's "habitual and deadening" submission to "spacetime" or space as "objective" geometric extension. What makes this possible is the capacity for the organization of space—conditioned, as it is, by the body—to destabilize the body's perceptual landing sites and thereby to call into play the body's normally imperceptible imaging landing sites. By altering the body's typical architectural landing sites, radical architecture perturbs the body, compelling it to draw on its "longitudinal" sense of space in order to right itself.

That is why the two methods of subverting the body's submission to spacetime—"to cause an overload of the familiar by putting surroundings forward in a manner so concentrated that they wax unfamiliar; and to have the body be so greatly and so persistently thrown off balance that the majority of its efforts have to go entirely towards the righting of itself"—are, in the end, *necessarily* complements of one another (*Architecture*, 8). It is also why, at bottom, all architectural landing sites are "hybrid—in part a perceptual and in part an imaging landing site" (21). By short-circuiting the body's perceptual grasp of space, architecture compels the body to concentrate on recalibrating itself as the correlate of its longitudinal imaging landing sites.

Arakawa and Gins' *Ubiquitous Site* ▪ *Nagi's Ryoanji* ▪ *Architectural Body* (1992–1994) submits its inhabitants to precisely this two-part recalibration of the body. The first of Arakawa and Gins' large-scale architectural surrounds, this work comprises a cylindrical building, 70 ft in length and 30 ft in diameter, which constitutes one-third of the Nagi Museum of Contemporary Art. *Ubiquitous Site* is quite literally a

FIGURE 4.4 Arakawa and Madeleine Gins, *Ubiquitous Site ▪ Nagi's Ryoanji ▪ Architectural Body* (1992–1994), view inside cylinder. (Courtesy of the artists, K. Furudate, and the Solomon Guggenheim Museum of Art.)

piece of architecture that refuses to recognize the vertical conventions of architecture: rather than a floor and ceiling surrounded by walls, the piece juxtaposes two sets of symmetrical surfaces, which flow more or less seamlessly into one another (see Figure 4.4). On the bottom and the top is a curved concrete "floor" equipped with a see-saw, a bench, and a metal bar; on the two sides are rock gardens set into sand.

FIGURE 4.5 Arakawa and Madeleine Gins, *Critical Resemblances House*, Site of Reversible Destiny—Yoro, Gifu Prefecture, Japan (1993–1995). (Courtesy of the artists, Mitsukiko Suzuki for NHK Technologies, and the Solomon Guggenheim Museum of Art.)

Further exploration reveals another symmetry set into this space because the large restraining wall running along one border of each transition from concrete "floor" to sand "wall" diagonally divides the entire space into two mirror-image segments. Insofar as the respective symmetries built into this space exist in internal tension with one another, they place architectural landing sites within the space that function precisely to catalyze a shift from the body's habitual perceptual grasp of space as extended to an imaging or longitudinal grasp of space as affective. Here, architecture is deployed in a most radical manner: its pregiven spatial conventions are dissolved in favor of a variant deployment of gravity, one that constitutes space through the body's self-recalibration.

Yet another example, the *Critical Resemblances House* (1985–1986), makes even clearer why imaging landing sites (and longitudinal perception) are instrumental to the forging of the architectural body (see Figure 4.5). Once again, the operative mechanism is a superposition of alternate spatial projections which functions to destabilize the body's perceptual grasp of space and trigger its self-recalibration through "alternate landing site configurations" made possible "by means of imaging landing sites" (*Reversible Destiny*, 154). The first of Arakawa and Gins' reversible destiny houses, *Critical Resemblances House* is composed of three levels of "reworked labyrinth" (defined as "groups of labyrinth-derived patterns of wall segments"). These levels include a rectilinear group placed on top of two curvilinear ones: one on the ground level and another in the basement.

Entering into this edifice consisting "primarily of entrances," the body is "invited to move through composite passageways—rectilinear above, curvilinear below—often in two opposing ways at once" (258). In phenomenological terms, this results in a radical deceleration of the body's passage through space because the normal perceptually guided negotiation of space yields to a longitudinal exploration that infolds imaging potential directly into the bodily constitution of space. "It could take several hours to go from the living room to the kitchen," claims the project description. "Parts of the kitchen or the living room reappear in the bedroom or the bathroom. It might take several days to find everywhere in the house that the dining room turns up" (258). In the end, this radical deployment of architecture catalyzes nothing short of a shift in the function of space: the process of passing through perceived space yields to that of dwelling with the imaging potential of space, what Arakawa and Gins aptly gloss as the "underside of things" (259).

Arakawa and Gins' architectural experiments thus expose the bodily source of architecture in its most extreme, indeed, bare form: for them, architecture comprises nothing short of an opportunity to alter "habitual and deadening" patterns of thought by soliciting the site where these patterns originate—namely, the body as imaging potentiality. Architecture, Arakawa and Gins bluntly state, "exists to provide landing sites" (*Architecture*, 121). That is why, ultimately, all architecture comes from the body: "What generates landing sites? The movement and power of the body. Through where does the body fall? Not through spacetime but through landing sites. In what does architecture have its origin? In the movements and exertions of body" (150).

By tapping the potential of bodily movement to create new landing sites, architecture supports the body's concretization of spacetime, its giving of time and space as the foundation for all real experience. Arakawa and Gins' work proffers many permutations of this technical exteriorization of embodiment. Consider, for example, the *Trench House*, which "accommodates and embodies the body's endless desire to draw close and be in rapport with virtually everything" (105). Consider *Reversible Destiny House I*, which offers a means for "a person to have a sense of her own extent" (99). Or, consider *Double-Horizon Public Housing*, designed to demonstrate the maxim that "to form the body endlessly is the purpose of the city" (121). In all of these cases, architecture is built out of the body; it comprises an instrument to tap the body's capacity to constitute space.

By positioning the body as the hinge that renders all space (potentially) architectural, Arakawa and Gins furnish a grounding point that will prove crucial as we explore the impact of digital design technology on space and, specifically, on the potential for space to become wearable. Their work foregrounds the role of the body as the "converter" of force into affect, thereby installing the infralinguistic, indeed infratactile, body at the very core of architectural framing.

The internal complexity of the infralinguistic body, following philosopher José Gil's conception, is precisely what informs its capacity for imaging or longitudinal perception. According to Gil, as we have seen in Chapter 1, the infralinguistic body (which, importantly, is different from the body as a biological, existential, or phantasmatic unity) mediates all forms of social power, including spatial organization and language; it does so not as a passive inscriptional surface, as in the early work of Foucault and the majority of today's theorists of the performative or socially constructed body, but rather as a wielder of power in its own right.[iv] Because its processing or conversion of force into affect is responsible for all meaning in the world, the infralinguistic body is instrumental in the production of all forms of social power.

As a contribution to the conceptualization of wearable space, Gil's work shows specifically how and why the body must be understood to be the source for the spatiality of space. By "exfoliating" itself into its concrete environment, the body creates spatiality as something like a field of energy:

> It is only through abstract form that information resulting from the spatialization of space is integrated. Because of its anatomical and physiological structure, the human body encodes information through its sense organs in a particular way. The form that this information takes is not, therefore, that of the perceived object (taken "in itself"), but also depends on the structure of the body. In this sense, infralanguage acts as a primary encoder, ... organizing multiple and diverse sensuality into a unitary form. ... perception thus depends on the body organizing space in a certain way. Bodily space is the product of the double investment of the body by space (the information coming from the physical world) and the investment of space by the

body (as a certain kind of receiver–encoder of this information).... The space of the body is made of plates, exfoliations, surfaces, and volumes that underpin the perception of things. These spaces "contain" the relations of the body to things, insofar as they are integrated in the body itself and insofar as they are translated among themselves. (130/129)[8]

This spatializing power of the body exemplifies the more general capacity of the infralanguage to decode forces into affects, to convert information originating in the material environment into meaningful experiences—experiences capable of affecting the body.[v] Because it posits the conjunction of "body proper" and "architectural surround" as the effect of a more fundamental indifferentiation between bodily exfoliation and spatial information, Gil's conception of the spatializing power of the body explains the mechanism for Arakawa and Gins' architectural body. More precisely, it restores a complex balance to the conception of the architectural body, making this latter not so much the result of a subordination of architecture to the body as a figure for the co-origination and coevolution of body and space.

3. THE "INTERIORITY" OF ARCHITECTURE

Among contemporary figures in architecture, Peter Eisenman, more than anyone else, has insisted on the irreducibility of embodiment in architecture. From his early theoretical engagement with what he termed the "motivatedness of the architectural sign" to his recent concern with "reading affective relationships in the somatic experience" of architecture, Eisenman has struggled with the embodied constraints endemic to architecture. Within the trajectory of this struggle, the digital occupies a privileged place. The formal liberation facilitated by digital design techniques fundamentally reconfigures the correlation of architecture and embodiment, transforming what originated as an indelible material constraint cosubstantial with the "architectural sign" into a dynamic aspect of the architectural framing of space. By means of a digital conversion, Eisenman's concern with the intrinsic embodiment of architecture has morphed into an embrace of the (human) body as, to borrow Gil's terminology, a converter of (spatial) forces into embodied affects.

To understand the significance of this transformation—and to appreciate why it renders Eisenman a singular figure among contemporary digitally-inspired architects—we need to revisit Eisenman's career-instigating insight into the specificity of the architectural sign. It is fairly well known, if little understood, that Eisenman distinguishes the architectural sign from all other regimes of signs on account of its "motivatedness"—the fact that it not only serves as a sign, but always also embodies its architectural meaning or function. The architectural sign can be considered to be motivated because the "sign and signified are one and the same thing":

> In architecture, a structural element such as a column is both a real column and the sign of a column. In language, on the other hand, the word *apple* is the sign of a real apple, but the real apple is also the sign of something else, such as the "Big Apple" or the sign of temptation in the Garden of Eden. There is already a metaphoric and therefore representational condition in the object *apple* that reaches beyond the object itself. Thus the real apple has both a conventional relationship to the sign *apple* and also becomes a sign of this other metaphoric relationship. Unlike the real apple, which is removed from its sign, the physical *column* is simultaneously an object and the sign of the object. It is a more complex reality than the apple. Initially because the column is a sign of itself, it can be considered as an indexical sign in that it receives its motivation from an internal, prior condition—the interiority of its being.[9]

Unlike the linguistic sign, which acquires a degree of freedom and creativity from the nonidentity of its referential and signifying functions, the architectural sign is constrained by a conflation of reference and signification, by the fact that it is what it signifies. A column or a wall is unavoidably a column or a wall—a material structural element of architecture—at the same time that it is a sign of that structural element within the discursive system of architecture.

This special status of the architectural sign holds an altogether ambivalent status for Eisenman; it is at once the material constraint architecture must struggle against *and* the condition of its identity as a cultural practice. It is only by bearing this ambivalence in mind that we will be able to grasp the complexity of what emerges as the key term of Eisenman's theory: namely, the "interiority" of architecture. Variously configured at different times during Eisenman's long career, this term accords architecture a kind of internal, though certainly evolving, unity and includes among its most important elements the "targets" of Eisenman's early practice: most notably, the geometric grid and the notion of grounding.

Indeed, Eisenman's career—at least up to the point when he began to deploy digital design techniques—can be summarized as a directed struggle against these elements of architectural interiority. In his House projects and his early institutional commissions, Eisenman's aim was to confront specific elements of that interiority in order to transform them from within—to preserve their architectural specificity in the very act of critiquing and modifying their signifying potential.

The advent of digital design in architecture punctuates Eisenman's ongoing struggle with the evolving interiority of architecture in a most significant way: it allows Eisenman to refunctionalize embodiment entirely, transforming it from an indelible aspect of the architectural sign (hence a kind of negative, if enabling, constraint) into an agent in the experience of architecture (hence a creative capacity rooted in the bodily spacing of architecture). This theoretical displacement from the embodiment *of the architectural object* to embodiment *in the experience of architecture* is signaled by a shift in Eisenman's ambivalence toward interiority. In the earlier, "predigital" phase of his career, Eisenman tended to view interiority as a problem to be deconstructed; in the aftermath of the digital revolution, by contrast, his emphasis falls squarely on defending interiority as that which gives architecture its material specificity.

Nowhere does this shift appear more pronounced than in Eisenman's criticism of the currently ascendant generation of younger architects, many of whom he helped to train:

> Reacting against an understanding of the diagram that characterized it as an apparently essentialist tool, a new generation, fueled by new computer techniques and a desire to escape its perceived Oedipal anxieties ... is today proposing a new theory of the diagram based partly on Gilles Deleuze's interpretation of Foucault's recasting of the diagram as "a series of machinic forces," and partly on their own cybernetic hallucinations.... [This theory] challenges both the traditional geometric bases of the diagram and the sedimented history of architecture, and in so doing ... question[s] any relation of the diagram to architecture's anteriority or interiority. (Diagram, 30)

Odd as it sounds given Eisenman's own theoretical debt to Deleuze in all of his work from the '90s, this criticism must be understood as a retrospective reaffirmation of the architect's basic commitment to interiority, even at those moments when it contradicted his primarily transitional, theoretical attachments.[vi]

What is ultimately at stake in this theoretical *différend* with the younger generation is the potential for affect to play a crucial constructive role in the formal genesis of space and, with it, the potential transformation of architecture into a process of embodied spatializing. For Eisenman, affect is the vehicle for the transfiguration of embodiment, and, as the conclusion of *Diagram Diaries* makes clear, its emergence as *the* crucial element of a new conception of architecture's interiority corresponds to a digitally facilitated metamorphosis of the diagram:

> The diagram has come full circle from the strategies of reading to the tactics of visceral experience. At the same time, the diagram seems to disappear from the built work. In projects such as the Virtual House, the Staten Island Institute, and the IIT student center, it becomes more or less a virtual entity, rather than being made explicit in the projects. This is because the diagram becomes more of an engine in the projects rather than something which transforms itself into a physical reality. The external diagram provided a series of formal relationships and organizations that when given form, structure, and function in an architectural context, *did not permit these forms to be understood as coming from a known interiority—that is, a sedimented relationship between form and function.* Lastly, and perhaps of equal importance, these diagrams shifted the focus of the reading strategy from its origin in formal relationships, and then linguistic and textual relationships, to the possibility of reading affective relationships in the somatic experience itself. (208–209)

In its digital instantiation, the diagram functions precisely to interrupt the conflation of sign and being (or sign and embodiment) that defined architectural interiority for Eisenman. Because it allows form to emerge from an architectural context without its being dictated by architecture's preinscribed interiority, the digital diagram provides nothing less than a vehicle for the transformation of that interiority. Effectively, the forms it generates are spared the condition of having to embody the things of which they are signs and thus freed to be embodied otherwise—that is, for Eisenman at least, to be embodied through the bodily affect that they catalyze.

This shift in the tenor of interiority is, I suggest, just what Eisenman means when he contrasts the indexicality of affect with that of architecture's traditional structural elements: the diagram, he contends,

> attempts to unmotivate place, to find within place space as a void, as a negativity or nonpresence to be filled up with a new figuration of the sign. This new figuration is no longer within a semiotic system

but is rather an index of affect, and, as affect, the void becomes a sign of not-presence, and thus the beginning of the transgression of the metaphysics of presence … (215)

By confronting us with a space that does not signify according to architecture's traditional interiority, diagrammatic "figuration" indexes something else—namely, the body—which it brings into the fold of architecture's spatializing activity. Viewed schematically, the diagrammatic process thus divides into two stages: first, it generates forms which disturb architecture's interiority; second, it triggers an affective reaction in the body that, in a certain sense, fills in the void of interiority left in its wake. If the former stage triggers a crisis of figuration, the latter stage invests the body with the infralinguistic, infratactile capacity to convert the force of this crisis into the somatic experience of affect. It literally produces a body-in-code.

We might say then that Eisenman's interest in the computer is more operational than ontological, that it forms part of his ongoing effort to disrupt the singular "motivatedness" of the architectural sign. "Digital information is a new kind of sign system which is no longer mechanical; it produces the possibilities of separation"—separation, that is, of the sign and its being.[10] Far from being the first "machinic architect," as Alejandro Zaera-Polo has dubbed him,[11] Eisenman might better be considered the first *affective architect*: Not only does he subordinate the function of the computer to the genesis of affective space, but he also correlates affection with the body in a manner that is anathema to the Deleuzean context so central for the younger generation of architects and theorists.

Indeed, Eisenman's subordination of the computer exposes the fundamental limitation of the machinic perspective of the neo-Deleuzeans: their utter failure to account for the specificity of exteriority, to explain how it bears concretely on the embodied experience of architecture. These latter are simply unable to take the crucial "third step":

Neither the process of the machinic nor any computer program can a priori produce such a trope [a trope in architectural space]. This is what young architects, weaned on computers, fail to realize. Computers may produce blobs and other self-generated formless aggregations, but these are in and of themselves not any more architectural than they are graphic or illustrational…. Thus, a third step in the process takes a turn away from an aspect of the machinic, its possibility of extraction, towards its more arbitrary and aleatory nature, by taking the blurred two-dimensional diagram of superpositions and projecting it into the third dimension.[12]

At stake in this "third step" is nothing less than the difference between a formal operation like folding and an interstitial process like spacing. As Eisenman sees it, the machinic perspective of his younger colleagues is insufficient on two, closely related counts: it only deals with the idea of becoming "as a state of the object" and it "does not differentiate between forming and spacing" (21). Because it leaves the traditional subordination of spacing to forming undisturbed, the machinic process is unable to disturb the traditional embodiment of architecture.

By contrast, precisely because it "remains untheorized" and without pregiven "value systems," spacing holds the potential to (re)embody architecture differently:

> In the context of architecture, spacing ... begins to suggest a possible figure/figure relationship which in turn suggests a new possibility for the interstitial. Spacing produces an other condition of the interstitial. The interstitial proposes a dissonant space of meaning. Where figure/ground was an abstraction, figure/figure is a figural condition that is no longer necessarily abstract. It is a space as a matrix of forces and sense. It is affective in that it requires the body ... for its understanding. The interstitial, then, is the result of a process of extraction which produces a figural as opposed to a formal trope, and it exists as a condition of *spacing* as opposed to forming, as a presence in an absence, that is between two conditions of figure as opposed to figure and ground. (32)

Derived from Deleuze's concept of the figural,[vii] Eisenman's conception of spacing transforms the problematic of motivatedness from a restrictive into an enabling constraint, thereby transfiguring the experiential horizon of architecture. As the means of liberating architecture from the task of discovering a figure in the ground, form in the preformed, spacing exposes the forces inhabiting spatial forms and opens them up to an alternate processing by the body—to the bodily conversion into affect that, extending Gil's analysis, we have theorized as the labor of infratactility.

The process of spacing speaks to the singularity of architecture as the quintessential art of framing for our time. Rather than catalyzing the production of an affective space in the body, as the most interesting digital art (arguably) does,[viii] digitally generated architecture marshals the spatializing capacity of the affective body toward the constitution of new kinds of spaces—interstitial spaces. Eisenman's conception of spacing thus amounts to a plea to conceive architecture as a machine for producing longitudinal experience in the sense defined previously. As a recipe for reconfiguring architectural interiority, spacing functions precisely by soliciting an affective embodiment *that exceeds the spatial bounds of the organic body*. It thus deploys the longitudinal dimension as a means to access the space "in-between" empirical space and bodily imaging potential. In sum, spacing enlists the longitudinal dimension of the affective body in the larger process through which architecture is constituted, coupling it to a longitudinal dimension of space from which it is inseparable.

4. INTERNAL RESONANCE

By thus incorporating bodily imaging potential, architecture trades in an interiority based on preexistent properties for an emergent "internal resonance" generated from the architectural framing of the material flux. As theorized by French philosopher of technology Gilbert Simondon (one of Deleuze's significant influences), internal resonance designates the capacity for certain systems to *mediate* between disparate levels of being—that is, to process potential energy ("the necessary condition for a higher order of magnitude") into organized and distributed matter ("the necessary condition for a lower order of magnitude").[ix,13] Specifically, internal resonance corresponds to a living system's capacity to bring disparate orders of magnitude into communication and thus to maintain the metastability that is the precondition of its ongoing individuation:

> The living being is also the being that results from an initial individuation and amplifies this individuation, not at all the machine to which it is assimilated functionally by the model of cybernetic mechanism. In the living being, *individuation is brought about by the individual itself* ... The living being resolves its problems not only by adapting itself—which is to say, by modifying its relationship to its milieu (something a machine is equally able to do)—but by modifying itself through the invention of new internal structures and its complete self-insertion into the axiomatic of organic problems. *The living individual is a system of individuation, an individuating system and also a system that individuates itself*. The internal resonance and

the translation of its relation to itself into information are all contained in the living being's system. (305)

As a form of permanent individuation internal to and constitutive of a system, internal resonance offers a concept of unity that does not rely on internal closure; specifically, it allows for the maintenance of an optimal level of creativity (*heterogenesis*) at the same time that it ensures the maintenance of the system (*autopoiesis*). Put another way, internal resonance permits a system to maintain its life-giving "communication" with the metastability of the material flux while at the same time giving the mechanism for a system to individuate itself—that is, to achieve a certain degree of autonomy vis-à-vis that metastability.

Although it may stop short of rendering architecture a living system, internal resonance accords it a capacity that is not available to it on the machinic paradigm of today's cyberartists: the capacity to transform its interiority by opening it to forces in the environment or, more precisely, by encompassing the body as a locus of such force.[x] In this way, internal resonance answers to the problematic that architecture faces in our contemporary informational culture: can and how can it maintain a minimal autonomy or system closure even as it embraces the "active, informational penetration of matter" carried out through the microchip and the development of so-called "smart" materials?[14]

Eisenman's particular recipe for internal resonance—the conjunction of digital deformation and affective bodily spacing—addresses the "softness" that, for architectural theorist Sanford Kwinter, has come to define the contemporary material domain, "a world where everything flows seamlessly together in real time" (227). Specifically, Eisenman's reconfiguration of architectural interiority through the internalization of forces and their conversion into affect articulates a "soft system"—a system "driven by its very 'softness'" or openness to the environment, "by its capacity to move, to differentiate internally, to absorb, transform, and exchange information with its surroundings, to develop complex interdependent sub- and supersystems whose global interaction ... creates secondary effects of damping and self-regulation" (210–211).

The emergent result of subsystems of digital deformation and bodily affect, Eisenman's soft system produces internal resonance specifically by introducing two concrete "delays" into the material flux: the extrusion of a third dimension (the figural) and the conversion of this matrix of forces into affect. This conjunction of digital and infralinguistic, indeed infratactile, translations functions to *process* the material flux in a way that parts company with the monist ontology central to the Deleuzean model embraced by younger architectural practitioners[xi.] Insofar as it selects forces and solicits their bodily conversion into affects, architecture is better seen as an *intervention into* the material flux designed to trigger new affections than as a *"phenomenological integration of the human nervous system into … multilevel, multiscaled networks and environments."*[15]

Accordingly, far from calling on architecture to "become computationally coextensive with the aggregate's unfolding, so that all reaction is instantaneous" (81), we must correlate its concrete task as a material practice in the information age with the longitudinal *indetermination* of the body—the way that the double delay of the digital and the affective allows the internalization of interactions with the material aggregate to constitute and maintain architecture's identity-conferring internal resonance. Does not just such an imperative motivate Eisenman's recent interest in a "new organicity" built on computation, "a new idea of flow and movement, which is a model of self-organizing, self-generating systems of organization"? (Eisenman, "Architecture," 110).

5. A NEW ORGANICISM

The correlation of computation and organicism becomes particularly pronounced in projects in which affect comes most centrally into play (Eisenman, you will recall, mentioned three in particular: *The Virtual House*, the *ITT Proposal*, and the *Staten Island Institute*). This correlation thus illustrates how the spatializing of the body and the affectivity that is its index are empowered by the computer-facilitated vectorization of space that has, following Eisenman's understanding in "Visions Unfolding: Architecture in the Age of Electronic Media," literally transformed our lifeworld: "The electronic paradigm directs a powerful challenge to architecture because it defines reality in terms of media and simulation, it values appearance over existence, what can be seen over what is. Not the seen as we formerly knew it, but rather a seeing that can no longer interpret."[16]

Not only does digital technology thus dematerialize architectural embodiment, but it also displaces vision from its privileged position as the foundation of architecture's interiority: "Architecture, unlike any other discipline, concretized vision. The hierarchy inherent in all architectural space begins as a structure for the mind's eye.... The interiority of architecture more than any other discourse defined a hierarchy of vision articulated by inside and outside" (86). In phenomenological terms, this transformation involves nothing short of an eclipse of the role of vision and a shift to a perceptual modality anchored in affect, proprioception, and tactility—anchored, that is, in the bodily infrastructure out of which vision emerges.[xii] In architectural terms, this same transformation calls on us to struggle against the specter of interiority under yet another guise: the longstanding privilege of vision and the one-point perspectival system upon which it is based.

To grasp how the vectorization of space triggers such a phenomenological and architectural revolution, let us turn to Eisenman's project for the Virtual House competition (1997). According to Luca Galafaro, one of Eisenman's assistants, this was the first of Eisenman's projects to use vectors in the place of hand-drawn models.[17] In mathematics, vectors are quantities "having direction as well as magnitude, denoted by a line drawn from its original to its final position" (OED). Because they have direction and density, vectors express forces or potentialities, rather than simply representing something already known. When they are used as the basis for architectural modeling, vectors liberate the architect from the need to convert a mental conception of space into a hand-rendered, axial drawing or modelization. Accordingly, vector modelization frees architecture from its rootedness in static spatial conditions: by injecting time into space, vectors unfold space as a field of intensity, a spatial field coequivalent to the matrix of potential connections it affords.

Virtual House was based on the memory of the spatial concept from Eisenman's *House IV* (1971), for which he wrote a text entitled "The Virtual House" (1987). Effectively, *Virtual House* deploys vector modelization to actualize the potential of the project that Eisenman considers his "first purely diagrammatic project"[xiii] and that Kurt Foster, in the Jury discussion to the Virtual House competition, describes as the summation of Eisenman's early House projects, where the "cube itself does not become the site of operations but a cube separated from itself."[18] In *Virtual House*, the potential field of interactions among the nine cubes of *House IV* is actualized via the expression of each potential connection as a vector.[xiv] Each vector unfolds a field of influence in which its virtual movement through time is actualized; this actualization is, in turn, visualized through the effect of each vector on the lines within its sphere of influence. In this way, the lines, with their constitutive

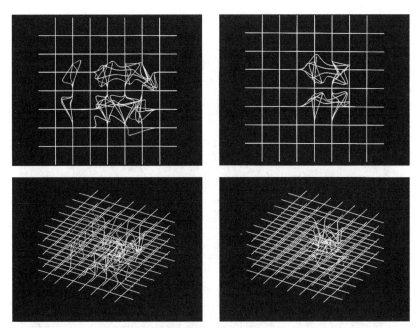

FIGURE 4.6 Peter Eisenman, diagrams illustrating genesis of the Virtual House project (1997). New spatial conditions are created through the movement and interrelation of vectors, permitting infinite variations. (Courtesy of the artist.)

geometric properties, become forces, and, because they emerge through a set of arbitrarily assigned constraints operating on one another as local forces, the traces left by these lines record the condition of each vector within the space (see Figure 4.6).

The "abstract machine" of *Virtual House* comprises two components arbitrarily constrained by parameters introduced by the architectural team. Thus, in a first operation, two of the original nine cubes are isolated from the rest and placed "side by side"; the computer reads each side of each cube from corner to corner, recording the traces of each reading. In a second operation, this process is repeated with the same two cubes "constrained" by one another; here the computer reads each process of constraint, again recording their traces. In this way, the interrelations between cubes become vectorial expressions of their potential connections within each operation and, importantly, across the two operations.

This process could be repeated for all permutations of the nine cubes and indeed (so long as new constraints could be found) potentially to infinity; however, the arbitrary selection of two cubes and two operations

FIGURE 4.7 Peter Eisenman, diagrammatic model of *Virtual House*. The lines outline surfaces and the interstitial spaces between them that await actualization by the operating program. (Courtesy of the artist.)

serves the architectural team's stated purpose to constitute "a single moment in the multiplicity of virtuality." This single moment bears witness to the possibility of deploying vector modelization to supersaturate a space with interstitial or figural relations because, despite its primary function as a theoretical exercise, what is at stake here is the machinic enumeration of potential connections within a spatial field or, put another way, a demonstration that space (at least as modeled with the aid of the computer) necessarily enfolds its virtual permutations (see Figure 4.7).

Its Deleuzean vocabulary notwithstanding, the project description of *Virtual House* seems to embrace the virtual more operationally than ontologically, as a means to liberate architectural space from the constraint of interiority rather than as an autonomous philosophical concept. Although this is already apparent in the arbitrary restriction of the machine to two cubes and two operations, it surfaces most forcefully in the necessity for the machine to stop by itself, at that point when the constraints produce a state of reduced activity or, more precisely, "when the differences in the system are so minimal that they are no longer perceptible" (23).

Effectively, the vector modelization of *Virtual House* maps the two cubes onto one another through two operations, and then maps these mappings onto each other so that the entirety of interstitial spaces contained within their differences is absorbed into the system. The result is a spatial form burgeoning with its potentiality, a spatial form that encompasses into itself the temporal unfoldings of all of its possible connections—in short, a "formal expression of the virtual." If this result makes it possible to "model in real space the actual time and movement of the abstract machine relations," this possibility bears the marks of architecture's singularity and its difference from philosophy. Only by freezing a segment or cross-section of the virtual material flux (in Kwinter's neo-Deleuzean sense) and exhausting its specific virtuality (the repertoire of potential interstitial connections it contains) can architecture actualize the virtual (see Figure 4.8). Put somewhat differently, it is only by actualizing the virtual that architecture can deploy it.[xv]

This is precisely how project designer Ingeborg Rocker understands the necessity for the machine to stop:

> When we talk about stopping the process, it is important that we don't limit architecture to its physicality, because *architecture is also about the process within the building, how it will be inhabited.* If we stop the process at a certain moment, we create spaces that maintain

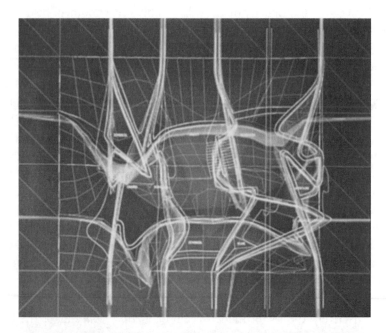

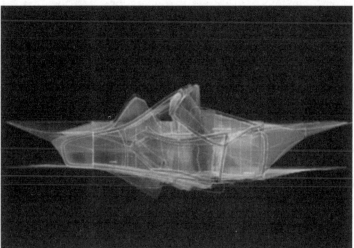

FIGURE 4.8 Peter Eisenman, first-floor plan and logitudinal section of the Virtual House project. Illustrates the function exploration of the interstitial spaces discovered through vectorial deformation and highlights the necessity to stop the process of variation by selecting one actualization. (Courtesy of the artist.)

the process or its programmatic aspects. (Rocker, in Foster, "Jury Discussion," 36, emphasis added)

For Rocker, the architectural constraint of the virtual is directly correlated with the capacity of embodied affect to transform architecture's interiority.

This observation returns us to our opening discussion of the singularity of architecture within the field of digital media, its privileged status as *the* art of the frame. We can now see that architecture must be differentiated from other aesthetic engagements with new media precisely because its vocation is to frame space *for inhabitation*: architecture alone deploys digital media to conjoin spatial form and embodied inhabitation. This vocation is inscribed into *Virtual House* through the architectural team's embrace of "incompletion" as the operative element of this confrontation of spatial form and embodiment. In *Virtual House*, the supersaturating of space through vector modelization yields a spatial form containing a field of forces: the result of a certain delimitation (and protoactualization) of the virtual, these forces can only be actualized as affects through the embodied inhabitation of this spatial form, which can be said to complete the space (though only provisionally), leaving it open to other affective responses and potential completions.

Through this coupling of formal incompletion and embodied inhabitation the virtual comes to infiltrate architecture; as against a simple and literal materialization of the immaterial, at issue here is a "working of architectural space that affects subject and object." The payoff is the coevolution of response and form so that the necessity of stopping the virtual at the level of form has as a *necessary* correlate finding a way to continue the virtual by other means—that is, through the affective inhabitation triggered by digitally synthesized spatial form. That is why the building's "realization" is the mode in which it "continues to become" (Rocker, "The Virtual," 23).

If *Virtual House* articulates the theoretical program for such a coevolution, Eisenman's project for the *Staten Island Institute of Arts and Sciences* puts it into practice (see Figure 4.9). The project is an ambitious attempt to cross-pollinate two architectural institutions—the ferry terminal and the museum—by breaking down architectural barriers that have long served to separate them:

Our idea is to take an established institution, the Staten Island Institute of Arts and Sciences and, instead of locating it in a nineteenth-century manner at the Snug Harbor parkland, place it in a

205

FIGURE 4.9 Peter Eisenman, project model for the Staten Island Institute project. (Courtesy of the artist.)

transformed and enlarged museum facility on top of the ferry terminal. In doing so, the waiting room will open up to become the atrium for the museum. Instead of the traditional museum experience, we propose a museum concept with several different and flexible museum venues. Thus the museum will house interactive displays of science and technology based on the Institute's permanent collection, a "kunsthalle" for large traveling exhibitions, and possibly a New York Sports Hall of Fame. In addition, there will be an IMAX-like theater, educational facilities, shops and restaurants available for all users of the terminal. Thus a new dimension of an intermodal facility would be introduced, bringing art, commerce, and travel into a new synthesis.[19]

In the more theoretical terms proper to Eisenman's architectural discourse, the project aims to deform what is perhaps the most fundamental element of architecture's interiority—the ground—by submitting it to the complex and contradictory forces of mobility that permeate this site. (According to Eisenman, the Staten Island ferry terminal is quintessentially "a place of movement": a nodal point for bus, car, and ferry transport used by over 18,000,000 people annually.) In his project, Eisenman channels these forces of mobility into a fluid spatial form that confronts the two kinds of places—static museum and dynamic ferry terminal—with one another and thus undermines the preexistent spatial interiority characteristic of each (see Figure 4.10).

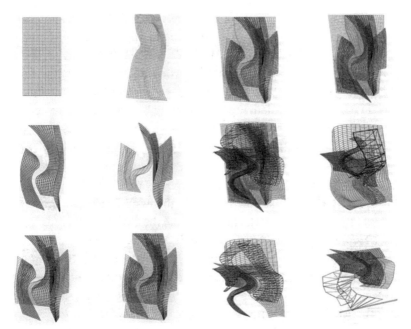

FIGURE 4.10 Peter Eisenman, diagrammatic models for the Staten Island Institute project. These diagrams illustrate the vectorial exploration of the interstitial spaces lying between the static museum and the dynamic ferry terminal. The spaces contain the potentiality for the genesis of new spatial forms. (Courtesy of the artist.)

Once again, digitally facilitated vector modelization furnishes the means to transform the axial synchrony characteristic of architecture—the synchrony of the "vertebrate axis of man" and the "horizontal symmetries of classical Greco–Christian space"—into the initial coordinates of a temporal virtualization that generates a spatial form supersaturated with the entire repertoire of interstitial spaces buried "in-between" these two axes. Here, vectors allow for the morphing of the static museum and the dynamic ferry terminal into one another so that the differences between them are absorbed as the potentiality of the new spatial form.

Unlike the morphing of cubes in *Virtual House*, however, this process of vector modelization is a means to an end, in the sense that it furnishes the generative source for the built form. In this role, vector modelization functions to supersaturate the built form with interstitial spatial potentialities that comprise so many triggers for (variant) actualization via embodied inhabitation. It is precisely this potential for inhabitation that

207

differentiates Eisenman's project from Frank Lloyd Wright's and Frank Gehry's Guggenheim Museums. Like these museum designs, Eisenman's deploys a "centroidal structure." However, whereas both Guggenheims deploy some kind of vertical central organizing axis, the spatial form of the *Staten Island Institute* envelops and twists on what is, in reality, a central void, effectively denying the orienting function of a large central axis that could link parts together in a continuous itinerary.

Insofar as it highlights the way in which the *Staten Island Institute* interrupts the narrative continuity characteristic of architecture—the "continuity between vertebrate man and axial building"—this comparison serves to expose just how integrally the experiential dimension is *built into* Eisenman's project. Although, like the Guggenheim museums, "it seems massed toward the center," in it "the subject moves across the striations, and is denied any continuous spiral." Moreover, "the smooth nature of the space is striated by deep V-shaped sections which begin to define a series of interlocking interstitial layers. The organizing principle of these layers comes from a resistance diagram of flows and vectors. The spatial experience becomes an incomplete narrative, a destination without end" (23).

In this regard, the *Staten Island Institute* culminates Eisenman's exploration of interstitial space in earlier projects like the *Wexner Center*, the *Columbus Convention Center*, and the *Aronoff Center*; here, specifically, what originated as a technique designed to interrupt linear spatial narrative is substantially complexified by the deployment of vector modelization.[xvi] Thus, "the linear nature of the warps and striations" of the earlier projects becomes "torqued into a centroidal mass" made all the more complex by its deceptive similarity to a central axis (23). In experiential (or "narrative") terms, as the separate architectural forms of museum and terminal interpenetrate (the waiting room literally becoming the museum hall), the itineraries characteristic of each blend together in the local flows of people moving through them.

Dissolved into "bands intersected by vibrant slits and deep V-shaped grooves," the architectural object no longer functions to guide the vertical body through horizontal space (Galafaro, 78); rather, as a continuously dilating fluid space, it draws on the "active, magmatic underground energy" of the site as a force capable of "displacing the body from its hierarchical, upright position within the axial system" (78). The result is a seepage of the spatial dilation onto the body as the conversion of this force into affect replaces the constituent material elements of the building as the index of the architectural sign.

By moving from the vectorial deformation of the site (liberation of the force of the interstitial) to its eventual longitudinal bodily inhabitation (processing of force as affect), this project exemplifies the refunctionalization of framing that is at stake in Eisenman's digitally inspired work and that confers a distinct architectural inflection on the concept of wearable space. Bluntly put, Eisenman transforms framing from an "objective" condition of the site into a process encompassing site, space, and body or, as I put it in *New Philosophy for New Media*, from a static, black-boxed technical frame to a dynamic bodily-generated one. Thus, he manages to displace the formal binary opposition—form vs. unform—that (with no small encouragement on his part) has been used to characterize his work.[xvii]

For the most recent Eisenman, the important task is *specifying the conditions for reframing*—how to deploy the potentiality of the site as the trigger for an embodied framing that brings together site, space, *and* body in the production of wearable space. Viewed in this context, we can see that Eisenman's interest in affect functions to displace the domain in which framing can be said to operate—to displace it *from* architectural form *to* the affective excess that, in the language of "Visions Unfolding," continuously unfolds alongside it. In this new vocation, framing foregrounds the necessity for what Eisenman has called the "third step": the confrontation of the smooth spaces of today's lifeworld (and computer modulation) with architecture's (constitutive) interiority. Thus, he can insist, once again with an eye toward the younger generation: "I am not interested in forming amorphic projects, rather I am interested in spacing the formless" (Zaera-Polo, "Interview," 20).

By "spacing the formless," bodily experience transforms the virtual excess of architectural space into a form not pregiven by, yet nonetheless inseparable from, architecture's constitutive interiority.[xviii] Such creative embodied framing, mobilized in the architectural construction of space, produces the condition of "wearable space," which can thus be considered a particular type of "digital any-space-whatever"[xix]—that is (following and extending the Deleuzean concept of the ASW), a production of space in which the body in effect forges an analogy where none preexists.[xx] In the context of architecture specifically, the production of a digital ASW through the body's infratactile capacity to convert force into affect explains how spacing can be understood as a dynamic operation of framing that manages to avoid grounding: it is an ongoing, embodied framing of space that is not given in this or that form, but only as an ongoing process open to the "longitudinal."[xxi]

Recalling Cache's argument, we can now appreciate just how much the privilege accorded architecture as the quintessential art of framing for our time owes to its constitutive embrace of the body.[xxii] Simply stated, embodiment is the operator of all interchanges between space and architectural interiority. It is from the bodily conversion of force into affect that new framings of space—dynamic framings "adequate to" the new spaces and, above all, the infospaces of the contemporary technosphere—always ultimately arise.

6. WEARING THE BLUR

How exactly do digital media contribute to architecture's privilege as the quintessential art of framing for our time? To answer this question, we must deepen our understanding of Eisenman's correlation of the digital with a certain refunctionalization of architectural interiority. How, we need to ask, does the digital effectuate an opening of the autonomy of the architectural sign such that it is made available for a re-embodiment through the bodily affects it triggers?

To address this crucial question, let us return to Diller + Scofidio who, as I shall now suggest, represent a legacy of Eisenman's efforts to retool architectural interiority that stands in marked contrast to the one currently pursued by today's so-called machinic architects. In a general sense, this divergence can be discerned from Diller + Scofidio's penchant to use technology against the grain, as a means of introducing delay into the temporal flux of contemporary experience. Rather than seeking to maximize productivity and efficiency, as capitalism preaches, or to make seamless contact with the material flux, as the machinic architects urge (following Kwinter's characterization), Diller + Scofidio deploy technologies as a means of introducing indeterminacy and instituting delay so that something unpredictable, something new, can emerge. The crucial question, then, will concern their use of digital media to open architectural interiority for the creation of new experiences.

In an insightful article that situates Diller + Scofidio's practice in relation to the '70s generation and, specifically, to John Hejduk and Eisenman, Michael Hays traces the singularity of Diller + Scofidio to their effort to expand the motif of interiority/autonomy beyond its narrow architectural embodiment. Whereas the "theory-practice alignment of the 1970s produced built (or at least buildable) objects (mostly private homes) that used elaborate formal devices to visibly lay bare the compositional procedures that had generated the object in the first place, that is, to represent the formative logic of the object *in the object itself*," Diller + Scofidio deploy the formalist code "in a different, higher register in which the new work sought to reveal the unintended presumptions that ostensibly autonomous architectural techniques had enabled or had tried to remove from the possibility of thinking."[21]

Thus, in early projects like *The withDrawing Room* (1987),

> The concern with the internal, autonomous working of architecture is not abandoned so much as folded into various discourses of context and exteriority, recalibrated according to what is sayable or thinkable in the ideolects of psychoanalysis, feminism, and other theoretical systems that seek to analyze the hidden structures of domestic life. Specific architectural forms, techniques, and operations, previously presumed to be purely self-reflexive, are now valued not for themselves, but rather for their ability to scan the domestic system they had tried to detach themselves from, map its ideological functions, and produce concepts whose ultimate horizon of effect lies outside of architecture "proper," in a more general sociocultural field. At this point in their work, then, "scanning" meant disclosing the extrinsic, ideological structures that contaminate and complicate the intrinsic, supposedly pure forms and techniques of architecture. (130)

A work that "disables, divides, and bisects" the walls and furniture of a century-old wood-frame house in San Francisco in order to expose "'the home's' organizational strategies: property rights, rules of etiquette, the marriage contract, and the public codes of a private residence,"[22] *The withDrawing Room* exemplifies Diller + Scofidio's constructive deployment of formalist procedures developed by Hejduk, Eisenman, and others as techniques specifically designed to address the problem of architecture's constitutive and constraining interiority. In Diller + Scofidio's hands, these formal techniques become instruments for a fundamental recontextualization of architecture in terms of the larger social codes and conventions—here (and often in the early work) conventions of domesticity—that inform the concrete embodiment of the architectural sign.

If this first phase of activity yielded a loosening of the scope of architectural embodiment, Diller + Scofidio's more recent work moves ever farther from the orthographic–geometric architectural apparatus of the '70s formalists. Indeed, beginning with their 1991 (unrealized) project *Slow House*, Diller + Scofidio have dedicated themselves to a more abstract recontextualization of architecture in terms of the sensory registers correlated with architectural embodiment. By deploying a strategy of direct defunctionalization of vision that has evolved from splitting to blurring, Diller + Scofidio now seek to interrupt the circuit connecting architectural interiority with the "nobility of vision" (to return to Jonas' term) and thus to effectuate an expansion, indeed an inversion, of that interiority by way of a shift in sensory registers from the visual to the proprioceptive, the aural, and the tactile. Accordingly, whereas the work of the '80s aimed to lay bare the "objective" conditions for the *real* experience of architecture, the work of the '90s aims to expose the "subjective"—or better, the "protosubjective"—conditions for the *real* experience of space.

Although this strategy of direct defunctionalization of vision certainly reaches its culmination in the *Blur Building*, it starts out as an attempt to split vision and thereby to catalyze an embodied synthesis—what Hays has called a "connective synthesis"—in the spectator-participant. Thus, in works such as *Para-site* (1989), *Jump Cuts* (1995), and *X, Y* (1997), Diller + Scofidio variously stage the presentation and consumption of irreconcilable images.

Developed for the Museum of Modern Art in New York, *Para-site* screened images from three live feeds—the revolving entrance doorway, the escalators in the lobby, and the doors to the sculpture garden—on monitors installed in a gallery. As a critique of the institutional ideology that views the museum as a place of decontextualized, pure vision, this work effectively bridges Diller + Scofidio's early examination of social conventions and their later critique of the primacy of vision. The viewing gallery contains unusable chairs variously mounted on the walls and ceiling, cut in half, and imprinted with texts by Michel Serres and Jeremy Bentham, and the images screened on the cantilevered monitors are oriented at 90° or 180° with respect to the floor. The effect of this installation is to split the viewer's perspective, to put into question the normal taken-for-granted nature of bodily orientation to the image so that embodiment becomes an issue. Thus, in addition to consuming (indeed, in order to consume) the images presented, the viewer must reconcile his or her embodied perspective with the inhospitable

FIGURE 4.11 Elizabeth Diller + Ricardo Scofidio, *Jump Cuts* (1995), digital video installation at the United Artists Cineplex Theater in San Jose, California, that decouples the video image from the embodied spatial orientation of the architecture containing it. (Courtesy of the artists.)

perspective(s) presented by the images and the defunctionalized institutional props contained in the gallery space.

In the later *Jump Cuts* and *X, Y,* Diller + Scofidio dispense with the domestic, institutional props, concentrating their attack on vision within the image. Both works record the insides of archetypal buildings—a movie theater and a pachinko parlor, respectively—from disorienting perspectives that survey movement from above. Installed at the United Artists Cineplex Theater in San Jose, California, *Jump Cuts* (1995) presented images of theater patrons riding the escalator (intercut periodically by movie trailers) on twelve liquid-crystal screens affixed to the outside of the theater building (see Figure 4.11). Here, the decoupling of the image from the viewer's embodied orientation—the decoupling already at issue in *Para-site*—is conjoined with (indeed, becomes the vehicle for) a critical intervention into architectural interiority, as Edward Dimendberg suggests:

> Uncoupling the video image from the actual spatial orientation of the architecture supporting it, these installations display alternate points of view in a manner that treats space as malleable, separable from the observer, and reprogrammable in new combinations. Mounted

on the façade of the cinema complex, *Jump Cuts* works by "flipping the building inside out, electronically" [citing a lecture by Diller]. It suggests the potential of digital technology to *shift the boundaries between architectural interiority and exteriority.*[23]

Because these and related works—*Loophole* (1992), *Overexposed* (1994–2003), and *Facsimile* (2003)—effectuate a displacement of architectural embodiment into the space outside the building, we might think that they make common cause with the formalist techniques designed to disembody the architectural sign. Yet, to confine our analysis to such an understanding would be to overlook the crucial role Diller + Scofidio increasingly come to place on spectator–participant embodiment as the "origin" of architecture.

Nowhere is this emphasis on embodied response more apparent than in their critical negotiations with the modernist ideology of transparency. In the unrealized project *Slow House* (1991), Diller + Scofidio juxtapose "natural" and technically mediated visual frames in order to foreground not only the inherent doubling of contemporary visual perception but also, and perhaps more importantly, the bidirectionality of the gaze, the fact that the preeminent technology of modernist architecture, glass, has opened the path to our massively surveillant society. Designed as a vacation home in Long Island, *Slow House* is a passage to a view: presenting a façade entirely occupied by a 4-ft-wide by 18-ft-high front door, the house widens as it curves around to the left, culminating 100 ft from the doorway in a large picture window that frames the ocean view (see Figure 4.12). By subordinating all of its elements to this framing function, the *Slow House* is a "house-frame," a piece of architecture that exposes the contemporary framing function of architecture in its barest imaginable form.

Yet, what results is hardly a celebration of architecture's primitiveness in relation to electronic and digital media; rather, as Diller + Scofidio point out, *Slow House* foregrounds architecture's conventionality, the inherent cultural contextedness of its mediation of vision. "Having thoroughly naturalized and internalized the normally 'invisible' visual codes of perspective and landscape depiction, we fail to recognize that the picture window is as much a cultural construct as the televisual image."[24] Indeed, if architecture can lay claim to a privileged role as the art of the frame, that is precisely because it is *more* technically advanced than television. "As advanced technology strives to dematerialize its hardware, leaving only its effects, is not the picture window, in fact, a

FIGURE 4.12 Elizabeth Diller + Ricardo Scofidio, *Slow House* (1991), unrealized project for a private vacation residence in Long Island. Juxtaposes picture window frame with television screen. (Courtesy of the artists.)

more advanced technology than the television set, in that its socially and economically driven mechanisms are virtually invisible, leaving only a simple frame?"[25]

As if to embed this question materially in the experience of the unrealized house project, Diller + Scofidio double the picture window with a small television monitor, placed directly in front of the window, that screens an electronically mediated landscape displaying a horizon that "is always out of register with that of the 'real' landscape visible through and mediated by the window."[26] The camera can pan and zoom by remote control, thus introducing perspectives at odds with the perspective of the embodied viewer–inhabitant; moreover, it can play prerecorded images if (for example) the view becomes obscured on account of foul weather or darkness. The end result of this juxtaposition of viewpoints is a technologization of nature, or rather, an exposure of the inherence of technics within nature: "as the image is manipulated and changed," the Project Description tells us, "nature becomes a slow form of entertainment" (103).

Can we say then that architectural framing functions to illuminate the ineliminability of framing as a process that is at once technical and embodied? Does this explain architecture's current privilege as the art of framing par excellence? Diller + Scofidio's reworking of *Slow House* as a gallery installation transforms the project's assault on unmediated vision into a thorough performative investigation of the embodied basis for the impossibility of pure transparency. Rather than simply juxtaposing two modes of framing landscape, at issue here is the bodily activity that arises as the agent of the "connective synthesis" solicited by such a juxtaposition.

Comprising twenty-four artifacts (drawings, models, and texts) displayed on liquid-crystal monitors mounted in freestanding frames in a gallery space, *The Desiring Eye: Reviewing the Slow House* (1992) foregrounds the oscillation between looking and reading as a kind of lure that prevents the embodied spectator from achieving pure vision. Thus, although it is true that the "layered grouping [of these displays] in the gallery space frustrates the possibility of gazing unobstructed from one end of the gallery to the other," as Dimendberg claims (75), far more important for the installation's performative impact is the mobile viewer's seduction by the image stations. Given the wealth of information framed by the individual displays (details about waterfront real estate, architectural details of the house, etc.), what the viewer experiences is

FIGURE 4.13 Elizabeth Diller + Ricardo Scofidio, The *Desiring Eye: Reviewing the Slow House* (1992), adaptation of Slow House project to a gallery setting. Foregrounds the oscillation between looking and reading as a lure preventing spectator from achieving pure vision. (Courtesy of the artists.)

the rich contextedness of the supposedly pure picture window view (see Figure 4.13).

That her interest in this context complicates and ultimately displaces the desire for total vision ultimately explains why the installation "literally deconstructs the modernist creed of architectural transparency," as Dimendberg suggests. It undermines the ideology of unmediated vision, of the picture window, "by laying bare its most fundamental premise: the body of the observer as it contemplates and is framed by architecture" (75). *The Desiring Eye*, then, moves from the questioning of the purity—the nobility—of vision staged in *Slow House* to a reckoning with the consequences of its contamination: namely, the exposure of embodiment as the "origin" of all architectural framing.

This exposure is just what is at stake in Diller + Scofidio's *Blur Building*, where the monumental framing of nature typical of the world exposition as an institution is undermined and displaced in favor of a framing via the slow time of bodily experience. As critic Ashley Schafer points out, in the *Blur* project as in the *Slow House*, technologies "produce nothing, or at least nothing that does not already exist; rather, they simply reframe the existing view by visually and temporally displacing it."[27] Not only does the project involve a shift from architectural interiority to exteriority, with the embodied spectator becoming the generator of "wearable space," but also, even more centrally to our concerns here, it foregrounds the imbrication of architecture with the digital, as Diller + Scofidio explain:

> The media event is integrated with the enveloping fog. Our objective is to weave together architecture and electronic technologies, yet exchange the properties of each for the other. Thus, architecture would dematerialize and electronic media, normally ephemeral, would become palpable in space. Both would require sophisticated technologies that would be entirely invisible, leaving only their effects. (*Blur*, 44)

The transduction of nature and technics exposed in earlier works like *Slow House* here becomes the very basis for a heightening of the creativity of embodiment. Accordingly, as the visual domination of space diminishes, the capacity of digital media to catalyze new embodied inhabitations of space, and thus new embodiments of architecture, grows. This, I suggest, is why Diller + Scofidio "needed technology to amplify the atmosphere of uncertainty, to technologize climate further," as they put it.[28] By vastly speeding up and artificially punctuating the fog environment's recursive self-regulation, Diller + Scofidio create an experiential atmosphere conducive to the exposure of embodied framing, of wearable space, as the origin of architecture.[xxiii]

A "defense mechanism against surveillance," as Aaron Betsky puts it, the technique of blur thus emerges as Diller + Scofidio's most recent strategy to exteriorize architectural interiority, to foreground it against the very context of incorporated conventionality that gives life to the social, not to mention formal, codings of architecture.[29] *Blur*, in short, allows habit to be suspended so that the unexpected and the unpredictable can emerge. That is why, for Betsky, Diller + Scofidio's ambition is

> to use the techniques of blur to make constructions in which one is never quite sure what one is experiencing, where one is, or how one should behave. The codes of behavior that tell us what to want and what to buy no longer work, as we don't know what we are meant to do. (35)

That this suspension of knowledge becomes an opportunity for creative embodiment serves to link Diller + Scofidio's "embodied conceptual art" to the corpuses of work we have explored previously. In perfect alignment with the architects' view of their project as part art and part architecture, we can place the *Blur Building* somewhere in the middle of the continuum stretching from Arakawa and Gins' instrumental (or artistic) deployment of architecture to throw the body out of balance to Eisenman's vectorial liberation of the interstitial potential of space to trigger affective response.

Like Arakawa and Gins, Diller + Scofidio deploy architecture as a means to catalyze a fundamental shift in the sensory economy of the body, from a frontal, visually dominant modality to a longitudinal modality that draws heavily on both hearing and touch, as well as properly bodily senses like proprioception. In contrast to Arakawa and Gins, they do this not only to uncover a truth about the body, but also to bring out the bodily component of spacing—the way that architecture, at least in this age of medial fluidity, must open itself out to the body as an environmental source of heterogenesis, of architectural exteriority, that is crucial to its ongoing individuation or internal resonance.

Like Eisenman, Diller + Scofidio invest space with the potential for triggering longitudinal experience, such that the shift in the body's sensory economy cannot be said to ensue solely from powers contained *within* the body, but rather to be the result of an encounter between the body and the longitudinal dimensions of space released through the crossover of architecture and electronic technologies. In contrast to Eisenman, however, this encounter of bodily affectivity and interstitial spacing is far more immediate, something that can be experienced explicitly within the confines of the bodily inhabitation of the blur. Indeed, in the *Blur Building*, space becomes wearable not as some abstract correlate of a distinct figural liberation of the interstitial, but rather as the condition for effectuating the interpenetration of architecture and media that is at once its primary phenomenological *and* architectural goal: the dematerialization of architecture into "atmosphere" and the becoming-palpable of electronics (the digital) as "habitable medium."

For these reasons, Diller + Scofidio's *Blur Building* is the quintessential expression of wearable space as a phenomenological and architectural condition directly tied to the massive infiltration of digital media into the contemporary lifeworld. It puts into action, on the cusp between architectural (in)form and the affective body, the program of sensory deterritorialization—specifically, the dethronement of vision—championed, in various ways, by Arakawa and Gins and by Eisenman. And it does so with a sensory immediacy that has the effect of inverting the function of architectural presence, transforming it into a source of affective intensity capable of making space wearable, not as an abstract design condition, but as a concrete phenomenological reality.

Accordingly, whereas Arakawa and Gins view sensory deterritorialization as a more or less ahistorical potential that inheres within the body and Eisenman conceives it as a specific correlate of a more general ontological shift in the materiality of culture, Diller + Scofidio explore it as a necessary consequence of the historically unprecedented interpenetration of body and media. They thereby bring a level of concreteness to Eisenman's keen understanding of the correlation between electronic media and a postvisual, affective phenomenology. What is at stake in the *Blur Building* is not simply a "seeing that can no longer interpret," but rather a wholesale short circuiting of the role of vision, such that the affective body is *literally* compelled to "space the void" (Eisenman, "Visions Unfolded," 84).

The *Blur Building*, in short, deploys the deformation of architectural form—the displacement of visible, planimetric enclosure by the amorphous, atmospheric fog enclosure—as a means to render the impact of the digital revolution experientially salient, to give us a sensory correlate – spatialized affectivity – to its deformations of space. Recalling the twin epigraphs to this chapter, we can now see why, precisely, the conjunction of a complete fluidity, respectively, between body and media (Picard) and body and space (Novak) allows space to become wearable. Although media make space flexible and invisible, it is embodiment that allows mediated space to be experienced sensorily, precisely as space made wearable.

The Digital Topography of *House of Leaves*

Zampanò only wrote "heater." The word "water" back there [in *The Navidson Record*]—I added that. Now there's an admission, eh?

Hey, not fair, you cry.
Hey, hey, fuck you, I say.[1]

For Mark Danielewski, perhaps the central burden of contemporary authorship is to reaffirm the novel as a relevant—indeed newly relevant— cultural form:

Books don't have to be so limited. They can intensify informational content and experience. Multiple stories can lie side by side on the page.... Words can also be colored and those colors can have meaning. How quickly pages are turned or not turned can be addressed. Hell, pages can be tilted, turned upside down, even read backwards.... But here's the joke. Books have had this capacity all along.... Books are remarkable constructions with enormous possibilities.... But somehow the analogue powers of these wonderful bundles of paper have been forgotten. Somewhere along the way, all its possibilities were denied. I'd like to see that perception change. I'd like to see the book reintroduced for all it really is.[2]

House of Leaves, the novel Danielewski wrote to reintroduce the book for all it really is, is a tour de force in typographic and media experimentation with the printed word. From its cover page and initial inset to its enigmatic final page, the novel defies standard expectations in a rich variety of ways. Making pseudoserious reference to the blue highlighting of hotlinks on webpages, the blue ink of the word "house" in the work's title transforms this keyword into something like a portal to information located elsewhere within and beyond the novel's frame. The color collage comprising the first inset page juxtaposes what looks to be a randomly selected group of common-use objects with snippets of manuscript copy as if to suggest some underlying equivalence between them. The final page—curiously situated *after* the index and credits page—bears the inscription "Yggdrasil" in the form of a "T" followed by four lines of text and a fifth line containing a single, large font, bold "O." A reference to the giant tree supporting the universe in Norse Mythology, the page startles in its apparent randomness, reinforcing the cosmological closure effected by the novel it culminates, yet shedding no new light on just what should be made of it.

Although these examples begin to expose the medial basis informing the novel's typographic play, they in no way exhaust its engagement with media. (The adjective "medial," by now adopted as a standard term in media studies, will here mark the specificity of analyses concerned with the materiality of the medium and of media generally.) Indeed, as we shall see, these examples form so many symptoms of what can only be understood (following Danielewski's aim to reintroduce the print book for all it really is) to be a *media-technical*, and not simply a stylistic or formal, shift in the function of the novel.

As Kate Hayles has argued, *House of Leaves* is obsessed with technical mediation and the complex media ecology that has been introduced and expanded since the introduction of technical recording in the nineteenth century. The broad outlines of a theory of the *media* revolution in literature have already been laid out in the work of self-proclaimed "media scientist" Friedrich Kittler, who, in *Discourse Networks 1800/1900* and *Gramophone, Film, Typewriter*, has catalogued the disenfranchisement of literature—its "devolution" from the exalted role of "universal medium" to a more humble vocation as one medium among others in a hybrid media ecology consisting of audio recording, image recording, and now digitization.[i] Yet, where Kittler seems content to identify the specific media forms—gramophone, film, and typewriter— as three broadly similar recording apparatuses, Danielewski takes pains to circumscribe the constitutive limitations of each and, in line with his previously stated aim, to champion the superiority of print.

Paradoxical as it sounds, the privilege of literature stems less from its capacity to ape the flexibility of technical media than from the novel's longstanding correlation with the body (the exemplar of which would certainly have to be Rabelais's *Gargantua and Pantagruel*). By updating this correlation in the context of today's complex and hybrid media ecology, Danielewski manages to submit the novel to a formal transformation, one that compels its adaptation to our allegedly "posthermeneutical" informational culture. It does so by treating the novel as a body subject to development and deformation.

In the broadest sense, such an updating of the novel's tie to the body is precisely what is at stake in its central thematic engagement—with the topological figure of a house that is larger inside than outside. The effort to document or otherwise make sense of this physically impossible object generates a series of mediations which, as Hayles has shown, stand in for the void of referentiality at the novel's core. Lacking the force of indexicality, these mediations can only acquire the force of conviction by eliciting embodied reactions in their fictional and actual readers. They garner their rhetorical effect by triggering what I shall call "reality *affects*."

The conjunction of the novel's host of mediations and the reader's embodied response comprises yet another type of body-in-code, one that is robustly distributed between the embodied selective framing of the singular reader and the peculiar embodiment of mediation that characterizes the novel in our contemporary culture. As a frame for the nonrepresentational impact of the digital, the novel furnishes a source of exteriorization for the embodied reader, taking her outside and beyond the scope of habitual existence and thereby allowing her to experience something new, something that would not be otherwise experientiable.

In this way, *House of Leaves* not only exemplifies the most general sense of virtuality as a dimension of human life—virtuality as the power of the imagination or, better, of the imaginary (following Cornelius Castoriadis[3])—but also specifies how language forms an important medium, perhaps *the* medium, for the actualization of this virtuality. By subordinating its orthographic function—recording something that exists elsewhere, *in absentia*—to its role as a trigger for the production of meaning via embodiment, *House of Leaves* exemplifies language's capacity to produce new images understood as material realities in their own right rather than as representations of something else, following Paul Ricoeur's conception. Indeed, the process of embodied response catalyzed by *House of Leaves* perfectly exemplifies how, as Ricoeur puts it, the "emergence of new meanings in the sphere of language generates an emergence of new images."[4]

More specifically, *House of Leaves* demonstrates how embodiment furnishes a medium for the passage between language and image, and thus how new linguistic formations—here, the deformation of the novel's body—can yield new experiences and thereby, as Ricoeur puts it, "shape reality." By tapping the power of the imaginary, of the imaginary as a bodily power, *House of Leaves* thus catalyzes the genesis of a myriad of bodies-in-code, each one corresponding to the concrete actualization of the text by a specific reader. Here, indeed, the role of code as a source of exteriority becomes synonymous with the role of the imaginary as an excess of embodiment, as a surplus intrinsic to individuation that furnishes the source for new acts of embodiment.

Given the novel's obsession with media and mediation, it is hardly surprising that the first of its many mediations is a film, *The Navidson Record*, compiled by Pulitzer Prize-winning photojournalist Will Navidson from videos made by him, his wife, Karen Green, and several of the characters involved in exploring the new house they moved into in order to begin afresh—the curious, "warped" house on Ash Tree Lane that turns out to be larger on the inside than on the outside. The events captured by this film come to us through the mediation of one Zampanò, a Borges-like figure, apparently named after the protagonist in Fellini's *La Strada,* who possesses a diabolical penchant for mixing real and fictional sources in an apparent bid to garner verisimilitude for his enterprise. (*House of Leaves*, in consequence, is littered with footnotes, an indeterminate number of which are pure inventions of its author.)

Left unfinished at his death, Zampanò's narrative in turn comes to us through yet another layer of mediation: that of the young tattoo artist's assistant, Johnny Truant, who assembles the pieces of the manuscript into a cogent order, and, in the process, adds a series of footnotes and appended documents that detail the destabilizing effects of the narrative on his already confused personal life. In yet another iteration of this framing structure, all of this material is said to come to us thanks to the efforts of a group of mysterious "editors," who have taken the work of Zampanò and Truant that initially—or so we are told—circulated on the Internet, and bound it together in book form, adding supplementary material allegedly worthy of the title of "second edition."

As if this bewildering proliferation of mediations were not enough, several further twists intensify the referential void at the novel's center.

In his introduction to the manuscript, Truant gives voice to his suspicions that the film does not exist:

> As I fast discovered, Zampanò's entire project is about a film which doesn't exist. You can look, I have, but no matter how long you search you will never find *The Navidson Record* in theaters or video stores. Furthermore, most of what's said by famous people has been made up. I tried contacting all of them. Those that took the time to respond told me they had never heard of Will Navidson let alone Zampanò. (xix–xx)[ii]

This mind-numbing evidentiary quandary is compounded by the even more startling revelation that Zampanò was "blind as a bat" and thus physically incapable of performing the job of mediation he has allegedly performed (xxi). Finally, jumping up a logical level, it has recently been suggested that Zampanò's identity as the main character in Fellini's *La Strada* makes him a fictional character *within* the fictional world of the novel, a fiction to the second degree.[iii] In the wake of this thorough imbrication of the fictional and the real, any effort to mark this separation is, in principle, impossible.

Far more important, however, than the epistemological hurdles these twists introduce are the ontological indifference underlying them and the definitive departure that it signals away from the tired postmodern agonies bound up with the figure of simulation. It is as if mediation has become so ubiquitous and inexorable in the world of the novel (which is, after all, our world too) that it simply *is* reality, *is* the bedrock upon which our investment and belief in the real can be built. "See," Truant announces with the confidence of embodied hindsight, "the irony is it makes no difference that the documentary at the heart of this book is fiction. Zampanò knew from the get go that what's real or isn't real doesn't matter here. The consequences are the same" (xx).

Far from an invitation to wax poetic about the simulacral pseudo-foundation of contemporary media culture, this deceptively flippant maxim betrays a disturbing willingness on Truant's part to accept the waning of the orthographic function of recording. As the reader soon discovers, this willingness—far from betokening a curiosity stemming from Truant's (admittedly curious) psychological profile—is simply a necessary consequence of the novel's play with mediation and undermining of any "sacred text." From Truant's sustained alterations of the text to the reported interventions of the unidentified editors, from Zampanò's impossible perceptual acts to (Truant's mother) Pelafina's unreliability as a conveyor of her own voice, the novel insistently stages the futility of any effort to anchor the events it recounts in a stable recorded form.

Although the deployment of these and other characters as figures for the end of orthography certainly betokens a shift away from traditional realism and psychological characterization, the novel's challenge—to generate belief without objective basis—becomes acute only when the role of the reader is taken into account. As Danielewski explains in an interview, the novel's true protagonist is the figure of interpretation—that is, the act of reading or the embodied reader:

> Let us say there is no sacred text here. That notion of authenticity or originality is constantly refuted. The novel doesn't allow the reader to ever say, "Oh, I see: this is the authentic, original text, exactly how it looked, what it always had to say." That's the irony of [Truant's] mother's letters [which are included as an appendix to the novel]: at first you probably just assume that, okay, this is the real thing, but then the artifice of the way they look starts to undercut everything, so you're not sure. Pretty soon you begin to notice that at every level in the novel some act of interpretation is going on. The question is, why? Well, there are many reasons, but the most important one is that everything we encounter involves an act of interpretation on our part. And this doesn't just apply to what we encounter in books, but to what we respond to in life. Oh, we live comfortably because we create these sacred domains in our head where we believe that we have a specific history, a certain set of experiences. We believe that our memories keep us in direct touch with what has happened. But memory never puts us in touch with anything directly; it's always interpretive, reductive, a complicated compression of information.[5]

Everything in this complex and rich novel—including everything that smacks of traditional realism (the investment in disturbed family dynamics, the oscillation among various focalizers, and so on)—is in the end subordinated to the task of posing the challenge of interpretation to the reader. The novel works, on the far side of orthographic recording, not by capturing a world, but rather by triggering the projection of a world—an imaginary world—out of the reader's interpretative interventions and accumulating memorial sedimentations.

Literally meaning "straight writing," the orthographic function of recording designates the capacity of various technologies to register the past as past, to inscribe the past in a way that allows for its exact repetition.

Despite its etymology, this function is neither limited to nor best exemplified by writing and, indeed, assumes its purest form in the technical domain—in the phenomenology of photography. Roland Barthes pinpoints this elective affinity between photography and orthography when, in *Camera Lucida*, he champions the specificity of photography as that technical medium capable of bringing together reality and the past:

> I call "photographic referent" not the *optionally* real thing to which an image or a sign refers but the *necessarily* real thing which has been placed before the lens, without which there would be no photograph. Painting can feign reality without having seen it. Discourse combines signs which have referents, of course, but these referents can be and are most often "chimeras." Contrary to these imitations, in Photography I can never deny that *the thing has been there*. There is a superimposition here: of reality and the past.[6]

This conjunction of reality and the past is the principle of photographic certainty and the basis for its specific intentionality; photography's noema, Barthes tells us, is "that has been" [*ça a été*].

Whereas Barthes takes pains to distinguish photography from other media, philosopher Bernard Steigler deploys Barthes' analysis as the basis for an account of orthography in general.[iv] Orthography, or "straight writing," has been adopted by Stiegler as a paradigm for technical recording, from writing to more recent, real-time, literal inscription technologies like phonography and cinema.[v] According to Stiegler, orthographic recording allows for the *exact inscription* of events and thus for their exact repetition, the possibility of experiencing *the same exact thing more than once* (the possibility upon which Stiegler's neo-Husserlian analysis of memory is based).[vi]

In his analysis of Barthes, however, Stiegler suggests that photography should be distinguished less for its technical singularity (which it shares with other mechanical inscription technologies) than for its exemplary resistance to phonocentrism: "The photo will in effect place us at a remove from 'phonocentric' temptations. And it will also permit us to discover that alongside orthographic writing there exist other types of exact registrations," an ensemble of "*orthothetic* memory supports" (*supports orthothétiques de la mémoire*) (Stiegler 1996, 24). What Stiegler has in mind here (on this point, his analysis certainly converges with Kittler's) is the host of technical recording instruments from photography to the digital computer—"straight-positing" (orthothetic) memory supports—that today function to inscribe our experience or rather, on

Stiegler's neo-Husserlian, phenomenological account, the memory of (our) experience.

Because of its dual principle—at once reality and the past—the photograph forms something of a paradigm for orthography: because it makes present a past that, however, cannot be a part of *my* past, that cannot be lived *by me*, photography insulates the past, the "that has been," even as it allows for its representification. Photography thus preserves the past in a way that avoids the phonocentric privilege of the present. Put another way, because its orthographic force stems from a technical (or, as Barthes says, a chemical) source, photography assures the autonomy of the past in the face of its inherent potential for representification. In this way, it forms a model that can help us conceptualize orthographic writing in its proper sense as the inscription of the past *as past* and not simply the copy of the voice, the writing down of the *phonē* (the voice):

> The meaning of literal orthothesis [*orthothèse littérale*] is not fidelity to the *phonē* as self-presence, but the literal registration of the past *as past*, as *passage* of the letter, or of the word [*parole*] *by* the letter—a certain mode of repeatability of the having-taken-place (if not of a having-been) of the play of writing. (Stiegler 1996, 48)

With his realization that it makes no difference whether the film is a fiction, what Johnny Truant effectively pronounces is precisely the *waning of the orthothetic function in general*. At stake here is more than simply the contamination of photographic orthothesis by the fictionalizing power of discourse; it is not just that, in the age of Photoshop, the alleged certainty of the photographic is subject to generalized suspicion. In question is the possibility for accurate recording per se, the capacity of technical inscription to capture what Danielewski celebrates, like Pynchon before him, as the singularity of experience.

In an age marked by the massive proliferation of (primarily audiovisual) apparatuses for capturing events of all sorts, from the most trivial to the most monumental, *House of Leaves* asserts the nongeneralizability (or nonrepeatability) of experience—the resistance of the singular to orthography, to technical inscription of any sort. This is precisely why *House of Leaves* is particularly well suited to theorize the medial shift in the function of the novel. As a corporeal palimpsest of the effects of mediation—including the mediation that it performs—*House of Leaves* practices what it preaches, always yielding one more singular experience, one more body-in-code, each time it is read.[vii]

1. THE DIGITAL

Danielewski observes that most people, if asked what *House of Leaves* is about, would say "it's about a house which is bigger on the inside than the outside" (Danielewski, "Conversation"). Put another way, the novel is about an *impossible* object, a referent that is absent not simply in the sense of being lost or unlocatable or even in the sense—common to all fiction—of lacking any existence whatsoever prior to and outside the fiction that conjures it up. *House of Leaves* is a realist novel about an object that, for precise technical reasons, cannot belong to the "reality" we inhabit as embodied beings: *even the fictional existence of this house is, in some sense, impossible.*[viii]

If we locate *House of Leaves* at the end of a long line of antimimetic novels—a line running from Sterne's *Tristram Shandy* to Calvino's *If on a Winter's Night a Traveler*—we can better grasp its (relative) novelty. Here, the referential impossibility is not narrative-based and epistemo-logically-focused so much as it is material: at bottom it stems from an incompatibility between the "topo-logic" of digital processing and the phenomenal dimension of human experience. *House of Leaves* is a narrative, as Kate Hayles has noted, that forthrightly admits the void at its center so as better to foreground the role of belief in its "reality" claim. Embodied belief is precisely the allegorical object of the hyperactive proliferation of mediation that comes to fill in the novel's central void.

Despite its referential impossibility, it remains the case that the house, as Hayles has astutely observed, "nevertheless enters the space of representation."[7] In a quite literal sense, it is the intrusion of the house into the lives of the novel's characters—not to mention those of its readers—that generates the narrative. This fact should not, however, be taken as license to interpret the house too narrowly as a figure for the novel in which it figures (a literal house of leaves). Although it certainly is that, the house must also and more fundamentally be viewed as a figure for the otherness of the digital as it enters thematically into the world of the novel and also as it punctures the surface of its textuality.

Not unlike the uneasy correlation between parameter-driven design techniques and built form in contemporary architecture (where the design possibilities materialized in the former vastly exceed the geometrical realities of the latter),[ix] what we encounter in this impossible house is a figure for a spatial dimension—a topological figure—that cannot find adequate representation in the forms of orthographic recording exhaustively inventoried by the novel. Its resistance to representation notwithstanding, this spatial dimension still manages to exert an immense impact as the very motor force driving both the host of recording technologies thematized in the novel and the recording technology that is the text.

This figural labor becomes quite explicit at the moment when Zampanò compares the house to an actual, physical icefall:

> Similar to the Khumbu Icefall at the base of Mount Everest where blue seracs and chasms change unexpectedly throughout the day and night, Navidson is the first one to discover how that place also seems to constantly change. Unlike the icefall, however, not even a single hairline fracture appears in those walls. Absolutely nothing visible to the eye provides a reason or even evidence of those terrifying shifts which can in a matter of moments reconstitute a simple path into an extremely complicated one. (68–69)

Here, through its difference from an actual, physical entity, we can see the house for what it is: a flexible, topological form capable of infinite and seamless modification; a postvisual figure immune to the laws governing the phenomenology of photography, cinema, and video; a logic of transformation whose output is disproportionate to its input. In this perspective, the house is nothing if not a figure for the digital: its paradoxical presence as the impossible absence at the core of the novel forms a provocation that, as we shall see, is analogous in its effects to the provocation of the digital.

That this analogy-by-effect surfaces most insistently at the point where the text's thematic concern with the digital coincides with its most extreme typographical deformation can hardly be a coincidence. Indeed, this point might be considered the culmination of the text's thematic engagement with the digital, the moment when this latter shades into a concern with the digital as a subterranean deformational force which threatens the integrity of the (traditional) text.[x] Chapter IX recounts "Exploration #4," in which the adventurer Holloway and his team encounter further evidence of the house's warped expansions as well as the bestial growl that, precisely by concretizing the unknown danger, will wind up driving Holloway out of his mind and ultimately to his demise.

Interspersed through the narration of this exploration and serving to interrupt its progression are a series of typological innovations—upside down and horizontal footnotes that literally carve into the space of the text. Certainly the highlight of this experimentation is, as Hayles has noted, footnote 144, a blue-lined frame, set near the top of the page and containing a (necessarily partial) list of everything that is *not* in the house. Because this list could be extended indefinitely, this footnote inscribes, in a particularly destabling manner, the way the outside world punctures the closure of the fictional world. The formal deformations to which it submits the novel put the latter's longstanding stability as a storage technology into question. This list of what is not in the house runs on through fourteen right-hand pages of the manuscript; in its appearance on the left-hand pages, it presents the text in reverse, as if the normally opaque text were suddenly rendered transparent or at least punctured by a see-through or reflective portal. This play with page layout and function culminates in a blank blue-outlined box followed, on the next page, by a solid-blue box, and on the next by a larger unframed box of blank white space imposed directly on and obscuring a single passage devoted to the capacity of digital technology to manipulate images.

Thus, although it playfully alludes to the capacity of text to mimic the effects of technical recording media, this culmination also foregrounds a deeper engagement of the text with digital technology. Made to coincide with a citation championing the improvements in real-time (analog) orthographic recording technology, the abrupt growth of the text box into an unwieldy blank field obstructing the text beneath hints at the potential disjunction between textuality and technical recording media.[xi] Here we can see clearly how the novel's thematic interest in coupling orthographic recording with textual deformation is a pretext for a more important argument concerning the rehabilitation of fiction in the wake of the digital.

That is why the previously invoked passage championing improvements in orthographesis goes on to conclude with a consideration of how the digital differs categorically from "low-end"—that is, analog, technology. Rather than extending the scope of orthographic recording, digital manipulation threatens to suspend the orthographic function of recording per se: "Digital manipulation allows for the creation of almost anything the imagination can come up with, all in the safe confines of an editing suite ..." (144). The digital here signifies the wholesale substitution of the productive imagination for the registration of the real—the triumph of fiction over documentation. It is in this sense that the fictional house can and must be understood as a figure for the digital: it challenges techniques of orthographic recording and, by evading capture in any form, reveals the digital to be a force resistant to orthothesis—the force of fiction as such.

2. MEDIA

Much more than just a thematic focal point, the impossible house that is larger inside than outside plays the role of catalyst for the events and actions that transpire within the novel. More than just a motor for narration, it triggers a media agon in which print's capacity to mimic technical orthographic recording attests not only to its flexibility, but also—far more significantly in my opinion—to its special aptitude for "documenting" the nondocumentable impact of the digital. Even as it reconfigures the novel from story-telling vehicle to interface onto a virtually limitless universe of information, the thematization of mediation serves first and foremost to foreground the paradoxical privilege enjoyed by print in today's new media ecology.

Consider, as an initial example, how the house jumpstarts the narrative: only once the house's peculiar spatial properties are discovered in Chapter IV do film and text acquire a plot. Prior to this moment, the void of narration had been filled by Zampanò's description of some altogether innocuous documentary footage from the daily lives of the Navidsons in their new house on Ash Tree Lane.[xii] Abruptly puncturing this static picture, the discovery of the house's transformation triggers a frenzied proliferation of recording that will drive the plot of film and text from this point forward. It is hardly insignificant that this proliferation occurs in direct response to a failure of technical orthography—the failure of ubiquitous Hi-8 video surveillance cameras to capture the house's uncanny transformation.[xiii] Indeed, this plot-instigating incident puts into play an odd logic that will recur throughout the narrative: rather than leading to a disinvestment in technical recording, as we might expect from such a bizarre event, orthographic failure will, time and again, only intensify orthographic desire.

Yet, even as it literally sets off an escalating multiplication of layers of mediation, this odd logic will also cause the relation between text and technical recording to evolve in ways that speak directly to the changing status of the literary in the new media ecology. As the resistance of the house to orthographic capture yields an ever more complex deployment of technical mediation (to the point where, in Exploration #4, photography, film, video, surveillance video, and sound recording are all deployed together), the text undergoes a kind of internal functional division. On the one hand, its apparent seduction by this escalating orthographic frenzy causes it to join the fray and demonstrate its flexibility as a form of media capable of mimicking other media; on the other hand, it differentiates itself from technical recording in what amounts to an assertion of the novel's privilege within today's complex media ecology. *House of Leaves* shows itself—and therewith the novel as such—to be the appropriate vehicle for documenting the incapacity of orthographic recording technology to document the impossible house—that is, the being of the digital that, as Friedrich Kittler says, today determines our experience.

Before exploring this privilege further, let us pause to take stock of the impact of this plot-instigating function of the house—specifically the way in which it correlates the structure and function of the narrative with the orthographic task thematized within the novel—on the other generic elements of the novel. Effectively, by placing Zampanò's narrative into a competition with recording media, *House of Leaves* subordinates traditional characterization to allegorical functions that serve the ends of media agon. (In general, my argument here builds upon observations made by Hayles in her consideration of characterization in *House of Leaves*.)

Consider, for example, the portrayal of Navidson. Navidson is, literally, a cipher for orthographic desire: all of the aspects that, traditionally speaking, contribute to well-rounded characterization—psychology, past experience, personal idiosyncrasies, and so on—are in his case mere subfunctions, indeed true epiphenomena, of this overriding function. This is why Navidson's character furnishes the emblem for the paradoxical correlation of orthographic failure and orthographic desire we have just observed:

> Perhaps one reason Navidson became so enamored with photography was the way it gave permanence to moments that were often so fleeting. Nevertheless, not even ten thousand photographs can secure a world, and so while Navidson may have worked harder, taken greater risks and become increasingly more successful, he was ultimately misled in feeling that his labor could make up for the love he was deprived of as a child and the ultimate sense of security such love bestows.... More than just snapping a few pictures and recording daily events with a few Hi 8s, Navidson wanted to use images to create an outpost set against the transience of the world. No wonder he

found it so impossible to give up his professional occupation. In his mind abandoning photography meant submitting to loss. (22–23)

What this passage so clearly shows is how Navidson's character encompasses both sides of the paradox of orthography. His history as a Pulitzer-prize-winning photographer, for example, stands just as clearly behind the desire that causes the family to retreat from the public domain as it does his inability to do so without documenting every step of the process.

Like character, relations between characters are also a direct function of the agon of media. Such relations develop only because and to the extent that they come together in the common task of documenting the impossible house. One striking instance appears in the renewal of Navidson's relationship with his brother, Tom—a relationship that, we are told, has been strained "for over eight years" (31). Although we might expect the coincidence of the house's transformation to occasion a reconciliation between these characters, this possibility is soon put to rest by nothing other than the house: "… the moment and opportunity for some kind of fraternal healing disappears when Tom makes an important discovery: Navidson was wrong. The interior of the house exceeds the exterior not by 1/4" but by 5/16"" (32).

This pattern holds for the remainder of the narrative, as if offering an allegory for the capacity of the house—because of the orthographic crisis that it occasions and figures—to subsume all possibility of independent character relations: at each point at which Will and Tom begin to address the substance of their estrangement (Will's success, Tom's drinking, etc.), some more pressing need related to the documentation of the house supervenes.

In an even more direct expression of its obsession with the problem of orthography, the novel enacts a subordination of face-to-face relations between characters in favor of ever more highly mediated forms. For example, Karen and Navidson communicate best across the distance of media interfaces: they speak to each other through Hi8 video diaries and learn more about one another, not to mention themselves, from viewing their documentations of the other than from any form of direct contact. One need only consider Karen's perspective on the relationship: her estrangement from Navidson mounts as his orthographic fervor intensifies, to the point that she feels compelled to abandon Navidson and the house. Only after having assayed her own documentation, "A Brief History of Who I

Love," can she begin to see Navidson "as something other than her own personal fears and projections." Through this mediation, Karen is able to witness how much Navidson "cherished the human will to persevere" and to glimpse the "longing and tenderness he felt toward her and their children" (368).

Even as it testifies to the irreducible complicity between character and mediation in this novel of mediations, this example also folds into itself supplementary layers of mediation which obscure even that measure of reconciliation that would seem to be effected between Karen and Navidson. Here, the fact that Karen's method is to let "Navidson's work speak for itself" could not be more significant. The Navidson she rediscovers is not the private Navidson that she so desires, but rather the Navidson that appears through the lens of *his* photographic mediation.

This conflation is symbolized by the conclusion of Karen's film which, despite showcasing material from Karen's own hand (a home video of Navidson and his children at play in their new home), serves above all to highlight the inadequacy of film as a documentary medium. Unable to follow Navidson's actions as he grabs their daughter Daisy and holds her up to the blinding sun, the film culminates in total overexposure, showing Navidson (and the children that tie Karen to him) simply "vanish[ing] in a burst of light," as if transmogrified into the materiality of film (368).

This recognition of the limitations of orthographic recording technology is not, however, restricted to localized "character" perspectives, but rather is woven increasingly tightly into Zampanò's unfolding narrative. At first this takes place thematically, as events reveal the utter impossibility of documenting that space. Following Exploration #3, in which the house appears for the first time in its immensity, the adventurer Holloway matter of factly pronounces the eclipse of orthography: "It's impossible to photograph what we saw" (86). For Zampanò, the force of this pronouncement suspends any lingering faith in the redemptive power of Navidson's extraordinary gift:

> Even after seeing Navidson's accomplished shots, it is hard to disagree with Holloway. The darkness recreated in a lab or television set does not begin to tell the true story. Whether chemical clots determining black or video grey approximating absence, the images still remain two dimensional. In order to have a third dimension, depth cues are required, which in the case of the stairway means more light. The flares, however, barely illuminate the size of that bore. In fact

they are easily extinguished by the very thing they are supposed to expose. Only knowledge illuminates that bottomless place, disclosing the deep ultimately absent in all the tapes and stills—those strange *cartes de visites*. (87)

Later, when it is taken up by Navidson, this contrast between orthographic illumination and some kind of deeper, sightless knowledge serves explicitly to introduce the superiority of print. In a snippet from "The Last Interview" detailing the rescue of Billy Reston (a document curiously missing from the inventory of supplementary materials assembled in the appendices, as Hayles underscores), Navidson recounts his discovery of the incongruity between mediated representation and reality:

When I finally went back to the house to retrieve the Hi8s, I couldn't believe how quickly it had all happened. My leap looks so easy and that darkness doesn't seem dark at all. You can't see the hollowness in it, the cold. Funny how incompetent images can sometimes be. (344)

Confirming the validity of Navidson's pronouncement, Zampanò goes on to observe that "only the interviews inform these events. They alone show us how the moments bruise and bleed" (344).[xiv]

This same pattern of mediation serving to highlight the comparative superiority of print over technical recording informs the novel's investment in the capacity of print to mimic and thereby subsume the operations of recording technologies like photography and film. Consider, for example, the text's simulation of the film running out, smack in the middle of the rescue. Spread out over the space of five pages (307–311, with slashes indicating page breaks) and located at various heights on the page, the following words are inscribed: "The film runs out here, / leaving nothing else behind but an unremarkable / white / / screen." Here the blank page functions as a material analog of the blank screen and the word "blank," giving a sensory correlate to the abrupt cessation of visual information that occurs when a film runs out or when the meaning of the word "blank" sinks in.

A closely related example helps show that the line between mimicry and the differentiation of media can be a very fine one. Just prior to this moment, as Navidson, Tom, and Reston seek to rescue Holloway's assistants, Jed and Wax, from the now homicidal and heavily armed Holloway, the film captures Jed's assassination in footage that would later permit frame by frame analysis "as diligent as any close analysis of the Zapruder film." If, like the Zapruder film, this documentary footage affords "ample information perhaps to track the trajectories of individual skull bits and blood droplets, determine destinations, even origins," it does not contain "nearly enough information to actually ever reassemble the shatter" or, in other words, to document exhaustively the irreversible process in which Jed's life transitioned over into death (193).

That such a transition can only be gestured at by both text and film becomes clear from the ensuing passage which, once again, unfolds over the space of several pages: "Here then— / the after / math /of meaning. / A life / time/ finished   between / the space of / two frames. / The dark   line   where   the / eye   persists   in   seeing / something   that was   never   there / To begin with" (193–205). In this case, the gradual unfolding of the text differentiates it from the filmic expression that it is attempting to simulate. Yet, it does so entirely to the advantage of the print medium; by contrasting its simulation to the filmic phenomenon of the afterimage—where what is seen is something extraorthographic, something imagined—this passage brings a depth and complexity to the representation of death that, as the novel suggests, simply cannot be achieved in a mechanical medium like film.

Certainly, we could follow Hayles's lead and add to these examples the many moments in which the typographical arrangement of the text functions to mimic the action depicted in the film (e.g., when the word "snaps" is stretched out over the space of three pages in imitation of the stretching of the rope holding the gurney as the stairway expands [294–296]). We could focus on moments when typography serves to produce cinematic effects of temporal acceleration and deceleration (e.g., the suspense generated by speeding up the turning of pages during the confrontation with Holloway [213–238] or the stasis achieved by the dense superimposition of several layers of footnoted text in Chapter IX). Yet, despite the undeniable testimony these typographical deformations lend to the mimetic flexibility of print text, we cannot overlook their prevailing *media-technical* function. More than signs of the text's capacity to subsume the function of other media, these deformations in the body of the novel are symptoms of the *impossibility of representing the digital, of its resistance to orthographic capture.*

3. BODY

If print nevertheless enjoys a certain privilege in the context of this representational impossibility, it must stem from something other than its orthographic capacity.[xv] Indeed, it can hardly come as a surprise that, in addition to the deformation of the generic and typographic conventions of the novel, the house also elicits fundamental changes in how we understand the novel as a process or, in other words, in how the novel—or rather how the activity of reading the novel—generates meaning.

If we bear in mind that the text we are holding in our hands has been transcribed by Johnny Truant, we can immediately appreciate how the "original" we are reading is already a copy and—given Johnny's addition to the text of footnotes recounting the personal transformation it elicits in him—how it is *a copy with a difference*. Simply put, it is a singular embodied reading of a "text" that does not exist in any other form, or at least that cannot be passed on to us in such a form. Indeed, Truant's mediation here presents a counterpart, within the domain of text, to the proliferating layers of orthographic mediation thematized in the narrative. As a postorthographic analogical mediation, Truant's narrative figures the act of reading as an act of copying with a difference—a difference borne directly by the body of the reader.[xvi]

Consider, in this respect, Truant's encounter, late in the text, with a group of musicians who had written song lyrics, "I live at the end of a Five and a Half Minute Hallway," based on a text they found on the Internet—the alleged first edition of *House of Leaves*. Given that this text includes an introduction and notes by Johnny Truant, the encounter creates a *mise-en-abîme* effect; specifically, it underscores the paradoxical existence of two different versions of the novel, only one of which (the one we are reading) could include Truant's notes about this encounter.

We are thus compelled to ask after the status of this section of the novel (Chapter XXI) and, more generally, whether Johnny's notes are properly located *inside* or *outside* its frame. As in the earlier mentioned passage in which Navidson reads *House of Leaves* by match and paper light (see endnote vii), here, the transfer of focus from postmodern epistemological play to orthographic critique is staged. In this respect, it is hardly surprising that Truant's interest in this text concerns the marginal notations added by the musicians and the larger question of orthographic exactitude they raise:

I thumbed through the pages, virtually every one marked, stained and red-lined with inquiring and I thought frequently inspired comments. In a few of the margins, there were even some pretty stunning personal riffs about the lives of the musicians themselves. I was amazed and shocked and suddenly very uncertain about what I had done. I didn't know whether to feel angry for being so out of the loop or sad for having done something I didn't entirely understand or maybe just happy about it all. There's no question I cherished the substance of those pages, however imperfect, however incomplete. Though in that respect they were absolutely complete, every error and unfinished gesture and all that inaudible discourse, preserved and intact. Here now, resting in the palms of my hands, an echo from across the years. (514)

Beyond signifying the author's loss of authority over his text and the merging of author and reader functions, this passage attests to Truant's simultaneous recognition of the singularity of his "reading" and the singularity of every other act of reading that might concretize his text. That is precisely why the pages he holds in his hand are at once "incomplete" and "absolutely complete." As the potential trigger for subsequent acts of reading—a trigger whose potential stems precisely from the failure of an orthographic fixing of the events recounted in the text—these pages are necessarily incomplete; however, as a cipher of Truant's experience of reading the text—an experience that exists only in his embodied actualization (as the perception of an *inaudible echo* from the past)—they are perfectly complete. As in the earlier "Navidson-matchlight" episode, the point here is not so much to introduce epistemic logjams as it is to foreground the correlation between the postorthographic condition and the role of singular readerly embodiment. This correlation yields a model of reading that I propose to call copying with a difference.

Not surprisingly, given the thematic and theoretical focus of *House of Leaves*, the reconfiguration of the novel as a copy with a difference is the direct payoff of the text's agon with other media. If the novel appears to be the victor in this agon, it is because it undergoes a fundamental transformation in its function. Liberated from its vocation as a means to stabilize, resurrect, and pass on the past—that is, to cash in a referential promise—the novel in its postorthographic form operates as a kind of machine for producing what we might call "reality *affects*" in the reader.

The payoff—or the realization—of the reader's singular concretization of *House of Leaves*, such a reconfiguration is anticipated from the very first page of *The Navidson Record*, where Zampanò urges the reader to ignore debates concerning the veracity of the film and to dwell instead on what is actually *in* the film: "Though many continue to devote substantial time and energy to the antinomies of fact or fiction, representation or artifice, document or prank, as of late the more interesting material dwells exclusively on the interpretation of events within the film" (3).

In what amounts to a compact allegory of its ironic, if not self-undermining, impact, the text's first reader, Johnny Truant, is unable to stick to such an interpretative strategy, despite his best intentions. Confronting Zampanò's later observation that "the best argument for fact is the absolute unaffordability of fiction," Truant makes a prescient observation of his own: Zampanò has, despite his hermeneutic injunction, managed to wander into "his own discussion of 'the antinomies of fact or fiction, representation or artifice, document or prank' within The Navidson Record. 196" (149, note 195). Yet, rather than bringing clarity, this observation brings only confusion: "I have no idea whether it's on purpose or not. Sometimes I'm certain it is. Other times I'm sure it's just one big fucking train wreck" (149, note 195).

The paradoxical impact of Zampanò's new critical asethetic is subsequently allegorized at the level of textual materiality, as Truant's observation is literally pierced from the outside—by the footnote that interrupts it only in order to continue it, but even more forcefully by the indecipherable, because utterly singular, free association it inspires from Johnny (which forms the content of that footnote):

> [196] 195 (cont.) Which, in case you didn't realize, has everything to do with the story of Connaught B. N. S. Cape who observed four asses winnow the air ... for as we know there can only be one conclusion, no matter the labor, the lasting trace, the letters or even the faith—no daytime, no starlight, not even a flashlight to the rescue—just, that's it, so long folks, one grand kerplunk, even if Mr. Cape really did come across four donkeys winnowing the air with their hooves.... (149, note 196)

In this expanding jumble of nonsensical associations, we encounter an effort—Truant's effort—to concentrate on interpreting events *within* the text that, paradoxically, can only succeed to the extent it abridges its imperative. Put another way, what appears to happen, from the moment the reader (with Truant as model) decides to concentrate *on what is given*, rather than *on the veracity of* what is given, is a shift in emphasis from the text (or film) as a referential object to the, as Barthes might say, *"necessarily* real" impact it has on the embodied life of its reader.

Following this transformation, however, the intentionality of the *"necessarily* real" impact undergoes a basic shift of orientation; no longer fixated on the past, it becomes emphatically future directed. In this sense, it is most significant that the digital—and the postorthographic text—correlates with the body in a fundamentally different way than does, for example, photography. Indeed, the flexibility of text—and hence its privilege—stem directly from this difference: whereas the orthographic function of technical recording emerges from a preexistent analogy with the body, the digital (and the postorthographic text) has no such ground.[xvii] Barthes' depiction of the photograph as an emanation from the body simply cannot characterize recording in the digital age:

> The photograph is literally an emanation of the referent. From a real body, which was there, proceed radiations which ultimately touch me, who am here; the duration of the transmission is insignificant; the photograph of the missing being, as Sontag says, will touch me like the delayed rays of a star. A sort of umbilical cord links the body of the photographed thing to my gaze: light, though impalpable, is here a carnal medium, a skin I share with anyone who has been photographed. (80–81)

By contrast, what is at stake in technical recording today is no longer an analog registration rooted in the correlation between technology and the body. In the age of Photoshop, the basis for Barthes' depiction—the profound tie linking the analog with the body—no longer holds.

Accordingly, we must fundamentally reconceptualize the relation between the body and technical recording. If, in Barthes' imagining, the body—direct carnal transmission—ensures the orthographic function of photography, today the body's no less fundamental mediating role must be introduced from the outside *as a supplement* to recording. The body must create analogy where there no longer is any or, more exactly, where none is *pregiven*. Rather than an inscription of the body as a stable trace of the past, what mediation in a digital environment involves is a supplementary, future-directed process of embodiment in which a carnal analogy with the digital is, as I put it in *New Philosophy for New Media*, forged as an "original" supplement (Chapter 6). Most important in this transformation is the liberation of the body from its function as a support or host for orthographesis. For this reason, it is hardly surprising that *House of Leaves* takes pains to champion the singularity of experience, whether of the characters *within* its several fictional frames or of readers situated *outside* some—but importantly, not all—of these frames.[xviii]

Consider, for example, the text's assertion that the various explorations of the house should be viewed less as collective experiences than as a conjunction of a host of singular ones: "As with previous explorations," Zampanò informs us in Chapter IX,

> Exploration #4 can also be considered a personal journey. While some portions of the house, like the Great Hall for instance, seem to offer a communal experience, many inter-communicating passageways encountered by individual members, even with only a glance, will never be re-encountered by anyone else again. Therefore, in spite of, as well as in light of, future investigations, Holloway's descent remains singular. (188)

This insight on Zampanò's part mirrors the conclusion of contemporary scientific researchers who, we are told, "believe the house's mutations reflect the psychology of anyone who enters it." Thus, "Dr. Haugeland asserts that the extraordinary absence of sensory information forces the individual to manufacture his or her own data" and "Ruby Dahl calls the house on Ash Tree Lane 'a solipsistic heightener,' arguing that 'the house, the halls, and the rooms all become the self—collapsing, expanding, tilting, closing, but always in perfect relation to the mental state of the individual'" (165).[xix] All of this leads Zampanò to conclude that in the case of Navidson's house:

> Subjectivity seems more a matter of degree. The Infinite Corridor, the Anteroom, the Great Hall, and the Spiral Staircase exist for all, though their respective size and even layout sometimes changes. Other areas of that place, however, never seem to replicate the same pattern twice, or so the film repeatedly demonstrates. (178)

Further evidence for this claim can be found, for example, in the chaotic and complexly mediated scene during which Tom, Navidson's brother, disappears for good as Navidson helplessly looks on. Here the correlation between singularity and spatial mutation creates a situation in which Tom's actions generate "spatial affects" that are subsequently countered by the variant spatial affects generated by Navidson's actions. Having retrieved Navidson's daughter, Daisy, from the house, Tom has, we are informed, "found his limit"; out of breath, he stops, kneels, and heaves for air, at which point:

> [The] floor carries him backwards ten or fifteen feet more and then for no apparent reason stops. Only the walls and ceiling continue their drunken dance around him, stretching, bending, even tilting.

> When Navidson returns to the window, he cannot believe his brother is standing still. Unfortunately, as Tom demonstrates, whenever he takes one step forward, the floor drags him two steps back. Navidson quickly begins to crawl through the window, and oddly enough the walls and ceiling almost instantly cease their oscillations. (346)

It is hardly insignificant that Tom's final disappearance is explicitly figured through photographic metaphors: "Only the after-effects create an image commensurate with the shutter like speed with which those walls snapped shut"; "In less time than it takes for a single frame of film to flash upon a screen, the linoleum floor dissolves, turning the kitchen into a vertical shaft. Tom tumbles into the blackness." Nor is it incidental that the narration of this event is tainted with the fragmentizing effects of mediation, as we learn from footnote 308: because of darkness and limitations of the Hi-8 video cameras deployed, the film had to be supplemented by Billy Reston's narrative, which is simply the retelling of what Navidson had earlier recounted to Reston.

One theory for why Navidson makes Reston "the sole authority" here concerns Navidson's insight into the incommensurability of past-oriented orthography and future-directed experience:

> By relying on Reston as the sole narrative voice, [Navidson] subtly draws attention once again to the question of inadequacies in representation, no matter the medium, no matter how flawless. Here in particular, he mockingly emphasizes the fallen nature of any history by purposefully concocting an absurd number of generations.... A pointed reminder that representation does not replace. It only offers distance and in rare cases perspective. (346, note 308)

As always in this text of ever proliferating mediation, after the many layers have been sorted, the one thing that remains "true"—"indubitable" in a perversely Cartesian sense—is the bodily impact of the effort to interpret. Thus the orthographic desire that forms the motor of the novel's plot sets the context for the singularity of embodied response. Likewise, the figuration of the house's subjective spatial mutations through media effects leads to an entirely different modality of conviction: the physiological.

Consider, in this respect, how Zampanò directs the discussion of subjective space toward more primitive processes of proprioception and somatic expression:

> No doubt speculation will continue for a long time over what force alters and orders the dimensions of that place. But even if the shifts

turn out to be some kind of absurd interactive Rorschach test resulting from some peculiar and as yet undiscovered law of physics, Reston's nausea still reflects how the often disturbing disorientation experienced within that place, whether acting directly upon the inner ear or the inner labyrinth of the psyche, can have physiological consequences. (179)

As Johnny's response makes clear, these embodied, nonconscious, practically autonomous processes confer the feeling of reality on mediated experience: "No doubt about that," he adds with wry irony, "My fear's gotten worse" (179, note 211).

This correlation between the house's spatial mutations and the singularity of experience finds an apt emblem in the figure of the Labyrinth. "In order to consider how distances within the Navidson house are radically distorted," Zampanò notes at the beginning of Chapter IX, "we must address the more complex ideation of convolution, interference, confusion, and even decentric ideas of design and construction. In other words the concept of a labyrinth" (109). Citing Penelope Reed Doob's *The Idea of the Labyrinth from Classical Antiquity through the Middle Ages*, Zampanò notes how the distinction between those who are inside the labyrinth and those who view it from the outside breaks down in considering Navidson's house, "simply because no one ever sees that labyrinth in its entirety." As a result, "comprehension of its intricacies must always be derived from within"—that is, through the singular experience of those inside it (114).

If this is true for the film as well, it is because the film is also an unsolvable labyrinth: there simply is no transition possible from the "continually devolving discourse" of the film—a discourse that promises discovery "while all along dissolving into chaotic ambiguities too blurry to ever completely comprehend"—to an embodied navigation of the house it mediates (114). In a now familiar pattern, this brush with the limits of technical orthography almost immediately shades into an account of the house as a figure for the digital. *This* house, Zampanò notes, defies the traditional means of escaping a labyrinth—for example, by keeping one hand on a wall and walking in one direction—because it "would probably require an infinite amount of time and resources" to be solved (115). *This* house, in other words, is a labyrinth *of unprecedented impossibility*: it presents truly irresolvable obstacles, rendering futile any "permanent"—that is, objectively mappable—solution: "Due to the wall-shifts and extraordinary size, any way out remains singular and applicable only to those on that path at that particular time. All solutions then are necessarily personal" (115).

This comparison of the house with the figure of an unobservable Labyrinth furnishes the genetic schema for *House of Leaves'* critique of orthography. Crucial here is the move, exemplified in the comparison, to *flip over* an initial aporia between mediation and experience in a way that reinvests the bodily dimension of experience that the aporia is designed to undermine. Thus, if experience is necessarily mediated by orthographic recording (film as exact registration of the past) and if such recording is necessarily incomplete (film as labyrinth), then there simply can be no transition from mediation to embodied experience. However, if what we are dealing with *in the first place* (the house as a figure for the digital) is something that cannot *in principle* be recorded—and here is where the flipping over occurs—then the aporia is a vicious one: no more adequate recording apparatus could potentially reconcile mediation and experience because the object in question *absolutely resists orthographic capture to begin with.*

If the house–labyrinth comparison forms an exemplary instance of this schema of reversal, that is because it takes the reader through this process (flipping over the aporia). The act of recognizing the house as a figure for the labyrinth of the digital—for an *impossible, unsolvable* labyrinth—catalyzes a fundamental shift of approach, an abandoning of the project of orthographesis thematized in the novel and a renewed concentration on the embodied, and thus necessarily partial, framing of information by the reader. To put it in the terminology of systems theory, which is germane here, the impossibility of an external, first-order observation of the entire system functions to ennoble second-order observations that take this impossibility—always from their singular standpoint within the system—as their content.[xx] No wonder, then, that Ruby Dahl, Zampanò's invented expert on space, "fails to consider why the house never opens into what is necessarily outside of itself" (165, note 202).

The reinvestment of what we might call bodily observation correlates directly with the reconfiguration of the novel as a copy with a difference. As yet another analog of the impossible, unrecordable house, the novel can only be said to exist through the series of embodied second-order observations to which it gives rise. If *House of Leaves* is able to speak *exemplarily* of this reconfiguration that is because it poses itself as one "medial presence" among others—as a specific medium (a house of leaves) with no pregiven privilege within the larger media ecology to which it necessarily belongs;[xxi] *House of Leaves* thereby opens itself to the infinite matrix of information outside it in a way that is almost unprecedented, even among contemporary novels. In this way, moreover, the novel is able to take the question of its specificity as its content.

This generic recursivity appears most strikingly in the digression on echo that opens Chapter V. Initially presented as a consideration prerequisite for understanding the importance of space in the film (and hence, by implication, of the house as an impossible labyrinth), the analysis of echo leads into a consideration of the Borgesian technique of indiscernible difference, a foray into the mythological resonances of echo, and a pseudoscientific exploration of the physiology of the echo. It finally culminates in a synaesthetic transformation of the process of hearing—a recalibration of hearing as sight—which testifies to its strongly embodied basis.

Distributed across these various interpretative domains, the figure of echo begins to take form as a model for the process of reading triggered by *House of Leaves*. Specifically, by articulating the mythic with the physical, Zampanò's analysis of echo correlates the act of reading with a hermeneutics of embodiment in which meaning simply *is* the entirety of the physiological impact of that act. In this articulation, the text's analysis of the physical conditions of echo functions to specify the embodied thresholds which serve to constrain the sonic phenomenon of the echo; the analysis of Echo's mythic heritage—from Ovid to John Hollander—re-envisions echo as a mode of *analog* repetition—that is, a conception of response marked by the *différance* of the body. The figure of Echo serves to introduce the maxim that will guide our construction of the novel as a copy with a difference: find the analog within the digital—that is, let your body re-enliven what is merely an exact copy, an orthographic inscription of the past as past.

Interweaving mythological and scientific accounts, the analysis of echo purports to unpack the "echoes reverberating within the word itself" (41). Together, the mythological and scientific accounts articulate "space" and "love" with one another:

> Myth makes Echo the subject of longing and desire. Physics make Echo the subject of distance and design. Where emotion and reason are concerned both claims are accurate.
> And where there is no Echo there is no description of space or love. There is only silence. (50)

By articulating space and love, myth and physics open an alternative relationship to the house, one rooted less in its blanket resistance to recording (its "digital autonomy") than in the concrete demands it makes on understanding. According to Zampanò, recognition of the imbrication of physics and myth is essential to the task posed to the novel's reader: "In order to even dimly comprehend the shape of the Navidson **house** it is … critical to recognize how the laws of physics in tandem with echo's mythic inheritance serve to enhance echo's interpretive strength" (47).

Indeed, as the text's exemplar for the strength of a bodily hermeneutics, echo forms a model for managing the impossible labyrinth of the house and thereby repudiates the supposed "descriptive limitations" that preface the analysis of the house as labyrinth. If the restriction of the echo "to large spaces" initially seems to restrict its capacity (as compared with a recording technology like film) to "consider how distances within the Navidson house are radically distorted" (109), following the analysis of the house as impossible labyrinth, where orthographic mediation is shown to be inadequate *in principle*, it is precisely this kind of restriction—insofar as it forms a correlate of embodied understanding—that is shown to be most necessary.

In what sense, then, can we understand echo to be the precondition for the description of space? Zampanò's analysis of the physics of sound explains how echo "defines," "limits," and "temporarily inhabits" space (46): the sonic phenomenon of echo transpires through the conjunction of distance and time. What matters most, as Zampanò reminds us, is "a sound's delay":

> The human ear cannot distinguish one sound wave from the same sound wave if it returns in less than 50 milliseconds. Therefore for anyone to hear a reverberation requires a certain amount of space. At 68 degrees Fahrenheit sound travels at approximately 1,130 ft per second. A reflective surface must stand at least 56½ ft away in order for a person to detect the doubling of her voice. (50)

The production of echo, the doubling of sound—sound's *différance*—requires that certain empirical conditions be met: the space inhabited by sound must be neither too small nor too large (there is no echo in a space of infinite dimensions just as there is none in a vacuum). Otherwise put, the sonic phenomenon must be calibrated to the thresholds and constraints of embodied hearing—hearing as it occurs in a concrete context and through a concrete apparatus.

These imperatives inform the double synaesthetic transformation of hearing at issue in Zampanò's analysis. To describe the "descriptive ability of the audible," Zampanò offers the following formula:

$$\text{Sound} + \text{Time} = \text{Acoustic Light} \qquad (47)$$

As a medium for measuring space, sound provides an acoustic analogy for light: like light, it is omnispatial and pervasive. For this reason, concludes Zampanò, "speaking can result in a form of 'seeing'" (47).

Following a contrast with animals that, we are told, use sound to create acoustic images and "see" the shape of sound, Zampanò modifies this formula. More accurate to the mode of imaging of the human eye, which is neither active nor passive and which merely requires an object to be illuminated, is the following formula:

$$\text{Sound} + \text{Time} = \text{Acoustic Touch} \qquad (47)$$

Sound measures distance and thus approximates the function of vision by translating distance into touch, by opening a bodily modality in which seeing is feeling. That is why, "to hear an echo, regardless of whether eyes are open or closed, is to have already 'seen' a sizable space" (50).

To grasp how this synaesthetic transformation and reembodiment of vision reconfigures the task of reading, we must turn to the mythological history. Myth, Zampanò notes, testifies to the insurgency of Echo who, despite suffering "total negation" of body and "near negation of voice," still manages "to subvert the gods' ruling." In so doing, Echo offers herself as a model for the reader, who is, after all, faced with the task of inhabiting an impossible spatial object, an object whose impossibility is a function of the disembodied logic of digital replication. Her example introduces the principle for the conversion that reading must effect; as Zampanò stresses, "her repetitions are *far from digital, much closer to analog*. Echo colors the words with faint traces of sorrow (the Narcissus myth) or accusation (the Pan myth) never present in the original" (41, emphasis added). Like Echo, the reader must breathe life into the orthographic, transforming it from an exact inscription of the past into the catalyst for the new, the unpredictable, the future.

Indeed, Echo furnishes an example of how—to adopt the language of information theory—information is turned into meaning: "Her voice has life. It possesses a quality not present in the original, revealing how a nymph can return a different and more meaningful story, in spite of telling the same story" (42). Just like Pierre Menard's echo of *Don Quixote* in the famous Borges story to which Zampanò compares it, the "exquisite variation" introduced by Echo marks the difference between information in a purely technical sense and information as intrinsically imbued with embodied meaning.

British cyberneticist Donald MacKay first introduced this important difference in his attempt to supplement Claude Shannon's mathematical theory of information with a theory of meaning. According to MacKay, there are two constituents of a unit of information: selection and construction. Selection corresponds to Shannon's technical conception of information and designates the probability of a message's likelihood, given the formal repertoire of choices.[xxii] Construction, on the other hand, specifies a larger context for selection—namely, the behavioral state of the receiver—by which MacKay means not simply cognitive predispositions but "visceral responses and hormonal secretions"—that is, the most primitive embodied faculties.[xxiii,8] For MacKay, information cannot be divorced from meaning because selection necessarily occurs in dirty, real-world situations in which embodied tendencies contaminate and thus actively contribute to the production of information.

MacKay's differentiation of meaning from the (purely technical) informational value of a message helps to flesh out the difference Zampanò has built into the phenomenon of the echo: the difference of reptition. By correlating meaning with the recipient's particular behavioral state rather than an observable change in his or her behavior, MacKay's theory encompasses situations involving the repetition of a message. Despite lacking informational value, a repeated message retains its meaning because this simply is the behavioral state it specifies, regardless of whether the receiver is already in that state.

By allegorizing this correlation of information with meaning, the myth of Echo operates an *epochē* of the phonocentric exactly opposite to that informing orthographic recording. Rather than preserving the past as a trace of the unlived (the past not lived by me), it serves to open the present moment of enunciation onto its uncanny doubling, to discover within it the possibility for an *analog* echoing that does not so much preserve the trace of the past as carry its force into the future in a way as unpredictable and singular as this or that reader's set of embodied predispositions.

A novel of ceaseless repetition across media, of mediation as repetition, *House of Leaves* ultimately proffers a model of reading as analog echoing. The exemplary instance of this model is Truant's "first read-ing" of the text. That is why, in a footnote added to Zampanò's discus-sion of echo, Truant recounts his self-transformation as an experience of the double synaesthetic crossing effected by the institution of echo as the mythico-physical condition of possibility for hearing. Musing on the "intensely personal nature" of Zampanò's consideration of echo in the orientation of the blind, Truant goes on to recount his own expanded and heightened visual capacities:

> But I saw a strange glimmer everywhere, confined to the sharp oscil-lations of yellow & blue, as if my retinal view suddenly included along with the reflective blessings of light, an unearthly collusion with scent & sound, registering all possibilities of harm, every threat, every move, even with all that grinning and meeting and din. (49)

This synaesthetic transfiguration gives Truant the possibility to hear and see in a noisy environment where, we are told, he and his friend Lude were prevented "from hearing correctly" and where Lude in particular remained "blind."

Truant's modeling of his response on the analogics of echo antici-pates later sections of the book in which he is led to postulate his sym-biotic relationship with Zampanò's narrative. In the most striking of these, Truant depicts himself as the nurturer and provider for the text, the source without which it would not exist:

> I wash the sweat off my face, do my best to suppress a shiver, can't, return to the body, spread out across the table like papers—and let me tell you there's more than just The Navidson Record lying there—bloodless and still but not at all dead, calling me to it, needing me now like a child, depending on me despite its age. After all, I'm its source, the one who feeds it, nurses it back to health—but not life, I fear—bones of bond paper, transfusions of ink, genetic encryption in xerox; monstrous, maybe inaccurate correlates, but nonetheless there. And necessary to animate it all? For is that not an ultimate, the ultimate goal? Not some heaven sent blast of electricity but me, and not me unto me, but me onto it, if those two things are really at all different, which is still to say—to state the obvious—without me it would perish. (326)

Almost immediately however—in yet another testament to the text's media self-reflexivity—this thought is abruptly turned around:

> There's something else.
>   More and more often, I've been overcome by the strangest feeling that I've gotten it turned around, by which I mean to say—to state the

not-so-obvious—without it I would perish. A moment comes where suddenly everything seems impossibly far and confused, my sense of self derealized & depersonalized, the disorientation so severe I actually believe—and let me tell you it is an intensely strange instance of belief—that this terrible sense of relatedness to Zampano's work implies something that just can't be, namely that this thing has created me; not me only it, but not it only me, where I am nothing more than the matter of some other voice, intruding through the folds of what even now lies there agape, possessing me with histories I should never recognize as my own; inventing me, defining me, directing me until finally every association I can claim as my own ... is relegated to nothing; forcing me to face the most terrible suspicion of all, that all of this has just been made up and what's worse, not made up by me or even for that matter Zampanò.

Though by whom I have no idea. (326)

Here then is the traditional equation of novel and body, now reconfigured for a media—or more precisely, a postorthographic—age. In place of the epistemological frisson generated by the *mise-en-abîme* of, for example, Borges' "Garden of Forking Paths," here we encounter a thorough recursivity between text and body. It literally makes no difference which is the container and which the contained because, in either case, the fictional narrative garners its "reality effect" through the reality *affects* it stimulates its readers to produce.

From this subtle reconfiguration of postmodern reflexivity, we can draw two important conclusions. First, Truant's transformation figures the response of every reader, showing how it encompasses the entirety of the bodily processing involved in reading the text and also how it is, necessarily, nondocumentable, utterly singular. Second, Truant's experience locates the correlation of the novel and the body *outside the frame of the novel* traditionally considered, thereby transforming it into something like an index of the creativity of embodied reading. Just as the novel undergoes bodily deformation as a result of its confrontation with recording media, so too does the reader undergo an embodied transformation which, in this most curious of mediations, manages to stand in for the referential absence at the core of the novel and thereby to confer reality on the physically, materially—and perhaps even logically—impossible fictional world it projects.

By enthusiastically shedding all aspirations to autonomy—aspirations that characterize the realist novel per se—*House of Leaves* comprises a veritable script for producing bodies-in-code. Although it is certainly constrained by the text's language (which provides a source for selectivity), reading as the production of bodies-in-code requires creativity from every one of its actual, flesh-and-blood readers. The source for the difference of repetition, for the analogics of echo, such creativity must stem directly from—and must necessarily capture, though in a nonorthothetic manner—the singular embodiment of each and every reader. That is why, in a final layer of mediation, the act of reading *House of Leaves* generates a potentially infinite proliferation of singular bodies-in-code

Notes

INTRODUCTION

i. Bach y Rita's work focuses on tactile prostheses for the blind and specifically on remapping vision through stimulation of the tongue. Krueger's work will be discussed later.

ii. "The brain is a media junkie" and "it wants the good stuff," notes venture capitalist Dan Mapes (Krantz, 24).

iii. Obviously, what Krueger means by "immersion" is a far cry from the picture of a passive media consumer dreamed of by today's media industries. Immersion here is something of a minimal condition for the establishment of a perceptuomotor circuit and, thus, for embodied human agency.

iv. What is crucial to obtaining agency in such environments, as Krueger clearly saw as early as 1974, is the capacity to interact with people in your environment exactly as you normally would. This would not be [possible] if you were wearing contemporary data goggles. This [difference] is important because most people have a variety of responsibilities and perform many different tasks. Only a few might be full-time artificial reality personnel. The rest would have to choose, moment by moment, whether to operate in an artificial reality or in the real world. [But] in fact, they will often want to be able to operate in both simultaneously. (Krueger 1993, 155)

v. According to Massumi:

Digital processing as such doesn't possibilize let alone virtualize. The digital is already exhaustively possibilistic. It can, it turns out, potentialize, but only indirectly, through the experiential relays the reception of its outcomes set in motion. Those relays may even more indirectly seed as yet uncoded possibilities: inventions.... Whatever inventiveness comes about, it is a result not of coding itself but of its detour into the analog. *The processing may be digital—but the analog is the process.* The virtuality involved, and any new possibility that may arise, is entirely bound up with the potentializing relay. It is not contained in the code. (Brian Massumi, "On the Superiority of the Analog," in Massumi 2002, 141-142).

vi. This, incidentally, is the way in which Lev Manovich interprets the phenomenon of digitization generally. See Manovich, 2000, Chapter 1.

vii. Bernard Stiegler is the thinker of the technical element of the sensible-transcendental and of the invagination of the empirical and the transcendental in the wake of technics. See Stiegler, 1998.

viii. Stiegler's critical reading of Leroi–Gourhan's empiricism engages the difficulties generated by such a concept of the origin. See Stiegler 1998, Part I, Chapter 3.

ix. It is not incidental that Lacan's analysis of the gaze, of *object a* as the gaze, identified radio and television as institutional supports for the gaze.

x. Ruyer's subjectivities form a complement to Leibniz's "little perceptions." I discuss Ruyer at length in *New Philosophy for New Media*, Chapter 5.

xi. Commenting on the concept of "reversed epiphenomenalism," Michel Piclin clarifies Ruyer's perspective:

The duality of the body and the spirit is illusory, Ruyer tells us, because our relation to the body is not of the order of having, but of the order of being: we do not *have* a body, we *are* an organism. The body is the organism seen by others; ... the organism, the body felt from within" (Piclin 1992, 161x).

xii. This priority can be seen clearly in the complexity of the observation (description) of an autopoietic organism (phenomenological unity):

Since it is a defining feature of an autopoietic system that it should specify its own boundaries, a proper recognition of an autopoietic system as a unity requires that the observer perform an operation of distinction that defines the limits of the system *in the same domain in which it specifies them through its autopoiesis*. If this is not the case, he does not observe the autopoietic system as a unity ... (Maturana and Varela 1980, 109).

In effect, Maturana and Varela distinguish two types of observation: one in which the autopoiesis complements the organism because it adopts the perspective of the organism and another that is allopoietic because it adopts a perspective external to the organism. Thus, to treat an autopoietic machine as autopoietic (and not as allopoietic), an observer must distinguish system from environment *in a manner which coincides with the system's self-specified boundaries*. Obviously, this necessarily also holds for the system observing itself.

xiii. I analyze this technophobia—the reduction of technology to a figure of thinking—at length in *Embodying Technesis: Technology beyond Writing*. The critique of Western metaphysical discourse for reducing technology lies at the heart of Stiegler's multivolume *Technics and Time* project (see volume 1, cited earlier).

xiv. I say "in the final instance" because Butler does as much as is possible to think the materialization of the body—that is, to think agency as materialization. Perhaps we could say that Butler's theory of gender performativity is the constructivist theory *least* guilty of externalism, with the important point being that it still is externalist. As I see it now, the commitment to externalism is a consequence of Butler's adherence to the Hegelian–Lacanian tradition of self-recognition, which privileges the visual and the objectifying role of the gaze. In this sense, my effort to develop a theory of embodiment using the resources of autopoietic theory (specifically, the privilege of the operational perspective) can be seen as an effort to counter the Lacanian hold (which is exercised even in the case of a critic, like Butler, who is otherwise critical) on thinking identity in our world today.

xv. "Without fragility, the body not only loses its sensibility, but also its capacity to apprehend the other in its own body. An infallible body is not only the translation of an omnipotence without default, it is perhaps also the refusal of the other in its specificity" (41).

xvi. Hayles, for instance, includes the instrumentalization of the body as the "first medium" as one of the four leitmotifs of the posthuman. See Hayles 1999, Introduction.

xvii. See Varela, "Organism: A Meshwork of Selfless Selves," (Varela 1991), for a delineation of the five primary levels of "selfhood." The term "individuation" comes from Gilbert Simondon, as does the concept of "excess"; Simondon's theory of individuation and of the preindividual basis for individuation as an ongoing process cosubstantial with living will become important for my analysis in Chapter 1.

xviii. When they note that "the interactive behavior of the observer as it is observed in the exhibition process is an integral part of the work" ("Images of the Body in the House of Illusion," in *Art @ Science*, 8), Fleishmann and Strauss recognize a recursive experiential dimension of the two works that, even if it remains too empirical, nonetheless opens the path toward this understanding.

CHAPTER 1

i. Krueger notes: "My term 'artificial reality' referred to this metaphor as much as to any particular means of implementing it. I deliberately made the term provocative and liked the fact that it was an oxymoron" (Turner).

ii. When Krueger observes that the term "artificial reality" was "more loaded [when he started] than it is now," he underscores his explicit and intentional desire to confront the flat-footed humanism of the art world whose "default position was outright hostility towards technology" and which associated technology with dehumanization. Now that the tides have shifted, we must lay stress elsewhere by insisting that the "artificial" does not stand in opposition to the "natural" and indeed forms an "originary" element of the natural. This is precisely what is at stake in Krueger's position as new media art pioneer.

iii. Krueger is clear concerning his endorsement of technogenesis as "originary" and its consequences for humanism: "I view technology as the essence of our humanity. An empty hand signals that our anatomy is incomplete until we pick up a tool. In addition, I consider technology an inevitable consequence of the laws of physics and therefore as natural as the birds and the bees" (Turner).

iv. Söke Dinkla characterizes the environment as one that puts into question assumptions governing everyday interaction:

> The *Glowflow*-environment irritates habitual spatial perception using visual and auditory means. While the sense of vision—essentially responsible for orientation in space—is disturbed through the experience of the light-emitting tubes, irritation of hearing also occurs through nearly unlocalizable noises. The result is a room

with apparently autonomous qualities, one with a life of its own, that counteracts everyday experience and that manifests above all in the sensorium of the visitor. Aside from these experiences, which vary greatly from one another in subjective terms, *Glowflow* offers no habitual possibilities to make meaning. It is in a certain sense empty of contents. (66)

v. As Dinkla notes, Krueger quickly became dissatisfied with the lack of clarity in the human–computer interaction comprising *Glowflow*: "On account of the indeterminacy of the correlation between visitor action and system reaction, Krueger ultimately came to strip *Glowflow* of any reactive qualities and to designate it instead as 'kinetic environmental sculpture'" (69).

vi. As Dinkla points out, Krueger's open environments show that "even *programmable* spaces can be influenced and structured through human action" (83).

vii. "The body without an image is an accumulation of relative perspectives and the passages between them, an additive space of utter receptivity retaining and combining past movements, in intensity, extracted from their actual terms" (Massumi 2002, 57).

viii. According to Gil,

> [I]t is in the body that the codes find their point of convergence and their first point of application: the very one that will allow language, and in particular symbolic language, to translate codes among themselves. This property of the body to be the home or the agent for the translation of signs can be designated by characterizing it as an *infralanguage*.

As Gil's analysis makes clear, the infralanguage forms a sensible-transcendental or infraempirical basis for sensory exchange as such (of which translation of signs is merely one privileged example). Importantly for our purposes here, the infralanguage also concerns the production of spatiality by the body:

> The space of the body is made of plates, exfoliations, surfaces, and volumes that underpin the perception of things. These spaces "contain" the relations of the body to things, insofar as they are integrated in the body itself and insofar as they are translated among themselves. The elaboration of these spaces in the course of the development of an infant's mobility and organic maturity implies their constitution as spaces decodable into

257

other spaces—that is, their constitution thanks to their activity of the decoder-body, or the infralinguistic body, each of which is thus connectable to others, associating, intermingling, and bonding according to the laws of a specific mechanism. (129)

ix. Head emphasizes how the body actively modifies "the impressions produced by incoming sensory impulses in such a way that the final sensations of position or of locality rise into consciousness charged with a relation to something that has gone before" (cited in Gallagher, 227).

x. According to Cole and Paillard:

The term "proprioception" has come to be used, among British physiologists, for those sensory signals that arise from the moving parts of the body, including the head segment and the vestibular apparatus of the inner ear. The visual sense, in contrast, is generally considered as being mainly devoted to exteroception ... Proprioceptive information is necessary for updating the postural body frame (or schema), whereas exteroceptive multimodal information, mainly visual, underpins the central representation and percept of the body image (Jonathan Cole and Jacques Paillard, "Living without Touch and Peripheral Information about Body Position and Movement: Studies with Deafferented Subjects," 247; 254).

See also Brian O'Shaughnessy, "Proprioception and the Body Image," especially 190–191.

xi. Here I am thinking of Renaud Barbaras, who puts much emphasis on Merleau–Ponty's admissions, in the Working Notes to *The Visible and the Invisible*, of the dead end or fundamental impasse of his earlier project. See *Desire and Distance: Introduction to a Phenomology of Perception*, tr. P. Milan (Stanford: Stanford University Press, 2005).

xii. According to Gil:

If there is no ideal posture, there is an abstract posture in the same sense [as there is] the abstract figure. This abstract posture is not a form (but each concrete posture has one, which can be described in terms of the position of the body before the throw, cardiac rhythm, degree of concentration, and so on), but a "form" of forms, which enables it to move from the one to the other, from one concrete posture to another.... the posture of the body "contains" the point situated at $x + k$ meters. But in this case the body-point relation is established via an exfoliation, a leaf/lamina of the space of the body. This is not just any lamina and not just any surface. It is built up progressively with the elimination of contingent and heterogeneous contextual factors. It concentrates its own energy, it is rhythm, because instead of an objective space around a point, only the point exists; instead of aleatory corporeal and psychic elements, the abstract posture implies the reduction of any other thing that relates to anything apart from lining up the point. This exfoliation is a rhythmed space that results from two forms being placed in an energy-based relationship: the body and the space of the point. It is a form of forms and a rhythm of forms. So if the notion of abstract posture is generalized, if all relations that could thus be made between the body and objects are considered, then we have an *abstract body*.... The infralanguage is the abstract body.... In the same way that an abstract posture allows the passage from one point to another, the abstract body, capable of elaborating abstract rhythms or figures from different contexts, allows the translation of one context into another. (135–136)

xiii. According to Merleau-Ponty:

[H]abit in general enables us to understand the general synthesis of one's own body.... every habit is both motor and perceptual, because it lies, as we have said, between explicit perception and actual movement, in the basic function which sets boundaries to our field of vision and our field of action. Learning to find one's way among things with a stick, which we gave a little earlier as an example of motor habit, is equally an example of perceptual habit. Once the stick has become a familiar instrument, the world of feelable things recedes and now begins, not at the outer skin of the hand, but at the end of the stick. (1962, 152)

xiv. For an interesting, if somewhat more general, discussion of the artifactuality of "real-time" teletechnologies, see Jacques Derrida and Bernard Stiegler, *Echographies of Television*. The problematic of "real-time" is the focus of *The Politics of Presencing*, the final volume of my trilogy on new media.

xv. Gallagher rightly discerns that, on Merleau–Ponty's account, the body image may in certain cases ultimately be affected by prostheses just as the body schema is: "This distinction [of image and schema in the case of technical extensions of the body] is not absolute, however, and may involve a temporal component. More permanent attachments to the body—such as prosthetic devices—can become incorporated into both the image and the schema of the body affecting our bearing and approach to the world in both conscious projection and movement" (Gallagher and Cole, 372–373). The crucial point here is that the body schema remains the basis for the eventual prosthetic modification of the body image; by first affecting the schema a prosthesis can come to modify the body image.

xvi. Lingis explicitly identifies the perspective presented by the body image as that of observation:

> To assume a posture is to contract a "body image": as we sit at our desk we have a sense of the visible shape with which we fill out a volume in the room; as we stretch our legs under the table we have a sense of how their position looks. The more our attention is absorbed in our task and our feeling in the orientation and rhythm of our forces, the more determinate is this perception of the sides and outer contours of a thing we form. This image is different from the patches of surfaces we are actually seeing and those we remember. It fills out the outer aspect of our body as it would be seen by someone viewing it from a distance sufficient to see the whole position or movement. (63)

xvii. A transductive relation is one in which the relation is primary in relation to its terms. See Gilbert Simondon, "The Genesis of the Individual."

xviii. He reports that people emerged from the CAVE "sweating, panting and red-faced! They really had to do physical work to interact with the system. People lay on the floor, jumped, kicked and danced. This in itself was proof that we have built a dramatically different type of CAVE experience" (Penny et al.).

xix. To do this issue justice, one would have to consider Bergson's curious and productive conceptualization of the image as an ontological dimension somewhere between the subjectivism of the pure image and matter. For a discussion of the image in Bergson, see Gilles Deleuze, *Cinema 1*, Chapter 1. I discuss the role of affectivity as a bodily contamination of pure perception and the image in *New Philosophy for New Media*, especially in the Introduction and Chapter 2.

xx. In *Volatile Bodies: Toward a Corporeal Feminism*, Elizabeth Grosz argues for the continuity between the body schema and the flesh:

> The notion of the body schema or postural model of the body outlined by Merleau-Ponty in *The Phenomenology of Perception* anticipates or provides the origins of the concept of the flesh in *The Visible and the Invisible*. The body is able to move, to initiate and undertake actions, because the body schema is a series, or rather a field, of possible actions, plans for action, maps of possible movements the body "knows" how to perform. The body schema is also the field in which the subject's cohesion and identity as a subject and its intimate incarnation in and as a particular body take place. The concept of the flesh is developed as an "ultimate notion" (Merleau-Ponty 1968: 140), not the union or compound of two substances, but "thinkable by itself," an elementary or foundational term, which "has no name in any philosophy" (139, 147), an *exemplar sensible*." While it does not displace perception as the thematic object of investigation, it is a more elementary and prior term, the condition of both seeing and being seen, of touching and being touched, and of their intermingling and possible integration, a commonness in which both subject and object participate, a single "thing" folded back on itself (Grosz 1994, 95).

xxi. Indeed, Merleau–Ponty goes on to suggest that such "postural impregnation" is necessary to avoid interoceptive solipcism:

> My perception of my body would, so to speak, be swallowed up in a cenesthesia if that cenesthesia were strictly individual. On the contrary, however, if we are dealing with a schema, or a system, such a system would be relatively transferable from one sensory domain to the other in the case of my own body, just as it could be transferred to the domain of the other. (118)

This dimension of commonality will become crucial in our analysis later.

xxii. Here is Lacan's definition: "The *mirror stage* is a drama whose internal thrust is precipitated from insufficiency to anticipation—and which manufactures for the subject, caught up in the lure of spatial identification, the succession of phantasies that extends from a fragmented body-image to a form of its totality that I shall call orthopaedic" (Lacan 1977, 4).

xxiii. Given what we have said earlier about the observational perspec-
        tive, it is interesting that Merleau–Ponty's explanation specifically
        addresses the distinction between the child's perception of the
        other's image and his or her own:

> Why does the specular image of one's own body develop
> later than that of the other body? According to Wallon
> (whose analysis we are following here), it is because the
> problem to be solved is much more difficult in the case
> of one's own body. The child is dealing with two visual
> experiences of his father [following Wallon's example]:
> the experience he has from looking at him and that which
> comes from the mirror. Of his own body, on the other
> hand, the mirror image is his only complete visual evi-
> dence. He can easily look at his feet and his hands but not
> at his body as a whole. (1964, 129)

Not without relation here is Penny's insistence on the user's capacity to see (parts of) his or her body as he or she experiences the
virtual world of *Traces*; as he points out, this capacity differentiates
CAVE environments from HMD VR: "When I first used a CAVE, I
was fascinated with the visceral sensation of collisions with virtual
objects. I realized that part of the disembodying quality of HMD
VR was because when you look down, your body is not there! In a
CAVE, you see your body colliding with virtual objects" (Penny).

xxiv.   In this respect, Merleau–Ponty's understanding supports Freud's
        suggestion, in *The Ego and the Id*, that the "ego is first and foremost
        a bodily ego" and that "the ego is ultimately derived from bodily
        sensations, chiefly from those springing from the surface of the
        body" (Sigmund Freud, *The Ego and the Id*, trans. J. Riviere [New
        York: Norton, 1960], 16.) Specifically, Merleau–Ponty's explana-
        tion for the doubling—rather than identity—of the interoceptive
        body and the specular body emphasizes the independent existence,
        and indeed preexistence, of the interoceptive body. It thus stands
        opposed to readings, like that of Judith Butler, which take Freud's
        concept of the ego as "the projection of the surface of the body" in
        the other direction—that is, which render the body an effect of the
        creation of the body ego. See Butler 1993, Chapter 1.

xxv.   See Laplanche, Jean and J-B. Pontalis, *The Language of
        Psycho-Analysis*.

xxvi.   Merleau–Ponty's discussion of doubling via the magic power or the
        image foregrounds the corporeal dimension of sensibility:

> Childhood is never radically liquidated; we never com-
> pletely eliminate the corporeal condition that gives us, in

the presence of a mirror, the impression of finding in it something of ourselves. This magic belief, which at first gives the specular image the value not of a simple reflection, of an "image" in the proper sense, but rather of a "double" of oneself—this belief never totally disappears. It re-forms itself in the emotional make-up of the adult. (1964, 138)

xxvii. It is also for this reason that the visual can be determined as a derivative mode of sensation (as indeed touch can be, in distinction from primary tactility):

Our images are predominantly visual, and this is no accident; it is by means of vision that one can sufficiently dominate and control objects. With the visual experience of the self, there is thus the advent of a new mode of relatedness to self. The visual makes possible a kind of schism between the immediate *me* and the *me* that can be seen in the mirror. The sensory functions themselves are thus redefined in proportion to the contribution they can make to the existence of the subject and the structures they can offer for the development of that existence. (1964, 138)

Obviously, this "schism" must not be identified with the primary schism of being, even if it represents its derivative or, to recall Lingis' term, its emanation.

xxviii. See Bernard Stiegler, "Derrida and Technology: Fidelity at the Limits of Deconstruction and the Prosthesis of Faith."

xxix. Following the important, indeed ground-breaking concept of Bernard Stiegler (1998, Part I, Chapter 3).

xxx. According to Anzieu,

Tausk showed particularly well that the syndrome of the "influencing machine" could only be understood by distinguishing between these two Egos: the psychical Ego continues to be recognized by the subject as his own, ... whilst the bodily Ego is not recognized by the subject as belonging to itself and the cutaneous and sexual sensations which emanate from it are attributed to the workings of an influencing machine in the service of a devious seducer/persecutor. (40)

xxxi. More generally, Anzieu helps us see why Bick's work, like his own, necessarily entails an analysis of technics. However, Anzieu does not recognize the depth of the technical element and thus is not responsible for the discovery of the essential technicity of the skin.

Nonetheless, his perspective is explicitly motivated by a concern with contemporary technics. Thus he cites the need for our culture to

> set limits … on the gigantic scale of scientific projects and economic enterprise, on the invasion of the private sphere by the media of mass communication, on the compulsion endlessly to break records at the cost of over-training and drug-taking, on the ambition always to go faster and further and to spend more … on the need to produce everything of which we are technically capable even when that means creating mechanical, architectural or biological monstrosities … and the threat posed by technological advances to the integrity of the human body and to spiritual freedom, to the natural reproduction of human beings and to the survival of the species. (6–7)

xxxii. As Anzieu explains, this distinction between a passive and an active protective shield goes back to Freud's 1895 *Project for a Scientific Psychology*; more specifically, it corresponds to Freud's distinction between contact barriers and the protective shield. See Anzieu, 71ff. I analyze the technical basis of this Freudian distinction and of its development from the *Project* to the "dead cortical layer" of *Beyond the Pleasure Principle*, in *Embodying Technesis: Technology beyond Writing*, Chapter 6.

xxxiii. See Olalquiaga, Celeste. *Megalopolis: Contemporary Cultural Sensibilities*. 2. I return to Olalquiaga's analysis in Chapter 2.

xxxiv. According to Anzieu,

> The specific instinctual cathexis of the muscular apparatus and therefore of the second skin is provided by aggressiveness (whilst the first tactile Skin Ego is cathected by the attachment, clinging or self-preservation drives): attack is an effective means of defense; it means taking the initiative, preserving oneself by keeping the danger at arm's length. (195)

xxxv. Per Brian Massumi's recipe for creating experimental nonvisual hypersurfaces. See Massumi, 2002, 191–192.

xxxvi. The installation, Couchot explains,

> establishes between the image-body and the spectator a sort of tactile and visual dialogue, without any other language than that of the body…. the spectator is not invited to retrieve [*retrouver*] the presence of the body of the art-

ist.… On the contrary, she is invited to give life to this body in animating it with her own body. (50)

xxxvii.   Barbaras goes even further in instituting the philosophical perspective that views the world and the body as ontology and phenomenologization, respectively. The endpoint of this analysis, at least where the body is concerned, is the dissolution of all body boundaries in favor of a generalized sensibility "that is without assignable subject":

> The self-relation that characterizes sensibility is accomplished only as self-difference, an exteriority in the form of a divergence between touching and touched hands. In truth, neither of the two hands is strictly speaking sensing or sensed; nowhere can one isolate a moment of pure consciousness or a moment of pure passivity. One must instead speak of an axis of equivalence—the possibility of changing roles—which is dismembered by what it joins together. Corporeity corresponds to the moment of difference; consciousness corresponds to the moment of reversibility, which is only the other side of the preceding moment.

The ultimate consequence of this understanding is to institute the *écart* as the operator of a sensory continuum and correspondence that remains distinct, however, from a *sensus communis* (because different senses disclose different worlds):

> This relationship can be generalized, as we have seen, to the other senses. Every sensation, vision or touch, is in accordance with every other through this possibility of reversion. Such is the sense of the flesh: a unity that is realized only as possibility of passage, equivalence without principle between singular sensibilities. Now, to the degree that this carnal unity merges with the articulation of its differences, it cannot be understood as a closed unity—*it also differs from itself*. (245)

xxxviii.   The description that follows owes much to the "Interval Trip Report" of Ars Electronica jury chairman (and influential media artist) Michael Naimark and it corresponds to the version of the work as it was originally presented. The report can be found on Naimark's Website: http://www.naimark.net/writing/trips/ars98trip. html, accessed 7/26/05.

CHAPTER 2

i. This passage is from Gaston Bacheland, *The Poetics of Space.*

ii. My description of this work borrows liberally from descriptions by Davis and Wettheim. See Eric Davis, "Osmose," and Margaret Wettheim, "Out of this World."

iii. It does, however, have an especially high profile for a virtual reality artwork, having been (together with Davies' later environment, *Ephemère*) experienced by a total of 35,000 individuals as of the last exhibition in Melbourne, Australia, in 2004. Davies has also informed me that both works, destined to run on Silicon Graphics machines, were reengineered to run on a PC. Email to the author, 9/20/05.

iv. Psychasthenia can be schematically defined as a disturbance in the relation between the self and the surrounding environment. See Roger Caillois, "Mimicry and Legendary Psychasthenia."

v. As far as is possible, I try in what follows to refrain from evaluating Gibson's substantive claim regarding perceptual invariants, reserving my commentary to how Gibson's work has been appropriated by VR researchers.

vi. Rheingold mentions the influence of Gibson on two central pioneers of VR: Scott Fisher and Michael McGreevy. See Rheingold, *Virtual Reality*, 143–144.

vii. Though this correlation is especially explicit in Gibson's *The Senses Considered as Perceptual Systems* (1966), where it forms the very topic of investigation, his early work, *The Perception of the Visual World* (1950), and his final work, *The Ecological Approach to Visual Perception* (1979), include extensive discussions of locomotion and haptic processes. See especially Chapter 13 of the latter work. Page numbers will be cited in the text.

viii. See Hillis, 125: "Texture gradients are seen as a way to overcome the vast storage and computational difficulties in modeling geometric form in VEs…" In this regard, Hillis mentions the ongoing research project of the Department of Computer Science at UNC Chapel Hill, aptly entitled "Virtual Backdrops: Replacing Geometry with Textures."

ix. In a related body of research, work on telepresence has linked the richness of tele-embodiment to success at getting technology "to support the body's role in face-to-face interaction." Thus, tele-embodiment functions neither via visual simulation nor through illusion, but by the functional duplication of the body's capacities in a variant environment. As John Canny and Eric Paulos note, "… we can best interact with others at a distance by recreating the affordances of our physical body with telepresence." See Canny and Paulos, "Tele-Embodiment and Shattered Presence: Reconstructing the Body for Online Interaction," 292.

x. This remains the case despite Steuer's understanding of virtual reality—*"defined as a real or simulated environment in which a perceiver experiences telepresence"*—as introducing "an alternative view of mediated communication in general," one that breaks with the notion that media are only important as a "conduit." Although Steuer's redefinition of virtual reality effectively breaks with a reductive understanding of it in terms of specific hardware and shifts the focus to the interaction between the mediated environment and the participant, it does not break with the standard notion that what is communicated in the telepresence circuit is information. If it is the case, as Steuer claims, that "[i]nformation is not transmitted from sender to receiver," this does not mean that the informational position is rejected. Indeed, what is experienced in mediated environments as Steuer describes them if not information? See Jonathan Steuer, "Defining Virtual Reality: Dimensions Determining Telepresence."

xi. Despite Gibson's embrace of an informational understanding of perception, his theory includes elements that could, potentially, serve to complicate such a view. By mentioning Gibson's differentiation of perceptual systems in relation to the variable of "breadth" (which "refers to the number of sensory dimensions simultaneously presented"), Steuer suggests as much:

> Breadth is a function of the ability of a communication medium to present information across the senses. J. J. Gibson (1966) defines five distinct perceptual systems: the basic orienting system, which is responsible for maintaining body equilibrium; the auditory system; the haptic, or touch, system; the taste–smell system; and the visual system. Inputs to several of these systems from a single source can be considered informationally equivalent (Gibson 1966). However, the redundancy resulting from simultaneous activation of a number of perceptual systems reduces the number of alterative situations that could induce such a combination of perceptions, and therefore strengthens the perception of a particular environment. (Steuer 1992, 81)

See Steuer, "Defining Virtual Reality," 81. Though Steuer here accepts the informational basis of Gibson's theory, we shall have occasion later not simply to question this, but also to rescue Gibson's

intriguing understanding of proprioception from the informational reduction it undergoes in his theory.

xii. Jones furthermore argues that the privilege placed by Western
philosophy on theory is simply a higher order extrapolation of this
privileged detachment of sight.

xiii. Indeed, one might understand Jonas' move here as an effort to
merge the generalized function of vision (which must be distinguished from the specific sense modality of sight) with the generalized function of touch. Hints in this direction can be found in his
discussion of the "mental side" of touch, which is closely bound up
with the generalized function of vision:

> There is more than mere coincidence in the fact that in his
> hand man possesses a tactile organ which can take over
> some of the distinctive achievements of his eye. There is a
> mental side to the highest performance of the tactile sense,
> or rather to the use which is made of its information, that
> transcends all mere sentience, and it is this mental use
> which brings touch within the dimension of the achieve-
> ments of sight. Briefly, it is the image-faculty, in classical
> terms: *imaginatio, phantasia*, which makes that use of the
> data of touch. Only a creature that has a visual faculty
> characteristic of man can also vicariously "see" by touch.
> The level of form-perception at the command of a crea-
> ture will be essentially the same for both senses, incom-
> mensurable as they are in terms of their proper sensible
> qualities. Blind men can "see" by means of their hands,
> not because they are devoid of eyes but because they are
> beings endowed with the general faculty of "vision" and
> only happen to be deprived of the primary organ of sight.
> (141–142)

We shall return to this deep correlation of vision and touch later,
in relation to the work of Merleau–Ponty. Incidentally, the differentiation of vision from sight bears on the misapplication of
Gibson's theory by VR researchers. As Hillis suggests, the latter seek
to extend to, in his terms, the necessarily interpretative faculty of
vision, what Gibson says about sight. (See Ken Hillis, *Digital Sensations*, 126–127; 132.) If we restrict Gibson's theoretical claims to
the domain of sight (as he suggests we should), what he says about
perceptual invariants begins to make more sense and indeed to
resonate with Jonas' similarly biologically inflected claim that "only
the simultaneity of sight, with its extended 'present' of enduring
objects, allows the distinction between change and the unchanging

and therefore between becoming and being" (144–145). Restricted in this way, Gibson's claims, at least potentially, leave room for processes of reception that would involve the "self-movement" of the observer and thus the role of other sensory modalities.

xiv. Using an apparatus that allowed an active kitten to move about freely while carrying a gondola containing another, passive kitten, Held and Hein demonstrated that active or voluntary movement was central to the development of sensorimotor skills. Thus, the active kittens developed normal sensorimotor coordination, but the passive kittens failed to do so. See Richard Held, "Plasticity in Sensory-Motor Systems."

xv. Incidentally, Jonas' imaginary case very nearly approximates the situation of what Bergson, in the first chapter of *Matter and Memory*, calls "pure perception." Like the winged seed endowed with eyes, pure perception simply registers the flow of images without correlating this flow with any organizational principle (for Bergson, bodily affection and personal memory) that could give it meaning. In Bergson, the notion of pure perception was only a *heuristic* device to illustrate how the body as a "center of indetermination" is simply one image among others in a universe of images and thus can be deduced from this universe (rather than being posited as something standing over against it, as in idealism and realism). When Deleuze generalizes Bergson's notion as the basis of his understanding of cinema (in the movement-image and the time-image), he makes the error that Jonas is accusing the philosophical tradition of making: lending vision an illegitimate autonomy from the lower sensory modalities of the body. (See Deleuze 1986). I develop a critical account of Deleuze's move in *New Philosophy for New Media*.

xvi. Like *Osmose*, *Ephémère* utilizes semitransparency and spatial ambiguity and an interface based on breath and balance. However, it moves beyond *Osmose* by foregrounding the temporality of the experience, rather than its spatiality and simplifying the spatial elements to three principle levels. Here is Davies' description of Ephémère:

> In seeking to deal with the ephemerality of life, this work expands the spatiality of *Osmose* to encompass temporality. While *Osmose* was based on spatial organization of various worlds, and stasis of most elements within (except flowing particles), *Ephémère* relies on the emergence and transformation of form, and the ebb and flow of visibility and audibility. *Ephémère* contains three horizontal levels: landscape, subterranean Earth, and interior body. The

landscape is constantly transforming through time. The relationships between the various elements and the participant are more interactive or inter-responsive. In *Osmose*, interaction was limited to navigation and the resulting ambiguous perceptual readings of gestalt-like compositions were dependent on the changing participant location (with the exception of the fully interactive sound). In *Ephémère*, gaze has been introduced as a means of interaction: rocks "open" when gazed upon, revealing landscapes which quickly fade, and in the earth, seed sprout if approached slowly with a steady gaze, blooming, then fading back into the earth. I introduced the interior flesh body as the substratum in *Ephémère* (quite a change from the software code that formed the base of the *Osmose* world) as a means of reaffirming the poetic correspondence or coequivalence between earth and body.... anecdotal responses from some of the three thousand people who have experienced *Ephémère* ... suggest that this second work feels much more interactive, and evokes a sensation of being swept up and away, without a secure unchanging place to return to (i.e., the clearing in *Osmose*), i.e., one has to surrender to the experience. (Karl O'Donaghue and Char Davies, "Interview with Char Davies." 3–4).

xvii.   Davies comments:

I think that by using a fully enveloping virtual environment, one can get closer to recreating the sensation of being ... I release people from these physical constraints and allow them to experience "being" in a slightly different way. It almost refreshes their perception, so they can rediscover what it feels like to be here when they come back out into the world. (Wettheim, "Out of this World," 1)

See also Char Davies, Artist's Statement, 01010101.

xviii. Though it is beyond the aim of the present purpose, the issue of gender in relation to psychasthenia and the lived spatiality of the body would concern the adequacy of representation as a means to account for it. On this score, let me simply note that I have certain reservations concerning Grosz's account of the "constitution of the subject's sexed body through various forces of signification and representation—the meaning the body has for others and for itself, its socioeconomic constitution as a subject, and, above all, the psychical, economic, and libidinal constitution of bodies as sexually differentiated, as sexually specific" (193). As I see it, this account too narrowly circumscribes the domain where sex matters. One would, instead, have to ask how sex enters into the phenomenal experience of lived spatiality as I here reconstruct it.

xix. In this respect, Davies' environments help demonstrate Irigaray's adherence to the technophobia constitutive of Western philosophy. For a critique of Irigaray along these lines, see Weiss, Chapter 6. The important question to pose here is whether this technophobia is necessary and, given the resonances of our analysis in Chapter 1 with Irigaray's privileging of tactility as primordial, whether there is reason to believe that it is not. The task then would be to specify what a technics of tactile indifferentiation, as this is thought out of the maternal, might look like.

xx. See also Caillois' footnote where he likens this instinct to the Freudian death drive ("Mimicry and Legendary Psychasthenia," 32, note 44).

xxi. For a critique of this technophobia in Heidegger, see Mark Hansen, *Embodying Technesis: Technology Beyond Writing*, Chapter 4, and Bernard Stiegler, *Technics and Time, volume 1: The Fault of Epimetheus*, Part II.

xxii. Caillois is here citing Minkowski, "Le temps vécu."

CHAPTER 3

i. On this point, see especially chapter 6, "Nations, Identities, and Global Technologies," in Poster's book.

ii. Lisa Nakamura examines the "whiting out" of race in her exposé of the conventions of chat-room culture ("Race in/for Cyberspace: Identity Tourism and Racial Passing on the Internet". This criticism is the inspiration for the essay collection, *Race in Cyberspace*, eds. B. Kolko, L. Nakamura, and G. Rodman (New York: Routledge, 2000). See especially the essays by Nakamura, Jennifer Gonzalez, and Beth Kolko.

iii. Apter predicts that "postcolonial theory and aesthetic practice will 'cyberize' themselves quite soon (if they haven't already), pushing the envelope of the politics of global subjectivity as they place the diaspora online" (223).

iv. See Lisa Nakamura's analysis of Internet advertising ("Where Do You Want to Go Today? Cybernetic Tourism, the Internet, and Transnationality" in *Race in Cyberspace*, 21–22).

v. Effectively, this means the conventions which govern believability of character in that medium or in a particular online community:

"Each individual is a character and participation is successful to the extent the character is believable by others" (15).

vi. Many would be quick to point out that gender, race, and class conventions not only structure the explicit possibilities for self-invention but also dictate the *ethos* of online interaction. See, for example, the introduction to Robert Markley's collection, as well as the Introduction to *Race and Cyberspace*.

vii. This claim finds verification in more empirical studies of chat-room behavior, such as that of Amy Bruckman, "Gender Swapping on the Internet," in *High Noon on the Electronic Frontier: Conceptual Issues in Cyberspace*, ed. P. Ludlow (Cambridge, MA: MIT, 1996).

viii. Poster suggests that the typed words on the screen take on the role played by the body in face-to-face discourse: "online interaction is disembodied communication like letters and print, where the enunciation is separate from the body of the sender. But the communication is like speech in that it is simultaneous. The important question is the way identity is performed in these contexts. Participants are interpellated by each other, suturing identity in performatives but the construction of the subject occurs entirely on the screen, determined entirely by the words entered on the keyboard" (75).

ix. In a general sense, my claim here follows arguments made by Lisa Nakamura and Jennifer Gonzalez. In her analysis of racial performance in the text-based Web space Lambda-MOO, Nakamura suggests that "everyone who participates is 'passing'" because "it is impossible to tell if a character's description matches a player's physical characteristics" (Nakamura 1995, 182). In her analysis of race and identity as digital assemblage, Gonzalez claims that "'passing' (or pretending to be what one is not) in cyberspace has become a norm rather than an exception" because "much of the activity online is about becoming the fantasy of a racial other" (Jennifer Gonzalez, "The Appended Subject: Race and Identity as Digital Assemblage," in *Race in Cyberspace*, 29).

x. Even a white male logging on as himself—that is, as a white male—must pass, in the sense that the text-body he creates can only garner "believability" from its participation in stereotyped norms.

xi. This *figure* of the body as residue is what *concretizes* the structural incompleteness of all performative interpellations—what *motivates* the formal iterability that maintains their openness.

xii. In this respect, it functions analogously to the mimicry through which women and minorities (and perhaps white men as well) become citizens: there, too, the lived reality of the body must be left wholly behind in order for the individual to acquire a "new body"—what Lauren Berlant calls a "prophylaxis for the person"—that will permit participation in a national fantasy ("National Brands/ National Body: *Imitation of Life*," 113).

xiii. Allucquère Rosanne Stone, *The War of Desire and Technology at the End of the Mechanical Age*, 17, cited in Foster, 139. If I am right to see in online interpellation a generalization of passing and if I am right that this generalization foregrounds the (at once constraining and enabling) role of the lived body as what gives existential meaning to representational modes of agency, then Stone's notion of multiple agency warranted to the physical body must be revised. Specifically, we must reject Stone's discursivizing of the virtual citizen:

> By means of warranting, [a] discursive entity is tied to an association with a particular physical body, and the two together ... constitute the socially apprehensible citizen.... Because so much of such an identity is discursive and is produced through the actions of texts, I have elsewhere referred to it as *legible* body, that is, as textually mediated physicality. *The legible body is the social, rather than the physical, body*; the legible body displays the social meaning of "body" on its surface, presenting a set of cultural codes that organize the ways the body is apprehended and that determine the range of socially appropriate responses. (Stone, 41, last emphasis added)

As I see it, this discursive conception of warranting forms the Achilles' heel of Stone's analysis. When she celebrates online multiplicity as a form of subjectivity that is liberating because it transcends the lived body, Stone displays a kind of euphoric Cartesianism, all too common in postmodern thinking, which views the body as the first prosthesis. Despite her efforts to retain the category of the physical body, it is all but impossible to fathom what role it could possibly have in underwriting the "transgendered body" that seems rather to be produced by the technological structure of the Internet. Indeed, Stone is unequivocal in proposing the naturalization of the transgendered body in cyberspace as an outright replacement for the physical body.

xiv. For this reason, cyberspace can plausibly be said to take up the legacy of "nonexpressive, nonhumanist modes of performing and producing 'blackness' and 'whiteness'" in African-American culture (Foster, 141).

xv. At the very least, this calls on us to take stock of the body's crucial role as the mediator of speech acts and other symbolic gestures in the process of interpellation. As Portuguese philosopher José Gil has brilliantly demonstrated, "symbolic efficiency" derives from the *activity* of the body as a translator between codes, the operator of what he calls the "infralanguage." It depends on the articulation of the force of language with the affective energy of the body: "For the [magical action of words] to have effects [on the body], words must release forces in the body; these forces must react directly on organs, on their physiology, and the body has to offer itself as a receptive surface of forces" (Gil, 143). In this respect, Gil's work forms a crucial corrective to the performative idealism of Butler and Stone: *because the body comprises the site where discursive force is constituted, it simply cannot be reduced to a product or materialization of discursive performance and it cannot be abstracted away as a mere prosthesis.*

On Gil's account, the body matters because it is the site where performative significations get correlated with the affects that grant them their meaning and substance. In relation to Poster's conception of interpellation as a purely formal process, it helps clarify how the physical body is not, and can never be, simply absent because it insists that, in order to make a difference, to matter, even something as formalized as the virtual "text-body" must be "translated" into affective bodily forces or, more simply, that it must somehow be made to have an impact on the physical body of the user. We can thus conclude that the lesson of online interpellation is precisely the lesson of Gil's analysis: interpellation is empty if it is not coupled with a bodily becoming; interpellated "identities" matter only insofar as they are translated into bodily forces.

For this reason, Gil's analysis helps us answer the question raised earlier concerning the function of online interpellation—that is, interpellation once it is freed from its social function. Rather than a vehicle for materializing a socially intelligible identity (and one that would in some way or other adequately express the user's actual identity or identity needs), as virtually every commentator on the phenomenon assumes, online interpellation forms something like a laboratory for experimenting with the process of translation that links represented identities with bodily affectivity. Certainly the documented prevalence of online gender- and race-bending would lend strong support to such an interpretation; indeed, as we might be tempted to ask, what else could be at stake here than the desire to explore how it would feel to be interpellated as an other, where "feel" means experiencing the symbolic reactions of others and of oneself as these are translated into bodily forces?

xvi. For a nuanced discussion of the imbrication of Fanon's critique of colonialism with gender politics, see Fuss, 27–36.

xvii.   Shohat and Stam seem oddly oblivious to the necessary interpella-
        tive *failure* that forms the enabling mechanism of a politics of affect,
        despite their full awareness of what the primacy affect enjoys in the
        domain of media culture:

> Within postmodern culture, the media not only set agen-
> das and frame debates but also inflect desire, memory,
> fantasy. By controlling popular memory, they can contain
> or stimulate popular dynamism. The challenge, then, is to
> develop a media practice by which subjectivities may be
> lived and analyzed as part of a transformative, emanci-
> patory praxis. The question of the political "correctness"
> of texts is ultimately less important than the question of
> *mobilizing desire in empowering directions.* The question
> then becomes: How can we transform existing media so
> as to mobilize adversary subjectivity? Given the libidinal
> economy of media reception, how do we crystallize indi-
> vidual and collective desire for emancipatory purposes?
> (166, emphasis added)

        This passage echoes the argument developed by Lawrence Gross-
        berg in *We Gotta Get Out of this Place: Popular Conservatism and
        Postmodern Culture.*

xviii. It is in this sense that we must reject Emily Apter's rejection of
        affect. Specifically, we must refrain from conceptualizing affect as
        a residue or simulation of a lost essence or identity, as Apter does.
        Although she is quite right to claim that affect takes up "where
        the critique of performativity leaves off: that is, at the point where
        antiessentialism has become a given and the market in identity-
        production is oversaturated," she is far too quick to condemn this
        upsurge of affect "as a return to 'easy[,]' to feelings washing about in
        a depoliticized space of the transnational commodity." As she sees
        it, affects can be nothing more than "the residue of the real; ghostly
        afterimages of attitudes, performances of human-ness, and attempts
        to simulate being a subject.... As the leftovers of instincts, as the
        residues of 'mythic' behaviors that haunt the staging of the subject,
        affects become crucial to sustaining the illusion of identity, however
        dismantled." "Affect," in short, "is about miming the human when
        the human has come increasingly to be embodied in posthuman
        constructions": "the aesthetics of affect clearly participate[s] in the
        identity politics of performative mimicry" (20).
            By thus confining the analysis of affects to a representational-
        simulational framework, Apter fails to appreciate their funda-
        mental tie to the body and their potential to open an entirely

different avenue for thinking community, one that welcomes the
bankruptcy of performativity as an opportunity to reforge a notion
of the human based on the commonality of embodied singularity.
The affects generated through the failure of online performative
indentification are not the happy, unifying, "easy" feelings Apter
describes. Indeed, by undermining identification via such culturally sanctioned individuating categories as race and gender, affects
cannot but be lived as confusing, if exhilirating, experiences of
bodily excess and singularity. Far from being "the 'theory lite' version of virtual subjects who have little real stake in national, ethnic,
or gender affiliations," affect thus emerges as the central category
of a conceptualization of the human as virtual in a very different
sense—as always in excess of any particular determination.

xix. "Relocating the Remains" has been documented in an exhibition
catalogue and accompanying CD-ROM (Piper, Keith. *Relocating
the Remains*). This catalogue contains an often insightful recapping
of Piper's evolution by Kobena Mercer, "Witness at the Crossroads:
An Artist's Journey in Post-Colonial Space." A version of the project
can be found on Piper's inIVA Website, www.iniva.org/piper. My
account of Piper's work addresses the CD-ROM, where what is at
stake is the effort to open Piper's work to the domain of the virtual,
to extend "the metaphor of the 'expedition' ... through a labyrinth
of user interactive 'virtual' spaces" (http://www.iniva.org/piper/
Cdrompage.html). The Website produces new versions of the three
spaces featured on the CD-ROM, in the process expunging all of the
works, both old and new, that were incorporated into the CD-ROM.
To my mind, the Website can at best suggest some of the effects
produced by the virtual extension carried out in the CD-ROM
and in particular by the works focusing directly on contemporary
technology. However, for an interesting analysis of the work that
focuses primarily on the Website, see Ashley Dawson, "Surveillance
Sites: Digital Media and Dual Society in Keith Piper's *Relocating the
Remains*."

xx. Mercer furthermore argues that Piper's work —specifically his
engagement with the world of sports—can be contrasted (favor-
ably) with the work of other black male artists like Glenn Ligon and
Byron Kim and Jean-Michael Basquiat on account of its "ability to
bring the analytical and the expressive into dialogue." He continues: "Piper takes account of identification as an emotional tie from
which one cannot extricate oneself at will" (58).

xxi. See Mercer, 54, for a subtle analysis of how Piper's work from the
early 1990s enacts this complexification.

xxii. As Piper recounts,

The shift away from grand globalizing themes, which characterized the earlier more prescriptive practice, had to do with a more immediately localized and focused perspective which was ready to embrace political alliances across race and ethnicity. By the late Eighties I was beginning to arrive at a position of exploring issues based on my personal interests, with a view that whether these issues gel on a subjective level with individual members or the audience is a question out of my hands, and that it is also to a degree independent of their membership in any particular social, ethnic, racial or gender constituency" (cited in Mercer, 54).

xxiii. For a discussion of the Foucauldian basis of Piper's work, see Sean Cubitt, "Keith Piper: After Resistance, Beyond Destiny." Mercer's discussion of Piper's evolution also makes reference to Foucault's conception of the imbrication of power and resistance. For example, "What distinguishes Piper's use of digital multimedia is his reflexive approach to the questions of power and knowledge intrinsic to the use of such visual technologies in surveillance and policing strategies that seek social control over the burgeoning chaos of urban space" (15). Like Cubitt, Mercer suggests that Piper gradually comes up against the limits of Foucault's model of knowledge/power, but goes one step further in citing Piper's concern with the emotional problematic of residual identification (what I am calling affect) as a means to complexify and move beyond the Foucauldian impasse. See, especially, 58 ff.

xxiv. For an account of the role of (in)visibility in art history, see Michele Wallace, "Modernism, Postmodernism and the Problem of the Visual in Afro-American Culture." Specifically, Wallace invokes the "paradox of invisibility": "On the one hand, there is no black difference. On the other, the difference is so vast as to be unspeakable and indescribable" (43).

xxv. As Mercer puts it, Piper actively uses the loss of certainty "as an opportunity to expand one's awareness of how the past has positioned the self in relation to others," to effect a "reconciliation across generations" and a "return to the enigma of the unknown past as a political obstacle to social reconciliation in a racially structured society" (67).

xxvi. As if to literalize the universality of this implication, by zooming in on its target and framing it with the clicking noise of the camera aperture, the interface implicates the viewer (again no matter who it may be) in the unavoidable violence of classification.

xxvii.   Poster links the contribution of the technologies of the virtual to their nonlocalization in physical space—that is, to the deterritorialization they accomplish, as well as their transitoriness:

> If cyberspace is the occasion of a great spiritual renewal of the planet, have we not surpassed in some sense the historic forms of ethnic identity and begun to move toward some as yet unknown relation of individual to group? … Linked to the continuously shifting global processes of textual, graphic, and aural formations, individuals in cyberspace cannot attach to objects in the fixed shapes of historic ethnicity." (169–170)

In my opinion, this (like the work of Pierre Lévy from which it draws) represents a massive overstatement of the impact of computer technologies on ethnicity which stems from the conflation of technology with archive. Rather, as I see it (and this is the burden of Piper's work), the archive forms the raw material which must be differentially actualized in a particular process of ethnicization. Rather than being (solely) the material support for the archive, technology facilitates this entire process.

xxviii. I borrow this term from Bernard Stiegler's brilliant analysis of Leroi–Gourhan in *Technics and Time 1: The Fault of Epimetheus*, 134–179.

xxix   I borrow this term "collective intelligence" from Pierre Levy. *Collective Intelligence: An Anthropology of Cyberspace*.

xxx.   As the mechanism for articulating figures of ethnicity that reflect their "electronic constitution in virtual spaces" (Poster 164), digital technology does not simply furnish a new, nonphysical place for memory, as Poster suggests; on the contrary, it brokers a new phase in the ongoing coevolution of the human and technology in the technico–social–cultural differentiation, characteristic of the human species, that French anthropologist André Leroi–Gourhan names (in specific opposition to genetic differentiation) *ethnic* differentiation. On this view, ethnicity has *always* been technical, in the sense that it coincides with the possibility for passing on memory that is nongenetically programmed, that is external to the individual: ethnicity is, in a word, "epiphylogenetic," to use Stiegler's felicitous term.

xxxi.   Piper, quotation from the "Background" section to "Tagging the Other," on the CD-ROM, "Relocating the Remains"; emphasis added.

xxxii.   Indeed, it is hardly incidental that the originally envisioned CD-ROM project was to have been titled after this work. In answer to a question about the racial construction of cyberspace, Piper explains why:

> [The CD-Rom that I'm currently working on] is provisionally entitled 'Caught Like a Nigger in Cyberspace,' and essentially it's an attempt to further explore what I saw as the particular ways in which black people have been characterized in terms of the digital domain, in terms of the ways in which our presence is often seen as transgressive, as the embodiment of threat and disorder. It's meant to have a computer game-type feel, even though it hasn't!" (Keith Piper, "In the Ring.")

xxxiii. Here is Deleuze's definition of the affection-image:

> There is therefore a relationship between affection and movement in general which might be expressed as follows: the movement of translation is not merely interrupted in its direct propagation by an interval which allocates on the one hand the received movement, and on the other the executed movement, and which might make them in a sense incommensurable. Between the two there is affection which re-establishes the relation. But, it is precisely in affection that the movement ceases to be that of translation in order to become movement of expression, that is to say quality, simple tendency stirring up an immobile element. (66)

xxxiv. Agamben has criticized Deleuze's deployment of the concept of the image in "Notes on Gesture," in *Means Without Ends*. Agamben argues that the gesture lies beneath the image.

xxxv. Here I mean the fact that it is—at least ostensibly—intended for all viewers. For this reason and despite the fact that video games have been shown to have built-in race and gender biases, Piper can use the video game interface as a signifier of that supposed universality.

xxxvi. Even though it ignores the phenomenon of contemporary techniques for direct intervention into the body which many see as a new phase of capital, one in which it is the body (and not just the image) that is capitalized. See the discussion in Muriel Combes and Bernard Aspe, "Retour sur le 'camp' comme paradigme biopolitique. Giorgio Agamben," (20,23). Agamben, of course, addresses biotechnology directly in *Homo Sacer* and *Remnants of Auschwitz*.

xxxvii. Simondon develops his analysis in the two volumes of his *thèse d'état*, *L'Individu et sa Genèse Psycho-Biologique* (Paris: Jerome Millon, 1995) and *L'Individuation Psychique et Collective* (Paris: Aubier,

1989). The introduction to the first has been translated into English as "The Genesis of the Individual" and appears in *Incorporations*, eds. J. Crary and S. Kwinter.

xxxviii. Indeed, Simondon's analysis of individuation parallels Agamben's understanding of potentiality as the potentiality *not to be*: in both cases, it is the domain of the nonactual—of the nonactual *in principle*, as *what need never be actualized*—that provides the margin of indetermination necessary for the subject to remain in continual genesis.

xxxix. It thus puts to work the very conception of the human advanced by Agamben: "There is in effect something that humans are and have to be, but this something is not an essence or properly a thing: *It is the simple fact of one's own existence as possibility or potentiality.*" (1993, 43).

xxxx. Muriel Combes and Bernard Aspe make a similar point with regard to Agamben's analysis of "bare life" in *Homo Sacer*. According to them, Agamben's intuition that politics is already contained within bare life requires a displacement of the couple *zoē/bios* as the basis for political thinking. Rather, the task is to "understand on which basis a collective subjectivation is constructed, to understand, for example, in what way *affective life*, already in itself something entirely other than mere life in the biological sense, is through and through [*d'emblée*] political, in what way the collective *as such* finds itself always already engaged" ("Retour sur le 'camp' comme paradigme biopolitique," 19). In a sense, Agamben's invocation of Simondon can be understood as responding to this injunction because it replaces the motif of *Homo Sacer*—namely, the search for an occulted indistinction between *zoe* and *bios*—with the concept of an internal relationality.

CHAPTER 4

i. Although the media component of the project as described here was scrapped due to financial constraints, the uncertain status of all of Diller + Scofidio's work on the cusp between art/architecture and theory emboldens me to treat it as an unrealized yet essential conceptual dimension of the *Blur* project. Put another way, in addition to being a temporary built project in the world, the *Blur Building* exists as work of embodied conceptual art preserved in the archive of traces that document its making and that include—as a central core of its drama—the media components.

ii. In *Matter and Memory*, Bergson argued that perception and affection were inseparable though distinct modalities of sensation:

> We must correct, at least in this particular, our theory of pure perception. We have argued as though our perception were a part of the images, detached, as such, from their entirety, as though, expressing the virtual action of the object upon our body, or of our body upon the object, perception merely isolated from the total object that aspect of it which interests us. But we have to take into account the fact that our body is not a mathematical point in space, that its virtual actions are complicated by, and impregnated with, real actions, or, in other words, *that there is no perception without affection. Affection is, then, that part or aspect of the inside of our body which we mix with the image of external bodies*; it is what we must first of all subtract from perception to get the image in its purity." (58; emphasis added)

Bergson's theory forms the basis for my account of new media in *New Philosophy for New Media*, where I argue that digital artists, in their efforts to distance themselves from cinematic conditions of perception, pursue a "Bergsonist vocation."

iii. In Bergsonist terms, we must differentiate two "extremes" related to the "body": on the one hand, the corporeal body and, on the other, the larger field of the "out-of-body" where the body merely propagates, and does not filter, images. Indeed, the body acts "like a magnetic field," encroaching on these two zones, winning over the out-of-body insofar as we can delay our reactions and winning over the mineralized body to the extent that we can punctuate our automatisms. Perception can be said to take place *only where both of these bodily actions are involved*, only when "there is an increase in the field of images between the out-of-body of interactions and the mineralized body of our automatisms" (147). What this means is that perception is contaminated by affection in two ways: first, following Bergson, through its accompaniment by an affective correlate in the perceiving body; second, through the nonperceived force of the longitudinal—that is, the way the milieu of interactions forms a "texture of sensation" that pervades and influences the body's framing of space.

iv. Here is how Gil contextualizes his intervention:

> This work is about the relations between power and the body. This does not mean those which result from the effects of the former on the latter.... Nor does it include

those which come from the action of the body on power, which covers a domain occupied by all sorts of ideologies and "liberatory" doctrines of the body. It is about the effects on the circulation of bodily powers that nourish formations of power in all fields. In other words, and we must stress this notion, it is not a question of studying *forces* ... according to their representational contents, but to grasp them in the way they function in their own right, that is, in the way they may differ from the signs and symbols that are attached to them. (xii)

v. In Gil's study, this conversion is best illustrated by the symbolic efficiency of myth: "Symbolic efficiency ... consists in 'remote control,' magical action of words on body parts. For this action to have effects, words must release forces in the body; these forces must react directly on organs, on their physiology, and the body has to offer itself as a receptive surface of forces"; as a "mediator between organs and discourse," the infralanguage "must necessarily articulate paths for the circulation of energy in discourse (forces) with paths for the circulation of energy in the body (affect)" (143). Generalized beyond the example of myth, Gil's project articulates nothing less than a theory of power as bodily power; in it, the infralinguistic body becomes the source for all meaning in the world, and meaning effectively converges with affect.

vi. From Eisenman's fully enlightened vantage point as author of the teleological recapping of his career, *Diagram Diaries*, the newer generation's theory of the diagram is fundamentally hampered by its "indifference" to the "three conditions unique to architecture": architecture's "compliance with the metaphysics of presence"; the "already motivated condition of the sign"; and its "necessary relationship" to a "desiring subject" (30). In their too enthusiastic embrace of models foreign to architecture, younger figures like Greg Lynn or FOA simply turn their backs on the motif of interiority, which is to say, on what, for Eisenman, constitutes the source of architecture's complex identity.

vii. Specifically, Eisenman appropriates Deleuze's conception of the extraction of the figural developed in his study of the painter Francis Bacon. Given the singular "presentness" of architecture, this process must be reconfigured in the domain of the architectural. Specifically, in painting the contour can be literally blurred through various spatial techniques; however, in architecture, no such blurring of the profile is possible because architecture must remain a "literal shelter." What is possible instead is a blurring of the diagram and with it the entire organization, such that it is "no longer seen as merely fulfilling a function of embodying its interior form" ("Processes of the Interstitial: Notes on Zaera-Polo's Idea of the Machinic," 28). By itself, however, this extraction of the diagram from its pregiven function cannot "guarantee" the modification of the traditional tropes of architecture. "The figural in itself," says Eisenman, "does not necessarily embody the tropes of architecture." Consequently—and this is what makes Eisenman's position so important—something more, a "third step," is needed to correlate the figural tropes given in the machinic with the transformation of architectural interiority.

As a step toward the production of nontraditional tropes in "real architectural space," this something more necessarily involves the body as a constitutive element of architecture's internal resonance: the correlate of the excess named the figural, the body's capacity to sense space affectively opens up new, invisible, and properly interstitial spaces:

> Architecture's being already has an internal consistency which could be considered machinic, that is, there could be tropes, already given which are not the same as a formal architectural trope which is always added to a functional container. Rather than a figural trope would be one that already exists prior to its unfolding in spatiotemporal coordinates. That is to say whether one considers figural tropes important to articulate or not is not the issue. Since their possibility already exists in a machinic process, they can only be repressed by choosing not to articulate them. If they are articulated, they will appear differently in space than they previously did as formal tropes. This difference can be seen, for example, in the trope of the *interstitial.*" ("Processes of the Interstitial: Notes on Zaera-Polo's Idea of the Machinic," 31)

viii. See my book, *New Philosophy for New Media,* for an account of digital art as a catalyst for bodily affectivity.

ix. For an account of Simondon's conception of individuation that differentiates his ontology from Deleuze's, see Mark Hansen, "Internal Resonance, or Three Steps Towards a Non-Viral Becoming."

x. For a critique of contemporary cyberarchitecture along these lines, see the analysis of structural engineer Harald Kloft and critic Andreas Ruby. In an account of Bernhard Franken's "BMW projects" that would apply equally to any number of contemporary projects, structural engineer Kloft shows how the deployment of parameter-driven processes renders form autonomous:

The actual form is achieved by arresting the process at a specific point and "freezing" the form. Franken describes the "freeze problem"—that is, "When do I say 'Stop' and freeze the process?"—as the key factor in this design method, for the process is launched without any specific idea of form, merely an idea of process, and then, as Franken puts it: "you wait for the form." This "subjective reality" generates a data record that defines only the external skin, which is fixed as a result of the design method. The consequences for the design of the structure are twofold. Firstly, the structure becomes formally an elemental component, because it constitutes either the internal spatial enclosure beneath the skin created by Franken or the skin itself becomes the structure, that is, external layer and internal layer are identical and only defined by the material thickness. Secondly, since the master form is fixed, optimizations to the structure cannot be implemented by means of changing the form. (Harald Kloft, "Structural Engineering in the Digital Workflow," in *Digitalreal: Blobmeister, First Built Projects*, 203).

By stripping formal genesis of any manual dimension and by rendering it a "qualitative multiplicity" (Deleuze), Franken's parameter-driven design technique successfully liberates architecture from the preinscription of form. Yet, as Andreas Ruby astutely points out, such liberation remains in force—at least in reference to digital architecture in its current state—only at the conceptual level, where architecture need not grapple with the material constraints of production and use. To his mind, the potential for digital design to stimulate a "new paradigm" remains largely unrealized:

What is currently promoted as "digital" architecture is marred by the fatal assumption that innovation in architecture is today mainly expressed through form.... With unrelenting eloquence, somewhat like an adolescent rebellion against the formal dogmatism of Modernism, the focus has been on visualizing what is believed to be its greatest asset—the extravagance of form—thereby ending up with a new dogmatism that is no less rigid. The fascination with the new digital processes for the creation of architectonic form is certainly understandable. But it is equally obvious that the formal experimentation they permit cannot by itself lead to a new architecture. (Andreas

Ruby, "Beyond Form: Architecture in the Age of Digital Reproducibility" in *Digitalreal*, 206–213; here 211–213)

xi. Though to be fair, some younger practitioners recognize the necessity for translation, following a slightly different trajectory than Eisenman's. Consider, for example, the practice of Reiser+Umemoto, an architectural firm directly inspired by Kwinter's conception of "computational coextensivity." The firm seeks to engage media "in the so-called solid-state," that is the state in which "material formations are inextricably linked to the computational logics inherent in materiality itself" (Jesse Reiser, Solid State Architecture).

In projects like the *Yokohama Port Terminal* and the *Kansai Library Project*, Reiser+Umemoto seek to catalyze the "lateral communication" between building structures and components as a means of allowing architectural materiality to express its potential. In the case of the Yokohama project, this was achieved by opening up the truss structure to the potential forces that are "inherent within" their definition as structure, but remain untapped without the "provocation of some outside force (of an adjacent structure)." In the proposal for the *Yokohama Port Terminal*, the structural system begins as a set of repeated trusses conceived as flexible at their control points. Subsequently, as other systems (e.g., roads, gardens, etc.) pass through them, they are deflected from their original structural function. This yields what Reiser provocatively calls a "resonance across elements," a resonance of material potentialities catalyzed solely through the extrafunctional "intermixing" of structural elements. Now Reiser specifically characterizes this practice in terms of its double engagement with media: as a material substance in its own right and as a virtual or informing potential.

To the extent that these two notions of media are folded together in the concept of the diagram, they operate the participation of architecture in what Reiser calls a "universal structure": the "dynamical diagram which has no essential origin and can be incarnated in multiple materials, scales and regimes." Whatever resonance there is between this conception and Kwinter's perspective is, as I have said, not accidental, but Reiser's effort to apply a continuous conception of the material flux to concrete problems of architectural design introduces something not found in Kwinter: the necessity, in a "second" stage, to *rematerialize* the diagram "in the stuff of architecture with all of its attendant phenomena." As Reiser recognizes, this modelization of architecture as a system in perpetual individuation "demands a renewed recognition of the integration of matter and effect."

285

Yet, to the extent that this integration demands a mediation—the conversion of force into affect—it necessarily brings in the body and indeed situates the body within the system of internal resonance operated by architecture. Otherwise put, if the liberation of the potentiality of matter manages to overcome architecture's traditional "rigidified structures," this is because it opens a whole new domain of sense (not signification): the domain of embodied affectivity. The forces actualized through the "lateral communication" of architectural structures "provoke ever-changing conditions of inhabitation" precisely and only through their impact on the body or, more precisely, on the body's dynamic production of space.

xii. On this point, see the analysis of Brian Massumi, *Parables for the Virtual: Movement, Affect, Sensation* (Durham, NC: Duke University Press, 2002), especially Chapter 6. I evaluate Massumi's understanding of the correlation of vision and proprioception in my book, *New Philosophy for New Media*, Chapter 6.

xiii. Eisenman, *Diagram Diaries*, 69. Given Eisenman's interest in differentiating himself from the younger generation of so-called diagrammatic architects, this has to be seen as reinscribing the insufficiency of diagrammatic play—in and of itself—to generate new spatial experience. In this sense, it is also hardly surprising that *House IV* witnesses the first appearance of "affect" in Eisenman's work (or at least in his retrospective summation):

> The House IV diagrams concerned the *being* of the diagram, such as the idea of *wallness*, as opposed to a mere plane. This was the first indication of the potential for affect to influence the diagram. The sign of wallness demanded overcoming not only the materiality of the object but also its function and meaning. (69)

xiv. The following description is a paraphrase of Ingeborg Rocker's project description, "The Virtual: the Unform in Architecture," 23.

xv. It is hardly surprising that this difference surfaces in Eisenman's intervention into the Jury discussion for the Virtual House competition. Unlike art, which "has no limits" and thus need not (and indeed cannot) ever stop, architecture—Eisenman insists—would not be architecture if it did not stop: "You shouldn't be asking architects, 'Why do these machines stop?' It's not architecture if they don't stop. 'Why do these machines enclose?' It's not architecture if they don't enclose. 'Why do these machines shelter?' They must shelter, or they become art" (Eisenman, in Foster, "Jury Discussion," 35).

xvi. Eisenman characterizes his work on the three just mentioned projects as

> primarily linear parts which attempt through various striations to deny their axiality and thus interrupt narrative. At the Wexner Center, two grids, each of which define[s] a different narrative axis, collide to disrupt not only each other's dominance but also each other's linearity. This collision is not marked by any formal entry point, thus the building does not provide entry for the subject into the narrative. At the Columbus Convention Center, while there is a linear axis parallel to the main street, the spatial striations of the volumetric mass of the building cross this axis, interrupting its linear continuity. At Aronoff Center in Cincinnati, while there is again an axial spine of circulation that runs the entire length of the building, the architectural narrative is defined by a wholly other geometry, that of a series of articulated volumetric boxes that twist, turn and step through the spine. ("Staten Island Institute of Arts and Sciences: Escape from New York (and the Guggenheim)," 23)

xvii. Specifically, the issue is not whether and how the trope of folding (or any other trope for architectural form) better captures the virtual dimensions of the site, as John Rajchman suggests in writing:

> There exists a "complexity," or a potential for folding, that is not contained within any frame or grid; on the contrary, a frame or grid only exists within a larger virtual complexity that exceeds it. What is thus implicit in a space, which it cannot frame, may at any point or moment break out of it and cause it to be reframed. (John Rajchman, "Folding," 18/20).

From Eisenman's final perspective, no trope can access the virtual without the mediation of embodied spacing.

xviii. As Eisenman explains in a 1997 interview with Zaera–Polo, he is interested in a "conceptual formlessness which requires a beginning … from a void, and produces form out of formlessness" (Zaera–Polo, "Interview," 20).

xix. This is a notion I have developed in my work on new media art. See *New Philosophy for New Media*, Chapter 6.

xx. Like the Deleuzean notion that is its source, the digital ASW exploits the untapped potential lurking in empirical spaces. (Deleuze develops the ASW in Chapter 7 of *Cinema 1: the Move-*

ment-Image, trans. H. Tomlinson and B. Habberjam [Minneapolis: University of Minnesota Press, 1986].) Yet, whereas the cinematic variant liberates spatial forces from their determination, deploying them "as they are expressed for themselves, outside spatiotemporal coordinates, with their own ideal singularities and their *virtual conjunction*," the digital ASW expresses a *supplementary* analogy that actualizes the virtual force of the digital *in the form of bodily affect*. In his study of the cinema, Deleuze links the cinematic ASW specifically to the shift in the experience of space following the Second World War, in which the human being was confronted with "disconnected" and "deserted" spaces that short-circuited the capacity to move and to act.

As if in response to this existential crisis, cinema invested space as a kind of character, freeing it from its function as "ground" for action and mining its "pure potential," its being as a "perfectly singular space, which has merely lost its homogeneity, that is, the principle of its metric relations or the connection of its own parts, so that the linkages can be made in an infinite number of ways." In the ASW, space becomes "a space of virtual conjunction, grasped as pure locus of the possible" (109). Matters are quite otherwise in the digital realm, where the problem is not how to reenergize disinvested space, but how to forge a connection between bodily lived space and the topological possibilities afforded by digital manipulation. Whereas the cinematic ASW emerges out of what is, in the end, a lapsed analogy between embodiment and spatiality, there is nothing similar to build upon in the case of the digital.

xxi. This is precisely why Eisenman insists that the processes of the machinic have no necessary correlation with the interiority of architecture. It is precisely what informs his characterization of the contemporary electronic era—and the central example of the fax—as autonomous from human interpretation: "noninterpretative vision" can and must be distinguished by the absence of any *originary* analogical correlation with human experience. As the experiential cipher of such an absence, noninterpretative vision is what makes framing necessary—framing, that is, as the activity of forging a *supplementary* analogy through the embodied activity of the receiver. As a figure for the production of such a supplementary analogy, the digital ASW helps explain how the body is capable of generating spatial experience from a purely intensive space, one without relation to any independent coordinates or external ground.

xxii. Indeed, in the expanded sense theorized by Cache, the body remains the "source" (no matter how occulted) for all derivative forms of (technical) framing, including those internal to architecture (e.g., the grid or the cube) as well as those external to it (the cinematic frame, the photograph, but also all the so-called "external texts," liquid crystals, brain waves, etc., to which Eisenman has had recourse in his recent work). In this respect, it is not without relevance that Eisenman's career can be understood as a progressive movement away from the cinematic metaphor to a notion of architectural framing that includes the body (embodied spacing). For an account of this movement, see R. E. Somol's "Dummy Text," the introduction to *Diagram Diaries*.

xxiii. In "Designing Inefficiencies," Ashley Schafer pinpoints the mechanism for this technification of the weather in *Blur*—namely, the 8-minute intervals in system self-regulation:

> This lag time made adjusting for lone gusts of wind impossible, and even gradual weather changes were accommodated slightly after the fact, producing a constant variation in the density, shape, and limits of the fog. This instability affected the form of the cloud as well as visitor's experience inside. The most intriguing areas of *Blur* were not those that manifested the architect-specified "acceptable fog quality," but those that, in the grip of this delay, were almost devoid of mist. Within 8 minutes ... those locations became the setting of dramatic visual, tactile, material, and aural transformation. On an auspiciously warm, humid, and variably windy day in June, I gravitated toward these fog-deficient areas, chasing the possibility of witnessing the change. The hiss of the nozzles grew louder as the water pressure increased—a process that took about a second—followed by large plumes of drenching mist that almost immediately reduced visibility to near zero. This profoundly apparent temporal displacement attenuates the relationship between cause and effect, *dissociating instruments of technology from means of control. In these intervals, Diller + Scofidio construct spaces in time that resist the modernist tyranny of efficiency by framing and questioning our present condition.*" (101, emphasis added)

CHAPTER 5

i. I discuss Kittler's conceptions of media separation and digital convergence at some length in "Cinema beyond Cybernetics, or How to Frame the Digital-Image."

ii. In a reversal altogether typical of Danielewski's novel, the categorical force of this declaration is put into question, though certainly not entirely undercut, by the editors' insertion of a supplementary section entitled "Contrary Evidence" and consisting of five exhibits—including a comic book depiction of the rescue scene, an architectural mock-up, and, most strikingly, a still image from the film, "Exploration #4"—all of which would seem to furnish contextual and, most importantly, indexical evidence of the film's existence.

iii. This is a claim advanced by Larry McCaffery and Sinda Gregory in Appendix 1 of their interview with Danielewski:

> Perhaps even more important than what these revelations about Zampanò's past may add to our understanding of [the] novel is what they imply about the overall narrative structure of *House of Leaves*. Once we assume that the Zampanò who wrote the novel in *House of Leaves* is literally the character Fellini created in *La Strada*, we are forced to revise our assumptions concerning the status of the world projected within Johnny Truant's framing narrative. That is, if Zampanò is only an imaginary character existing in a work of art, then everything else in the framing tale involving Johnny—including his mother, his (re)construction of the manuscript, and everything relating to the world in which this framing tale occurs—would necessarily also have to be "unreal," even in the sense of the imaginary "real" posited in most works of fiction. (Danielewski, "Haunted House—An Interview with Mark Z. Danielewski," 126)

Although this analysis is certainly correct, it is merely one of many examples in the novel of paradoxical fictional framing, and thus it serves as part of what I am taking to be the novel's sustained assault on orthography, the inscription of the past as real and exactly repeatable.

iv. Indeed, Barthes categorically distinguishes photography from cinema, which is said to sweep away and deny the pose, the "thought of that instant, however brief, in which a real thing happened to be motionless in front of the eye" (78).

v. Stiegler has developed a broad-ranging and original philosophy of technology in the last decade. His ongoing project, *Technics and Time*, now comprises three volumes: *The Fault of Epimetheus*, *La Désorientation*, and *Le Temps du Cinéma et la Question du Mal-Être*. Stiegler's basic argument is that the human has always been technologically exteriorized and has evolved following the operation of "epiphylogenesis"—evolution by means other than life (i.e., via the passage of cultural knowledge). In volumes 2 and 3, Stiegler turns his attention specifically to contemporary technologies and develops a forceful argument for the primacy of culturally sedimented, technically stored memory as the condition of possibility for the human synthesis of memory and hence for the experience of time. The core of this analysis concerns Stiegler's critical expansion of Husserl's account of internal time consciousness and the distinction between primary retention and secondary memory. In this expansion, Stiegler introduces a third form of memory, "tertiary memory," which is defined as the storage of experiences *not lived by present consciousness* that nonetheless become available for adoption by that consciousness. This mechanism is precisely that of cultural inheritance, and Stiegler's great merit is to show how much it is intertwined with technics and how it is inseparable from the issue of our human experience of time. For further discussion of Stiegler's project, see Hansen 2004 ("Time").

vi. Stiegler develops a complex account of how memory serves to condition perception that expands Husserl's account in the *Lectures on the Phenomenology of Internal Time Consciousness* (1905). According to Stiegler (here following Derrida's deconstruction in *Speech and Phenomena*), "primary retention" (the now of perception, including the "just-past" that is retained for a short interval as part of the present) is contaminated by secondary retention because the inclusion of the past (even the just-past) in the present introduces the role of memory, and hence imagination, into the inscriptional modality of perception. Stiegler builds on this deconstruction of Husserl by demonstrating, in great detail and with great force, that primary and secondary retention are in turn made possible by the prior existence of what he calls "tertiary retention," meaning the inscription or exact recording of the past that has never been lived by present consciousness so that it becomes available to be representified by that consciousness. Much of the force of Stiegler's analysis comes from his correlation of tertiary memory—and thus the entire Husserlian apparatus of memory—with technical recording. It is, Stiegler reasons, only with the possibility to experience the exact same temporal event (or "temporal object") more than once that the contamination of primary by secondary retention becomes manifest. See Stiegler 1996, Chapter 4.

vii. The novel repeatedly brings home this transfer of focus from postmodern epistemological play to orthographic critique. Consider, for example, the passage documenting Navidson's efforts to read, by matchlight (and "paperlight"), the one book he brought with him on his explorations of the house: a text called (not surprisingly) *House of Leaves*. As the passage detailing the so-called "Navidson-match question" hilariously recounts, Navidson had only one pack of matches (from the Learnèd pub outside Oxford, England), which, despite being "good matches," only afford him time to read six pages of the novel. Accordingly, to proceed with his reading, Navidson is forced to use already read pages as "raw material" to produce light. Despite the "calculations" of obviously fictional researcher Hans Staker, which, we are told, turn out to be "more a form of academic onanism, a jerk of numeric wishful thinking," rather than anything to do "with the real world," Navidson is "forced to light the cover of the book as well as the spine" causing him to burn his fingers and lose some of the text. Left in the end with one page and one match, Navidson literally consumes and allows to be consumed the last remnant of the book:

> First, he reads a few lines by match light and then as the heat bites his fingertips he applies the flame to the page. Here then is one end: a final act of reading, a final act of consumption. And as the fire rapidly devours the paper, Navidson's eyes frantically sweep down over the text, keeping just ahead of the necessary immolation, until as he reaches the last few words, flames lick around his hands, ash peels off into the surrounding emptiness, and then as the fire retreats, dimming, its light suddenly spent, the book is gone leaving nothing behind but invisible traces already dismantled in the dark. (467)

We experience here an inversion of the postmodern topos of the *mise-en-abîme*: stripped of its epistemologically debilitating impact, this episode of Navidson reading the text in which he figures as a fictional character functions to foreground the equivalence between the two forms of consumption—reading and material destruction—thematized here. The point then is to emphasize the absence of any "sacred text"—literally instanced by the destruction of Navidson's copy of *House of Leaves*—and the primacy of the singular act of reading that forms its necessary correlate.

viii. Here, to avoid confusion, we should note that *House of Leaves* is not a science fiction novel, which makes its engagement with the impossible distinct from that engagement constitutive of science fiction as a literary genre.

ix. For a useful discussion of this uneasy correlation in the world of today's so-called "cyberarchitects," see Kloft (198–205). Kloft conceives this tension as that between form and performance:

What is currently promoted as "digital" architecture is
marred by a fatal assumption that innovation in architecture is today mainly expressed through form. No doubt,
the topological geometry is presumed to be the basis for an
adequate formal language. With unrelenting eloquence,
somewhat like an adolescent rebellion against the formal
dogmatism of Modernism, the focus has been on visualizing what is believed to be its greatest asset—the extravagance of form—thereby ending up with a new dogmatism
that is no less rigid. The fascination with the new digital
processes for the creation of architectonic form is certainly understandable. But it is equally obvious that the
formal experimentation they permit cannot by itself lead
to a new architecture…. One can only hope that architecture will resist such trivialization and, having discovered
the form of this new paradigm, will go on to discover its
performance. (204–205).

x.   If this is the case, it is hardly surprising that *The Navidson Record*
begins with an invocation of the digital as its guiding theme:

While enthusiasts and detractors will continue to empty
entire dictionaries attempting to describe or deride it,
"authenticity" still remains the word most likely to stir
a debate. In fact, this leading obsession—to validate or
invalidate the reels and tapes—invariably brings up a col-
lateral and more general concern: whether or not, with
the advent of digital technology, image has forsaken its
once impeachable hold on the truth. (3)

It is not insignificant that this introductory passage ends with a
footnote that directs the reader to Chapter IX, precisely the point
where this thematic concern shades over into a symptomatology of
the impact of the digital on the text.

xi. The citation is attributed to one Murphy Gruner, who informs us
that "as the recording time for tapes and digital disks increases, as
battery life is extended, and as camera size is reduced, the larger the
window will grow for capturing events as they occur" (144).

xii. Though devoid of any consequential narrative action, this prelimi-
nary section does serve to reveal the potential tension between
literary narrative and visual recording that will become central to
the novel as a whole. When Zampanò seeks to reconstruct the film
Navidson "set out to make" from the seemingly straightforward
surveillance images and the innocent intentions motivating the
project, he very deftly illustrates the medial difference between film

and text, where what can only be the accurate registration of an innocent intention in film becomes, in effect, a portent of events to come. Thus, film transfigures Navidson's intention simply "to create a record of how Karen and I bought a small house in the country and moved into it with our children," to "see how everything turns out" (8). "In many ways," Zampanò observes, "the opening of *The Navidson Record* … remains one of the more disturbing sequences because it so effectively denies itself even the slightest premonition about what will soon take place on Ash Tree Lane" (8). Once the house is revealed to be a physically impossible topological figure, however, this division of labor between technical recording and writing—simple registration of the event vs. imaginative supplementation—breaks down, and the two forms of media become far more complexly interarticulated.

xiii. "… The motion sensors were never triggered.… Virtually a week seamlessly elided, showing us the family as they depart from a house without that strange interior space present only to return a fraction of a second later to find it already in place, almost as if it had been there all along" (28). Mediated through Navidson's surveillance system, the house's transformation registers as a deformation of the temporality of daily life, an erasure of the duration of lived experience that leaves instead a practically seamless punctual transition: life compressed to fit the limits of recording.

xiv. This theme of the superiority of writing to technical recording is reiterated countless times throughout Zampanò's narrative, always in close correlation with the impossible figure of the house. Thus, for example, the drawings of Navidson's children are celebrated for their capacity to capture "the awfulness at the heart of the house". In contrast to the stark, sanitized perfection of the photographic renderings, "the shallow lines and imperfect shapes" of these drawings "narrat[e] the light seeping away from their lives" (315). Embodying the force of imagination over the merely reproductive, these examples attest to the truth of (invented?) photography critic Kadina Ashbeckie's claim that "technology's failure is over[]un by the onslaught of myth" (335).

xv. I must therefore take issue with Kate Hayles' reading of the novel as a celebration of the medial flexibility of print. "The computer," Hayles writes, "has often been proclaimed the ultimate medium because it can incorporate every other medium within itself. As if learning about omnivorous appetite from the computer, *House of Leaves*, in a frenzy of remediation, attempts to eat all the other media" (781). Beyond its implicit (and in my opinion, inadequate) view of the digital computer as a mere extension of the orthographic project of technical recording media, Hayles' reading significantly downplays the way in which the deformations of the text point to the failure of print and the novel as *recording* technologies (or, in the terminology Hayles borrows from Jay David Bolter and Richard Grusin [and, ultimately, from Marshall McLuhan], "remediations" of such technologies). Hayles can thus remain blind to the extraorthographic vocation of the text which, as my reading suggests, can only be worked out through a consideration of embodied response.

Here, the mediation of the text by its reading—by Johnny Truant's reading and by ours—must be differentiated from other layers of mediation and, as I shall argue, accorded a certain privilege. I would nonetheless wholeheartedly concur with Hayles' conclusion that "*House of Leaves* recuperates the traditions of the print book—particularly the novel as a literary form" and that "the price it pays for this recuperation is a metamorphosis so profound that it becomes a new kind of form and artifact" (781).

xvi. As I see it (and as my argument in this section will substantiate), Truant holds a privilege within the novel precisely because of his status as the "first reader" of Zampanò's narrative. I am therefore in disagreement with Danielewski, who, in a recent interview, claims that "there are many ways to enter *House of Leaves*" ("Haunted House," 111). Certainly the reader can follow the suggestion of footnote 78 on page 72 and read the letters in Appendix II-E from Johnny's institutionalized mother, Pelafina, before resuming the narrative. Perhaps some readers will make their way to *House of Leaves* by first reading *The Whalestoe Letters* (the independently published, enhanced edition of these letters); nevertheless, whatever information these letters furnish about Pelafina serves first and foremost to introduce further information about Johnny: in short, they are subordinate to his function as narrator/first reader. In a sense, this situation is well captured by Larry McCaffery's experience of following the path suggested by footnote 72: MacCaffery's return to the text is affected by his reading of the letters, but without in any way changing his reliance on Johnny as the primary mediator of the story and model of interpretation. McCaffery recounts:

> Once I finished her letters and returned to page 72, several things had occurred. First, it was now clearer to me that the author of this book had a much wider range of styles and voices than I had suspected up to that point. And second, throughout the rest of the novel, I was very aware that I now had a completely different perspective on Johnny Truant than if I had not turned from page 72 to appendix E. ("Haunted House," 112)

If McCaffery was "quite literally reading a different book from the one most other readers would be reading," it was still a book whose primary narrator is Johnny Truant. Truant's privileged position requires a similar subordination of the potential themes that Pelafina's letters make available, such as family dysfunction. One need only consider the example of her typographically complex letter of January 3, 1988 (p. 627), which forcefully demonstrates that her letters are not direct conveyances of her inner voice and that her character is a figure for the necessary mediation of the voice, the living present, the self-identical self. Because Pelafina simply could not have typeset the complex overlay of the word "forgive" on the typewriter available to her, her letter confronts us with evidence of the irreducibility of mediation: her alleged "direct" expressions are thoroughly mediated and subject to all of the interpretative intrusions that comprise the novel's sustained assault on orthography. The important point here is that any effort to recuperate a level of thematic interpretation falters in the face of the material–epistemological–ontological hurdles the text insistently sets into place everywhere the reader turns.

xvii. This claim forms the basis of my analysis of the digital in *New Philosophy for New Media*.

xviii. As we shall see shortly, the text asserts the impossibility of being outside all frames—something that would amount, following the governing analogy with the digital, to processing raw digital data directly, without any mediating interface.

xix. As if this were not sufficient to prove the point at hand, the narrative goes on to enumerate various instantiations of the theory of subjective space, including Günter Nitschke's notion of "experienced or concrete space"; Michael Leonard's conception of the "'sensation of space' where the final result 'in the perceptual process is a single sensation—a "feeling" about that particular place ...'" (175); Kevin Lynch's concept of the *personal* basis for the emotional cognition of environment; and Jean Piaget's understanding of the perception of space as "a gradual construction" (177).

xx. See Tabbi (2002) for an interesting account of contemporary fiction in the context of systems theory.

xxi. The term "medial presence" comes from Rick Poyner's review of the novel in *Artbyte*, as cited in Tabbi (145, note 3).

xxii. Accordingly, information in the technical sense can be defined as a statistical measure of uncertainty equal to the logarithm taken to base 2 of the number of available choices. Thus, if a message can be specified following five binary steps or choices, the statistical measure of uncertainty (or information) can be specified as: $C = \log_2 32 = 5$.

This logarithm allows the message to be specified probabilistically, without any recourse being made to its meaning. See the discussion in Hayles 1990, Chapter 2.

xxiii. For a discussion of MacKay's "whole theory of information," see Hansen (2002). For further discussion, see also Hayles 1999.

References

INTRODUCTION

1. Krantz, Michael. "Television That Leaps Off the Screen," *The New York Times*, July 3, 2005, Section 2, pp. 1/24.
2. Grau, Olivier. *Virtual Art: From Illusion to Immersion*, trans. G. Custance (Cambridge, MA: MIT Press, 2003), 247.
3. Krueger, Myron W. "An Easy Entry Artificial Reality," in Alex Wexelblat, *Virtual Reality: Applications and Explorations* (Boston: Academic Press Professional, 1993), 161.
4. Jeremy Turner, "Myron Krueger Live," *C-Theory*, 25, 1-2, Article 104 (1992).
5. Damasio, Antonio. *The Feeling of What Happens* (New York: Harcourt, Brace and Co., 1999), 171.
6. Merleau–Ponty, Maurice. *The Phenomenology of Perception*, trans. C. Smith (London: Routledge & Kegan Paul, 1962), 139–141.
7. Millon, Alain. *La Realité Virtuelle: Avec ou sans le Corps?* (Paris: Éditions Autrement, 2005), 17. hereafter cited in text.
8. Sedgwick, Eve K. and Adam Frank. "Shame in the Cybernetic Fold: Reading Silvan Tomking," *Critical Injury 21* (Winter 1995), 513.
9. Deleuze, Gilles. *Difference and Repetition,* trans. P. Patton (New York: Columbia University Press, 1995) and Irigaray, Luce *An Ethics of Sexual Difference.* trans. C. Burke and G. Gill (Ithaca: Cornell University Press, 1993).
10. Kittler, Friedrich. *Gramophone, Film, Typewriter*, trans. G. Winthrop–Young and M. Wutz (Stanford: Stanford University Press, 1999), Preface.

I discuss Kittler at length in *New Philosophy for New Media*, Chapter 3, and in "Cinema beyond Cybernetics."

11. Ruyer, Raymond. *La Conscience et le Corps* (Paris: Librarie Félix Alcan, 1937), 27.

12. Piclin, Michel. "Conscience et Corps, "in Raymond Ruyer, de la Science a la Théologie, eds. L.Vax and J-J. Wunenburger (Paris: Editions Kimé, 1992), 161.

13. Olalquiaga, Celeste. *Megalopolis: Contemporary Cultural Sensibilities* (Minneapolis: University of Minnesota Press, 1992), 2. See Part II, Chapter 2, Section 2 in this book.

14. Fleishmann, Monika and Wolfgang Strauss. "Images of the Body in the House of Illusion," in *Art @ Science*, eds. C. Sommerer and L. Mignonneau (Vienna/New York: Springer Verlag, 1997), 7 (citation from ms. copy).

15. Fleishmann, Monika, cited in Stephen Wilson, *Information Arts: Intersections of Art, Science, and Technology* (Cambridge, MA: MIT Press, 2002), 750.

16. Fleishmann, Monika and Wolfgang Strauss, cited in Derrick de Kerckhove, "Externalizing Consciousness: Meditation on the Work of Monika Fleishmann and Wolfgang Strauss," in *Art @ Science*, eds. C. Sommerer and L. Mignonneau (Vienna/New York: Springer Verlag, 1997), 1 (citation from ms. copy).

CHAPTER 1

1. Krueger, Myron. "An Easy Entry Artificial Reality," in Alex Wexelblat, *Virtual Reality: Applications and Explorations*. Boston: Academic Press Professional, 1993, 161; hereafter cited in text.

2. Turner, Jeremy. "Myron Krueger Live," *C-Theory*, 25.1-2, Article 104, 1/23/02, available at www.ctheory.net, unpaginated, emphasis added; hereafter cited in text.

3. Rheingold, Howard. *Virtual Reality* (New York: Simon and Shuster, 1991), 143-44.

4. Krueger, Myron. *Artificial Reality*, 2nd ed., cited in Söke Dinkla, *Pionere Interactiver Kunst* (Karlsruhe: ZKM/Ostfildern: Cantz, 1997), 67; hereafter cited in text.

5. Cameron, Andy. "Dinner with Myron, or: Rereading *Artificial Reality 2*: Reflections on Interface and Art," in *aRt&D: Research and Development in Art* (Rotterdam: V2_NAi Publishers, 2005), 18; hereafter cited in text.

6. Gallagher, Shaun. "Body Schema and Intentionality," in *The Body and the Self*, eds. J. Bermúdez et al. (Cambridge, MA: MIT Press, 1995), 228; hereafter cited in text.

7. Gallagher, Shaun and Jonathan Cole. "Body Image and Body Schema in a Deafferented Subject," *The Journal of Mind and Behavior*, 16.4 (Autumn 1995): 369–390, here 371; hereafter cited in text.

8. Merleau–Ponty, Maurice. *Phenomenology of Perception*, trans. C. Smith (London: Routledge & Kegan Paul, 1962), 99, emphasis added; hereafter cited in text.

9. Penny, Simon, Jeffrey Smith, and Andre Bernhardt. "Traces: Wireless Full Body Tracking in the CAVE," paper presented at the ICAT Virtual Reality Conference, Japan, December 1999, available at www.ace.uce.edu/Penny/works/traces/traces.html.

10. Penny, Simon. "Traces: System and Network," available at www.ace.uce.edu/Penny/works/traces/traces.html; hereafter cited in text.

11. Lingis, Alphonso. "The Body Postured and Dissolute," in *Merleau–Ponty: Difference, Materiality, Painting*, ed. V. Fóti (NJ: Humanities Press, 1996), 64.

12. Schilder, Paul. *The Image and Appearance of the Human Body* (New York: International Universities Press, 1950), 226–227.

13. Merleau–Ponty, Maurice. *The Visible and the Invisible*, trans. A. Lingis (Evanston: Northwestern University Press, 1968), 255–256, last emphasis added; hereafter cited in text.

14. Merleau–Ponty, Maurice. "The Child's Relations with Others," trans. W. Cobb, in *The Primacy of Perception*, ed. J. Edie (Evanston: Northwestern University Press, 1964), 116; hereafter cited in text.

15. Weiss, Gail. *Body Images: Embodiment as Intercorporeality* (New York: Routledge, 1999), 13; hereafter cited in text.

16. Bick, Esther. "The Experience of the Skin in Early Object Relations," in *Surviving Space: Papers on Infant Observation*, ed. A. Briggs (London: Karnac Books, 2002), 55; hereafter cited in text.

17. Anzieu, Didier. *The Skin Ego*, trans. C. Turner (New Haven: Yale University Press, 1989), 193; hereafter cited in text.

18. Schiphorst, Thecla. "Bodymaps: Artifacts of Touch (The Sensuality and Anarchy of Touch)," *Dance & Technology Zone*, http://www.art.net/~dtz/schipol.html, accessed 7/25/05, emphasis added.

19. Edmund Couchot, "Présence et Présent du Corps dans les Arts Interactifs," in *Pour une Ecologie des Media: Art, Cinéma, Vidéo, Ordinateur*, eds. M. Klonaris and K. Thomadaki, (Paris: A. S. T. A. R. T. I., 1998), 50.

20. Renaud Barbaras, *The Being of the Phenomenon: Merleau–Ponty's Ontology*, tr. T. Toadvine and L. Lawlor (Bloomington: Indiana University Press, 2004), 199.

21. Merleau–Ponty, Maurice. *Nature: Course Notes from the Collège de France*, ed. D. Séglard, trans. R. Vallier (Evanston: Northwestern University Press, 2003), 217; hereafter cited in text.

22. Hegedüs, Agnes. "Handsight," www.aec.at/en/archiv_files/19921/ E1992_101.pdf, accessed 9/12/05.

23. Hegedüs, Agnes. [Description of *Handsight*], http://csw.art.pl/new/ 99/7e_agndl.html, accessed 9/12/05.

24. Duguet, Anne-Marie. *Déjouer l'Image: Créations Électroniques et Numériques* (Paris: Éditions Jacqueline Chambon, 2002), 117.

25. Stiegler, Bernard. *Technics and Time, volume 1: The Fault of Epimetheus,* trans. R. Beardsworth and G. Collins (Stanford, CA: Stanford University Press, 1996), Part I, Chapter 3.

26. Simondon, Gilbert. *Du Mode d'Existence des Objets Techniques* (Paris: Aubier, 1989), 245.

27. Benayoun, Maurice. "A Photo-Safari in the Land of War," http://www. benayoun.com/Aframe_crea.html, accessed 7/26/05.

28. See Zizek, Slavoi. *Welcome to the Desert of the Real* (New York: Semiotext, 2002).

29. Stiegler, Bernard. *La Technique et Le :Temps,* 2: La Desorientation (Paris: Galilee, 1996).

30. Benayoun, Maurice. "From Virtual to Public Space: Toward an Impure Art," *cast01: understanding mixed reality,* 29, available as a pdf file at http://netzspannung.org/cat/servlet/CatServlet?cmd=netzkollektor &subCommand=showEntry&lang=en&entryId=41198.

31. Lozano–Hemmer, Rafael. "Relational Architecture," available at http:// www.fundacion.telefonica.com/at/rlh/eprlh.html, accessed 7/13/05.

32. Lozano–Hemmer, Rafael. "Re:Positioning Fear," http://rhizome.org/art-base/2398/fear/, accessed 7/13/05.

33. Massumi, Brian. "Expressing Connection: Relational Architecture," in *Vectorial Elevation: Relational Architecture 4* (Mexico City: Conaculta and Ediciones San Jorge, 2000), 184–185.

34. Adriaansens, Alex and Joke Brouwer. "Alien Relationships from Public Space: A Winding Dialog with Rafael Lozano–Hemmer," in *Transurbanism* (Rotterdam: NAI/V2_Institute, 2003), downloaded from http://www.fundacion.telefonica.com/at/rlh/ecomisario.html, 7/13/05.

CHAPTER 2

1. Fisher, Jennifer. "While it affords diverse modes of engagement," www. immerscence.com/JFisher-Parachute-B.htm, 2.

2. Rajah, Niranjan. Excerpt from "The Representation of a New Cosmol-ogy," www.immerscence.com/Nrajah-B.htm., 1.

3. Pesce, Mark. "Cathedrals of Light," excerpt from *The Playful World,* www.immerscence.com/Mpesce-PlayfulWorld-B.htm (2000), 2.

4. Davies, Char, as cited in Eric Davis, "Osmose, *Wired*, 4.08 (August 1996)."

5. Bergson, Henri. *Matter and Memory*, trans. N. M. Paul and W. S. Palmer (New York: Zone, 1991).

6. Sutherland, cited in Hillis, Ken. *Digital Sensations: Space, Identity, and Embodiment in Virtual Reality* (Minneapolis: University of Minnesota Press, 1999), xxi.

7. Biocca, Frank. "Virtual Reality Technology: A Tutorial," *Journal of Communication* 42.4 (Autumn 1992), 27. In this passage, Biocca cites VR researcher Fred Brooks.

8. Gibson, James J. *The Perception of the Visual World* (Boston: Houghton Mifflin, 1950); *The Senses Considered as Perceptual Systems* (Boston: Houghton Mifflin, 1966); and *The Ecological Approach to Visual Perception* (Boston: Houghton Mifflin, 1979).

9. Campbell, Jeremy. *Grammatical Man: Information, Entropy, Language, and Life* (New York: Simon and Shuster, 1982), 203–204. Page numbers will be cited in the text.

10. Wann, John and Simon Rushton."The Illusion of Self-Motion in Virtual Reality Environments," *Behavioral and Brain Sciences* 17.2 (1994), 338.

11. Held, Richard and Nathaniel Durlach. "Telepresence, Time Delay, and Adaptation," in *Pictorial Communication in Virtual and Real Environments*, ed. S. Ellis (New York: Taylor & Francis, 1991), 235; henceforth cited in the text.

12. Krueger, Myron. "Artificial Reality: Past and Future," in *Virtual Reality: Theory, Practice, and Promise,* ed. S. Helsel and J. Paris Roth (Westport, CT: Meckler, 1991), 19.

13. Steur, Jonathan. "Defining Virtual Reality: Dimensions Determining Telepreference," *Journal of Communication* 42.4 (Autumn 1992), cited in Hillis, 15.

14. Biocca, Frank and Jaron Lanier, "An Insiders View of the Future of Virtual Reality," *Journal of Communication*, 42.4 (Autumn 1992), 164.

15. Jonas, Hans. *The Phenomenon of Life* (Chicago: University of Chicago Press, 1982), 135–136; henceforth cited in the text.

16. Davies, Char. Artist's Statement, 01010101, Whitney Museum 2001, www.whitney.org.

17. Olalquiaga, Celeste. *Megalopolis: Contemporary Cultural Sensibilities* (Minneapolis: University of Minnesota Press, 1992), 2.

18. Grosz, Elizabeth. "Lived Spatiality: Spaces of Corporeal Desire," in *Culture Lab*, ed. B. Boigon (Princeton: Princeton Architectural Press, 1993), 187; henceforth cited in the text.

19. Caillois, Roger. "Mimicry and Legendary Psychasthenia," tr. J. Shepley, October 31 (Winter 1992), 28; henceforth cited in the text.

20. Damasio, Antonio. *Descartes's Error: Emotion, Reason, and the Human Brain* (New York: Avon Hearst, 1995).
21. Merleau–Ponty, Maurice. *The Phenomenology of Perception*, trans: C. Smith (London: Routledge, 1962), 99; henceforth cited in the text.
22. Merleau–Ponty, Maurice. *The Visible and the Invisible*, trans. A. Lingis (Evanston, IL: Northwestern University Press, 1968), 136 (translation modified).
23. O'Donaghue, Karl. "Virtual Ecology." www.immerscence.com/KODonohue-Thought-B.htm, 4.

CHAPTER 3

1. Poster, Mark. *What's the Matter with the Internet?* (Minneapolis: University of Minnesota Press, 2001), 3; henceforth cited in the text.
2. Shohat, Ella and Robert Stam. "From the Imperial Family to the Transnational Imaginary: Media Spectatorship in the Age of Globalization," in *Global/Local: Cultural Production and the Transnational Imaginary*, Eds. R. Wilson and W. Dissanayake (Durham: Duke University Press, 1996), 165; henceforth cited in the text.
3. Apter, Emily. *Continental Drift* (Chicago: University of Chicago Press, 1999), 223.
4. Agamben, Giorgio. *The Coming Community*, trans. M. Hardt (Minneapolis: University of Minnesota Press, 1993), 64; henceforth cited in the text.
5. Foster, Thomas. "The Souls of Cyber-Folk: Performativity, Virtual Embodiment and Racial Histories," in *Cyberspace Textuality: Computer Technology and Literary Theory*, Ed. M.-L. Ryan (Bloomington: Indiana University Press, 1999), 141.
6. Lott, Eric. *Love and Theft: Blackface Minstrelsy and the American Working Class* (New York: Oxford, 1993), 113.
7. Fanon, Franz. *Black Skin, White Mask*, trans. C. L. Markmann (New York: Grove, 1967), 110; henceforth cited in the text.
8. Butler, Judith. *Excitable Speech: A Politics of the Performative* (New York: Routledge, 1997), 2.
9. Fuss, Diana. "Interior Colonies: Frantz Fanon and the Politics of Identification," *Diacritics* 24.2–3 (Summer–Fall 1994), 20–42, here 21.
10. Mercer, Kobena. "Witness at the Crossroads: An Artist's Journal in Post-Colonial Space," in K. Piper, *Relocating the Remains* (London: Institute of International Visual Arts, 1997), 58.
11. Agamben, Giorgio. "Une Biopolitique Mineure," Interview with Giorgio Agamben, *Vacarme*, December 1999, www.vacarme.eu.org/article255.html, 9.

CHAPTER 4

1. Picard, Rosalind W. *Affective Computing* (Cambridge, MA: MIT Press, 1997), 229.
2. Novak, Marcos. "Eversion: Brushing against Avatars, Aliens and Angels," *AD: Hypersurface II*, 69:9–10 (September–October 1997), 74.
3. Eisenman in Zaera-Polo, Alejandro. "Interview with Peter Eisenman," *El Croquis* 83 (1997), 21–35.
4. Cache, Bernard. *Earth Moves: The Furnishing of Territories*, trans. A. Boyman (Cambridge, MA: MIT Press, 1995), 2.
5. Diller + Scofidio. *Blur: the Making of Nothing* (New York: Harry Abrams, 2002), 44; hereafter cited in the text.
6. Arakawa and Madeleine Gins. *Reversible Destiny—Arakawa/Gins* (New York: Guggenheim Museum, 1997), 12; henceforth cited in the text.
7. Arakawa and Madeleine Gins. *Architecture: Sites of Reversible Destiny* (London: Academy Group, 1994), 19; henceforth cited in the text.
8. Gil, José. *Metamorphoses of the Body*, trans. S. Muecke (Minneapolis: University of Minnesota Press, 1998), 130/129.
9. Eisenman, Peter. "The Diagram and the Becoming Unmotivated of the Sign," in *Diagram Diaries* (New York: Universe Publishing, 1999); hereafter cited in the text.
10. "Architecture in the Digital Age—Interview with Peter Eisenman," in *Dialogue* 34 (2000), 108–109.
11. Zaera-Polo, Alejandro. "The Making of the Machine: Powerless Control as a Critical Strategy," in *Eleven Authors in Search of a Building*, ed. C. Davidson (New York: The Monacelli Press, 1993). See also Zaera-Polo, "Eisenman's Machine of Infinite Resistance," *El Croquis* 83 (1997), 50–63.
12. Eisenman, Peter. "Processes of the Interstitial: Notes on Zaera-Polo's Idea of the Machinic," *El Croquis* 83 (1997), 29; hereafter cited in the text.
13. Simondon, Gilbert. "The Genesis of the Individual," trans. M. Cohen and S. Kwinter, in *Incorporations*, ed. J. Crary and S. Kwinter; hereafter cited in the text.
14. Kwinter, Sanford, "Soft Systems," in Culture Lab 1, ed. B. Boigon (Princeton: Princeton Architectural Press, 1993), 227; hereafter cited in the text.
15. Kwinter, Sanford. "Flying the Bullet, or When Did the Future Begin?" in Rem Koolhaas, *Conversations with Students* (Princeton: Princeton Architectural Press, 1996), 89; hereafter cited in the text.

16. Eisenman, Peter. "Visions Unfolding: Architecture in the Age of Electronic Media," in Luca Galafaro, *Digital Eisenman: An Office of the Electronic Era* (Basel: Birkhäuser Publishers for Architecture, 1990), 84; hereafter cited in the text.

17. Galafaro, Luca. *Digital Eisenman: An Office of the Electronic Era* (Basel: Birkhäuser Publishers, 1999), 66.

18. Foster, Kurt. "Jury Discussion," *ANY*, no. 20 (1997), 33.

19. Eisenman, Peter. "Staten Island Institute of Arts and Sciences: Escape from New York (and the Guggenheim)," *Casabella*, no. 658 (July–August 1998), 22–23; hereafter cited in the text.

20. Rouyer, Rémi. "L'Historie en Perspective: Entretien avec Peter Eisenman," *Architecture Intérieure Créé*, no. 252 (2000), 35.

21. Hays, K. Michael. "Scanners," in *Scanning: The Aberrant Architectures of Diller + Scofidio* (New York: Whitney Museum of American Art, 2003), 130; hereafter cited in the text.

22. Diller, Elizabeth and Ricardo Scofidio, Project Description for *The With Drawing Room*, in Scanning, 128.

23. Dimendberg, Edward. "Blurring Genres," in *Scanning*, 68; emphasis added; hereafter cited in the text.

24. Diller + Scofidio, cited in Dimendberg, 72.

25. Diller + Scofidio, cited in Dimendberg, 75.

26. Diller, Elizabeth and Ricardo Scofidio, Project Description for *The Slow House* in *Scanning*, 103.

27. Schafer, Ashley. "Designing Inefficiencies," in *Scanning*, 97.

28. Diller, Elizabeth and Ricardo Scofidio, "Interview with Laurie Anderson," in *Scanning*, 148.

29. Betsky, Aaron. "Display Engineers," in *Scanning*, 35; hereafter cited in the text.

CHAPTER 5

1. Danielewski, Mark. *House of Leaves*. New York: Pantheon, 2000, 16; hereafter cited in the text.

2. Danielewski, Mark. "A Conversation with Mark Danielewski," with Sophie Cottrell, http://www.randomhouse.com/boldtype/0400/danielewski/interview.html, accessed 4/28/02.

3. Castoriadis, Cornelius. "Radical Imagination and the Social Instituting Imaginary," in *The Castoriadis Reader*, ed. D. A. Curtis (Oxford: Blackwell, 1997).

4. Ricoeur, Paul. "The Function of Fiction in Shaping Reality," in *A Ricoeur Reader: Reflection and Imagination*, ed. M. J. Valdés (Toronto: University of Toronto Press, 1991), 122.

5. Danielewski, Mark. "Haunted House – An Interview with Mark 2. Danielewski," with Larry McCaffery and Sinda Gregory, *Critique* 44.2 (Winter 2003), 121.
6. Barthes, Roland. *Camera Lucida: Reflections on Photography*, tr. R. Howard (New York: Hill and Wang, 1981), 76.
7. Hayles, N. Katherine. "Saving the Subject: Remediation in *House of Leaves*," *American Literature* 74.4 (December 2002), 788. I am indebted to Hayles for her provacative commentary on the role of mediation in the novel.
8. MacKay, Donald. *Information, Mechanism, Meaning* (Cambridge, MA: MIT Press, 1969), 54.

Bibliography

Adriaansens, Alex and Joke Brouwer. "Alien Relationships from Public Space: A Winding Dialog with Rafael Lozano–Hemmer," in *Transurbanism*. Rotterdam: NAI/V2_Institute, 2003, downloaded from http://www.fundacion.telefonica.com/at/rlh/ecomisario.html, 7/13/05.

Agamben, Giorgio. *The Coming Community*, trans. M. Hardt. Minneapolis: University of Minnesota Press, 1993.

———. *Homo Sacer: Sovereign Power and Bare Life*, tr. D. Heller-Roazen. Stanford: Stanford University Press, 1998.

———. *Remnants of Auschwitz*: The Witness and the Archive, tr. D. Heller-Roazen. New York: Zone Books, 2002.

———. "Une Biopolitique Mineure." Interview with Giorgio Agamben. *Vacarme* (December 1999), 9, available at www.vacarme.eu.org/article255.html, accessed 3/20/02.

———. *Means without Ends*, trans. V. Binetti and C. Casarino. Minneapolis: University of Minnesota Press, 2000.

Anzieu, Didier. *The Skin Ego*, tr. C. Turner. New Haven: Yale University Press, 1989.

Apter, Emily. *Continental Drift*. Chicago: University of Chicago Press, 1999.

Arakawa and Madeleine Gins. *Architecture: Sites of Reversible Destiny*. London: Academy Group, 1994.

———. *Reversible Destiny—Arakawa/Gins*. New York: Guggenheim Museum, 1997.

Aspe, Bernard and Muriel Combes. "Retour sur le Camp comme Paradigme Biopolitique," *Multitudes* 1 (March 2000), available at http://multitudes.samizdat.net/article.php3?id_article=206, accessed 3/20/02.

Bachelard, Gaston. *The Poetics of Space*, trans. M. Jolas. Boston: Beacon Press, 1964.

Barbaras, Renaud. *The Being of the Phenomenon: Merleau–Ponty's Ontology*, trans. T. Toadvine and L. Lawlor. Bloomington: Indiana University Press, 2004.

Barthes, Roland. *Camera Lucida: Reflections on Photography*, trans. R. Howard. New York: Hill and Wang, 1981.

Benayoun, "From Virtual to Public Space: Toward an Impure Art," *cast01: understanding mixed reality*, 29, available as a pdf file at http://netzspannung.org/cat/servlet/CatServlet?cmd=netzkollektor&subCommand=showEntry&lang=en&entryId=41198.

Benayoun, Maurice. "A Photo-Safari in the Land of War," http://www.benayoun.com/Aframe_crea.html, accessed 7/26/05.

Bergson, Henri. *Matter and Memory*, trans. N. M. Paul and W. W. Palmer. New York: Zone Books, 1991.

Berlant, Lauren. "National Brands/National Body: *Imitation of Life*, in H. Spillers, *Comparative American Identities: Race, Sex and Nationality in the Modern Text*. New York: Routledge, 1991.

Bermúdez, José, Anthony Marcel, and Naomi Eilan (eds.). *The Body and the Self*. Cambridge, MA: MIT Press, 1995.

Betsky, Aaron. "Display Engineers," in Diller + Scofidio, *Scanning: The Aberrant Architectures of Diller + Scofidio*. New York: Whitney Museum of American Art, 2003.

Bick, Esther. "The Experience of the Skin in Early Object Relations," in *Surviving Space: Papers on Infant Observation*, ed. A. Briggs. London: Karnac Books, 2002.

Biocca, Frank. "Virtual Reality Technology: A Tutorial," *Journal of Communication* 42.4 (Autumn 1992).

Biocca, Frank and Jaron Lanier, "An Insider's View of the Future of Virtual Reality," *Journal of Communication* 42.4 (Autumn 1992).

Boigon, Brian. *Culture Lab I*. Princeton: Princeton Architectural Press, 1993.

Bolter, Jay David and Richard Grusin. *Remediation: Understanding New Media*. Cambridge, MA: MIT Press, 1999.

Borges, Jorge Luis. "The Garden of Forking Paths," in *Collected Fictions*, trans. A. Hurley. New York: Viking, 1998.

Bruckman, Amy. "Gender Swapping on the Internet," in *High Noon on the Electronic Frontier: Conceptual Issues in Cyberspace*, ed. P. Ludlow. Cambridge, MA: MIT Press, 1996.

Butler, Judith. *Bodies That Matter: On the Discursive Limits of "Sex."* New York: Routledge, 1993.

———. *Excitable Speech: A Politics of the Performative*. New York: Routledge, 1997.

Cache, Bernard. *Earth Moves: The Furnishing of Territories*, trans. A. Boyman. Cambridge, MA: MIT Press, 1995.

Caillois, Roger. "Mimicry and Legendary Psychasthenia," trans. J. Shepley, *October* 31 (Winter 1992): 17–32.

Cameron, Andy. "Dinner with Myron, or: Rereading *Artificial Reality 2*: Reflections on Interface and Art," in *aRt&D: Research and Development in Art*. Rotterdam: V2_NAi Publishers, 2005.

Campbell, Jeremy. *Grammatical Man: Information, Entropy, Language, and Life*. New York: Simon and Shuster, 1982.

Canny, John and Eric Paulos, "Tele-Embodiment and Shattered Presence: Reconstructing the Body for Online Interaction," in *The Robot in the Garden*, ed. K. Goldberg. Cambridge, MA: MIT Press, 1999.

Castoriadis, Cornelius. "Radical Imagination and the Social Instituting Imaginary," in *The Castoriadis Reader*, ed. D. A. Curtis. Oxford: Blackwell, 1997.

Cole, Jonathan and Jacques Paillard, "Living without Touch and Peripheral Information about Body Position and Movement: Studies with Deafferented Subjects, in *The Body and the Self*. Cambridge, MA: MIT Press, 1995.

Couchot, Edmond. "Présence et Présent du Corps dans les Arts Interactifs," in *Pour une Ecologie des Media: Art, Cinéma, Vidéo, Ordinateur*, eds. M. Klonaris and K. Thomadaki. Paris: A.S.T.A.R.T.I., 1998, 46–54.

Cubitt, Sean. "Keith Piper: After Resistance, beyond Destiny." *Third Text* 47 (Summer 1999): 77–86.

Damasio, Antonio, *Descartes's Error: Emotion, Reason, and the Human Brain*. New York: Avon Hearst, 1995.

———. *The Feeling of What Happens*. New York: Harcourt, Brace and Co., 1999.

Danielewski, Mark. *House of Leaves*. New York: Pantheon, 2000.

———. "A Conversation with Mark Danielewski," with Sophie Cottrell., http://www.randomhouse.com/boldtype/0400/danielewski/interview.html, accessed 4/28/02.

———. "Haunted House—An Interview with Mark Z. Danielewski," with Larry McCaffery and Sinda Gregory, *Critique* 44.2 (Winter 2003), 99–135.

Davies, Char. Artist's Statement, 01010101, Whitney Museum 2001, www.whitney.org.

Davis, Eric. "Osmose," *Wired*, 4.08, www.wirednews.com/wired/archive/4.08/osmose_pr.html (August 1996).

Dawson, Ashley. "Surveillance Sites: Digital Media and Dual Society in Keith Piper's *Relocating the Remains. Postmodern Culture* 12.1 (2001).

de Kerckhove, Derrick. "Externalizing Consciousness: Meditation on the Work of Monika Fleishmann and Wolfgang Strauss," in C. Sommerer and L. Mignonneau. *Art @ Science*. Vienna/New York: Springer Verlag, 1997.

Deleuze, Gilles. *Cinema 1: The Movement-Image*, tr. H. Tomlinson and B. Habberjam. Minneapolis: University of Minnesota Press, 1986.

———. *Difference and Repetition*, trans. P. Patton. New York: Columbia University Press, 1994.

Derrida, Jacques and Bernard Stiegler, *Echographies of Television*, trans. J. Bajorek. Cambridge: Polity Press, 2002.

Diller, Elizabeth and Ricardo Scofidio, *Blur: the Making of Nothing.* New York: Harry Abrams, 2002.

———. "Interview with Laurie Anderson," in Diller + Scofidio, *Scanning: The Aberrant Architectures of Diller + Scofidio.* New York: Whitney Museum of American Art, 2003.

———. *Scanning: The Aberrant Architectures of Diller + Scofidio.* New York: Whitney Museum of American Art, 2003.

Dimendberg, Edward. "Blurring Genres," in Diller + Scofidio, *Scanning: The Aberrant Architectures of Diller + Scofidio.* New York: Whitney Museum of American Art, 2003.

Dinkla, Söke. *Pionere Interaktiver Kunst.* Karlsruhe: ZKM/Ostfildern: Cantz, 1997.

Doob, Penelope Reed. *The Idea of the Labyrinth from Classical Antiquity through the Middle Ages.* Ithaca: Cornell University Press, 1990.

Duguet, Anne-Marie. *Déjouer l'Image: Créations Électroniques et Numériques.* Paris: Éditions Jacqueline Chambon, 2002.

Eisenman, Peter. "Visions Unfolding: Architecture in the Age of Electronic Media," in Luca Galafaro, *Digital Eisenman: An Office of the Electronic Era.* Basel: Birkhäuser Publishers for Architecture, 1990.

———. "Processes of the Interstitial: Notes on Zaera-Polo's Idea of the Machinic," *El Croquis* 83 (1997): 21–35.

———. "Staten Island Institute of Arts and Sciences: Escape from New York (and the Guggenheim)," *Casabella*, no. 658 (July–August 1998), 22–23.

———. "Architecture in the Digital Age—Interview with Peter Eisenman," in *Dialogue* 34 (2000): 108–109.

———. *Diagram Diaries.* New York: Universe Publishing, 1999.

———. "The Diagram and the Becoming Unmotivated of the Sign," in *Diagram Diaries.* New York: Universe Publishing, 1999.

Fanon, Frantz. *Black Skin, White Mask*, trans. C. L. Markmann. New York: Grove Press, 1967.

Fisher, Jennifer. "While it Affords Diverse Modes of Engagement," www.immerscence.com/JFisher-Parachute-B.htm.

Fleishmann, Monika and Wolfgang Strauss, "Images of the Body in the House of Illusion," in C. Sommerer and L. Mignonneau. *Art @ Science.* Vienna/New York: Springer Verlag, 1997.

Foster, Kurt. "Jury Discussion," *ANY* no. 20 (1997).

Foster, Thomas. "The Souls of Cyber-Folk: Performativity, Virtual Embodiment, and Racial Histories," in *Cyberspace Textuality: Computer*

Technology and Literary Theory, ed. M-L. Ryan. Bloomington: Indiana University Press, 1999.

Freud, Sigmund. *The Ego and the Id*, trans. J. Riviere. New York: Norton, 1960.

Fuss, Diana. "Interior Colonies: Frantz Fanon and the Politics of Identification." *Diacritics* 24.2–3 (Summer–Fall 1994): 20–42.

Galafaro, Luca. *Digital Eisenman: An Office of the Electronic Era*. Basel: Birkhäuser Publishers, 1999.

Gallagher, Shaun. "Body Schema and Intentionality," in eds. J. Bermúdez et al. *The Body and the Self*. Cambridge, MA: MIT Press, 1995.

Gallagher, Shaun and Jonathan Cole. "Body Image and Body Schema in a Deafferented Subject," *The Journal of Mind and Behavior*, 16.4 (Autumn 1995): 369–390.

Gibson, James J. *The Perception of the Visual World*. Boston: Houghton Mifflin, 1950.

———. *The Senses Considered as Perceptual Systems*. Boston: Houghton Mifflin, 1966.

———. *The Ecological Approach to Visual Perception*. Boston: Houghton Mifflin, 1979.

Gil, José. *Metamorphoses of the Body*, trans. S. Muecke. Minneapolis: University of Minnesota Press, 1998.

Gonzales, Jennifer. "The Appended Subject: Race and Identity as Digital Assemblage," in eds. B. Kolko et al. *Race in Cyberspace*. New York: Routledge, 2000.

Grau, Olivier. *Virtual Art: From Illusion to Immersion*, trans. G. Custance. Cambridge, MA: MIT Press, 2003.

Grossberg, Lawrence. *We Gotta Get Out of this Place: Popular Conservation and Postmodern Culture*. New York: Routledge, 1992.

Grosz, Elizabeth. "Lived Spatiality: Spaces of Corporeal Desire," in B. Boignan. *Culture Lab I*. Princeton: Princeton Architectural Press, 1993

———. *Volatile Bodies: Toward a Corporeal Feminism*. Bloomington: Indiana University Press, 1994.

Hansen, Mark. *Embodying Technesis: Technology beyond Writing*. Ann Arbor: University of Michigan Press, 2000.

———. "Internal Resonance, or Three Steps towards a Non-Viral Becoming," *Culture Machine* 3 (March 2001): http://culturemachine.tees.ac.uk/frm_f1.htm.

———. "Cinema beyond Cybernetics, or How to Frame the Digital-Image," *Configurations* 10.1 (Winter 2002): 51–90.

———. *New Philosophy for New Media*. Cambridge, MA: MIT Press, 2004.

———. "The Time of Affect, or Bearing Witness to Life," *Critical Inquiry* 30 (Spring 2004): 584–626.

Hayles, N. Katherine. *Chaos Bound: Orderly Disorder in Contemporary Literature and Science*. Ithaca: Cornell University Press, 1990.

———. *How We Became Posthuman: Virtual Bodies in Cybernetics, Literature and Informatics.* Chicago: University of Chicago Press, 1999.

———. "Virtual Creatures." *Critical Inquiry* (Winter 1999): 1–26.

———. "Saving the Subject: Remediation in *House of Leaves*," *American Literature* 74.4 (December 2002), 779–06.

Hays, K. Michael. "Scanners," in Diller + Scofidio, *Scanning: The Aberrant Architectures of Diller + Scofidio.* New York: Whitney Museum of American Art, 2003.

Hegedüs, Agnes. [Description of *Handsight*], http://csw.art.pl/new/99/7e_agndl.html, accessed 9/12/05.

———. "Handsight," www.aec.at/en/archiv_files/19921/E1992_101.pdf, accessed 9/12/05.

Held, Richard. "Plasticity in Sensory-Motor Systems,' in *Perception: Mechanisms and Models*, eds. R. Held and W. Richards. San Francisco: W. H. Freeman, 1972.

Held, Richard and Nathaniel Durlach, "Telepresence, Time Delay, and Adaptation," in *Pictorial Communication in Virtual and Real Environments*, ed. S. Ellis. New York: Taylor & Francis, 1991.

Hillis, Ken. *Digital Sensations: Space, Identity, and Embodiment in Virtual Reality.* Minneapolis: University of Minnesota Press, 1999.

Irigaray, Luce. *The Ethics of Sexual Difference*, trans. C. Burke and G. Gill. Ithaca, NY: Cornell University Press, 1993.

Jonas, Hans. *The Phenomenon of Life.* Chicago: University of Chicago Press, 1982.

Kittler, Friedrich . *Discourse Networks 1800/1900*, trans. M. Metteer with C. Cullens. Stanford, CA: Stanford University Press, 1990.

———. *Literature, Media, Information Systems: Essays*, ed. J. Johnston. Amsterdam : G+B Arts International, 1997.

———. *Gramophone, Film, Typewriter*, trans. G. Winthrop–Young and M. Wutz. Stanford, CA: Stanford University Press, 1999.

Kloft, Harald. *Digital Real: Blobmeister, First Built Projects.* Basel: Birkhäuser, 2001.

Kolko, B., L. Nakamura, and G. Rodman (eds.). *Race in Cyberspace.* New York: Routledge, 2000.

Krantz, Michael. "Television That Leaps Off the Screen," *The New York Times*, July 3, 2005, Section 2, pp. 1/24

Krueger, Myron W. "Artificial Reality: Past and Future," in *Virtual Reality: Theory, Practice, and Promise*, eds. S. Helsel and J. Paris Roth. Westport, CT: Meckler, 1991.

———. *Artificial Reality II.* Reading, MA: Addison–Wesley, 1991

———. "An Easy Entry Artificial Reality," in Alex Wexelblat, *Virtual Reality: Applications and Explorations.* Boston: Academic Press Professional, 1993.

Kwinter, Sanford. "Flying the Bullet, or When Did the Future Begin?" in Rem Koolhaas, *Conversations with Students*. Princeton: Princeton Architectural Press, 1996.

———. "Soft Systems," in *Culture Lab I*, ed. B. Boigon. Princeton: Princeton Architectural Press, 1993.

Lacan, Jacques. *Ecrits: A Selection*, trans. A. Sheridan. London: Tavistock Publications, 1977.

Laplanche, Jean and Jean-Baptiste Pontalis. *The Language of Psycho-analysis*, trans. D. Nicholson-Smith. New York: Norton, 1973.

Lévy, Pierre. *Collective Intelligence: An Anthropology of Cyberspace*, trans. R. Bononno. New York: Plenum Trade, 1997.

Lingis, Alphonso. "The Body Postured and Dissolute," in *Merleau–Ponty: Difference, Materiality, Painting*, ed. V. Fóti. New Jersey: Humanities Press, 1996.

Lott, Eric. *Love and Theft: Blackface Minstrelsy and the American Working Class*. New York: Oxford University Press, 1993.

Lozano–Hemmer, Rafael. "Re:Positioning Fear," http://rhizome.org/artbase/2398/fear/, accessed 7/13/05.

———. "Relational Architecture," available at http://www.fundacion.telefonica.com/at/rlh/eprlh.html, accessed 7/13/05.

MacKay, Donald. *Information, Mechanism, Meaning*. Cambridge, MA: MIT Press, 1969.

Manovich, Lev. *The Language of New Media*. Cambridge, MA: MIT, 2000.

Markley, Robert (ed.). *Virtual Reality and Its Discontents*. Baltimore: Johns Hopkins University Press, 1996.

Massumi, Brian. "Expressing Connection: Relational Architecture," in *Vectorial Elevation: Relational Architecture 4*. Mexico City: Conaculta and Ediciones San Jorge, 2000.

———. *Parables for the Virtual: Movement, Affect, Sensation*. Durham, NC: Duke University Press, 2002.

Maturana, Humberto and Francisco Varela, "Autopoiesis: the Organization of the Living," in *Autopoiesis and Cognition: the Realization of the Living*. Dortrecht, Holland and Boston: D. Reidel Publishers, 1980.

McLuhan, Marshall. *Understanding Media: the Extensions of Man*. New York: McGraw–Hill, 1964.

Mercer, Kobena. "Witness at the Crossroads: An Artist's Journal in Post-Colonial Space," in *Relocating the Remains*, K. Piper. London: Institute of International Visual Arts, 1997.

Merleau–Ponty, Maurice. *The Phenomenology of Perception*, trans. C. Smith. London: Routledge, 1962.

———. "The Child's Relations with Others," trans. W. Cobb, in *The Primacy of Perception*, ed. J. Edie. Evanston, IL: Northwestern University Press, 1964.

———. *The Visible and the Invisible*, trans. A. Lingis. Evanston, IL: Northwestern University Press, 1968.

———. *Nature: Course Notes from the Collège de France*, ed. D. Séglard, trans. R. Vallier. Evanston, IL: Northwestern University Press, 2003.

Millon, Alain. *La Realité Virtuelle: Avec ou Sans le Corps?* Paris: Éditions Autrement, 2005.

Minkowski, Eugen. "Le Temps Vécu," *Etudes Phénoménologiques et Psychopathologiques*. Paris, 1933, 382–398.

Naimark, Michael. "Interval Trip Report," http://www.naimark.net/writing/trips/ars98trip.html, accessed 7/26/05.

Nakamura, Lisa. "Race in/for Cyberspace: Identity Tourism and Racial Passing on the Internet," *Works and Days* 25/26, 13.1/2, 1995.

Novak, Marcos. "Eversion: Brushing against Avatars, Aliens and Angels," *AD: Hypersurface II*, 69:9–10 (September–October 1997), 72–76.

O'Donaghue, Karl. "Virtual Ecology." www.immerscence.com/KODonohue-Thought-B.htm.

O'Donaghue, Karl and Char Davies, "Interview with Char Davies." www.immerscence.com /NewMediaNotes-B.html, 1999.

Olalquiaga, Celeste. *Megalopolis: Contemporary Cultural Sensibilities*. Minneapolis: University of Minnesota Press, 1992.

Penny, Simon. "Traces: System and Network," available at www.ace.uce.edu/Penny/works/traces/traces.html.

Penny, Simon, Jeffrey Smith and Andre Bernhardt, "Traces: Wireless Full Body Tracking in the CAVE," Paper presented at the ICAT Virtual Reality Conference, Japan, December 1999, available at www.ace.uce.edu/Penny/works/traces/traces.html.

Pesce, Mark. "Cathedrals of Light," excerpt from *The Playful World*, www.immerscence.com/Mpesce-PlayfulWorld-B.htm, 2000.

Picard, Rosalind W. *Affective Computing*. Cambridge, MA: MIT Press, 1997.

Piclin, Michel. "Conscience et Corps," in *Raymond Ruyer, de la Science à la théologie*, eds. L. Vax and J-J. Wunenburger. Paris: Éditions Kimé, 1992.

Piper, Keith. *Relocating the Remains*, includes CD-ROM. London: Institute of International Visual Arts, 1997.

———. "In the Ring," Interview with James Flint, 1.6.1997, www.rhizome.org/print.rhiz?405, accessed 5/3/02.

———. www.iniva.org/piper.

Poster, Mark. *What's the Matter with the Internet*. Minneapolis: University of Minnesota Press, 2001.

Rajah, Niranjan. "The Representation of a New Cosmology," www.immerscence.com/Nrajah-B.htm.

Rajchman, John. "Folding," in *Constructions*. Cambridge, MA: MIT Press, 1998.

Reiser, Jesse. "Solid State Architecture," www.reiser-umemoto.com/books/monograph/ssa/ssa.htm, accessed 12/21/01.

Rheingold, Howard. *Virtual Reality.* New York: Simon and Shuster, 1991.
Ricoeur, Paul. "The Function of Fiction in Shaping Reality," in *A Ricoeur Reader: Reflection and Imagination*, ed. M. J. Valdés. Toronto: University of Toronto Press, 1991.
Rocker, Ingeborg. "The Virtual: the Unform in Architecture," *ANY*, no. 20 (1977).
Rouyer, Rémi. "L'Historie en Perspective: Entretien avec Peter Eisenman," *Architecture Intérieure Créé*, no. 252 (2000).
Ruby, Andreas. "Beyond Form: Architecture in the Age of Digital Reproducibility" in H. Kloft, *Digital Real: Blobmeister, First Built Projects*. Basel: Birkhäuser, 2001, 206–213.
Ruyer, Raymond. *La Conscience et le Corps.* Paris: Librarie Félix Alcan, 1937.
Schafer, Ashley. "Designing Inefficiencies," in Diller+Scofidio, *Scanning: The Aberrant Architectures of Diller + Scofidio.* New York: Whitney Museum of American Art, 2003.
Schilder, Paul. *The Image and Appearance of the Human Body.* New York: International Universities Press, 1950.
Schiphorst, Thecla. "Bodymaps: Artifacts of Touch (The Sensuality and Anarchy of Touch)," *Dance & Technology Zone*, http://www.art.net/~dtz/schipo1.html, accessed 7/25/05.
Sedgwick, Eve Kosofsky and Adam Frank. "Shame in the Cybernetic Fold: Reading Silvan Tomkins," *Critical Inquiry* 21 (Winter 1995): 496–522.
Shohat, Ella and Robert Stam. "From the Imperial Family to the Transnational Imaginary: Media Spectatorship in the Age of Globalization," in *Global/Local: Cultural Production and the Transnational Imaginary*, eds. R. Wilson and W. Dissanayake. Durham: Duke University Press, 1996.
Simondon, Gilbert. *L'Individuation Psychique et Collective.* Paris: Aubier, 1989.
———. *Du Mode d'Existence des Objets Techniques.* Paris: Aubier, 1989.
———. "The Genesis of the Individual," in *Incorporations*, eds. J. Crary and S. Kwinter. New York: Zone Books, 1992.
———. *L'Individu et sa Genèse Physico-Biologique.* Paris: Jerôme Millon, 1995.
Sommerer, Christa and Laurent Mignonneau. *Art @ Science.* Vienna/New York: Springer Verlag, 1997.
Spillers, Hortense. *Comparative American Identities: Race, Sex and Nationality in the Modern Text.* New York: Routledge, 1991.
Steuer, Jonathan. "Defining Virtual Reality: Dimensions Determining Telepresence," *Journal of Communication* 42.4 (Autumn 1992): 73–93.
Stiegler, Bernard. *La Technique et le Temps, volume 2: La Désorientation.* Paris: Editions Galilée, 1996.
———. *Technics and Time, volume 1: The Fault of Epimetheus*, trans. G. Collins and R. Beardsworth. Stanford, CA: Stanford University Press, 1998.
———. *La Technique et le Temps, volume 3: Le Temps du Cinéma et la Question du Mal-Être.* Paris: Editions Galilée, 2001.

———. "Derrida and Technology: Fidelity at the Limits of Deconstruction and the Prosthesis of Faith," in *Jacques Derrida and the Humanities: A Critical Reader*, ed. T. Cohen. Cambridge and New York: Cambridge University Press, 2001.

Stone, Allucquère Rosanne. *The War of Desire and Technology at the End of the Mechanical Age.* Cambridge, MA: MIT Press, 1995.

Tabbi, Joseph. *Cognitive Fictions.* Minneapolis: University of Minnesota Press, 2002.

Turner, Jeremy. "Myron Krueger Live," *C-Theory*, 25. 1-2, Article 104 (1992), available at ctheory.net.

Varela, Francisco, "Organism: A Meshwork of Selfless Selves," in A. Tauber, *Organism and the Origins of Self.* Dordrecht and Boston: Kluwer Academic, 1991.

Wallace, Michele. "Modernism, Postmodernism and the Problem of the Visual in Afro-American Culture," in *Out There: Marginalization and Contemporary Culture*, eds. R. Ferguson et al. New York: New Museum of Contemporary Art/Cambridge: MIT Press, 1990.

Wann, John and Simon Rushton, "The Illusion of Self-Motion in Virtual Reality Environments," *Behavioral and Brain Sciences* 17.2 (1994).

Weiss, Gail. *Body Images: Embodiment as Intercorporeality.* New York: Routledge, 1999.

Wettheim, Margaret. "Out of this World," www.immerscence.com/MWeitheim-NewSc-B.htm (1999).

Wilson, Stephen. *Information Arts: Intersections of Art, Science, and Technology.* Cambridge: MIT Press, 2002.

Zaera–Polo, Alejandro. "The Making of the Machine: Powerless Control as a Critical Strategy," in Eleven Authors in Search of a Building, ed. C. Davidson. New York: The Monacelli Press, 1993.

———. "Interview with Peter Eisenman," El Croquis 83 (1997): 21–35.

———. "Eisenman's Machine of Infinite Resistance," El Croquis 83 (1997): 50–63.

Zizek, Slavoi. *Welcome to the Desert of the Real.* New York: Semiotext, 2002.

Index

1937